SIGNS OF THE GREAT REFUSAL

Before you start to read this book, take this moment to think about making a donation to punctum books, an independent non-profit press,

@ https://punctumbooks.com/support/

If you're reading the e-book, you can click on the image below to go directly to our donations site. Any amount, no matter the size, is appreciated and will help us to keep our ship of fools afloat. Contributions from dedicated readers will also help us to keep our commons open and to cultivate new work that can't find a welcoming port elsewhere. Our adventure is not possible without your support.

Vive la Open Access.

Fig. 1. Detail from Hieronymus Bosch, *Ship of Fools* (1490–1500)

First published in 2023 by punctum books, Earth, Milky Way.
https://punctumbooks.com

ISBN-13: 978-1-68571-162-7 (print)
ISBN-13: 978-1-68571-163-4 (ePDF)

DOI: 10.53288/0488.1.00

LCCN: 2023951545
Library of Congress Cataloging Data is available from the Library of Congress

Book design: Hatim Eujayl
Cover design: Vincent W.J. van Gerven Oei
Cover photo: View of office cubicle looking south — Skinner Meat Packing Plant, Main Plant, 6006 South Twenty-seventh Street, Omaha, Douglas County, NE. Library of Congress Prints and Photographs Division Washington, DC. HAER NE-12-A-26.

punctumbooks
spontaneous acts of scholarly combustion

HIC SVNT MONSTRA

Tedd Siegel

Signs of the Great Refusal

The Coming Struggle for a Postwork Society

Contents

Acknowledgments

Writing nonfiction in the absence of an institutional platform makes one especially beholden to a supportive personal community. As a result, there are a number of people to thank for their fellowship, support, and encouragement. Foremost of among these, I'd like to thank Matt Young, my husband of almost three decades now, for helping me, in myriad ways, to accept life's twists and turns, and to transmute frustration and disappointment into creative undertakings. Second, for similar reasons, I'd like to thank my parents, to whom this book is dedicated.

Unique among my community of support, there is also my longtime friend and collaborator Steve Heikkila. Steve and I met in the PhD program called Philosophy, Interpretation, and Culture at Binghamton University in the early 1990s, and we have continued to talk philosophy and politics on a daily basis ever since, even though both of us ended up in business careers. When we cofounded the blog site *In Dark Times* (indarktimes.com) together in 2016, I had not written a single word unrelated to my employment in sixteen years. Since that time, under the umbrella of the blog's intellectual friendship, I produced approaching half a million words of blog content, and the daily practice is one of the main things that has made this project possible.

There also are a number of people who have provided me with mentorship. Special thanks for mentoring relating to this project in particular go out to Tyrus Miller, Peggy Delaney,

Bernard Leboeuf, Arturo Giraldez, and Liz Devitt. Additional thanks for general encouragement are also due to the following people: Michael Schwab, Caree Brown, Donald Dufford, Scott Parker, Susan Giraldez, Rohanna Shultz, Diana Austin, Nathan Westrup, Lisa & Doug Charnock, Johan Schimmel, Ashoka McCormick, Tim & Jen Lewis, Bill McCalpin, Bill Jacobson, Marc Romano, Rodney and Lisa Siegel, Amy Bronstone, Joanne Reiter, Martin Spierings, Nelson Graff and David Reichard, Lisa Crouch, Brian Fulfrost, Siobhan O'Meara Kelley, Jack Rosenberg, Martin Chemers, Barbara Goza Chemers, Aimee Beckstrom Escalante, Michael Ritter and Peter Toscani, and Leobardo and Alma Ruiz.

Finally, a heartfelt thanks is due to the leadership team and staff of punctum books for their support. For those of us engaged in contemporary critiques of capitalism, publication by a leading open access publisher makes it possible to align the values found in the book with the publication of the book itself, and for this I am very thankful.

For my parents, who taught me the value of hard work

The Great Refusal takes a variety of forms.

—Herbert Marcuse,
An Essay on Human Liberation

Foreword

I am honored to be called upon to be an early reader of Tedd Siegel's *Signs of the Great Refusal: The Coming Struggle for a Post-work Society.* The author was my university colleague at the outset of this project, which he says has roots dating back to 2016, marking the election of Donald J. Trump to the US presidency and the beginning of Siegel's collaboration on a long-form blog site dedicated to analyzing our current "dark times." Back then, he was in an administrative staff role working at the university research/industry interface defined by such terms as "tech transfer," "commercialization," and "innovation," while I was in a campuswide academic administrative role. We connected personally through our common background in the study of the humanities and professionally on a number of university tasks that seemed to me to emanate from a world very different from anything my humanistic training had prepared me for. Our on-duty conversations were taut, Excel spreadsheet-mediated discussions of business issues, such as federal contracts or space policy at the university's Silicon Valley sites or research support policies, but our off-duty talk engaged a far more diverse set of topics and values than those at work: for example, the legacy of AIDS activism and activist art; the strengths and shortcomings of Jürgen Habermas's social theory; the quirky pedagogy of Georg Lukács's "students" Ágnes Heller and Ferenc Fehér, who were among Siegel's teachers during his graduate studies at the New School for Social Research. It was all "Critical Path Method" on one side of the door, and *Kritische Theorie* on the other.

Reading *Signs of the Great Refusal,* I can now more fully grasp that for quite a while, Siegel has kept his analytic eye trained on precisely this deep chasm I am describing between the value production to which our shared work in office had to be directed and the values that informed our talk when we left the office. Notably, Siegel is very skeptical about any therapeutic healing *of* work through humanistic values, arguing rather for recovery *from* work as it now functions for vast numbers of people. Nor does he envision spicing up work's meaningfulness with a few pinches of spirituality and aesthetics. So-called reflexive or creative or self-directed work is, in his view, just more of the same brew so long as a single sort of value continues to be the goal and organizing principle of work in contemporary society: surplus value extracted in the interest of profit.

Siegel is withering in his critique of such exercises in rebranding contemporary work. These have latterly taken on a bad aroma, particularly since the disruptions experienced by millions of workers during the COVID-19 pandemic and their massive "exit" from their workplaces in response to the organizational disintegration they had witnessed. Yet at the same time, it should not be lost how strongly Siegel's critical argument is grounded not only in a negative judgment of actually existing work today, but also in positive normative beliefs oriented toward the future: Contemporary workers, individually and collectively, are worthy of richer, freer existences grounded in autonomous decisions about how to value their lives and those of others (including nonhuman lives), and to achieve this autonomy we must liberate ourselves from the immiserating order of alienated labor. The first formulation has its legacy in the Enlightenment and especially Kant; the latter, of course, in Marx.

I won't summarize here Siegel's argument against work; he does that thoroughly in his introductory chapter and expounds it in a prismatic treatment throughout the book's various chapters and topics. But I will underscore some notable features of his approach and material. First, I want to point out that *Signs of the Great Refusal* is—I would say, in the best sense—a "bookish" book. That is, it traverses a remarkable range of reference points in recent publications, both academic and extra-academic. Like Kafka's "K." searching for the door that will lead outside the Castle, Siegel picks up the items of his bibliography like keys to the apparently sealed chamber of work, hoping that one or more will help him turn the massive lock. (K. does eventually find an open door, but Kafka didn't finish the novel, so we don't know if this ever resolved K.'s predicament.)

One of the rewards of reading Siegel's work is, in fact, receiving a cogent précis of writings offering context for his critique. His books come from a scrappy range of genres and publication venues, including Marxist theory and leftist publications, academic studies, and texts of a more popular hortatory mode. His goals and standards of discrimination regarding these texts are not always the professional ones of the university scholar, but rather those of a "mobilized" erudition critically sifting for hints, indices, and conceptual tools in the service of making the still-obscure goal of the refusal of work more tangible.

In passing, I will observe that I do not think it ancillary to Siegel's approach that as an activist and theorist he comes out of, and to some extent also addresses his work to, an independent intellectual milieu that especially became visible to me in the first decade of the 2000s. At that time, a certain counterpublic sphere emerged for theoretical and critical writing that was not dependent on institutions of higher education or academic presses, as was especially evident in new publications venues, including the blog scene and in independent presses, such as Zero and Repeater Books. Though some of the original energy associated with this extra-academic discourse network has ebbed, it inspired a number of experiments both in and outside the academy in short-form, public-facing, and open-access publication that continues today.

As I read *Signs of the Great Refusal,* I found myself thinking about how, precisely, to characterize the mode or genre of this book. In many respects it is manifestly a work of theory and critique. Yet it is also an unconventional journey across an archipelago of discourses that are not necessarily themselves in direct communication. Rather, they are connected by Siegel's far from self-evident intellectual itinerary, traversing leftist critiques of neoliberal ideology, Marx's value theory, arguments from and with Hannah Arendt, questions of mental health and illness, criticisms of mindfulness and neuroscience, conceptions of the public sphere and its deformation or decline, and Italian autonomist post-Fordist theories about technoscience, immaterial labor, and virtuosity (with an occasional one-liner about Plato thrown in for good measure).

For reasons I will soon explain, however, it was Ernst Bloch who kept coming to mind as I read the book. This is certainly not on stylistic grounds; Siegel's firm dedication to a vernacular treatment of even abstruse theoretical discourse has nothing of the expressionist philosophical prose Bloch was wont to write. Nor is it even that Siegel's basic argument about a collective, transformative exit from work might be considered by many, even on the left, to be "utopian"—a term that Bloch did much to rehabilitate from its often negative connotations in the Marxist tradition. It is rather because of a metaphor that Bloch adopted for a certain mode of discourse he took as a philosophical model for his own thought and writing: *colportage*.

Historically, the *colporteur* was a distributor of religious pamphlets, Bibles, and popular books to a rural population whose literacy was increasing. *Colportage* is a *portmanteau* word evoking a picture of a rider on a horse with a miscellany of books hung around its neck (French, *cou*) for travel. For Bloch, the image was appealing for its connection with a plebian public, for such literature's role in stimulating the popular imagination with new and sometimes fantastical (i.e., "utopian") content, and for its adumbration of a kind of publicness that could circulate around and beyond the metropolitan centers of power.

But it also appealed to Bloch for the sheer incongruous variety of the *colporteur*'s wares, in which religious texts might share a discursive space with salacious novels, fantastic adventure stories, or stories of travel to distant and exotic parts. He found this discursive promiscuousness salutary and generative, taking inspiration for his own montage-like juxtapositions of philosophy, folktales, political commentaries, literary and musical observations, and whatever else might be material to his prospecting for the utopian moment among the richness of human thought and culture.

I think I perceive a similar impulse in Siegel's wanderings through his own labyrinth of books. He draws us into the confusions of our contemporary situation and carries us deeper into them with many a surprising argumentative turn. Yet in the end, his reading and our reading of him can only take us so far. When we put our books down, we remain in this current world from which, he believes, we must keep seeking the exit. Will we come out together on the other side? Siegel keeps our eyes trained on a still-dim horizon; a horizon, he states, that will only open truly when work-as-we-know-it no longer holds us in its thrall.

Tyrus Miller
Irvine, California, 2023

Preface

Almost anywhere one chooses to look, there is evidence that long-standing expectations surrounding the experience of work and the structure of wage-based society are breaking down. Included in this are expectations around social benefits, job stability and the availability of full-time work, collaborative management cultures, worker-friendly regulatory regimes, and the role of automation and technology in job roles, work performance, and surveillance. The COVID-19 pandemic has served to "rend the veil" of corporate PR, so that beneath the continued rhetoric of partnership and teamwork, one can see clearly the dull glint of underlying structures of domination and coercion. But the issues with work and wage-based society actually go far deeper, and precede pandemic-era disputes over work rules, work/life balance, and mass resignations by years, if not decades.

This book is about these deeper issues surrounding the collapse of wage-based society, its division of social labor, and the revocation of its implicit "social contract," namely, that "if you are prepared to work hard, you can expect to make a living that will support a decent life for yourself and those closest to you." As a blanket reappraisal, it also involves beginning to imagine the transition to a postwork society, where the conditions of work and social experience generally have been radically transformed. In this respect, *Signs of the Great Refusal* should be understood as aligned with present international debates and explorations found under the headings of postwork theory, the antiwork movement, and degrowth economics.

But where others strive to envision the particulars of this world-to-come, elaborating an array of specific postwork imaginaries, or emphasizing generative policies to bring about new and transitional forms, I have chosen to remain focused on prospects for active resistance or refusal. In my view, it's important to try to think about postwork as a political struggle, even if the chances of this materializing must be rated as being rather dim. *Signs of the Great Refusal* thus concerns the status of the postwork *political* imaginary, as a necessary condition for a politics of refusal that would be capable of deploying successful strategies and tactics. Social and political conditions that we find unacceptable generally tend to generate a will to negation, and along with it a change in consciousness. But what really matters is whether the various "signs" of this refusal can grow into a mass movement for change, or what, following Herbert Marcuse, one might call a form of "the Great Refusal."

In an article on "postwork" for *The Guardian,* British journalist Andy Beckett writes that work "increasingly forms our routines and psyches, squeezing out other influences" and does so to such an extent that "the things we rely on to give life meaning, like religion, party politics, and community fade away."[1] And yet it is also true, he does not fail to point out, that *work is not working, for ever-more people, and in ever-more ways.* And Beckett goes on to count the ways: as subsistence (i.e., the problem of the working poor); as a source of social mobility and self-worth (college graduates making you a latte); as precarious; as pointless, and even socially damaging; as incredibly stressful, and thus bad for your health; as poorly distributed (people have too much or too little); and finally, as something endangered,

1 Andy Beckett, "Post-Work: The Radical Idea of a World without Jobs," *The Guardian,* January 19, 2018, https://www.theguardian.com/news/2018/jan/19/post-work-the-radical-idea-of-a-world-without-jobs.

and maybe facing extinction as the result of increasing automation. *Signs of the Great Refusal* explores the issue of "postwork," for example, by questioning the priority of the so-called work ethic, asserting the value of nonwork activity, and by theorizing the end of work in and through the trajectory of advanced technological capitalist society.

The growing body of literature on the problem of work today tends to present readers with what I consider to be an unacceptable either/or: either it encourages people to lean in and further commodify themselves as successful human capitals, embracing some version of the prosperity gospel, or it offers palliative care for the commodified, neoliberal self (capitalist spirituality's projects of self-optimization, recovery, and wellness). In response, this book is offered as a kind of an intervention in insufficiently radicalized mainstream debates about the future of work. *Signs of the Great Refusal* is thus meant to be synergistic with various other titles that might be described as "leftist critiques of work with a practical intent." In the spirit of Kathi Weeks's *The Problem with Work* (2011), therefore, the objective here is also to contribute to overcoming "inattention to work within political theory," and thereby to challenge the privatization of work, promote the understanding of work as a social relation, and to encourage a cross-class politics of refusal of work-as-we-know-it. The framing hypothesis of the book is that if there is a chance that something like "the Great Resignation" could turn out to be a form of "the Great Refusal," it is necessary to first overcome various capitalist realist dogmas about work, and to recognize and to understand the trajectory of wage-based society in the post-Fordist, digital age.

The interrelated provocations of several books have continually inspired and informed my efforts to think about the postwork political imaginary as a condition for a politics of refusal, including three in particular: Mark Fisher's *Capitalist Realism* (2009), Moishe Postone's *Time, Labor, and Social Domination* (1993), and Peter Fleming's *Resisting Work: The Corporatization of Life and Its Discontents* (2014). Fisher's concept of capitalist realism lays down a kind of a gauntlet, showing how and why we have great difficulty imagining alternatives to capitalist society because of the totalizing way that the satisfaction of human need has been fundamentally restructured and preformatted by the prevailing social logic of capitalism. Postone's theoretical account of how abstract labor as a form of social domination continually weaves and maintains capitalist social relations shows precisely how this operates and came into being, and why framing resistance only in terms of an everyday understanding of class antagonism misses something intractable and pernicious about capitalist social relations in the post-Fordist, neoliberal era. Finally, Fleming's exploration of whether and in what way it is possible to "wake up" from the structural fantasies of capitalist realist ideology opens the space of a practical, social, and political response. His description of how the control society's reliance on internal self-policing, via market incentives and coercion, becomes undermined by the logic of late capitalism, causing the appearance of "cracks" sets the stage for my initial consideration of autonomist-Marxist approaches to resistance found in the work of John Holloway, Bifo Berardi, and André Gorz, ideas that are also taken up again in chapter 17.

Most of the chapters included in this book were written over a two-year period starting in late 2019. But the origins of this project, as with so many things, reside in a very personal response to trauma. The sensibility of this book was actually forged out of two powerful shocks. The first of these was the 2016 election of Donald J. Trump as president of the United States. In the ensuing surprise and disbelief, my friend Steve Heikkila and I cofounded a new political blog site called *In Dark Times* (indarktimes.com), which was dedicated to overcoming liberal postpolitics/antipolitics, something we saw as being necessary for an effective, broad-based resistance to the rising tide of white nationalist authoritarianism in US society. The articles posted on indarktimes.com thus chronicled a deliberate process of political self-radicalization. It was hoped that our effort to give various radical/leftist ideas a serious hearing might be useful for others who also aspired to join the ranks of the "dissident professional-managerial class (PMC)."

As for the second trauma, some months before millions of people started loudly bemoaning their pandemic working conditions, I had found myself already at home on a medical leave from a senior management position, beginning my recovery from chronic PTSD/anxiety, and counting down the days until I could officially begin my early retirement. As one might imagine, an important part of this process was to try to understand how I had ended up so burned out and despairing. Beyond the specifics of my own experience, I wanted to understand what it was about *work itself* that had become so untenable. I knew that I was far from alone in feeling forced to tap out early, despite a whole raft of potential implications and consequences. Thinking about all of this also made me want to situate this experience of work, and myself, in a much more precise way. I wanted to achieve a clearer understanding of despair over work as a sort of a generational happening, as something unique to this moment in US history and enterprise, and I especially wanted to try to understand it properly as a specific sort of a class position, one replete with both blinders and action potentials.

Finally, the trajectory of this book also reflects a determination on my part to try to make the most of a highly eclectic resume. I spent the first half of my twenties participating in and witnessing community and street activism as part of the gay rights movement and the politics of HIV/AIDS across the 1980s. In my later twenties to my mid-thirties, I was a PhD student in philosophy at the New School for Social Research, undertaking a dissertation project in moral and political philosophy under the late Ágnes Heller. Instead of finishing and pursuing an academic career, however, I ended up in Silicon Valley, where for twenty years I worked as a program manager in enterprise software, semiconductor, and optical telecom, and then as a manager of university/Silicon Valley research and educational partnerships (NASA, other federal agencies, and private industry). The diverse set of these experiences are all represented here, resulting in a philosophical polemic that might be described, however awkwardly, as "de-fetishizing, work-related, activist theory." By weaving together current affairs, political and social theory, and aspects of personal narrative, *Signs of the Great Refusal* aims to introduce a selected set of notions derived from autonomist Marxism to the increasingly disaffected, younger generations of the professional-managerial class among others.

The overall arc of this book represents a sincere effort (however misguided it may be) to offer a different sort of narrative about "the future of work" to the generation of the professional classes in the United States now coming of age, one I hope is bristling with heretofore unfamiliar, radical ideas. I say "misguided," because I recognize that it has always been intrinsic to the outlook of those of us in the professional classes to assume, out of an overabundance of confidence, that there is nothing we don't already know, or, barring this, that among the small number of things we don't know, there is nothing that is terribly important. With the recent shattering of liberalism's core social and political assumptions, however, I think it is safe to say that this class confidence has all but completely evaporated. The immediate effect is a painful and disorienting loss of compass, but there may yet be a silver lining: there are at least some signs of a new willingness to challenge all manner of well-worn dogmas or received ideas that now only serve highly entrenched interests (e.g., those of corporate, governmental, and media elites).

INTRODUCTION

From the Great Resignation to the Great Refusal

> Quitting is, in some ways, the sad resort of an individualized working class. Unorganized, you can quit.
>
> —Jacob Rosenberg, *Mother Jones,* February 2022

It started in the spring of 2021, growing in intensity across the summer and fall. After an initial wave of pandemic-related layoffs and widespread uncertainty that caused many people to just hunker down, there was a sudden jump in the "monthly quit rate," reflecting what came to be known as "the Great Resignation." The rate had never exceeded 2.4 percent at any point over the last twenty years, but it suddenly climbed above 3 percent. Per the Bureau of Labor Statistics, there were 4 million people who quit in July, 4.2 million in August, 4.4 million in September, and then 4.5 million in November 2021.[1]

1 Twenty-year quit rate numbers are from the Bureau of Labor Statistics, and are graphed on the Economic Policy Institute website (Total Hires, Layoffs, and Quits, 2000–2022), https://www.epi.org/indicators/jolts/. The 4 million quits figure for July 2022 is taken from Ian Cook, "Who Is Driving the Great Resignation?," *Harvard Business Review,* September 2021, https://hbr.org/2021/09/who-is-driving-the-great-resignation. The EPI figure is consistent with this reporting. The 4.4 million for September 2021 is

How, then, to account for a tight labor market during a period of recession and high unemployment? In the corporate media, and among the economic intelligentsia, words such as "puzzling" and "mysterious" came up again and again in attempts to explain it.[2] Initially, some suggested that it was just pent-up "quit demand" from the pandemic, and wasn't really a thing. Others tried to make some sort of a skills-gap argument, as had been made in relation to labor market disruptions after the 2008 crash. Some claimed that the change resolved to the decision, on the part of some frontline workers in the early days of the pandemic, to find new jobs that would allow them to work from home, and to have some schedule flexibility to care for children and other family members. Among conservative out-

---

taken from Nelson Lichtenstein, "Are We Witnessing a 'General Strike' in Our Own Time?," *The Washington Post,* November 18, 2021, https://www.washingtonpost.com/outlook/2021/11/18/are-we-witnessing-general-strike-our-own-time/. The EPI figure for this month is a bit lower, at 4.25 million. Finally, the 4.5 million figure for November 2021 is from Jacob Rosenberg, "Workers Got Fed Up. Bosses Got Scared. This is How the Big Quit Happened. And What it Means," *Mother Jones,* January–February 2022, https://www.motherjones.com/politics/2022/01/record-quits-great-resignation-labor-workers-pandemic/. EPI's graph also tracks with this figure.

2 "We haven't seen anything quite like the situation we have today": Daniel Zhao, labor economist with Glassdoor, quoted in Hannah Cox, "What Is The Great Resignation of 2021? (If You Don't Know, You'll Want To Read This)," *FEE Stories,* July 8, 2021, https://fee.org/articles/what-is-the-great-resignation-of-2021-if-you-dont-know-you-ll-want-to-read-this. Also, "A variety of reasons have been offered for this situation": Tim Smart, "Study: Gen Z, Millennials Driving 'The Great Resignation,'" *US News & World Report,* August 26, 2021, https://www.usnews.com/news/economy/articles/2021-08-26/study-gen-z-millennials-driving-the-great-resignation. Or: "The emergence of what looks like labor shortages even though employment is still […] below pre-pandemic levels and even further below its previous trend — remains somewhat mysterious": Paul Krugman, "Is the Great Resignation a Great Rethink?," *Seattle Times,* November 7, 2021, https://www.seattletimes.com/opinion/is-the-great-resignation-a-great-rethink/. "It's hard to know what to make of the enormous churn now taking place in the American workplace": Nelson Lichtenstein, "Are We Witnessing a 'General Strike' in Our Own Time?" *The Washington Post,* November 18, 2021, https://www.washingtonpost.com/outlook/2021/11/18/are-we-witnessing-general-strike-our-own-time/.

lets, "blame" for the quit rate was placed at the feet of extended unemployment benefits, government assistance to families, and student loan deferrals, which they said had encouraged laziness.

For still other analysts, the story became about trying to understand what was going on in the most affected sectors of the economy, specifically low-paid, frontline service industry jobs in hospitality and leisure, retail and food services, health care, and teaching. The narratives in these cases had more to do with creating a sense of mystery where there really wasn't one, by asking, for example, mostly rhetorically, "why nobody wants to work anymore." The real mystery here, however, was why it was so hard to grasp what was going on with essential workers burned out under pandemic conditions with little or no incentives, something that ought to have been well within the capabilities of behavioral economics.

In *The Guardian,* as with other leftist outlets that tend to focus more on the conditions of unionized workers, the story was all about "Striketober," since there was an uptick in strike-related activity at companies such as John Deere, Kellogg, and Kaiser Permanente, along with actions by Hollywood production employees and some food production workers.[3] Angered during the pandemic after years of seeing scant improvement in pay and benefits, many unionized workers went on record that they wanted something back, given that they had continued to show up, and companies were raking in record profits. By contrast, *Fortune* ran a story that August that reacted to survey data showing that many younger employees were planning to change jobs in the coming year.[4] Relying on "a new study from Adobe" that confirmed that it was GenZ that was actually leading the

3 Steven Greenhouse, "Striketober Is Showing Workers' Rising Power — but Will It Lead to Lasting Change?," *The Guardian,* October 21, 2021, https://www.theguardian.com/us-news/2021/oct/23/striketober-unions-strikes-workers-lasting-change.

4 Rachel King, "What's Fueling 'The Great Resignation' among Younger Generations?," *Fortune Daily,* August 26, 2021, https://fortune.com/2021/08/26/pandemic-burnout-career-changes-great-resignation-adobe/.

the Great Resignation to labor agitation after World War II rather than to the period of Civil War Reconstruction.[10] After the war, he says, there was a pent-up need for workers to "get something back after their contributions to the war effort, and the corporate sector's huge war-time profits." Workers who were left wondering "why they had to sacrifice so much, or why some people got so much while they worked for scraps," Rosenberg said, joined unions and went on strike. Today, by contrast, with stagnant wages, a threadbare safety net, and low unionization, he says, something else happened — a lot of people up and quit. If we want to characterize the Great Resignation in general terms, therefore, Rosenberg suggests, it makes sense to see the entire hodgepodge of elements (organized labor action, early retirements, walkouts, burnout, generational change) as a resistance to the status quo — as what he calls a "wildcat year of *enough*." Workers are pissed off and burned out. Millions of people decided, either by choice or by pressure, that they were done.

Given the experience of work across multiple demographics in recent decades, Rosenberg thinks that rising wages alone will only go so far. But he also says that because this highly individualized mass happening was triggered by a confluence of specific recent events, we should be skeptical about how much lasting change we can expect, and we should also be prepared for some kind of a backlash. Rosenberg, Lichtenstein, and others may be right to have characterized the Great Resignation as a sort of a mass wildcat strike. There are at least some signs that this could further solidify, and become more of a self-conscious worker revolt, one generative of a new kind of cross-class worker solidarity, uniting the 99 percent, so to speak. Here I have in mind various ideas that have been offered about how combining community-based politics and services-industry labor organizing in new ways might produce a more effective counterhe-

---

10 Jacob Rosenberg, "Workers Got Fed Up. Bossed Got Scared. This Is How the Big Quit Happened. And What It Means," *Mother Jones*, January-February 2022, https://www.motherjones.com/politics/2022/01/record-quits-great-resignation-labor-workers-pandemic/.

gemonic practice. The basic direction can be seen going back to Ira Katznelson (*City Trenches: Urban Politics and the Patterning of Class in the United States* [1981]), and more recently, Jane McAlevey (*No Shortcuts: Organizing for Power in the New Gilded Age* [2016]), for example. It is the wish animating this book as a whole, therefore, that something like the Great Resignation could yet turn out to be a form of "the Great Refusal."

The Great Refusal as the Deep Grammar of the New Left

Before proceeding further, it should be pointed out that the term "the Great Refusal" comes to us from Herbert Marcuse as part of his early and influential attempt—across several books—to theorize the general significance of what came to be called "the New Left" in the 1960s. The Great Refusal thus generally refers to the aggregated social movements of resistance against advanced capitalist forms of domination that operate *in the absence of* any discernable revolutionary working-class consciousness. Nonetheless, Marcuse tends to be remembered, first and foremost, as the philosophical guru of the youth counterculture, because he was able to grasp, in a theoretical form, what has been referred to as "the deep grammar" of the movement.[11] As Wini Breines pointed out about the notion of the Great Refusal back in the late 1980s, Marcuse recognized that political demands are different from political goals, and that therefore "the issue is not the issue."[12] At the surface level, the New Left and the counterculture were organized around certain issues that gave the movement its impetus. But Breines says that "the American student move-

11 Peter N. Funke, Andrew T. Lamas, and Todd Wolfson, "Bouazizi's Refusal and Ours: Critical Reflections on the Great Refusal and Contemporary Social Movements," in *The Great Refusal: Herbert Marcuse and Contemporary Social Movements,* eds. Andrew T. Lamas, Todd Wolfson, and Peter N. Funke (Philadelphia: Temple University Press, 2017), 13.

12 Wini Breines, *Community and Organization in the New Left* (New Brunswick: Rutgers University Press, 1982), 18, 23.

ment of the 60s was about the necessity of revolt. Students [...] wished to create a world turned upside down."[13]

As I read *An Essay on Liberation* once again after many years, there are several things that tend to stand out as wildly optimistic from the perspective of contemporary experience. For example, there is Marcuse's hopeful view that the spread of a "surrealist form of protest and refusal" in the 1960s was enacting a kind of a Kantian "contest of the faculties" carried out in the streets. Marcuse proposed that this supposed liberation of the productive imagination might come to direct science and technology as such in a utopian direction, that is, as deployments of human energies that would give substance to Nietzsche's notions of a *gaya scienza* and a transvaluation of values. His related claim that "the psychedelic experience" actually represented a related search for "a new sensorium, a revolution in perception" has not aged terribly well either.[14] Also problematic today, even on its face, is the notion that the working class, understood as the traditional industrial proletariat, somehow remains the historical "agent of revolution," and as such is "in itself" even though it has come to share the "counter-revolutionary needs of the middle classes" and so is not yet "for itself." The displacement of most industrial manufacturing away from the developed world belies the need to continue to rethink the meaning of labor and work under post-Fordist, neoliberal capitalist conditions. In a related vein, Marcuse would need to be updated in order to account for how crisis-prone capitalism has become, to register the effects of increasing inequality, and to theorize the diversity of new forms of domination that have emerged.[15]

What has continued to be relevant, for lack of any better option, is the notion that there is an immediate need to "loosen the hold of enslaving needs" created by the exploitative power of corporate capitalism, even if, as Marcuse says, "the search

13 Breines, *Community and Organization*, 18.
14 Herbert Marcuse, *An Essay on Liberation* (Boston: Beacon Press, 1969), 30, 33, 37.
15 Funke, Lamas, and Wolfson, "Bouzazizi's Refusal and Ours," 15–16.

for other specific historical agents of revolutionary change in the advanced capitalist countries is indeed meaningless."[16] Marcuse's legacy in this domain resides in his having been the first to theoretically situate the emancipatory potential of the prefigurative politics of non-working-class, cultural forms of resistance, and thus also the successive waves of new social movements and identity politics thereafter.[17] The happening of this kind of revolt, he says, signals the need for Marxism to rethink utopian politics. "Utopian" should no longer be taken to mean that which has "no place," "but rather should mean that which is blocked from coming about by the power of established society."[18]

The Great Refusal and Contemporary Social Movements

Most of those of the Left concerned with the politics of refusal today, and who reference Marcuse, tend to write about the relevance of the Great Refusal for understanding new social movements. For example, in the foreword to the anthology *The Great Refusal,* Angela Davis says that Marcuse must be acknowledged for reinterpreting Marxism in ways that embrace the liberation struggles of all those marginalized by oppression, and she says that the Black radical tradition can be described as a manifestation of the Great Refusal.[19] In the opening chapter of that book, Marcuse's legacy is then explored in relation to the most recent spontaneous revolts, such as the Arab Spring, *Gilets jaunes* ("yellow vests") in France, the Occupy movement, and the Ferguson Black Lives Matter protests. For both good and ill, the editors indicate, these movements encompass certain dynam-

16 Marcuse, *An Essay on Liberation,* 79.

17 From a purely theoretical standpoint, the story of the rise of various new social movements and the politics of identity would also have to include the trajectory and influence of various types of "post-Marxism" after '68, including certain strains of poststructuralism, the Budapest School, the reception of Laclau and Mouffe's *Hegemony and Socialist Strategy* in the mid-1980s, and postcolonial theory.

18 Marcuse, *An Essay on Liberation,* 3.

19 Angela Y. Davis, foreword to Lamas, Wolfson, and Funke, eds., *The Great Refusal,* viii.

ics that constitute the dominant logic of resistance of our times, descending from the New Left: coalitions of diverse actors and fronts of struggle, a commitment to nonhierarchical and prefigurative forms of organizing, consensus decision-making, a distrust of existing institutions, and varieties of personal politics, which, as Breines also says, are "neither based in the industrial working class, nor centered around strictly political and economic demands."[20]

Here in *Signs of the Great Refusal,* I leave it to others to explore whether or not these recent cases of prefigurative politics have been successful, in what ways, and to what degree. There are interesting debates going on about this style of politics as compared to deep organizing, for example. For a recent critique of prefigurative politics in general, see Jonathan Matthew Smucker, *Hegemony How-To: A Roadmap for Radicals* (2017). Needless to say, there are also many people with roots in movements of resistance making the case for an intersectional politics of identity. By contrast, the jumping-off point for this book may be found, at least in part, via Marcuse's observation from *An Essay on Liberation* that "the Great Refusal takes a variety of forms,"[21] and from the conviction that an increasingly mass resistance to the contemporary experience of work under post-Fordist, neoliberal capitalism should be counted among the forms of the Great Refusal.

As I reread *An Essay on Liberation,* it's interesting to note that despite its valorization of the student movement, counterculture, and resistance in minority communities, there is also a significant sprinkling of remarks concerning resistance to work. For example, Marcuse's techno-utopian optimism fuels his belief that a postwork society in which "the necessities of life ceases to demand the aggressive performance of earning a living"[22] is actually within our grasp, and that "the stupefying and enervating pseudo-automatic jobs of capitalist pro-

20 Breines, *Community and Organization,* xxv.
21 Marcuse, *An Essay on Liberation,* vii; see also 3–6.
22 Ibid., 5.

gress might be abolished.[23] Its striking to recognize that even when he is writing about the student movement per se, and under conditions where organized labor shares the stabilizing, counter-revolutionary needs of the middle classes, these sorts of considerations are never very far away.[24] The youth revolt, he says, represents a "refusal to grow up," to perform normally in a society that "compels the vast majority of the population to earn their living in stupid, inhuman, and unnecessary jobs."[25] Recognizing that "even the most totalitarian technocratic-political administration depends, for its functioning on [...] a positive attitude toward the usefulness of their work, and toward [...] the repressions enacted by the social organization of work,"[26] Marcuse says in the final paragraphs that the "anarchic element is an essential factor in the struggle against domination."[27] He sees in the growing spread of, for example, inefficiency, resistance to work, refusal to perform, and even negligence and indifference, the signs of a possible mass politics of refusal. In this respect, one can see that there is at least a dotted line of connection to be drawn between Marcuse's conceptions, influential in American identitarian struggles, and the European (Italian and French) tendency of autonomist Marxism.

Outline and Plan of the Book

Signs of the Great Refusal: The Coming Struggle for a Postwork Society is divided into three major parts, which represent three different (but closely related) narrative arcs. The first part contains a critique of entrenched notions about work that still have currency, despite their status as increasingly hollow dogmas.

The second part seeks to answer the question of whether the impossibility at the heart of contemporary capitalism can be activated in some way to escape the conditions of work-as-we-

23 Ibid., 21.
24 Ibid., 16.
25 Ibid., 62.
26 Ibid., 83.
27 Ibid., 89.

know-it. To get to a viable politics of refusal, we need deeper understanding of the overall meaning and significance of work in the modern age, and more specifically, in the post-Fordist digital age. How then should we understand abstract labor and projects of emancipation today?

Since the popular pattern of refusing work today is generally found in individual searches for self-optimization, wellness, and recovery in the face of debilitating work-related illnesses and conditions, the third part begins by exploring 'the ambiguities of healing.' The direction of these chapters is informed by the imperative to find a way to avoid an unacceptable either/or, that of either remaining complicit with things that make us sick (post-Fordist, neoliberal wage labor, consumer culture) or else to withdraw into some personal health/wellness project. How should one orient oneself with respect to projects of recovery, mindfulness, wellness today?

Finally, the last few chapters consider where one can find conditions for genuine self-renewal, if the collapsing of our occupational, pseudo-public sphere limits our choices for social belonging, undermining community psychology's health and wellness prescriptions. At the end, this line of questioning is redirected into an exploration of the conditions for a politics of the refusal of work. Taken together, the three main arcs, which are written in somewhat different registers, are meant to capture all the major elements I have been able to identify as essential for the constitution of the postwork political imaginary, something necessary for the establishment of a viable politics of refusal of work-as-we-know-it.

Chapter Summaries: Part I

Chapter 1 describes the project as the characterization of a postwork political imaginary in support of a politics of refusal. It delineates contemporary conditions of work today by looking at key ideas from David Graeber's *Bullshit Jobs,* Elizabeth Anderson's *Private Government,* and Peter Fleming's *Resisting Work* as a way to capture the extent to which work has become purposeless, authoritarian, and increasingly reliant on our personal "biopower."

Chapter 2 offers an initial specification of what it means to adopt an attitude of refusal as a strategy of resistance to the post-Fordist, neoliberal cocktail of overwork, exploitation, and precarity. Whereas chapter 1 emphasizes "work-as-we-know-it," this chapter is focused more on the "refusing" part. Given the pervasive culture of capitalist realism supporting the present post-Fordist, neoliberal hegemony, there is a need to account for the cultural space of refusal. This chapter thus evaluates certain signs that such a cultural space may be emerging by looking at a nascent, generationally specific cultural revival of interest in Diogenes the Cynic, Melville's *Bartleby the Scrivener,* and Henry David Thoreau's *Walden.*

Chapter 3 explores the ways in which Ivan Illich and Mark Fisher each direct our attention to various "social paradoxes" of capitalism, undermining capitalist realism as a means to generate a politics of refusal. Both seek to reassert the radical autonomy of the commons and the right to be useful to oneself and others in ways not tied to market productivity in the commodity-intensive society.

Chapter 4, as part of the critique of capitalist realist dogmas, challenges various attitudes toward idleness and leisure in capitalist society, evaluating various attempts to recover a positive valuation of idleness. The first section starts by considering works by Paul Lafargue, Karel Čapek, and Bertrand Russell. For contemporary inspiration, there is a section on Thom Hodgkinson's *How to Be Idle: A Loafers Manifesto,* and Devon Price's *Laziness Does Not Exist.* Contrasting views of leisure in Thorsten Veblen's *Theory of the Leisure Class* and Josef Pieper's *Leisure the Basis of Culture* are also explored. The final section evaluates Brian O'Connor's recent attempt to situate idleness as part of a theory of freedom, but with caveats.

Chapter 5 introduces Arthur Waskow's interpretation of the biblical concept of "Jubilee" in the light of the global experience of pandemic. It also challenges capitalist culture's insistence on ever-expanding productivity, citing Waskow's ideas concerning the need for cycles of rest, renewal, and debt forgiveness, as also recommended by economist Michael Hudson.

Chapter 6, given the highly fractured state of working-class consciousness under post-Fordist conditions, considers prospects for a generational politics of refusal of work. It includes a close reading of Malcolm Harris's *Kids These Days,* and reconsiders traditionally Marxist-inspired claims that generational politics amounts to nothing more than a socialism of fools.

Chapter Summaries: Part II

Chapter 7's objective is to unpack the meaning of work and labor in the modern age by exploring competing accounts in Hannah Arendt's *The Human Condition* and Karl Marx's *Capital.* This chapter covers Arendt's account of premodern conceptions of labor and work, up until the modern discovery of labor power, and the abandonment of premodern conceptions of work in favor or labor.

Chapter 8 juxtaposes Arendt's position on the meaning of modern work as wage labor with Marx's mature labor theory (labor power, abstract labor, and commodity fetishism).

Chapter 9 compares Arendt and Marx once more, this time on the question of emancipation. If we accept that modern wage labor, in its abstractness, is labor in alienated form, then how should we understand prospects for emancipation?

Chapter 10 offers consideration of three different accounts of how we might "reweave the social" in a manner incompatible with capitalism in the post-Fordist digital age: John Holloway's *Crack Capitalism,* Bifo Berardi's *The Soul at Work,* and André Gorz's *Reclaiming Work.*

Chapter 11 sketches Gorz's account of the rise of a supranational state of capital, in which capital itself has become committed to an exodus from its own proper form of society. It then considers Gorz's claim that it is now time for a commensurate exodus of labor into what he calls the "multiactive society." Post-*Operaismo* theories of refusal and exodus are introduced here, to be taken up again and deepened in chapter 17.

Chapter Summaries: Part III

Chapter 12 begins with the recognition that much of what goes by the name of "self-help," "self-care," and "self-optimization" has been thoroughly co-opted and enlisted to meet the needs of capital. The soul, as Bifo Berardi says, "has been put to work." What can be the vector from alienation to autonomy if work has harnessed the parts of ourselves that used to be left over when the work day was done? These concerns are explored by sketching out the ideas of three critiques that dare to question the value of our corporate-sponsored search for mindfulness, wellness, and happiness. Ronald Purser, Jeremy Carrette and Richard King, and Barbara Ehrenreich converge in describing the bricolage of mindfulness and wellness techniques and imperatives as forms of capitalist spirituality, amounting to a neoliberal technology of the self. So understood, capitalist spirituality is designed to help people to better adjust to their present conditions, and to accept them as given, in the interest of overcoming things like employee disengagement and burnout in order to maintain productivity and profit.

Chapter 13 extends the critique of capitalist spirituality to include the behavioral neuroscience of happiness in contemporary popular culture. Whereas the chapter 12 account of mindfulness as capitalist spirituality relies on a narrative of the privatization of religion in the twentieth century, this chapter enlists William Davies's description of the modern project of happiness management, and traces its origins in the privatization of utility as seen in the transition from classical economics to marginalism.

Chapter 14 begins with the question, "Where can we find the conditions for genuine self-renewal today?" Since the increasing collapse of our occupational, pseudo-public sphere is directly implicated in our current epidemic of work-related illness, and so limits our broader options for social belonging, it behooves us to understand the dynamics of the collapsing public sphere. In this chapter, therefore, three different patterns of explanation for this long process of dissolution are introduced, patterns that, following Richard Sennett, I refer to as those of "the moralist camp," the "historicist camp," and the "Marxist camp." This chapter focuses upon Barbara Ehrenreich's *Dancing in the Streets* and Robert Putnam's *Bowling Alone* as examples of the first type.

Chapter 15 continues the preceding analysis of the meaning and significance of "the collapse of the public sphere" by showcasing two examples from the "historicist camp," namely, Arendt's presentation of ancient and modern versions of the *res publica* in *The Human Condition,* and Sennett's contrasting account in *The Fall of Public Man.* Where Arendt denies the existence of a distinctly modern public realm, Sennett offers an assessment of the modern public sphere as a certain universe of social relations, but his version lacks a consideration of the bourgeois public sphere's structure and political function, and its subsequent dialectic and crisis.

Chapter 16 completes the preceding analysis by describing two positions from the "Marxist camp," specifically Jürgen Habermas's description of the trajectory of the liberal model of the public sphere from emergence to crisis in *The Structural Transformation of the Public Sphere,* and Oskar Negt and Alexander Kluge's *Public Sphere and Experience,* which describes the public sphere's continued spectral existence and what purposes it serves, and proposes the emancipatory potential of counterpublics.

Chapter 17 considers the concrete case of the Italian *Operaismo* movement from the late 1960s and 70s and beyond, as reflected in the writing of Mario Tronti, Sergio Bologna, Paolo Virno, Hardt and Negri, and others. As an example of a politics of refusal of work in the post–World War II period, *Operaismo* is explored here as a living laboratory for understanding the interplay between the postwork political imaginary and the politics of refusal under a set of real-world conditions.

Part I

Energizing a Politics of Refusal

1

Prologue: The Refusal of Work-as-We-Know-It

> "The copies, the copies," said I hurriedly.
> "We are going to examine them, there — "
> and I held towards him the fourth quadruplicate.
> "I would prefer not to," he said, and gently disappeared behind the screen.
>
> — The Lawyer, in Herman Melville, *Bartleby the Scrivener*

Something quite momentous is happening with respect to our cross-class experience of work in the post-Fordist, digital age — or, following people such as Antonio Negri, Peter Fleming, and Kathi Weeks, what I like to call "work-as-we-know-it," in order to keep attention upon work as something historical, and thus not immutable.[1] Septuagenarian baby boomers in lead-

1 See for example, Peter Fleming, *Resisting Work: The Corporatization of Life and Its Discontents* (Philadelphia: Temple University Press, 2015), 4. In the introduction, Fleming writes, "This book aims to convince the reader that we can actually live comfortably and happily without work as we know it." In the early chapters, I use this construction as part of a counter-factual assertion – refusing work-as-we-know-it refers to the impulse to reject work as it is increasingly experienced today, by more and more people across class and other demographics, under neoliberal, post-Fordist condi-

ership positions throughout US society (both liberals and their antagonists on the authoritarian Right) continue to insist that the ascendancy of unfettered market capitalism in all domains is in fact the very meaning of human freedom. Increasingly, however, larger and larger swaths of GenX, millennials, and Zoomers just know that something has gone terribly wrong. This is not something they know, first and foremost, because they have become swayed by some slick re-packaging of an alternative economic and political ideology. They know it (somewhat differentially) in and through the direct effects of work-as-we-know-it. They know it as the flowering of a kind of generational truth. They know it in their bones.

For many Gen Xers, this awareness has come to the fore through a new and distinctive experience of debilitating burnout, becoming chronic long before they reach the age of Medicare and Social Security. For the millennials and Zoomers, on the other hand, it's by way of growing doubts about "signing on the bottom line" because the deal being offered (work yourself to death for the next thirty years while you build your human capital) requires each of them to take out a mortgage on the self that they know they can never pay off. The deferral of most personal goals to an imagined future, in exchange for laboring continually for the goals of their employers, lies exposed as a rotten deal. What does it mean to be against work, to want to refuse the conditions of work-as-we-know-it today, not as a refusal to be useful to oneself and others, or as an unwillingness to participate in the GDP, but as an awakening demand for the general re-politicization of work and work-based society? What

---

tions. In later chapters, work-as-we-know-it comes into view via the set of specific characteristics that describe the new reality of work in the US: an increasingly universal cocktail of post-Fordist precarity, highly financialized enterprises, bullshit jobs, neo-rentier debt peonage, authoritarian terms of employment, blurry barriers between work and private life, and stress-related illnesses. In the final set of chapters, it is also seen to refer to our collective sense of living in two spheres: a semi-public occupational sphere that has taken the place of the bourgeois public sphere, and a truncated private sphere defined by leisure and the imperative to externalize contents of an inner life.

if it's true that many Gen Xers, millennials, and Zoomers (in their diversity, and each for their different reasons) have already begun to refuse to accept work-as-we-know-it? If so, then it's at least possible that a meaningful plurality could be on the verge of "waking up" from what Mark Fisher,[2] following Slavoj Žižek, has called the "structural fantasies of capitalist realism," the "ideological DNA" carrying the instructions for all the various possibilities found within the present post-Fordist, neoliberal capitalist hegemony.

The Politics of Refusal and the Postwork Political Imaginary

A necessary condition for the emergence of a genuine politics of refusal (in relation to the contemporary experience of work) is the opening up of a specific kind of alternative cultural space, one I would like to refer to here as *the post-work political imaginary.* In making this claim, I am following a trail first blazed by leading figures in the contemporary degrowth movement, such as Serge Latouche,[3] who has adopted the idea of "the social imaginary" first developed by Cornelius Castoriadis in his magnum opus, *The Imaginary Institution of Society* (1975). By referring to this alternative cultural space as the post-work *political* imaginary, however, I also embrace various efforts to further radicalize this approach. For example, I am in broad agreement with Giuseppe Feola, who writes in "Degrowth and the Unmaking of Capitalism"[4] that the activity of critiquing dominant significations and elaborating alternative social imaginaries (all in the service of conceptual decolonization) needs to be wedded explicitly to tactics and strategies for unmaking capitalism, that

2 Mark Fisher, *Capitalist Realism: Is There No Alternative?* (Winchester: Zero Books, 2009), 13.

3 Serge Latouche, "Decolonization of Imaginary," in *Degrowth: A Vocabulary for a New Era,* eds. Giacomo D'Alisa, Federico Demaria, and Giorgios Kallis (New York: Routledge, 2014), 117–20.

4 Giuseppe Feola, "Degrowth and the Unmaking of Capitalism: Beyond 'Decolonization of the Imaginary'?," *International Journal for Critical Geographies* 18, no. 4 (2019): 977–99.

is, to various types of acts of refusal. So, whereas Nick Srnicek and Alex Williams employ the term "post-work imaginaries" in *Inventing the Future: Postcapitalism and a World without Work* (2016), generally using it as an umbrella term for the specification of what a postcapitalist world of work will actually look like, I use the term "post-work political imaginary" to describe characteristics, features, and notions that must be thought of as central to a politics of refusal of work-as-we-know-it.

As conservative ideologues will tell you, the very idea of "society" is something imaginary. In making this assertion, however, they mean that society literally does not exist—that it is in fact a null set—because, as everyone knows, there are only market relations, the state, families, and, well, churches, and anything outside the set of activities derived from these things either do not exist, should not exist, or, at the very least, need to be aligned with the aforementioned things that have real social significance. The use of the term "imaginary" on the part of Latouche, Castoriadis, and others, by contrast, derives instead from a set of rarefied ideas concerning the function of the productive imagination in the constitution of experience, ideas that come down to us from Kant and the Romantics, make a notable appearance in Sartre, and appear in the psychoanalytic thought of Jacques Lacan, to whom this notion is most proximally related. The Lacanian triad of "imaginary-symbolic-real," as a way to define fundamental orders of being, can be seen to form a conceptual backdrop for Castoriadis's particular take on social constructionism, which amounts to a sort of an ontology of cultural formation and development.

In Castoriadis, the radical imaginary functions as both the foundation of culture and the basis of all subsequent cultural products. As Luis Prádanos writes in *Post-Growth Imaginaries* (2018), "Social realities are constructed according to certain dominant conceptions and postulates about humans and their relation to one another and the world."[5] These key concepts are

5 Luis Prádanos, *Postgrowth Imaginaries: New Ecologies and Counterhegemonic Culture in Post-2008 Spain* (Liverpool: Liverpool University Press,

recognized as ultimates, or cultural first things, from which all other significations are seen to arise. For example, Prádanos tells us that the dominant capitalist social imaginary reduces social reality to "the competition among individuals to maximize their economic gain in a naturalized market economy," and that it "assumes that unlimited growth in the productive forces is the central objective of human existence."[6] Relying on the postulation of various social significations to maintain itself, he says, the capitalist social imaginary also ignores, dispossesses, disciplines, and criminalizes alternative positions.[7] For Latouche and the degrowth movement, therefore, the project of the decolonization of the social imaginary starts with the recognition that imaginary social significations are hegemonic — they build a *sensus communis* (common sense) that installs a particular worldview as the universal horizon of a society, which permeates social institutions and cultural values, and they normalize (mask) their ideological function as something ahistorical and politically neutral.

How, then, to go about finding an exit from the dominant pro-growth imaginary, and do so in a way that could somehow lead to the unmaking of capitalism? Giuseppe Feola finds fault with Latouche's approach to decolonizing the social imaginary, in that he regards it as overly focused upon cultural critique, building awareness, and such. Outside this domain, Feola says, he only talks about things such as abstaining from using certain technologies, or about how natural disasters opens up certain kinds of opportunities for new, organic forms of socialization. The treatment of the mechanisms of decolonization has been very piecemeal, and if we look around for examples of successful strategies of resistance, what we find up to now, he says, is quite sparse. Feola agrees with Giorgios Kallis and Hugh March

2018), 11.

6 Prádanos, *Postgrowth Imaginaries,* 11.

7 Ibid., 12.

in that "the role of social conflict remains under-examined in decolonizing the imaginary."[8]

Seeking a remedy, Feola references various anti-capitalist strategies and tactics to enrich the decolonization narrative. From projects of everyday resistance found within the system of capitalist industrial production and innovation, Feola calls out tactics such as false compliance, foot-dragging, refusal to compete, and things such as petty theft and sabotage under the most exploitative conditions, where the conditions warrant. He considers how transformation of social practices (both technology-driven and not) create changes in everyday life that lead to new subjectivities that have the potential to be more oppositional to the existing capitalist hegemony. He also calls out some recent attention to the dynamics of social and political refusal from within cultural anthropology, specifically the work of Carole McGranahan. Refusal, McGranahan says, can be more than just "saying no."[9] It can be something generative, in that it can open up a new kind of political space. Since refusal involves the removal or reconfiguration of attachments, connections, and shared goals, it can represent an effort to reframe or redirect certain expectations, relationships, and outcomes. Finally, refusal can be counter-hegemonic, because those who refuse challenge the legitimacy of the existing order. In this respect, refusal needs to be seen as something willful and hopeful rather than something passive and just desperate. Something is refused, McGranahan says, in the hope of something better.

In "Culture as Creative Refusal,"[10] anthropologist and anarchist David Graeber also has some interesting things to say about self-conscious acts of refusal as a mechanism by which new social orders are created, and he offers some provocative (albeit premodern) examples for our consideration. Graeber starts by reflecting on a minor motif found in Marcel Mauss,

8 Feola, "Degrowth and the Unmaking of Capitalism," 982.

9 Carole McGranahan, "Theorizing Refusal: An Introduction," *Cultural Anthropology* 31, no. 3 (2016): 319.

10 David Graeber, "Culture as Creative Refusal," *Cambridge Anthropology* 31, no. 2 (2013): 2–6.

having to do with some striking examples of the "nondiffusion" of cultures. Whereas Mauss was generally convinced that human societies are in constant contact, such that the entire Pacific region could be considered a single zone of cultural exchange, the question of why certain traits are clearly not diffused demanded an explanation. Why is it that Algonquians in Alaska refused to adopt Inuit kayaks, despite those kayaks being self-evidently more suited to the environment than their own boats? And why did the Inuit refuse to adopt Algonquian snowshoes? Mauss concludes (and Graeber agrees) that with respect to things of this sort, it makes sense to see cultures as something like self-conscious political projects that have their basis in creative refusals. Following Gregory Bateson, Graeber finds the driver for this process in a heretofore unrecognized kind of complex schismogenesis—social orders are actively created, out of rejections or refusals of other ones.

By way of example, Graeber describes the effigy mound culture of Wisconsin, which (per Michael Taussig and Peter Lamborn Wilson) he says stood in stark contrast to the Mississippian and Hopewell mound builders, in that their cultural monuments were created by a scattered population with no signs of social hierarchy, or even systematic farming, much unlike the mound builders to their south, but evidently in reaction to them.[11] Unlike the surrounding cultures that "preceded them, surrounded them, invaded them, and superseded them," the effigy mound builders (again following Wilson) consciously and by choice remained hunter-gatherer, and eschewed class structure, use of metal, social violence, warfare, kingship, aristocracy, human sacrifice, and cannibalism.[12] Graeber takes things still further, however, speculating about the much vaunted ecological consciousness of northeast woodland societies. In rejecting urbanization, he says, they were not at all primordial, but reflected instead a conscious "political project" on the part of populations encountered by Europeans that rejected the very

11 Graeber, *Creative Refusal*, 3.
12 Ibid.

hierarchical, urban civilizations that had "mysteriously vanished some generations immediately before."[13] Graeber also sees similar traces from around the globe, in "the anarchist societies of southeast Asia," and in the "'heroic societies" of the Bronze Age. These societies rejected the values of nearby urbanized cultures, and were characterized instead by decentralized aristocracy without a principle of sovereignty, by social mobility, and by game-like contests to establish individual worth. They were also famous for gift-giving, resistance to accumulation for its own sake, and for a lack of enthusiasm for the use of money and commerce.[14]

In recounting some aspects of Graeber's highly suggestive (and somewhat fantastical) account of the role of complex schismogenesis or creative refusal in the history of civilization, the objective here has been to provide a sense of precedent. It has been to identify some examples that might help to cement the connections between the politics of refusal, on the one hand, and the role of alternative sociocultural imaginaries in the founding of new social orders, on the other, which is the primary focus of this book. To realize something like a broad-based politics of refusal in relations to the conditions of work as it exists today, there must first be an alternative, postwork political imaginary. As an explicitly political imaginary, oriented toward the struggle for a postwork society, it must be one that contains a number of different elements. It first requires a set of symbolic elements, for example, critiques of a variety of ideas about work found within the dominant, capitalist culture that maintain the work relation as something completely privatized, and thus nonpolitical. Along with this, as a political imaginary, it must also contain action-oriented elements, such as an overall narrative concerning the trajectory of wage-based society in the digital age that can support a politics of refusal of work-based society. Finally, it must also provide an understanding of our currently

---

13 Ibid.

14 Ibid., 4–5.

collapsing "occupational, pseudo-public sphere" in a way that encourages the creation of new, post-work counter-publics.

Bullshit Jobs, Private Government, Refusing Work

To understand the new reality of work in the United States, it's useful to consider some examples of the burgeoning contemporary literature that situates this experience in a broader historical and sociopolitical context, with various angles of vision. It is my contention that there is a common thread of "refusing work-as-we-know-it" that runs through these books, and that each, in their own very small way, causes the enveloping neoliberal capitalist realism to tremble. Consider, for example, David Graeber's *Bullshit Jobs,* which struck quite a nerve when it first came out in 2018. Almost everybody, it seems, knew people who fit the descriptions in the rogues' gallery of human types that Graeber found inhabiting our office complexes ("Flunkies," "Goons," "Duct Tapers," "Box Tickers," and "Taskmasters").[15] But after the fun of these modern "Canterbury Tales" had begun to subside, the discussion in the reviews continued to deepen because of Graeber's interesting way of framing things. A bullshit job, he writes, "is one that even the person doing it secretly believes it need not, or should not, exist [...] [and] 40% of workers say their jobs make no difference."[16]

In a 2018 interview in *The Economist,* Graeber says that the really radical thing about his book is that it proceeds on the assumption that the 40 percent are largely correct—their jobs really are as pointless as they think they are.[17] Graeber goes on to add that the thing that most surprised him was how hard it appears to be for so many people to adjust to boredom and purposelessness. Instead of reconciling themselves to getting some-

15 David Graeber, *Bullshit Jobs: A Theory* (New York: Simon & Schuster, 2018), 28.

16 David Graeber, "Bullshit Jobs and the Yoke of Managerial Feudalism," *The Economist,* June 29, 2018, https://www.economist.com/open-future/2018/06/29/bullshit-jobs-and-the-yoke-of-managerial-feudalism.

17 Ibid.

thing for nothing, "the overwhelming majority report themselves to be utterly miserable. They report depression, anxiety and psychosomatic illnesses that would magically disappear the moment they were given real work, and escaped awful sadomasochistic workplace dynamics."[18]

In framing things in this way, Graeber actually invites us to identify with the rather hopeless people working the bullshit jobs, rather than to point the finger at them as a parasitic class of people who "need to be made to pull their own weight." He takes this approach, because he understands the people who occupy these roles as having done so not by choice, but rather because of what he refers to as "the yoke of managerial feudalism." To understand what he means, therefore, one must also understand certain things about the contemporary purview of finance capitalism. First, one must recognize that bullshit jobs are especially concentrated in what is called the FIRE sector (finance/insurance/real estate), and in health and education, among some others. The general rule of thumb is that the more a company's profits are derived from finance rather than from actually making and selling anything, Graeber writes, the more the administrative and managerial ranks are padded with bullshit jobs. Second, he claims, one must see that an economy driven by finance capitalism isn't really capitalism anymore—at least not in any sense that would be recognizable to "Adam Smith, Karl Marx, or, for that matter, Ludwig von Mises or Milton Friedman."[19] If bullshit jobs seem to defy the logic of capitalism, he adds, it's because our present economic system is increasingly just an elaborate system of rent extraction, and in this it "most closely resembles medieval feudalism." The existence of bullshit jobs therefore, provides the army of flunkies one would expect to find in such a system.

---

18 Ibid.

19 Graeber, *Bullshit Jobs*, 190–91.

"Oh, God, are all jobs bullshit jobs?"

More than a year after its first publication, new reviews of *Bullshit Jobs* and follow-on interviews with Graeber were still coming out in print, and for reasons other than the sluggishness of the publication cycle. In a July 2019 review in *Current Affairs,* Nick Slater and Oren Nimni wrote, "Isn't this a long time to wait to review it? To this we say that, [...] if anything, Graeber's book is even more relevant today than when it was first published, because the foul trends it examines have only grown stinkier since then."[20] Along with the account of the proliferation of bullshit jobs, Graeber had also invoked "the bullshitization of real jobs." Trying to think through the difference between real jobs and bullshit ones, or what aspects of jobs were real and what bullshit, reviewers Slater and Nimni despairingly asked, "Oh, God, are all jobs bullshit jobs?" "Should anyone be concerned if blockchain startups struggle to find software engineers to design their shitty apps?" At the most basic level, however, they were unnerved because they recognized that bullshit jobs "invoke an intense cognitive dissonance [...] because they shouldn't be able to exist under capitalism [...] companies with bloated advisory boards and expensively useless brand consultants should perish at the hands of their leaner rivals."

Current Affairs had thus set about to review *Bullshit Jobs* in mid-2019 not just because the foul trends it described had grown more odious — it was because they had begun asking themselves some of the more troubling questions the final chapters of the book raised about the current phase of late capitalism. These include questioning whether and in what way it makes sense to describe work as productive or unproductive. What is it that gives work that is considered to be useful it's supposed value? Is it really correct to simply say that commodity market prices decide the degree to which goods or services satisfy a want/ need? As Graeber has commented, "Anyone who has a bullshit

20 Nick Slater and Oren Nimni, "Bullshit Jobs," *Current Affairs,* August 20, 2019, https://www.currentaffairs.org/2019/08/bullshit-jobs.

job […] is aware that the market is not an infallible arbiter of value."[21] If work today is 40 percent bullshit, and we as a society suffer this growing bullshitization because capitalism is, strictly speaking, no longer capitalism, then how do we escape this predicament? Having felt compelled to begin to question the value of work per se, Graeber does not then resort to moralizing about the virtue of work. Instead, he eases down the road of refusing work-as-we-know-it: "If it is really true that as much as half the work we do could be eliminated without any significant effect on productivity, why not just re-distribute the remaining work so that everyone works four-hour days? Or four-day weeks? Why not shutter down the global work machine?"[22]

Private, Arbitrary, and Unaccountable

In summarizing aspects of *Bullshit Jobs,* my primary interest has been to show how Graeber's view of the nature and origins of contemporary bullshitization (and our apparent lack of concern about it) raised questions and led to recommendations that actually cause our capitalist realism to start to glitch. It does so, because by definition "capitalist realism" is the naturalizing of a set of social, political, and economic structures in order to deny the possibility that there could be viable alternatives. Something similar is also at work in Elizabeth Anderson's *Private Government* (2017). Like Graeber, Anderson is also asking questions that cause a significant cognitive dissonance about the contemporary experience of US capitalism. She asks, "Why do we talk as if workers are free at work, and that the only threats to individual liberty come from the state?"[23] We have the "language of fairness and distributive justice to talk about low wages and inadequate benefits," Anderson says, but "we don't have good ways to talk

21 Graeber, *Bullshit Jobs,* 200.

22 Ibid., 194.

23 Elizabeth Anderson, *Private Government: How Employers Rule Our Lives (And Why We Don't Talk About It)* (Princeton: Princeton University Press, 2017), xx.

about the way bosses rule workers' lives."[24] For example, there is the case of Walmart, which prohibits employees from exchanging casual remarks while on duty, calling this "time theft"; Apple inspects retail employees' personal belongings upon arrival at the office, making them wait in line for up to a half hour of unpaid time; Tyson Foods prevents poultry workers from using the bathroom; and millions of workers nation-wide are made to take suspicion-less drug tests, and are pressured to support employer-favored causes and political candidates. Despite all this going on, "American public discourse is also mostly silent about the regulations employers impose upon their workers."[25] Most workers are unaware that only about half of us enjoy even partial protection for off-duty speech from employer meddling.[26] Anderson says that only 25 percent of the population has a full and clear-eyed understanding that they are subject to dictatorship at work (including governance of their after-work activity).[27]

It appears that the condition for a new public discourse about work really only emerges with the changing condition of work for another 55 percent, who have up to now enjoyed all manner of de facto negative liberties for which they really have no legal entitlement. They have enjoyed these liberties, Anderson says, because "market pressures, social norms, lack of interest, or simple decency keep most employers from exercising the full scope of their authority."[28] It is the contractual relation between most employers and their employees that turns out to be the real center of Anderson's book. Her primary intent is to find language that can expose this relation to be one of "private, arbitrary, and unaccountable government over the vast majority," and in so doing, also explain the ruling ideology that has continued to mask and downplay its importance.

---

24 Ibid., xix.
25 Ibid.
26 Ibid., 40.
27 Ibid., 63.
28 Ibid.

As should be clear, Anderson's purpose here is not to simply add something to the traditional leftist discourses of the labor movement. She is concerned instead with what I call "work-as-we-know-it." It encompasses the experience of millions of people, most of whom have nothing to do with Fordist industrial production, or even with the broader, unionized services sector. Many of them work under post-Fordist conditions of precarity. Many of the people perform white collar, management-level work. It's in this broader context of the experience of work that Anderson offers new language: "We need to revive the idea of private government as a tool to discern [...] relevant factors of our current workplace governance."[29]

The Authoritarianism of the Workplace

What then, does Anderson mean by private government? She is fully aware that, to contemporary ears, it sounds like something of a contradiction: "Isn't everything in the private sphere part of individual liberty, and everything subject to public [government or state] control a constraint on individual liberty?"[30] To begin with, the term "government" need not apply only to the state, and thus need not, as such, be associated with things public, as is the case under a republican democracy: "Government exists wherever some have the authority to issue orders to others, backed by sanctions, in one or more domain of life."[31] Next, there is the notion of what is private. What is private can be thought of in two senses — what is private *to you* (your business and no one else's except or unless you say so), and what is private *from you* (not your business, even if it otherwise concerns you). So, you are subject to private government whenever you are subordinate to authorities who can order you around and sanction you, and the authorities say it is none of your business

29 Ibid., 41.
30 Ibid., 44.
31 Ibid., 42.

what orders it issues and why it sanctions you, so that you have no standing to demand that anything be taken into account.[32]

Private government is thus government that has arbitrary, unaccountable power over those it governs. So, contrary to the position that says that government only applies to the state, and everything in the private sphere is about individual liberty, it is in fact the case that liberty can be constrained by private governors in domains kept private from the state. Anderson wants to describe "work-as-we-know-it" in these stark terms (she literally calls the terms of contemporary employment-at-will a "communist dictatorship")[33] in order to provide a counterweight to some very deeply inscribed narratives about work that completely ignore the experience of most people in the workforce: "A large class of libertarian-leaning thinkers and politicians cannot perceive half the economy. The half that takes place after the employment contract is accepted."[34]

Why, then, are workers subject to dictatorship, and why does this condition persist, almost without comment? The inability or refusal to see the authoritarianism of the workplace, it turns out, rests on fundamental delusions about market capitalism that enables it and reinforces the willful blindness concerning work-as-we-know-it. The narrative about the free market being more or less equal to human freedom writ large, Anderson explains, originated in a tradition of "free market progressivism" from the seventeenth century to the early nineteenth century. The political economists of that time assumed that free men operating in free markets would be independent artisans, merchants, and participants in small-scale manufacturing enterprises, rather than wage laborers. Thus, it made sense, she writes, to equate economic liberty, free markets, with things such as autonomy, self-sufficiency, and independence. But the industrial revolution dramatically altered the assumptions on which this hopeful "free market progressivism" rested. With the changed con-

32 Ibid., 43–45.

33 Ibid., 38–39.

34 Ibid., 58.

ditions that came with industrialization — significant numbers of people performing wage labor in large, capital-intensive organizations — we see instead the rise of widespread workplace authoritarianism under cover of the rhetoric of laissez-faire liberalism. And yet, Anderson writes, the full-throated advocates of unencumbered capitalism today continue to speak as if their preferred system of production upholds individualism. Given our current reality, she counters, doing so is a "mis-deployment of a hopeful, pre-industrial vision of what market society would deliver." As a result, "we are working with a model of our world that omits the relations between employers and employees within which most of us work."[35]

Freedom to Choose Your Own Leviathan?

The stubborn holdover of this early modern tradition of market progressivism, so long after its relevance, Anderson says, occurs because of a fundamental delusion about market capitalism. The delusion, it turns out, is nothing other than a central tenet of economic liberalism, that there is a formal equivalence between the salaried worker and the employer, where both are seen as subjects free to dispose of their property, be it labor power, on the one hand, or capital, on the other, and to exchange it at its proper value in the market. This "superficial symmetry" of the employment contract, as Anderson refers to it, lies increasingly exposed as such today, where neoliberalism increasingly withdraws the worker protections that used to be the hallmark of a liberal, mixed economy. In the central sections of her second chapter, Anderson zeroes in on the crux of the matter by interrogating the liberal economists' "theory of the firm."[36] In the period immediately following World War I, a group of economists looking at transactional cost theory changed their focus from thinking about markets to thinking about organizations (corporate partnerships). Per Anderson, the theory of the firm

35 Ibid., xxii.
36 Ibid., 50.

purports to offer "politically neutral, technical, economic reasons why most production is undertaken by hierarchical organizations, with workers subordinate to bosses, rather than by autonomous individual workers."[37]

Although this theoretical project contained important insights into the organization of production in advanced economies (capital-intensive economies of scale doomed the prior market egalitarianism), "it fails to explain the sweeping scope of authority that employers have over workers." Most importantly, "it provided resources for denying it," in terms that "reflect and reinforce an illusion of workers' freedom that also characterizes much of public discourse." It's true that the existence of firms brought down the transaction costs associated with production, Anderson says, but these efficiencies are established primarily through the centralized authority that comes with management hierarchy: "The key to the superior efficiency of hierarchy is the open-ended authority of managers" in the context of incomplete contracts that do not specify everything a worker must do.[38]

The theory of the firm thus explains why firms exist in hierarchies of authority, but it does not explain, Anderson says, the sweeping scope of that authority over workers' off-duty lives, inasmuch as "their choice of sexual partner, political candidate, or Facebook posting has nothing to do with productive efficiency."[39] Instead, these theorists soft-pedal and paper over the issue at hand. For example, she references Ronald Coase, the founder of the "theory of the firm," who says that the essence of the employment contract is that it should only state the limits to the power of the entrepreneur."[40] This tends to suggest that the limits of the employer's powers are therefore an object of negotiation and communication between the parties, but in the vast majority of cases, "outside collective bargaining or for higher-level employees this is not true."

37 Ibid.
38 Ibid., 52.
39 Ibid.
40 Ibid., 53.

But Anderson reserves the "shamelessness award" for two other luminaries in this subfield of economics, Armen Alchian and Harold Demsetz, who write that "the firm has no power of fiat, no authority, no disciplinary action any different in the slightest degree from ordinary market contracting between any two people [...] I can fire my grocer by stopping purchases from him or sue him for delivering faulty products."[41] In response to this dubious example, Anderson reminds us that in the employment contract, "workers cannot separate themselves from the labor they have sold; in purchasing command over labor, employers purchase command over people."[42] It is indeed the case that, under employment-at-will, workers may quit for any or no reason, but quitting is nonetheless not equivalent to firing your boss, and quitting often imposes greater costs on workers than being fired does.

Despite what these theorists (and laissez-faire liberalism in general) would have us believe, "the firm" is not merely a nexus of contracts among independent individuals. "Let us not fool ourselves," Anderson writes, "into supposing that the competitive equilibrium of labor relations was ever established by politically neutral market forces mediated by pure freedom of contract [...] every competitive equilibrium is established against a background assignment of property rights and other rights established by the state."[43] Through the laws regulating corporations, labor laws, and such, the state establishes the default constitution of workplace governance, and it is a form of authoritarian private government where, "under employment-at-will, workers cede all their rights to their employer except those specifically reserve for them by law." Workers under such free-market conditions are free in a certain sense, — but only free to choose their own Leviathan.[44]

41 Ibid., 54.
42 Ibid., 57.
43 Ibid., 60.
44 Ibid.

The evaporation of middle-class entitlement reveals the sham at the center of economic liberalism that presents a de facto equivalence between the capitalist and the wage laborer, or under neoliberalism, finance capital and human capital. If it is true that as much as 80 percent of the population (those who are not self-employed, or among the class of workplace dictators) are subject to intolerable conditions by work-as-we-know it, then the potential exists, Anderson concludes, to insist upon greater human freedom by making the private government under which they work "a public thing, accountable to the governed."[45]

Tired Bodies, Anxious People, and Numb Personalities

To complete this initial survey (provided here to show that some idiosyncratic and pugnacious academics are picking up on the vibe), consider also Peter Fleming's *Resisting Work* (2014). As with Graeber and Anderson, Fleming's interest is situated in the gap between the experience of work-as-we-know-it, and the hegemonic ideology and rhetoric of contemporary post-Fordist, neoliberal capitalism. But whereas Graeber writes about the increasing purposelessness of workers under the conditions of finance capital, and Anderson writes about the authoritarianism of the at-will employment contract, Fleming is mostly concerned with how contemporary capitalism's reliance on our personal biopower (our very life energies from daily life and socio-cultural domains) is actually a feature, and not a bug. Fleming frames the issue of how our jobs are increasingly sucking us dry (by erasing the distinction between work and private life in order to get us to exploit ourselves) in terms of the contemporary discourse of biopower and biopolitics inspired by Michel Foucault.

In doing so, Fleming seeks to open up space for explicit resistance. Within post-Fordism, he says, there has been a qualitative change in our relationship to our jobs. Our jobs are more

45 Ibid., 65.

intimate to us, more reliant on our interpersonal aptitudes and emotional intelligence. Neoliberal capitalism "has us constantly concerned with its problems, integrating them into our life problems in order to get things done."[46] Under these conditions, life itself is now drawn into the logic of production, especially since the control logic of post-Fordist organizations augments supervisor management with horizontal forms, such as self-managed teams and the like. Another important takeaway is that in harvesting the social commons, employers leave us with "the burnt-out remains [...] tired bodies, permanently anxious people, and numb personalities."[47] We know that overwork and precarity are largely manufactured, and that the rise of biopower in and around the workplace is "inexorably linked to the shifting tactics of capitalist regulation." But can the impossibility at the heart of contemporary capitalism really be politically activated to oppose and escape work?[48]

First, there is the problem of what Mark Fisher in *Capitalist Realism* calls "centerlessness." For anyone who wants to oppose work-as-we-know-it, who is the target of opposition? "Is it the boss, the co-worker, or ourselves?" Given that the power of work over our lives today is so embodied and socialized, "it behooves us to partially revise what we mean by resistance, its target, and its objectives concerning the future and non-future of work." Resistance against work is no longer resistance against capitalism, in the sense of fighting for a better deal within its parameters, especially because there is a growing perception that "neoliberal capitalism is irrevocably bereft of future promise."[49] Nor does refusal have to do with work-life balance programs, which he says have always been a ruse to reconcile us to our own exploitation. Needless to say, it also does not mean advocating for lassitude or for some sort of privileged, romanticism.

---

46 Peter Fleming, *Resisting Work: The Corporatization of Life and Its Discontents* (Philadelphia: Temple University Press, 2015), 5.

47 Ibid., 3–4.

48 Ibid., 19.

49 Ibid., 20.

To refuse work-as-we-know-it, Fleming says, is to assert the radical autonomy of the commons — biopolitical workers are not seeking to withdraw into solitude, or bourgeois individualism, but rather to escape back into collective life, reclaiming the public labor that we already are. This sort of autonomy, along with detachment, are central concepts for understanding emerging approaches to labor that are starting to be seen around the world. There is the beginning of a radical repossession movement among the disenfranchised working classes, (which now includes almost everybody). The important thing to recognize, he concludes, is that these postwork worlds are not in some faraway inscrutable future.[50]

50 Ibid., 20–21.

2

Signs of the Great Refusal

> Every age, and especially our own, stands in need of a Diogenes.
>
> —Jean-Baptiste Le Rond d'Alembert, *Miscellaneous Pieces in Literature, History, and Philosophy*

In this book I am exploring the implications of what I take to be an increasingly broad-based societal realization: the overall conditions of work-as-we-know-it are becoming *quite intolerable.* As it turns out, explaining what is meant by "refusing work-as-we-know-it" and deflecting the standard Panglossian neoliberal objections ("shame on you; nobody has ever had it so good!") proves to be a rather multifaceted undertaking. In this chapter, I want to say something more about what it means to adopt an attitude of refusal as a strategy of resistance to the intensifying post-Fordist and neoliberal cocktail of overwork, exploitation, and precarity. Whereas chapter 1 emphasized the work-as-we-know-it part, this chapter is focused more on the refusing part. Given the pervasive culture of capitalist realism[1] supporting the

1 By use of Mark Fisher's term "capitalist realism," I mean to refer to the hegemonic ideology of neoliberal capitalism, which asserts, reinforces, and maintains the naturalization of a specific set of social, political, and economic structures, in order to deny the possibility that there could be viable alternatives. Capitalist realism makes market logic the touchstone

present neoliberal hegemony, there is a need to account for the emerging *cultural space of refusal* before considering the other elements of the postwork political imaginary and the various modes of a politics of refusal. Along with the changing experience of work, it is my view that there is also a new and distinctive cultural mood arising in response to these same conditions. This new cultural mood and/or ethos of refusal also appears to me to be a millennial-specific, generational happening. This is important, because if it takes root, it could turn out to be even more decisive for the bromides of contemporary capitalist realism than the sort of ideology critiques previously described.

Thematizing the Space of Refusal

When I was a master's student at The New School in the early 1990s, I vividly recall taking a first class with the American philosopher Richard Bernstein about the politics of modernity/postmodernity. When it came time to define and describe postmodernity and/or postmodernism in the opening lecture, Bernstein struck a Heideggerian pose and declared that the postmodern was best described as a *Stimmung*, or what he called a "cultural mood." To be honest, some of us were shocked. We were expecting something having to do with the cultural logic of late capitalism, à la Fredric Jameson. A mood? That's really all you got? And yet here I am, thirty years later, appropriating this dubious critical language of "cultural mood." Nonetheless, if the

for everything found within the general cultural field, preemptively formatting and shaping desires, aspirations, and hopes so as to be consistent with capitalist culture. Support for the notion that capitalist realism refers to the functioning of a hegemonic ideology is provided by Fisher himself in Mark Fisher and Jeremy Gilbert, "Capitalist Realism and Neoliberal Hegemony: A Dialogue," *New Formations* 80/81 (2013): 89–101. In response to Gilbert's introduction of this interpretation, Fisher says, "The hegemonic field which capitalist realism secures and intensifies is one in which politics itself has disappeared. What capitalist realism consolidates is the idea that we are in the era of the post-political [...] the (essentially 1990s) idea of the post-political [...] was always a cover for neoliberal hegemony" (90). In chapter 3, I address capitalist realism specifically in some detail.

phrase "refusal of work-as-we-know-it" is going to be meaningful in the ways intended, it is essential to talk about a certain cultural mood or ethos that first creates the collective "space of refusal." Otherwise, refusal can be too easily mischaracterized and dismissed via a raft of predictable charges — individual laziness, romanticism, and/or privileged position.

For a sense of what this is all about, consider the carefully chosen titles (and underlying intentions) of two fairly recent books written by millennial authors who are clearly speaking to their peers: Jenny Odell's *How to Do Nothing: Resisting the Attention Economy* (2019) and Mark Greif's, *Against Everything* (2017). What do these titles tell us? They tell us, straightaway, that things one would generally consider to be bad or even indefensible, such as "doing nothing" and "being against everything," are in fact somehow meaningful, and that understood in the right way (because the world is actually upside down) they need to be seen as important, even essential. This is how the kind of cultural space I am describing is created at the level of "nuts and bolts."

Odell: The Value of Certain Nothings

A closer look at the introduction to Odell's book provides additional confirmation. At the most basic level, the book is about what she calls "disengaging from the attention economy." Odell is an artist, and until 2021 was an adjunct professor of digital arts at Stanford. But this is no mere self-help book about remembering to put down our devices, or even a straightforward discussion about how contemporary technology is changing our everyday experience, presumably for both good and ill. She describes the book as a "field guide to doing nothing as an act of political resistance to the attention economy."[2] What sticks out here is the word "political." In what way is resisting being directed by the attention economy political? The use of this

2 Jenny Odell, *How to Do Nothing: Resisting the Attention Economy* (Brooklyn: Melville House, 2019), xi.

word tells us that Odell is concerned about much more than just overcoming technological mediation and overoptimization of free time in the name of work/life balance.

Another immediate giveaway is the introduction's title, "Surviving Usefulness." Odell wants us to recognize that the attention economy's power derives from living in a world "where our value is determined by our productivity." The book is thus "for any person who perceives life to be more than an instrument, and therefore something that cannot be optimized." She goes on to say that the stakes are actually higher than just the individual recovery of the sort of things "that give life meaning," which are often found by way of "accidents, interruptions, and serendipitous encounters." When we are being directed by the attention economy, we are bereft of the time and space that is necessary to carry on some version of a collective life, to exist as what Hannah Arendt, following Aristotle, calls *homo politicus.* The stakes are thus also cultural, she adds, since the "narrowing horizon for things deemed unproductive" results in impatience with anything "nuanced, poetic, or less than obvious." These nothings, Odell says, cannot be tolerated, because they "cannot be used or appropriated, and provide no deliverables." In general, the point of doing nothing, "isn't to return to work refreshed and ready to be more productive, but rather to question what we currently perceive as productive." The nothing she proposes "is only nothing from the point of view of capitalist productivity."[3]

There is a lot more to say about what Odell means by doing nothing (more on this below, the section on Diogenes, Bartleby, and Thoreau). What I hope is starting to become clear, however, is that Odell is valorizing "doing nothing" and "surviving usefulness" as an explicit strategy. She is trying to challenge what Mark Fisher calls the "condition of capitalist realism," which he says concerns the "pre-emptive formatting and shaping of desires, aspirations, and hopes by capitalist culture."[4] The valorization of

---

3 Ibid.

4 Mark Fisher, *Capitalist Realism: Is There No Alternative?* (Winchester: Zero Books, 2009), 9.

"nothings that cannot be used or appropriated, and provide no deliverables" is thus necessary, because the attention economy, she writes, "hijacks and frustrates our most basic desires and then profits from them."[5] To resist-in-place "is to make oneself into a shape that cannot be easily appropriated by a capitalist value system."[6] Doing this, it turns out, begins with a specific sort of "doing nothing" where we learn "to redirect and enlarge our attention." To resist-in-place is to stake out this territory that lies somewhere between withdrawing (or escaping or dropping out) and simply remaining within the framework of the attention economy.

Greif: To Figure Out What Living Is For

Now consider also the preface to Greif's *Against Everything*. Although Greif is also a professor at Stanford, he says the essays in his book were written in his twenties and thirties, and previously published in the journal *N+1*, which he cofounded. There is a specific reason, inherent to the overall logic of the work, as to why it makes sense for him to publish a collection of what otherwise (in an academic setting) might be considered his juvenilia. Greif writes that the essays "reflected an effort, in my twenties and thirties, to try to figure a few things out. What I was living for, principally, and why so much around me seemed to be false and contemptible, yet was accepted without a great collective cry of pain."[7] In writing in this way, Greif's strategy is to reinaugurate and then reenact a specific sort of a philosophical journey. In doing so, he is following in the footsteps of Henry David Thoreau, who wrote in *Walden*, "To be a philosopher is not merely to have subtle thoughts [...] it is to solve some of the great problems of life, not only theoretically, but practically."[8] Next, Greif tells us that whereas "a lot of books tell you how

5 Odell, *How To Do Nothing*, x–xi.
6 Ibid., xvi.
7 Mark Greif, *Against Everything* (New York: Vintage Books, 2016), ix.
8 Henry David Thoreau, *Walden* (San Bernardino: Black and White Classics, 2004), 9.

to do things you are supposed to do, but better, this book asks about those things you are supposed to do." He says he wants to know whether we really do these things, and if so, for the reasons supposed. Also, if it turns out that the true reasons are not the ones usually proclaimed, then it might also be that "the right reasons to do things, to be good and true and righteous" are in fact wrong. Young Greif asks, as Thoreau asked, "What if the usual wisdom is unwise?"[9]

But what specifically are these things of which he speaks? As it turns out, he means all manner of things concerning the body as understood through popular culture, including exercise, sex, food, and child-rearing, among others. There are also essays on popular music, reality TV, and YouTube. Animating his concern, across the various essays, however, is his sense that "the ceaseless grooming and optimizing of ordinary life stands in the way of finding out how else we could spend our attention and energy."[10] Along with what reverberates within the book title, then, perhaps you hear in the opening part of Greif's preface some echoes of Thoreau, for example, from *Walden:* "The greater part of what my neighbors call good, I believe in my soul to be bad [...] one generation abandons the enterprises of another like stranded vessels"; also, "men labor under a mistake. The better part of man is soon plowed into the soil for compost."[11]

But Greif is doing more than merely providing echoes of Thoreau. At the outset, I referred to *Against Everything* as a kind of a reenactment of *Walden,* and suggested that this reenactment is the deeper philosophical purpose of the book, its true *raison d'être.* In the second half of the preface, this reenactment starts: "I can imagine someone asking, 'Against everything?' I'll tell you what this impulse means to me." Following this, Greif tells a decisive story from his own childhood, about how he actually grew up going on walks around Walden Pond with his mother, who told him stories about Thoreau, about how he had

9 Greif, *Against Everything,* x.
10 Ibid.
11 Thoreau, *Walden,* 4.

written in his book that things people considered superior, were often inferior, that the best things might not belong to anybody per se, and that work was overrated. Greif and his mother would play a kind of a game. His mother would point out every "folly driving to the pond or coming home: billboards, luxury cars, malls, political signage, mansions [...]."[12] Greif's portion "was to figure out exactly what his critique and alternative could be." As a result, for Greif, already from an early age, to be a philosopher was "to be a mind that was unafraid to be against everything." When he finally read *Walden* at seventeen, he says he had an experience he's had with only a handful of books — "of knowing I didn't deserve to finish it until I would no longer have to cast down my eyes, abashed, in the presence of its words. That kind of growing up, I thought uneasily, could take a lifetime."[13]

In reading the essays that come after this preface, we are meant to understand Greif's various observations, ruminations, and reflections in a distinctly Thoreau-like register, as an enactment of what it means to ask "what life is for," and how to dwell in such questions, at least for a time, "as a way of life." This is what binds the diversity of things found within *Walden*. Whether he is reflecting on nature, the practices of "the Hindoos," building a house, comparing the ancients and the moderns, fretting over home economics, or wondering at the citizens of Concord, Thoreau does so as part of a grand, youthful personal experiment within a larger, young national experiment.

Finally, if the directness of Greif's book seems somehow disarming, even immature, and thus not in accord with what Thoreau refers to as the "subtle thoughts" one would expect from a philosopher,[14] it's because he has followed Thoreau in the need to valorize this specific sort of youthful reflection, warts and all. He does so, I believe, in order to show that young people should be free to take this journey without inhibition, and to do so before the vagaries of work have managed to "plow them into

12 Ibid., xi.
13 Ibid., xii.
14 Thoreau, *Walden*, 9.

the soil for compost." In this sense, *Against Everything* has a lot in common with Odell's "field guide for doing nothing as an act of political resistance to the attention economy,"[15] which has the dedication, "To my students."

Diogenes, Bartleby, and Thoreau

Picking up the thread from Odell's book again, let's recall that she was advocating for something she referred to as "resisting-in-place" by making oneself "into a shape that cannot be easily appropriated by a capitalist value system." One of the ways that we do this is to survey the "history of refusal."[16] For such examples, Odell turns to Diogenes of Sinope, Melville's Bartleby the Scrivener, and Thoreau. "Diogenes, Diogenes." I can hear you mulling it over. Diogenes the Cynic? Lives in a barrel? Barks like a dog? That Diogenes? The one Plato called "Socrates gone mad?"[17] Yes, that one. Diogenes, Odell writes, "has much to teach us about how to refuse."[18] Unlike Socrates, Diogenes is not concerned to teach the noble youth the meaning of virtue, seeing no point in helping to prepare them to lead a society he considered to be upside down. Instead, he practiced what Odell characterizes as a kind of in-your-face performance art, and she goes on to relate some of the still shocking stories of Diogenes's behavior. Odell's purpose, in looking to Diogenes, is something more than just to point out that "stories like his contribute to our vocabulary of refusal, even centuries later."[19]

It's hard not to laugh when Diogenes disses Alexander the Great, but Odell wants us to see that Diogenes can provide more than just a "locus for our wish" to do likewise. Her major point, which also provides the throughline for the seemingly incongruous triplet of Diogenes/Bartleby/Thoreau, is that "faced with unrelenting hypocrisy," Diogenes "did not flee [...] nor did he

15 Odell, *How To Do Nothing*, xi.
16 Ibid., xxi.
17 Ibid., 65.
18 Ibid., 68.
19 Ibid.

like Socrates kill himself," but rather "neither assimilated nor exited society," living instead "in the midst of it, in a state of refusal."[20] Odell says that the decision "to participate, *but not as asked*" (my emphasis) is what produces a third space, or what I have been calling here the "space of refusal." It is also what connects the "I'd prefer not to" of Bartleby the Scrivener to Diogenes the Cynic. The added twist, of course, is that Bartleby's acts of refusal happen in a Wall Street law firm, as a scene of resistance to white-collar working conditions. As for Melville and Thoreau, they are connected via their common acquaintance with Ralph Waldo Emerson, and mutual engagement with his ideas. They share a milieu, both writing about working conditions in the northeast, with nearly simultaneous publication. But Odell doesn't simply focus on Thoreau's writing on civil disobedience here. She also wants us to see the connectedness of Bartleby's strange performance of resistance to Thoreau's odd spectacle, his Walden Pond "experiment in subtraction," as Slavoj Žižek would say.

If Odell were the only one making these connections and showcasing them, this summary of her account of the history of refusal might be interesting but not especially noteworthy. But along with Odell, Greif's *Against Everything* is also peppered with thoughts on Epicurean *ataraxia* and austerity, Stoic *apatheia*, and, of course, the cynicism of Diogenes, along with continual (albeit often subterranean) ruminations on Thoreau. This, however, is really just the tip of an iceberg. In various places, and in different combinations, Diogenes, Bartleby, and Thoreau seem to keep popping up. Bartleby has been embedded in academic political discussions about "what is to be done?" for quite some time.[21] As with Odell, the focus of these discussions

20 Ibid.

21 See Jacques Derrida, *The Gift of Death, Second Edition / Literature in Secret,* trans. David Wills (Chicago: University of Chicago Press, 2008); Gilles Deleuze, "Bartleby; or, The Formula," in *Essays Critical and Clinical,* trans. Daniel W. Smith and Michael A. Greco (Minneapolis: University of Minnesota Press, 1997), 68–90; Michael Hardt and Anotnio Negri, *Empire* (Cambridge: Harvard University Press, 2001); and Byung-Chul

is on how it might be possible to "do something" in a way that is not easily appropriated and assimilated by market logic, with its tendency to prestructure any and all movements of resistance. But Bartleby has found his way into (albeit highly educated) popular culture also. See, for example, this recent humor piece on Bartleby the Scrivener in *McSweeney's*, "I Cannot Recommend My Former Co-Worker Bartleby for Your Scrivening Position."[22] Odell is right to string together Diogenes, Bartleby, and Thoreau. Where Bartleby is found, it is often the case that Diogenes and Thoreau are not very far away. The thread of connection among them is the (lately) smoldering possibility of a widespread recovery of the attitude of classical cynicism under conditions of late capitalism.

Walden Three: Thoreau and the Question of the Political

I want to say something more about Thoreau, so that those who look to him for inspiration, such as Greif and Odell, are not accused of political quietism, on the false assumption that Thoreau is merely advocating for a withdrawal from society and a "return to nature." When we read Thoreau's *Walden* as an extended meditation on labor and work in relation to a set of more elevated "ends of man," it makes sense that he should become the nineteenth-century poster boy for the contemporary refusal of work-as-we-know-it. But unless one continually foregrounds the idea that conditions of labor and work are such that "men lead lives of quiet desperation," it's easy to miss why Thoreau does not stand for a withdrawal from society and an avoidance of politics.

Han, *The Burnout Society,* trans. Erik Butler (Stanford: Stanford University Press, 2015). Žižek's many mentions of Bartleby's "I would prefer not to" are legion, but see the last section of *The Parallax View* (Cambridge: MIT Press, 2006), his magnum opus.

22 Rebecca Christopher, "I Cannot Recommend My Former Co-Worker Bartleby for Your Scrivening Position," *McSweeney's,* March 22, 2018, https://www.mcsweeneys.net/articles/i-cannot-recommend-my-former-coworker-bartleby-for-your-scrivening-position.

In 2015, *The New Yorker* published a highly polemical article by Katherine Schulz, "The Moral Judgements of Henry David Thoreau."[23] Since the article appears to have been written specifically to thwart the budding Thoreau/Walden revival, it's worth stepping through some of her claims in order to draw out what is still left to be said here. The centerpiece of Schulz's criticism is the claim that Thoreau actually had little interest in or feeling for other people, and therefore should be recognized primarily as a failed moralist. She writes near the end of the article that *Walden* is "a book about how to live that says next to nothing about how to live with other people." Ridiculing his asceticism, Shultz paints a picture of Thoreau as an oddly pedantic, Puritan Calvinist who is hopped up on transcendentalist steroids. Thoreau "never met an appetite too innocuous to denounce. He condemned those who gathered cranberries for jam [...] food was bad, drink was bad, even shelter was suspect [...] he recoiled from the idea of a doormat." She is not aware "of any theology which holds that the road to hell is paved with doormats."

Since there is indeed an air of madness about this stuff (as there is with Diogenes, living in an overturned barrel), it's hard to argue that this polemical arrow does not find its mark. But Shultz really goes out of her way to be completely noncomprehending of asceticism and the choice of personal austerity in general. The last time I checked, asceticism and austerity have a rather long religious and philosophical pedigree, and are found in almost every period of every culture on earth, save perhaps that of the contemporary bourgeoisie, hopped up on consumerist steroids. Schulz's generalized noncomprehension of asceticism leads her to the conclusion that "Walden is not a paean to living simply; it is a paean to living purely, with all the moral judgment the word implies." From here, once again, it is religious moralism and transcendentalism that explain why Thoreau so thoroughly rejects the opinions of others, moves away

23 Kathryn Schulz, "The Moral Judgments of Henry David Thoreau," *The New Yorker,* October 12, 2015, https://www.newyorker.com/magazine/2015/10/19/pond-scum.

to Walden Pond, and supposedly looks down on other people, especially his Concord neighbors. All of this also leads her to frame Thoreau's remarks about lived experience as hopelessly burdened by metaethical problems. She says she doesn't know what he means when he says he wants to separate what is life from what is not life, and she weirdly characterizes the statement "the mass of men lead lives of quiet desperation" as an unsubstantiated allegation.

Contrary to the popular, straw man version of Thoreau as "our national conscience, urging us to be true to ourselves and to live in harmony with nature," Schulz wants to show up Thoreau as a hypocrite and a solipsist. Further challenging the view of *Walden* as "the story of voluntary exile from society, an extended confrontation with wilderness and solitude," Schulz points out that in 1845, Walden Pond was scarcely more off the grid than Prospect Park, Brooklyn, is today. The commuter rail to Boston ran along the pond's southwest side, she says, and he could (and did) walk home to Concord several times a week in only about twenty minutes, and often had large numbers of guests visiting him in the cabin. Reaching a final apotheosis of unfairness, Shultz writes, "Rather than compare him to Emerson, Muir, or Garrison, he is closer to Ayn Rand—suspicious of government, fanatical about individualism, egotistical, elitist, convinced other people lead pathetic lives, but unwilling to help them."

Thoreau and Ayn Rand? Really? In order to counter the basic charge that Thoreau is a solipsist, a failed moralist, and a hypocrite, in favor of the view (found in Greif and Odell) that he is more like a modern version of a classical Cynic, it makes sense here to take a partial step back. If one grasps Thoreau's underlying concept of experience, *Walden* need not be encountered, as Schulz finds it, as "an unnavigable thicket of contradiction and caprice," and Thoreau's desire to "live deep and suck out all the marrow of life" and to "put to rout all that was not life"[24] really need not be all that mysterious. One merely has to forgo

24 Thoreau, *Walden*, 51.

Schulz's end-of-history, capitalist-realist assumption that every asceticism is an unwarranted fanaticism, because in our present neoliberal capitalist reality, we are already living in the best of all possible worlds.

To Learn What Life Has to Teach

When I was a graduate student in philosophy, we didn't read Thoreau, except perhaps *On Civil Disobedience* in an applied ethics course. American philosophy was the pragmatists, including Charles Sanders Pierce, and maybe the transcendentalists (i.e., Emerson). To the extent that we thought about "philosophy as a way of life," it came up in ancient ethics, and via Foucault, as a bridge to the writing of Pierre Hadot.[25] We pondered Heidegger's negative-theological pieties on the meaning of "dwelling,"[26] but didn't give any thought at all to what Thoreau had to say about shelter. Like Schulz, I didn't think Thoreau's "house building and bean planting and whatnot" had anything to teach me about what life has to teach me.

For those who have not read it, the opening section of *Walden,* called "Economy," is a heartfelt reflection on labor and work, and is permeated with a kind of a bitter soul-sickness that gives the book its overall propulsion. Watching the spectacle of his fellows in their barns and at their plows, Thoreau asks himself, "Why should they begin digging their graves as soon as they are born? The laboring man has no time for anything but to be a machine."[27] Thoreau's reflections on the condition of the townsmen of Concord are also strikingly contemporary: "always trying to get into business, and trying to get out of debt [...] always promising to pay, tomorrow, and dying today, insolvent [...] making yourself sick, that you may lay up something

25 See Pierre Hadot, *Philosophy as a Way of Life,* trans. Michael Chase, ed. Arnold I. Davidson (Malden: Blackwell, 1995).

26 See Martin Heidegger, "Building, Dwelling, Thinking," in *Poetry, Language, Thought,* trans. Albert Hofstadter (New York: Harper Colophon, 1971), 145–61.

27 Ibid., 4.

against a sick day [...] the slave driver of yourself."[28] Reflecting on his neighbors, he says he finds that "they have been toiling, twenty, thirty, or forty years that they may become the real owners of their farms."[29] Since for him the cost of a thing is "the amount of "what I call life which is required to be exchanged for it, immediately or in the long run,"[30] it is clear that Thoreau thinks that this is too high a price to pay for a dwelling.

From here, the narrative mood shifts. When we consider what is the chief end of man, and what are the necessities of life, Thoreau says that "it appears as if men had deliberately chosen the common mode because they had preferred it to any other [...] but it is never too late to give up our prejudices. No way of thinking or doing, however ancient, can be trusted without proof."[31] There is a world of mere appearances, Thoreau wants us to understand, and human life is in a disordered state (Socratic/Cynical). What kind of proof would alleviate this additional skeptical stance? Thoreau answers, "Here is life, a great experiment, untried by me [...] we might try our lives by a thousand simple tests."[32] He proposes to examine first the necessities of life, how they are obtained, and what attitude toward them one ought to take (he considers food, shelter, clothing, fuel). Then the discussion turns to consideration of luxuries and comforts, and to voluntary poverty and austerity. The general thrust is captured when he says that "when he obtains those things which are necessary [...] there is another alternative than to obtain the superfluities; and that is to adventure on life now."[33]

It's also important to point out, given what Schulz has said, that Thoreau is very direct and clear about for whom *Walden* is written: "I don't mean to prescribe rules to strong and valiant natures who will mind their own affairs, whether in heaven or in hell." Nor is he addressing "those who find encouragement in

28 Ibid., 5.
29 Ibid., 19.
30 Ibid., 18.
31 Ibid., 6.
32 Ibid., 6–7.
33 Ibid., 9.

precisely the present condition of things [...] I do not speak to those who are well-employed [...] but mainly to the mass of men who are discontented, and idly complaining of the hardness of their lot, or of the times [...]."[34] Finally, in case there is still the temptation to see him as a do-gooder, looking down his nose: "I never knew, and never shall know, a worse man than myself."[35] One last rejoinder on the question of "withdrawal from society." Initially, Thoreau says, he goes off to live at the pond just to cut expenses while he figured out how to start a small business.[36] *Walden* might have been a "LinkedIn article" about how to be an effective small businessperson, but it isn't. His sojourn turns instead into a kind of a laboratory for an experiment in living, and for what Odell has called "refusing in place." Like Descartes, sitting in his stove-heated room to stay warm and contemplating the wax, Thoreau creates a spectacle of himself, bracketing prior experience and arguing from first principles. Perhaps, with all this in mind, you think that this sort of *epoché* (suspension of judgment by bracketing assumptions) is either something wholly antiquated, belonging to the distant past or merely a form of adolescent activity. That is all well and good. But tell it to the tiny house movement; tell it to the millions of people trying to find paths to wellness and recovery from work-related stress; tell it to the people who decide to Marie Kondo their lives.

From Walden Pond to Zuccotti Park

Just before the account of the history of refusal in Odell's *How to Do Nothing,* there is a chapter titled "The Impossibility of Retreat." Faced with the need for digital detox, "we might conclude that the answer is to turn our back on the world, temporarily, or for good."[37] Here too, she tries to make the case for a third

34 Ibid., 10.
35 Ibid., 44.
36 Ibid., 12.
37 Odell, *How To Do Nothing,* 30.

way, something other than either temporary life hacks designed for increasing productivity once back at work or saying goodbye permanently and neglecting our responsibility to the world. Odell is skeptical of dreams of permanent retreat from society. She thinks that fully utopian attempts to begin with a blank slate as were attempted in some 1960s communes "lead to a technocratic solution where design has replaced politics, presaging the libertarianism of Silicon Valley tech moguls."[38] Relying on Robert Houriet's *Getting Back Together*, Odell points out that there was a sort of a "second stage" to the communal experiments. Facing "unfinished geodesic domes, crops gone wrong, and arguments over how to raise children," the naïve optimism gave way in some places to a "more rigid and less idealistic approach" epitomized by B.F. Skinner's novel *Walden Two*.[39]

For Skinner, she says, utopian experimentation takes a scientific turn. Odell writes that "in the void left by politics, the emphasis in *Walden Two* lies on the aesthetic (better design, more efficient, etc.)." Skinner addressed problems such as exhaustion of resources, pollution, overpopulation, and nuclear threat, but he fails to mention the Viet Nam War, or struggles over racial equality.[40] Since the question for Skinner was not how power could be redistributed or injustice redressed, but how technical problems might be solved, Odell sees a direct line between Skinner and Peter Thiel, for whom the future requires a total escape from politics.[41] Since democracy and freedom are incompatible, the task is to build a machinery of freedom that ultimately makes the world safe for capitalism. By contrast, Odell invokes the possibility of what she calls "collective refusals" in which individuals align with each other to form flexible structures that can hold open the space of refusal. Here again, she posits a third space, "not of retreat or withdrawal—but of refusal, boycott, and even sabotage," a space that she says is "like

38 Ibid., 38.
39 Ibid., 44–45.
40 Ibid., 48.
41 Ibid.

a "crowd of Thoreaus, refusing in tandem," in a "spectacle of noncompliance."[42]

It remains to say a few words about how it is that Greif also gets it. To begin with, where Odell describes some high points in the history of refusal, Greif writes instead about what one might call "the rise of eudaimonic hedonism" in bourgeois European culture, starting sometime in the nineteenth century.[43] Under this cultural shift, Greif says, the pursuit of happiness becomes the quest for experience. But since happiness is ambiguous, and pleasure evanescent, "you amass experiences," and you inevitably learn that "they're not enough, and never will be enough."[44] Into the breach of this experience of nihilism (each and every moment is lost to time and leaves a residue of perpetual loss), there arises various attempts to radicalize experience as some sort of a solution. Greif says that by the 1850s, there are actually two radical solutions offered: the aestheticism of Flaubert, where you perceive the world as art and must make of your life a work of art, and the perfectionism of Thoreau, where you charge yourself with weighing and choosing, with changing yourself.

Greif thus acknowledges that Flaubert withdrew to Croisset and Thoreau to Walden in order to figure out "how to survive their time."[45] It's possible that these methods "make people appear to withdraw from the living." It's true that "Flaubert and Thoreau seemed hermited, by the standards of their friends."[46] But then he adds, similarly to Odell, "against the obvious criticism of these solutions as solipsistic, the efforts to remake your inside world inevitably turns you outward."[47] Greif also understands, along with Odell, that there are a number of reasons why Thoreau's reflections converge on the building of a simple cabin in the woods, and why it is connected to Diogenes in his barrel. It's not that everyone should consider withdrawing into an iso-

42 Ibid., 77.
43 Greif, *Against Everything*, 86.
44 Ibid., 79.
45 Ibid., 87.
46 Ibid., 92.
47 Ibid.

lated natural setting—rather, it's about austerity as an attempt to recover a certain kind of autonomy and conviviality. Odell writes, "Solitude, observation, and simple conviviality should be recognized not only as ends in and of themselves, but inalienable rights belonging to anyone lucky enough to be alive."[48] The philosopher occupied a cabin, Greif writes in his concluding section, "because he wished to live outside all houses [...] Occupy Wall Street occupied a park in the financial center of the United States, not because they wanted to sleep outdoors, but because its participants wanted to live in a democracy."[49] It's important to remember, Greif writes, "that jail is the other notable site with which Thoreau [...] is associated, after the cabin and the pond."[50]

Many Thoreaus, Refusing in Tandem

I've tried to dispel a number of different preconceptions that are likely to arise about the cultural space of refusal, as an element of a postwork political imaginary, and as such as a condition for some sort of a politics of refusal (of work-as-we-know-it). But this underlaboring, to steal a phrase from John Locke, is incomplete if I don't address "privileged position" along with its close relatives, solipsism and romanticist withdrawal. After all, who, precisely, is really free to refuse the most general of working conditions? It is certainly true, as Odell has written, that whatever refusal might mean, "some can more easily afford to refuse than others."[51] At the level of group ideology rather than individual action, however, there is a kind of tipping point with respect to immiseration that apparently brings things out into the open. This is because some people's misery counts for more than others on the terrain of public discourse. Once the middle class and the professional classes join the ranks of the miserable,

48 Odell, *How To Do Nothing*, xi.
49 Greif, *Against Everything*, 293.
50 Ibid., 297.
51 Odell, *How To Do Nothing*, 82.

it starts to become possible to talk about the problem at the level of the system itself.

In Elizabeth Anderson's *Private Government,* as we discussed in chapter 1, her major explanation for the gap between the (increasingly miserable) experience of work-as-we-know-it and the dominant neoliberal capitalist ideology is that, at least until recently, there was an aggregate class of people who "do not find the situation so bad."[52] She includes in this professors and students, the self-employed, and the many in the professional classes who have thought themselves exempt from the most onerous aspects of their employment contract's range of discretion. If it is the case, as Odell also writes, that refusal requires a degree of latitude, "a margin enjoyed at the level of the individual," it is also true, she says, appearing to agree with Anderson, that this margin "has been shrinking for a long time now."[53] And once "there is a growing perception that neoliberal capitalism is irrevocably bereft of future promise," as Peter Fleming writes, and that neorentier finance capital "must increasingly gain sustenance from the living communities and rich sociality of the ninety-nine percent," then the extent and texture of collective misery opens up at least the possibility of collective action.[54] If the dominant ideology cannot manage, per Abraham Lincoln, to "fool all of the people all of the time," then the question becomes, following Fleming, "Can the impossibility at the heart of contemporary capitalism be politically activated to oppose and escape work?"[55] I believe that the answer to this question is yes. But I believe that the emergence of an action potential in this regard has to start with a generational culture change that opens up the space of refusal as a meaningful proposition. I realize that I have cited evidence only from within a very edu-

52 Elizabeth Anderson, *Private Government: How Employers Rule Our Lives (and Why We Don't Talk about It)* (Princeton: Princeton University Press, 2017), 62.

53 Ibid., 84.

54 Peter Fleming, *Resisting Work: The Corporatization of Life and Its Discontents* (Philadelphia: Temple University Press, 2014), 20, 7.

55 Ibid., 19.

cated, literary domain. But in the darkest times, ideas have a way of jumping over the firebreak. It may turn out to be the case that this distinctly changed cultural mood is already busy discovering itself.

3

Rethinking Usefulness (Amid the Collapsing Fantasies of Capitalist Realism)

> The struggle for an equitable distribution of time and power to be useful to self and others outside employment [...] has been effectively paralyzed.
>
> — Ivan Illich, *The Right to Useful Unemployment*

The Useless Philosopher-President of Ireland

In a speech to a group of students gathered for a reception at Áras an Uachtaráin in 2019, the diminutive, soft-spoken, and hugely popular president of Ireland, Michael D. Higgins, made some startling remarks that generated headlines.[1] The speech, which opened the ceremony for the Young Philosopher Awards, had all the hallmarks of a traditional convocation address. But its departures from this format were what made it notable. If the press reports are accurate, Higgins told the gathered young people that they were "not born just to be useful." Various articles

1 See, for example, Mike Colagrossi, "You Weren't Born Just to Be 'Useful,' Irish President Tells Students," *Big Think*, May 17, 2019, https://bigthink.com/the-present/young-philosophers/.

reporting on the remarks differ as to the precise language used, and there appears to be no available video of the address. Luckily, Higgins gave a similar speech at the same event in 2017, and that version is available on YouTube in its entirety, almost thirty minutes long, which seems like rather a lot to ask of high schoolers.[2] It is thus possible to piece together what he was intending.

President Higgins's 2017 remarks are framed by a critique of what he calls "the narrow utilitarian approach to education," understood primarily as preparing young people for the labor markets. Instead, access to education, he believes, should first and foremost be understood as training for citizenship, for being able to ask and answer difficult questions, to exercise historical judgment, and to address perennial questions, such as "What is justice?" for one's own time. Decrying the inevitability of a culture focused exclusively on individual performance, career advancement, and the like, Higgins reminds those assembled that "freedom is not just freedom of the market" and that we need to raise citizens who "place humanity and solidarity at the heart of what they do" rather than settling for them to be "citizens seeking mere survival in a society–economy relationship that is poorly understood." When I try to absorb the significance of a contemporary world leader, a head of state, actually saying these sorts of things, I must admit that I end up somewhat bereft of my faculties. My first reaction was actually to imagine the faces of concerned parents near the back of the room. But as my friend Steve Heikkila very thoughtfully reminds me, this unbidden image relies upon a stereotype, and anyway the Republic of Ireland is not a Protestant country. I have invoked President Higgins here because his intentional devaluing of usefulness, which amounts to an impassioned plea to awaken us from the fantasies of capitalist realism, is at the heart of this chapter.

It's important to note here that Higgins appears to be in complete agreement with Jenny Odell. In the introduction, "Surviv-

---

2 Áras an Uachtaráin, "Speech by President Higgins at a Reception to Launch Irish Young Philosopher Awards," *YouTube,* November 17, 2017, https://www.youtube.com/watch?v=Os20UivqNBI.

ing Usefulness," Odell rejects the notion that we should simply accept living in a world where "our value is determined primarily by our productivity," since life itself is not a mere instrument, and so stands higher than any optimization imperative. Like Higgins, Odell denounces the narrowing horizon for "things deemed unproductive," not just because they give meaning to people as individuals, but because capitalist productivity's intolerance for these "nothings" robs us of the time and space necessary to carry on some version of a collective life. We are completely immersed in work, and when not at work, immersed in the busy activity of consuming the goods and services that we need in order to live. Sucked dry of our biopower, we have consented to a pattern of life that seriously endangers our species-level persistence as *homo politicus.*

In the following sections, which describe aspects of *The Right to Useful Unemployment* by Ivan Illich along with Mark Fisher's *Capitalist Realism,* I again consider Odell's basic strategy of valorizing "nothings" as a form of resistance in order to make ourselves "into a shape that cannot be [...] easily appropriated by a capitalist value system."[3] This time around, however, I try to draw out what was only implicit in chapters 1 and 2, that is, how it is that refusing work-as-we-know-it is intimately connected to overcoming the fantasies of capitalist realism. Perhaps you are asking, But why Ivan Illich? I must confess that I had previously scanned his work only briefly many years ago, and saw in him something rather typical of the 1970s — a popularizing, leftist-humanist polemicist who railed against the excesses of consumer society, someone in the mold of Erich Fromm or Paul Goodman. Revisiting his work in light of the issues explored in this book, however, I have come to the conclusion that Illich is very much the progenitor and avatar of the current trend toward the refusal of work-as-we-know-it. His concerns encompass both the critique of capitalist ideology with respect to work and the aspect of a culture of refusal from chapters 1 and 2. Personal

3 Jenny Odell, *How To Do Nothing: Resisting the Attention Economy* (Brooklyn: Melville House, 2019), xvi.

austerity. Seeking an escape back into some form of autonomous life. The politics of conviviality. Rethinking usefulness. It's pretty much all in there.

How Our Pervasive Capitalist Realism Begins to Crack

I've been exploring the possibility that it might actually make sense for all of us (collectively) to begin to refuse the conditions of work-as-we-know-it. It's a rather outrageous idea, I do realize. Especially since I'm not talking about petitions for better pay and improved working conditions on the part of the organized industrial labor force. I have in mind something much more expansive and fundamental, something that necessarily concerns all "wage laborers," including not just the service industry and FIRE (finance, insurance, real estate) sector's white-collar and pink-collar contributors, but also tech workers, middle managers, and even members of the professions. What then are the conditions of work-as-we-know-it, which so extravagantly call forth such a nontraditional form of solidarity on the part of a heretofore nonexistent collective subject? They aren't hard to come by. Think post-Fordist precarity; think financialization of everything; think the bullshitification of jobs; think neorentier debt peonage; think increasingly authoritarian employment contracts; think the erasure of the barrier between work and private life, and the enlistment of everyone's life energy on behalf of the company; think exhaustion, stress, anxiety, depression, and despair.

In chapters 1 and 2, I repeatedly made reference to the role of "capitalist realism" in promoting and sustaining this very unhappy trajectory. I contend that the pervasive ideology of capitalist realism is one of the major things that stands between ourselves and the possibility of a truly different experience of work, one less totalizing, less intrusive, less precarious, less soul-sucking. The reason for this has everything to do with the particular kind of society in which we now live. As both Fisher and Fleming have pointed out, following Gilles Deleuze, today we are increasingly living in what are called "control societies."[4] Whereas the previous "disciplinary society" (as described by Foucault[5]) is generally characterized by enclosure (the family, the school, the factory, the prison), control societies exhibit a new and different type of domination. This kind of disciplinary regulation, Fleming writes, "does not seek to contain the subject of power. Instead, it utilizes its inherent and self-productive qualities."[6] How does this utilization manifest itself? To begin with, where the corporation (with its various incentives and inducements) replaces the factory, "the disciplinary tropes of spatial confinement and docile bodies" are less important.[7]

The factory, Deleuze said, constitutes individuals as discontinuous producers of energy within what, from the viewpoint of capital, is essentially an aggregate body. But corporations, by contrast, constantly motivate individuals to think of themselves as human capitals, motivating rivalries and internal competition via modulations of salary and other incentives, and especially by inviting a set of indefinite postponements—in the control society setting, it turns out, one is never finished with anything. Fisher writes, "Education is a lifelong process [...] training [...] persists for as long as your working life continues [...] [and] work, you take home with you."[8] In this way, the spatially limited surveillance of the disciplinary society is replaced, in large part, by internal policing that is prompted by the operation of markets. There is, of course, quite a lot more to say about the nature of surveillance today—Deleuze was writing about this thirty years ago, before the widespread deployment of data mining, predictive analytics, artificial intelligence, and other such

4 Gilles Deleuze, "Postscript on the Societies of Control," *October* 59 (Winter 1992): 4.

5 See Michel Foucault, *Discipline and Punish: The Birth of the Prison,* trans. Alan Sheridan (New York: Vintage Books, 1979).

6 Peter Fleming, *Resisting Work: The Corporatization of Life and Its Discontents* (Philadelphia: Temple University Press, 2014), 27.

7 Ibid., 28.

8 Mark Fisher, *Capitalist Realism: Is There No Alternative?* (Winchester: Zero Books, 2009), 22.

technologies. But with all of this in mind, one can see how this basic mode of domination turns out to be highly dependent upon capitalist realism. Fisher says that it is dependent upon the naturalizing of a set of social and political structures reliant on the fantasy that "resources are infinite, the earth itself is merely a husk which capital can, at a certain point, slough off like a used skin, and that any problem can be solved by the market."[9]

Between ourselves and effective resistance to work-as-we-know-it lies what the poet William Blake referred to as our "mind forg'd manacles." To refuse the conditions of work requires us to first recognize that our collective experience of work is historically and socially conditioned, and that the form of domination under which we live everywhere attempts to prefigure our needs, our wishes, and our hopes according to its market logic. It is capitalist realism that tells us that we have arrived at the end of history, and that the future is as bereft of utopian energies as the present, and that "there is no alternative" (TINA).

If the increasingly immiserating experience of work actually begins to undermine the effectiveness of the various inducements and postponements upon which the control society relies, then the pervasive capitalist realism that undergirds work-as-we-know-it begins to crack. If the cracks become wide enough, and the ideology that equates human freedom exclusively with market freedom becomes too improbable, then large numbers of people may actually start to breakout of the "non-enclosure" that replaced the disciplinary panopticon of previous social institutions. This is especially the case because advanced capitalist society, asserting the end of history, is functioning in a manner largely bereft of any and all utopian energies. If nothing else, once work is exposed as something socially constructed and thus historically determined, there is an opportunity to decide that work-as-we-know-it is not destiny and thus not necessarily on an unwavering course to achieving its most dystopian potentials.

9 Ibid., 18.

The Strange Case of Ivan Illich

Illich is a rather difficult figure to describe. I tend to regard the half-Croatian, stateless Illich as sort of a spiritual casualty of World War II, a wandering anarchistic leftist who never got on board with the postwar liberal project, and whose skepticism about the human costs of economic development programs and so-called modernization peaked in the 1970s right when liberalism's own confidence seriously began to falter. A one-time Catholic priest, Illich took up a post ministering to the immigrant communities of Washington Heights in Manhattan upon his ordination in 1951. After that, he became vice rector of the Catholic University of Puerto Rico in 1956, where he was very vocal in his criticism of the Church's role in economic development in Latin America. In 1960, he was fired from the university, and he then traveled around Latin America, by bus and on foot.

It wouldn't be totally off base, in my view, to regard him in his travels as an Anthony Bourdain figure, as sort of an amateur cultural anthropologist intensely interested in realness wherever he could find it. Or maybe a comparison with Michael Taussig or Tobias Schneebaum might be even closer to the mark.[10] It seems pretty clear that one of the things Illich witnessed was the progressive debasement of previously self-reliant agrarian communities as they became dependent upon the liberal welfare state in the interest of economic development. Illich eventually settled in Cuernavaca, Mexico, where he opened a social research institute that came to be known as CIDOC (Centro Intercultural de Documentación). He continued to provide radical critiques of the role of missionaries in Latin America, until he got so crosswise to Opus Dei types at the Vatican that he was forced to shut down. Illich then renounced the priesthood, and began the period of his most productive literary work, during the 1970s.

10 Michael Taussig is an Australian anthropologist most famous for his firsthand accounts of shamanic practices in South America; see *Shamanism, Colonialism, and the Wild Man* (Chicago: Univesity of Chicago Press, 1987). Tobias Schneebaum was an anthropologist and activist; see *Wild Man* (New York: Viking Press, 1979).

The Right to Useful Unemployment came out in 1978, and is not among Illich's most-read works. Illich's first book, *Deschooling Society* (1971), was the work that made him something of a literary star, and he was seen as a fellow traveler with Paolo Freire, who was making a simultaneous splash with his own ideas about educational reform. In the end, the radicalism of Illich's critique of professionalism turned out to be too much for Freire, and they became estranged, but Illich and Paul Goodman (*Growing Up Absurd*, 1960) were friends until the end of Goodman's life.

Illich and the Politics of Conviviality

The basic meaning of Illich's title, *The Right to Useful Unemployment,* is given to us succinctly in a set of statements rather late in the book: "People have been dispossessed of their usefulness unless they are gainfully employed," and "The struggle for an equitable distribution of time and power to be useful to self and others outside employment [...] has been effectively paralyzed."[11] Illich agrees with Odell and Irish president Higgins (and for that matter, most women, who do all manner of unpaid work in the interest of society). He wants to rethink the meaning of usefulness in a way that decenters market productivity. But Illich's overall narrative under this umbrella is quite a bit more ambitious than even this would suggest. His opening strategy is similar to that of a number of more recent writers considered here thus far. He draws our attention to some universal experiences in market-intensive societies in order to reframe otherwise traditional labor narratives focused on the industrial working class. Because we measure material progress by growth in GDP, "and we measure social progress by the distribution and access to commodities," Illich writes in chapter 1, "socialism has been debased to a struggle against handicapped distribution, and welfare economics has identified the public

11 Ivan Illich, *The Right to Useful Unemployment and Its Professional Enemies* (London: Marion Boyars Ltd., 2000), 58, 88.

good with opulence."[12] Instead of buying into these underlying assumptions, Illich proposes to describe what he calls another "distinct and under-theorized kind of poverty."

Since market dependence has led to a widespread loss of what he calls "autonomous and creative life," he thinks it necessary to focus on a kind of "industrialized impotence" that affects both rich and poor, an experience not captured where the focus is exclusively upon the economic markers of industrial poverty. Economists, Illich says, "have no effective means of including in their calculations the society-wide loss of a kind of satisfaction that has no market equivalent."[13] This is not to say that Illich is not also concerned with inequality per se: "I am of course so clearly committed to a radically equitable distribution of goods, rights, and jobs that I find it almost unnecessary to insist on our struggle from this side of justice," he writes in the foreword.[14] Illich's primary concern here is with what he calls the "negative internalities of modernity," which he identifies as, for example, "time-consuming acceleration, sick-making healthcare, and stupefying education."[15] Per Illich, total dependence upon commodities creates a crisis condition, which then brings in "the needs creators and managers, the doctors, diplomats, bankers, and assorted social engineers."[16] We end up with such things as "educators who live on society's alienation, and doctors who prosper on the work and leisure that have destroyed health."[17] Where this kind of poverty reigns, attempting to live "without access to addictive commodities is rendered impossible or criminal — or both."[18] Illich names this concern with the equality of modern poverty rather than upon inequality the "politics of conviviality."

12 Ibid., 24.
13 Ibid., 30.
14 Ibid., 15.
15 Ibid., 14.
16 Ibid., 19.
17 Ibid., 20.
18 Ibid., 9.

Illich's Call for a Copernican Revolution in Values

Illich's critique of modern, market-intensive society is nothing if not radical. One can see why this approach, which is implicitly focused upon the moment of "emergence from subsistence" at the beginning of the modern age, would not get a lot of popular purchase, even in the face of the social, political, and economic pathologies of the last twenty-five years of the twentieth century, which have led us to yearn for more organic communities. Even during the tumult of the 1960s, only a small minority seriously dreamed of living in premodern communities as if there was some utopian content made available by doing so. Also, given the scope of mass society, it seems hard to imagine on the face of it that such a pattern of life could really be scalable for billions of people. However, one can also see why there would be a resurgence of interest in all of this just now, given the almost total eclipse of community life.

Putting aside his implicit criticism of socialist strategy, Illich is in some sense more orthodox in his Marxism than most of the orthodox Marxist critics, since his core ideas devolve upon the eclipse of use values in all aspects of social life in favor of exchange values. When Illich talks about "impoverishing wealth" or "paralyzing affluence" or "modernized poverty," he is zeroing in on how capitalist market logic has fundamentally changed human-needs satisfaction in the age of bourgeois liberalism. The professionalization of everything, the need for experts to help you negotiate all aspects of even everyday life (with the associated load of administrative actions and bureaucratic challenges) substitutes industrial goods and services for an intangible set of "nonmarket values" that Illich deems to be nonetheless essential: "The generation of non-marketable use values must inevitably occupy the center of any culture that provides a program of satisfactory life to the majority of its members."[19]

All of this leads him to pose a stark choice, a kind of a Kierkegaardian either/or: either "produce another new bill of

19 Ibid., 27.

goods, or take a new approach to needs and their satisfactions." The first choice, he says in the section "The History of Needs," "leads to acceptance of market edicts, the second means drawing down the curtain on absolute market dominance and fostering an ethic of austerity."[20] Carrying out this sort of "social inversion," Illich writes, is to refuse to continue to see consumer goods and professional services at the center of our economic system. Instead, we should insist upon moving use values created and valued by people (what he calls "convivial austerity") to the center of our experience.[21] In this sense, what he is describing is thoroughly consistent with the notion of a politics of refusal that I am exploring here. Illich says that to choose convivial austerity in this way, so as "to produce use values against disabling enrichment," depends on nothing less than a Copernican revolution in our perception of values.

Fisher on Realism and the Real

The first sections of Fisher's *Capitalist Realism* follow a trajectory remarkably similar to that of Illich just described, even though Fisher starts where this opening salvo from Illich ends — with the need for some sort of Copernican revolution in our thinking. Invoking a phrase attributed to Fredric Jameson or to Žižek — "It is easier to imagine the end of the world, than it is to imagine the end of capitalism" — Fisher says that this observation gives the sense of what he means by the term "capitalist realism." The term denotes more than just the ideological assertion of the superiority of capitalism, or even the assertion that unfettered capitalism is the only viable political and economic system; it captures the sense in which *capitalism itself has rendered it literally impossible to even imagine a coherent alternative to it.*

Like Illich, Fisher locates this effect in the manner in which capitalism has restructured the satisfaction of human needs. To

20 Ibid., 34.
21 Ibid., 36.

begin with, he tells us, there is the way that capitalism, through its system of equivalence, subsumes and consumes all previous history by assigning a monetary exchange value to all cultural objects. This "massive desacralization of culture" also heralds a turn from engagement to spectatorship. The result, however, is an ad hoc reinstallation of all cultural codes, even those previously derived from a putative transcendent law—the limits of capitalism are defined pragmatically and improvisationally, on a playing field to the horizon line at history's end. The term "capitalist realism" is thus needed in order to describe the pervasive sense of cultural exhaustion and sterility that is widely experienced "after postmodernism." Cultural postmodernism, per Fisher, was all about "hijacking and recuperation, and was concerned with subversion and incorporation." However, under the neoliberal capitalist condition, we are dealing instead with pervasive "pre-corporation," that is, the preemptive formatting and shaping of needs, desires, aspirations, and hopes by capitalist culture.[22]

To capture what all this really means, Fisher gives us some examples. He points out that today we live in a reality where neoliberal capitalism has installed what amounts to a business ontology, one where it is simply obvious that everything in society should be run like a business. He reminds us that we live in a reality where poverty, famine, and war can all be presented as inevitable, because a set of social, political, and economic structures have been afforded the force of natural law. Finally, he points to the persistent fantasy that holds that Western consumerism, far from being implicated in the system of global inequalities, can itself solve them, since all we have to do is to buy the right products.[23]

Capitalist realism cannot generally be seen directly. But it becomes visible in the reflected light of other social phenomena. For example, when we continue to dutifully recycle our trash, because it's the right thing to do, even when we know most of

22 Fisher, *Capitalist Realism*, 9.
23 Ibid., 16–17.

it isn't being recycled, capitalist realism can be seen. Likewise when we attack the homeless rather than the causes of homelessness. The notion of capitalist realism is thus offered as a means to express the way in which capitalist ideology is seen to function today. The role of ideology is "not to make a case for something, the way that propaganda does."[24] This is because "the fundamental level of ideology is not that of illusion masking the real state of things, but that of an unconscious fantasy structuring our social reality itself."[25]

For most of us in the Anglophone world, to be told that the Real is something we collectively assert or posit, and that the concomitant realism is the stabilization of a regime of truth and power, is somewhat difficult to swallow. Nonetheless, beyond any specific assertion of reality, and its associated realist supporting claims, Fisher insists, there is also the unknowable thing-in-itself, the Real, that for which it is offered as a sufficient representation, but in relation to which it must inevitably fall short. Following Žižek and Lacan, Fisher also wants us to recognize that in all accounts of the Real (as something that resists all symbolization), there is more than a dash of longing and frustrated wish fulfillment. These assertions of wholeness, he says, are often traumatized by horrifying ruptures and incursions of Realness into the reality principle's everyday symbolic order. The sublimity of large-scale natural disasters is offered as a case in point, as are unnatural monsters, aliens, and other ghouls from horror genres.

Given this account of the dynamics of capitalist ideology, not so much as propaganda, but as a set of persistent fantasies constitutive of a fundamental pattern of social life, where is an effective challenge supposed to come from? One strategy, Fisher asserts, could involve invoking the Real underlying the reality that capitalism presents to us.[26] To awake from capitalist realism is to glimpse the Real behind the naturalized reality, and

---

24 Ibid., 12.

25 Ibid., 13, 18.

26 Ibid., 18.

to thereby witness the failure of capitalist incorporation or precorporation of human needs, aspirations, and hopes. The most obvious example, Fisher says, is the climate crisis, which invokes the Real because of its increasingly undeniable and irrecuperable exigency (capitalism is the only viable political economic system versus capitalism is primed to destroy the entire natural and human environment).

But Fisher thinks there are also good examples of various "social paradoxes" of capitalist ideology that also seriously threaten capitalist realism: there is the growing number of people suffering from mental health disability, which neoliberal capitalism continues to treat as a natural phenomenon, like the weather, with no connection to politics and social causation. There is the strong ideological assertion that capitalism is somehow antibureaucratic, as opposed to socialism, despite the obvious proliferation of what Fisher calls "market Stalinism" and, of course, there is the phenomenon we've seen Graeber call "bullshit jobs."[27]

Illich on Paradoxical Counterproductivity

Similar to Fisher, Illich also wants to direct our attention to a set of "social paradoxes" of capitalism as a way to help bring about his "Copernican revolution in values" and a new politics of conviviality. To do this, he takes aim at the professional classes along with commodification rampant in market-intensive society. A critique of what he terms the "disabling professions" is introduced in order to complete the picture of the generalized, radical alienation of people in society from organic-needs generation and the exercise of use values in the conduct of their affairs, individually and collectively. Illich's rather startling unmasking of the professional ethos, as both a form of class domination and an assault on autochthonous cultural life,[28] is initially somewhat disorienting, and this is something that is not lost on him: "Is

27 Ibid., 19–20.
28 Illich, *The Right to Useful Unemployment,* 38.

it not irresponsible to undermine the trust of the man in the street in his scientifically-trained teacher, physician, or economist? Is it not perverse to denigrate the very people who have the knowledge to recognize and service our needs?"[29] In reply, Illich says that "the age of professions will be remembered as the time when politics withered, when voters entrusted to technocrats the power to legislate needs, the authority to decide who needs what, and a monopoly over the means by which needs shall be met."[30]

The problem with the array of professional services that we all rely upon (and for which we pay handsomely) in our market-intensive society is that they create and/or shape the needs that they then serve, and that they are complicit with elites and/or the state that have afforded them monopolies, so that in their functioning they most closely resemble cartels. This is a matter of serious concern because of what he calls "the perversity of generated needs"; recall "time-consuming acceleration, stupefying education, and sick-making medicine." The professions must be indicted along with the capitalist financiers, Illich insists, because doing so is necessary to expose "the disparate antipathy between the ideal for the sake of which the service is rendered, and the reality that the service creates." Our major institutions, Illich writes, "have acquired the uncanny power to subvert the very purposes for which they were originally engineered and financed [...] their principal product is paradoxical counter-productivity."[31]

If we need more examples, Illich says things like this in the section "Enabling Distinctions": "Healthy homes are transformed into hygienic apartments where one cannot be born, cannot be sick, and cannot die decently. Not only are helpful neighbors a vanishing species, but also liberal doctors who make house calls. Workplaces fit for apprenticeships turn into mazes of corridors that permit access only to functionaries with

29 Ibid., 40–41.
30 Ibid., 46.
31 Ibid., 67.

identities pinned to their lapels."[32] Illich says it would be a mistake to attribute counterproductivity per se to "negative externalities" as mere side effects of economic growth, things such as pollution, congestion, and the like. Rather, he wants us to see, it's something more fundamental, and it "arises from the paralysis of the person who can no more exercise his autonomy in an environment designed for things."[33] He also says that there is no "rebellion against the huge disabling service delivery system" because of the "illusion-generating power that these same systems possess."[34] One can see in all of this, consistent with Fisher, the specter of the Real, peeking out from behind capitalist realism. And though it is likely true that most individual professionals care about their clients, it is also true that they are complicit with a larger societal pattern of disempowerment. Despite the "mask of care," in the end "the waning of the current professional ethos is a necessary condition for the emergence of a new relationship between needs, contemporary tools, and personal satisfaction."[35]

On the Right to Plant Veggies

In July 2019, National Public Radio reported a story, "After a 6-Year Battle, Florida Couple Wins the Right to Plant Veggies in Front Yard."[36] According to the article, a Florida couple had been growing vegetables in their front yard for nearly two decades, because their house is south-facing and the backyard is mostly in the shade. Then a local ordinance was tightened to forbid vegetable gardens in the front of a house, and the couple were told to dig up their plots or face steep daily fines for every day out of

32 Ibid., 66.

33 Ibid., 72.

34 Ibid., 67.

35 Ibid., 40.

36 Laurel Wamsely, "After a 6-Year Battle, Florida Couple Wins the Right to Plant Veggies in Front Yard," *KCUR Radio,* July 3, 2019, https://www.kcur.org/2019-07-03/after-6-year-battle-florida-couple-wins-the-right-to-plant-veggies-in-front-yard.

compliance. Then they went to court. After a six-year legal battle, they won "the freedom to grow healthy food on their own property."

Surely, one doesn't have to be a radical libertarian in order to conclude that it's socially counterproductive (and paradoxical) to tell people they can't grow food on their only reliable sun patch, because everyone knows you're supposed to engage in wage labor so that you can buy food and services, rendering the growing of some nice veggies a form of antisocial behavior. I mention this dismaying municipal legal fight over kale and squash because this story captures a lot of what is at stake when Illich talks about *the right to be useful to ourselves and others in ways not tied to our market productivity.* It is thus also connected to what is happening when Odell writes about "surviving usefulness," and the president of Ireland tells a group of students that they were "not born just to be useful." Activity, effort, achievement, or service, Illich says, when conducted outside of hierarchical relationships, and unmeasured by professional standards, represents a threat to a commodity-intensive society. Autonomous activity comes to be seen as a form of deviance because of the manner in which it detracts from employment and thus GNP.

Illich ends by calling for what he refers to as a "politically-generated convivial austerity." This is the style of life he envisions in a postindustrial economy where "people have succeeded in reducing their market dependence and done so by protecting, by political means, a social infrastructure [...] used primarily to generate use values."[37] In more or less complete agreement, Fisher says that we need a new struggle over work and who controls it, and thus an assertion of much greater worker autonomy, together with the rejection of certain kinds of labor (e.g., excessive auditing and other aspects of bullshitification). What is really needed, Fisher concludes, are new forms of resistance to managerialism, including the rejection of a universal business ontology applied to all types of human endeavor, a refusal of the facile naturalization of mental health epidemics, and a new style

37 Illich, *The Right to Useful Unemployment,* 94.

of personal austerity that refuses excessive consumerism — if we are less reliant on endless goods and services, we needn't work ourselves to death to pay for them.[38]

This chapter has revolved around the emerging political importance of reasserting the notion that it is work that is parasitic upon life, rather than the other way around. Hence the theme of rethinking usefulness, so that it means something other than "contributes to the GNP" and holds a job that pays well enough to afford all manner of consumer goods and a thicket of newly essential services. Since, along with Illich, Fleming (*Resisting Work: The Corporatization of Life and Its Discontents*) is among the great champions of refusing work today, it is fitting to give him the last word. In the final part of his book, Fleming remarks that "when our jobs become the index for living as such," our various job-related fears become existential and seemingly without object, because "widespread anxiety and hopelessness are built into the very logic of work today."[39] This is why it is vital to remember that what he calls "the commons," understood as living social labor, is always something in excess of the reductions that our jobs seek to place upon it. It has most often been the tendency to see the corporation (capital) as a kind of first mover, and then labor as the resisting subject. But "to appreciate how neoliberal control is counteracted and subverted by workers today," he writes, "we must be sure to avoid surveying the scene from the viewpoint of capital."[40] Today, where workers everywhere seek an "escape back into life," it is the corporation that must be seen as the resisting party. The old way of looking at things cedes way too much constitutive energy to an otherwise ossified system, Fleming says. Instead, we need to recognize that work today is "a rather extreme ritual linked to a dying capitalist project."[41] To refuse work today, therefore, is to assert the radical autonomy of the social commons.

38 Fisher, *Capitalist Realism*, 79–80.
39 Fleming, *Resisting Work*, 126.
40 Ibid., 127.
41 Ibid., 128.

4

Reclaiming Idleness from the Work–Laziness–Leisure Nexus

As we live a life of ease
Every one of us
Has all we need
Sky of blue
And sea of green

— The Beatles, "Yellow Submarine"

Comparing painter Georges Seurat's much celebrated *A Sunday Afternoon on the Island of La Grande Jatte* with his somewhat less famous *Bathers at Asnières,* we are invited into a certain kind of dialogue, a contrapuntal reflection on the differences between idleness and leisure. Looking at these paintings, what do we see? *Grande Jatte* shows affluent, middle-class figures, smartly dressed for a Sunday in the park, engaged in various acts of what Veblen called "conspicuous leisure," performing their "pecuniary emulation" of the leisure class, playing their part in what Guy Debord later referred to as "the society of the spectacle." *Asnières,* by contrast, shows working-class men and boys, idling in midday stillness on the banks of the Seine, the workaday world of industrial Paris visible in the background. Idleness and leisure, as this suggests, indicate a differential signification—leisure and idleness are not the same. Where leisure is generally something consistent with existing, hegemonic social arrangements, and is even sanctioned within capitalist relations of production, idleness is something else, something considered to be a vice, something thought to be identical with, or at least akin to, laziness, which these dominant interests everywhere aggressively oppose.

Thierry Paquot's *The Art of the Siesta* (2003) opens his own meditation on idleness by surveying the many instances of midday repose found in European painting since the Renaissance. In works such as Bruegel the Elder's *The Land of Cockaigne* and *The Harvesters,* we see "a dream of indolence, rest, and abundance," and the "courtesans, bathers, and prostitutes that populated the canvasses of Orientalists, Impressionists, Pointillists, and Fauves are as indolent as they are active at their siestas."[1] This is not to deny that the numerous situations depicting figures in states of repose in modern painting can be seen to stem, in large part, from the formal requirements of naturalistic depictions of the human body. Likewise, it is not to deny that many such situations find their *raison d'être* in stylistic references to traditional, premodern subjects, both Greco-Roman and biblical. Rather, it is simply to point out that in the "innumerable *déjeuners sur l'herbe*" (lunches in the grass) we also find individuals "surrendering themselves, or just about to surrender themselves, to the siesta."[2] Paquot writes, "Manet, Monet, Lautrec, Gaugin, and many more have depicted the arresting passage of time, that break in the day, that time to oneself [...] it would never form the central theme or title of a painting, but its presence is indisputable."[3]

Paquot wants us to regard these scenes of daytime idling, these representations of the siesta, as referring to something that is "more than just the act of falling asleep or dozing in the

1 Thierry Paquot, *The Art of the Siesta* (London: Marion Boyars Ltd., 2003), 17.
2 Ibid., 18.
3 Ibid., 19.

middle of the day."[4] The creation and reception of such scenes in the modern period, he thinks, inevitably must also involve an implicit statement about "the growing ubiquity of homogeneous, abstract time, the regularity of which imposes a discipline upon natural rhythms."[5] Seen in this light, he says, the siesta functions as a metaphor for "the capacity we have to dictate the use of our own time rather than submitting to time imposed by society."[6] In the siesta, time becomes a kind of a singularity that shapes daily existence through a dialectic of tension and relaxation. Through its rhythm, it supports an experience of human life as a succession of experiences "whose order is not always apparent."[7] Drawing on E. P. Thompson's *The Making of the English Working Class* (1966), Paquot points out that already by 1700, European societies were entering the familiar landscape of industrial capitalism, with its "timesheets, timekeeper, and informers to find and expose indolent and tardy workers."[8] In eighteenth- and nineteenth-century European societies, where time was ceasing to be "a succession of experiences, but rather a collection of hours, minutes, and seconds,"[9] scenes of country-dwellers and field workers harmonizing their time with that of nature reflect a reaction to "the discipline of the industrial process having escaped the confines of the factory floor."[10]

The valorization of idleness today and the defense of the siesta as a cultural institution, therefore, are intended by Paquot as a "strategy of resistance against the continued production of global time," which he says "has infiltrated everywhere, shamelessly presenting itself as self-evident, self-defining, and incontestable."[11] At first blush, imagining how this might be effective can be hard to do, especially for those with a radical

4 Ibid., 57.
5 Ibid., 32.
6 Ibid., 57.
7 Ibid., 51.
8 Ibid., 36.
9 Ibid., 32.
10 Ibid., 34.
11 Ibid., 71.

bent. We quite naturally tend to envision the path to a changed reality to be found by means of dramatic calls to political action. Here, though, Paquot wants us to try to imagine the myriad ways in which individual experience and social life might change if significant numbers of people insisted on experiencing time differently, and lived the course of the day according to a different rhythm. In this respect, what Paquot has in mind here is reminiscent of Jenny Odell's claim that in some contexts "doing nothing" can be an act of political resistance. The various stubborn nothings, Odell says, "which produce no deliverables, can't easily be used or appropriated by the dominant capitalist value system."[12]

Both Paquot and Odell thus also share a family resemblance to things such as the "culture jamming" movement of the 1980s, and especially with what Debord and the members of the Situationist International from the 1960s called *détournement*, which can be translated roughly as "hijacking." Recognizing how capitalism had proved surprisingly adept at recuperating or recommodifying radical culture, projects under the umbrella of *détournement* sought to "negate this negation." By hijacking elements of mainstream media representation to produce subversive messages designed to disrupt capitalist social relations, they sought to expose mass society as a form of domination, even if significant prospects for meaningful collective action remained elusive. Under this overarching banner of political surrealism, for example, Debord proposed something he called the *dérive* ("drift/drifting") as a "psychogeographical" activity designed to induce a kind of behavioral disorientation. An idle ramble through urban landscapes, the dérive was meant to be a radical encounter with social space stripped of the "programming of everyday social relations" dictated by capitalism.[13] If Paquot is

12 Jenny Odell, *How to Do Nothing: Resisting the Attention Economy* (Brooklyn: Melville House, 2019), xvi.

13 See esp. Guy Debord, "*Détournement* as Negation and Prelude," and "Theory of the *Dérive*," in *Situationist International Anthology*, ed. and trans. Ken Knabb (Berkeley: Bureau of Public Secrets, 2006), 67–68 and 62–66.

right in insisting that the integrity of the siesta should be seen as part of a process to reclaim our right to inhabit time, to assert its noncommercial use in the name of autonomy, then it behooves us to reach for a deeper understanding of how it is that idleness is actually something worthy, and thus something distinct from laziness, and from leisure. Since capitalist ideology unequivocally equates idleness with laziness, and seeks instead to promote leisure, the negation of this negation of idleness has a role to play within the broader intention to challenge our pervasive capitalist realist understanding of work in the modern age.

Some Early Polemics in Praise of Idleness

Notable political tracts encouraging resistance to work, and that deal with the thorny nexus of "idleness-laziness-leisure," can be found as far back as the late nineteenth century. Most famous among these early efforts is the pamphlet *Le Droit à la paresse* ("The Right to Be Lazy") written by Karl Marx's son-in-law, Paul Lafargue, and first published in 1880. Lafargue was writing in the aftermath of the failed revolutions of 1848, and what Marxists like to call the "bourgeois sellout" of the peasantry and industrial working class. The pamphlet was written as a kind of a warning to the French polity about what was in store for them, based on the things he had seen of industrial working conditions in England. Lafargue thus took aim at the so-called right to work that had rather spectacularly substituted for "the right to property," which had been a hallmark of the French Revolution's struggle against feudalism.[14]

Lafargue challenged what he called the "sacred halo that economists, moralists and priests have placed over work."[15] Proclaiming instead a "right to be lazy," Lafargue wrote that "the sons of the heroes of the terror have allowed themselves to be

14 Paul Lafargue, *The Right to Be Lazy*, ed. Bernard Marszalek (Chicago: Charles H. Kerr Company and AK Press, 2011), 22, 51.

15 Ibid., 23.

degraded by the religion of work."[16] Refusing the fifteen-hour day (and also reformist calls for a twelve-hour day), he argued polemically instead that the proletariat must "proclaim the right of laziness, a thousand times more noble than the anemic rights of man concocted by the metaphysical lawyers of the bourgeois revolution."[17] The defiant and semisatirical embrace of laziness, therefore, was meant as a rejection of calls from some quarters for more leisure time, for an assimilation of the working class to bourgeois values and patterns of living. It was also meant as a way of taking a stand against the constant drumbeat, coming from capitalist elites, that industrial workers should limit their expectations, reduce their needs, suppress their joys and passions, and curb any independence, all under the umbrella of "rooting out laziness." Lafargue consistently invokes "laziness" (*paresse*) and rarely mentions "idleness" (*oisiveté*), but it appears that he sometimes means "idleness" rather than "laziness," for example, when he goes so far as to refer to "laziness" as "mother of the arts, and noble virtues."[18] Perhaps if his purposes had been less polemical, he might have given some thought to idleness rather than simply embracing laziness as a way to oppose "work/leisure."

By contrast, in his 1923 reflection, *In Praise of Idleness,* the Czech playwright and critic Karel Čapek draws a strong distinction between idleness and laziness (and also leisure). He starts by announcing, "I would like to be idle today," and then goes on to describe his view of what idleness is and what it is not. Without calling out leisure by name, he says that idleness is not leisure: "Going out is not idling. Nor reading nor sleeping, because neither the one nor the other is idling. Nor amuse myself, nor rest, because idleness is neither relaxation or amusement." Rather, "idleness is the absence of everything by which a person is occupied, diverted, distracted, interested, employed, annoyed, pleased, attracted, involved, entertained, bored,

16 Ibid., 28.
17 Ibid., 34.
18 Ibid., 41.

enchanted, fatigued, absorbed, or confused."[19] What then is idleness? Čapek says that idleness is nothing, a negation, an intentlessness, a lack-purpose. Idleness is also not wasting time, nor is it "the mother of sin," since it "yearns for nothing." Also, idleness is not laziness. Laziness is neglecting to do something that ought to be done, and, anyway, anyone resting is doing something useful, in that one is preparing for future work. In closing, Čapek can only say that idleness "is something perfect, and rare," and that "when a person is through idling, he arises and returns as if from another world."[20]

It is not easy to discern whether or not Bertrand Russell ever read Čapek, but in 1932 he published his own work by the same title, *In Praise of Idleness,* where he uses "idleness" and "leisure" somewhat interchangeably (for Russell, it appears that idleness essentially coincides with an equal opportunity for the judicious use of leisure). As was the case with Lafargue, Russell is intent on contesting the widespread dogma that work is in itself something virtuous, as a condition for his call for a four-hour workday. Russell employs a sort of a rudimentary hermeneutics of suspicion to arrive at the origin of the "gospel of work." Work, he says, is actually of two kinds: there is altering the position of matter at or near the earth's surface relative to other such matter," and there is the activity of "telling other people to do so." There is also a third kind, which is "the giving of advice as to what orders should be given."[21] Having established this macro-division of labor, Russell then points out that there is a "class of landowners, who are idle, and whose idleness is made possible by the industry of others."[22]

For Russell, since work is nothing at all virtuous, leisure is also nothing vicious. Quite the contrary. Leisure "is essential to

19 Karel Čapek, "In Praise of Idleness," trans. Norma Comrada, in *Toward the Radical Center: A Karel Capek Reader,* ed. Peter Kussi (New Haven: Catbird Press, 1990), 241.

20 Ibid., 243.

21 Bertrand Russell, *In Praise of Idleness and Other Essays* (New York: Routledge, 1996), 3.

22 Ibid., 4.

civilization." Historically speaking, the problem with idleness/leisure is that until recently it has been "rendered possible for the few by the labor of the many."[23] Since the transformations wrought by the Great War, however, and with the aid of modern technology, it has now become possible to distribute leisure justly. Were it not for the fact that capitalist society continues to insist that work is a duty and a virtue, Russell says, we could "cut the hours of work per day down to four."[24] The problem standing in the way is just this: the idea that the poor should have leisure "has always been shocking to the rich."[25]

Russell goes on to say that if the ordinary wage earner worked just four hours per day, and assuming a "moderate amount of sensible organization," then there would be enough for everybody, and no unemployment.[26] Of course, it isn't entirely clear what Russell, in his understated way, means by "a moderate amount of sensible organization." It would not be unreasonable, given his statements elsewhere, to assume that he is actually referring to the enactment of some sort of socialist utopia (by either revolutionary or nonrevolutionary means) where industry would exist to meet human needs rather than valorize capital, and that in the future we could simply abjure the extraction of surplus value.

Russell does not tarry over the significant problem of implementation raised by this suggestion. Instead, he continues on with the exploration of his major point, namely, that leisure, if distributed fairly, is a species of the good. In response to the oft-made point by the wealthy that the poor would not know how to use so much leisure, Russell concedes that the wise use of leisure is indeed a product of "civilization and education," and says that if it is ultimately true that "men would not know how to fill their days," then this can only be a condemnation of the modern world as such.[27] Nonetheless, he still insists that, "without a con-

23 Ibid., 5.
24 Ibid., 6.
25 Ibid., 7.
26 Ibid., 8.
27 Ibid., 11.

siderable amount of leisure, a man is cut off from many of the best things," and he reasserts that if working hours were reduced to four a day, "which should entitle a man to the necessities and elementary comforts of life," then "the rest of his time should be his to use as he sees fit."[28] To the extent to which leisure is problematic, once again, it is because work-based society everywhere inculcates a passive, lower, or debased form of leisure (going to cinemas, watching football matches, listening to the radio), which he says is appropriate for people whose energies are fully taken up with work. If men will not be tired in their spare time, Russell says, "they will not demand only such amusements as are passive and vapid." In a world where no one is compelled to work more than four hours per day, "every person possessive of scientific curiosity will be able to indulge it, every painter will be able to paint without starving," and, above all, "there will be happiness and joy of life instead of frayed nerves, weariness, and dyspepsia."[29]

With this summary account of Lafargue, Čapek, and Russell, we can see three different (and only partially satisfactory) strategies for attempting to "reclaim idleness" in relation to work-based society's prevailing notions about laziness and leisure. Lafargue, who doesn't distinguish between idleness and laziness, defiantly embraces laziness as a way to oppose "work/leisure." Čapek, for his part, goes out of his way to draw a strong distinction between idleness and laziness (and also leisure), and makes the implicit claim that idleness, because of its lack of all positive determinations, as a kind of transport, represents a kind of freedom. Russell, in his turn, innovates in yet another direction, and equates idleness with a higher form of leisure, which is something distinct from the debased, lower form in which it appears in wage-based society. To get a sense of how stubborn a jumble this remains, it is useful to next consider some contemporary treatments of the subject.

---

28 Ibid., 12.
29 Ibid., 14.

A Sampling of Some Contemporary "Idleness Manifestos"

In *How to Be Idle: A Loafer's Manifesto* (2004), satirist Tom Hodgkinson (who was the founding editor of *The Idler* magazine in the early 1990s) offers a highly whimsical account of the idler's experience. He steps through a series of idling competencies that he says make up the ideal idler's day, beginning at 8 am, when other people are knocking about getting ready for work. The book has very charming line drawings situated throughout the text, and looks and feels a lot like *Winnie the Pooh.* Each chapter title begins with an hour designation (10 am: Sleeping In; 3 pm: The Nap). It isn't hard to imagine this set of nonadventures making up the life of some other possible world's adult Christopher Robin, forced to move on from his hundred-acre wood, but still aimlessly rambling.

Per *The Idler's* Wikipedia entry, Hodgkinson's aim has been to make idling into something to aspire towards rather than reject, by combining the aesthetics of 1990s slacker culture and pre-industrial revolution idealism. Along with Samuel Johnson's letters on idling from the eighteenth century, however, Hodgkinson looks for inspiration closer to home via an American tradition, drawing on Whitman, Twain, and Thoreau as ingredients for an antidote to the main tradition of work-obsessed Puritanism, Methodism, Horatio Alger, and the prosperity gospel. "The idea that idleness is good," Hodgkinson writes in the preface, "goes against everything we have ever been taught [...] this book seeks to recover an alternative tradition in literature, poetry, and philosophy, one that says not only is idleness good, but that it is essential for a pleasurable life."[30] Sampling just the first three chapters, which deal with getting up in the morning, one can easily see Hodgkinson's strong affinity for the main observations made by Čapek in defense of idleness and those made by Paquot.

30 Tom Hodgkinson, *How To Be Idle: A Loafer's Manifesto* (New York: Harper Perennial, 2007), xiii.

Starting with the idler's early morning hours, Hodgkinson reflects on "early to bed, early to rise," and how we are generally taught that idleness is a sin. With increasing intensity across the nineteenth century, Christianity teaches bed guilt.[31] Whereas in times past, the Catholic Church might have had an equal number of things to say about the entire list of cardinal sins, a special focus on sloth/*acedia* grew up during the industrial revolution in order to "convince the masses of the benefits of tedious, disciplined toil."[32] It suited the new avatars of progress to promote a culture of early rising "specifically among the working classes." Hodgkinson reminds us, once again, that before machines and factories, work was a much more haphazard and less structured affair. For example, preindustrial weavers, as Thompson shows in detail, were self-employed and worked when they chose, maybe weaving eight or nine yards on a rainy day, and then only two or three on other days, before turning to other work and sundry jobs "about the lathe and in the yard."[33]

The idea of the job as the answer to all woes, individual and social, Hodgkinson writes, is one of the most pernicious myths of modern society, one that persists into the present day where we are subject to a steady stream of self-help guidance on strategies to become even more productive and hardworking. And yet, creative people have consistently argued otherwise: G. K. Chesterton, for example, made the opposite point, arguing that "greatness and late rising are natural bedfellows," and attacked the idea that early rising is morally good, and staying in bed is morally bad. Based on this and similar testimony, "lying in bed should not be seen as a selfish indulgence, but as an essential tool for any student of the art of living," says Hodgkinson.[34] Governments don't like the idle, because they win no awards for either production or consumption, aren't easily monitored, and are quite literally out of control, but it remains the case that

31 Ibid., 7.
32 Ibid., 9.
33 Ibid., 19.
34 Ibid., 10, 11, 30.

"long periods of idleness are needed by any creative person in order to develop ideas […] it is while prone that ideas come."[35] The claim that idleness is a waste of time, therefore, is a damaging notion put about by its spiritually vacant enemies. Echoing Čapek, Hodgkinson defends idleness by saying that creative people need thinking time away from the myriad distractions of everyday, domestic life.

In *Laziness Does Not Exist* (2021), psychologist Devon Price makes use of a strategy similar to Lafargue, forcefully insisting, despite the book's title, upon our "right to be lazy." Since the chances that Price means to employ some form of dialectical logic here are very slim indeed, the apparent violation of the logical principle of identity is best explained by an equivocal use of terms. Price's assertion of "the right to be lazy" and also claiming that "laziness does not exist" is explained by the conviction, implicit throughout the book, that there is a meaningful sense in which "laziness is not laziness," but rather exists as a judgment that capitalist culture everywhere levels against idleness. Where people try to "cram every waking moment with activity," and yet still feel disappointed in themselves, even in the midst of burnout, sleep deprivation, and stress-related illness, Price says, it's because they have internalized something she calls "the laziness lie."[36]

The "laziness lie," therefore, is the internalized belief that, deep down, I'm lazy and worthless, and that because of this, I always have to work incredibly hard, making work the absolute center of my life to overcome my essential laziness and achieve some measure of worth. Price says that the laziness lie has three main tenets: your worth is your productivity, you cannot trust your own feelings and limits, and there is always more that you could be doing. The idea that laziness is always a bad thing is a worldview that is literally ruining lives. People deemed to be lazy are struggling to survive in a demanding, workaholic culture that berates them for having basic needs, one of which is

35 Ibid., 32, 34.
36 Devon Price, *Laziness Does Not Exist* (New York: Atria Books, 2021), 9.

the need for downtime. Her book "is a full-throated defense of the behaviors that get maligned as laziness."[37]

In order to rethink laziness, Price uses most of the first chapter to address the question, "Where does the laziness lie come from?" The answer she gives is consistent with the other accounts described here. As an American phenomenon, the laziness lie first arrives via Puritanism's Protestant work ethic, becoming generalized as a way to motivate people in a society structured by slaveholding and indentured servitude, and finally becoming a mechanism for controlling the working poor as such during the industrial revolution. Where the Puritans apparently felt no sympathy for people who lacked motivation, since it merely highlighted their lack of election and predestination, so too, in our own time, people who believe the laziness lie believe that economic reform, legal protections for workers, and welfare programs are unnecessary. Those who have an interest in succeeding just need to pull themselves up by their bootstraps, and thus anyone who lacks motivation has only themselves to blame.[38]

In a world beholden to the laziness lie, Price says, "many of us feel we have to hide our desire for free time."[39] The normative judgment of laziness makes us hide our need for idleness. In rethinking laziness, therefore, Price wants us to see that those actions we typically write off as laziness can actually help us to both heal and grow, and can bring satisfaction to our lives, if we stop distrusting our feelings. This is certainly all well and good. And yet, for all this effective special pleading, there are those who will still want to object (quite rightly I believe) that laziness remains a vice, at least under certain conditions. And though it's true that laziness in many cases is not actually laziness (because it is really idleness), it is also true that not all cases of laziness can be reduced to idleness, either.

37 Ibid., 10.
38 Ibid., 23–26.
39 Ibid., 42.

In a revealing aside, Price describes an argument with a student who insisted that her account didn't square with his experience that there are people who, lacking any obvious challenges, "still don't care enough to get anything done."[40] In reply, Price divides the unmotivated into three types—the depressives, the procrastinators, and the apathetic—and for each finds an underlying, and *a posteriori,* or nonmoral cause. The depressed, she says, are exhausted, and it's not a moral failure for the exhausted to "let their responsibilities drop." As for the procrastinators, they actually care quite a lot—maybe even too much—about doing well, and become paralyzed. Luckily, "there are strategies and treatments for what ails them." As for the truly apathetic, Price says that in the face of this, we really have to ask why they find things "otherwise thought to be important to be pointless." She says that it usually comes down to the fact that they have been mistreated in some way.[41]

Since the topic of this chapter is reclaiming idleness, and not a defense of laziness per se, it is not necessary here to take what would be the obvious next step, and attempt to situate Price's stance in the light of various articulations of the problem of moral motivation. This is especially true because Price herself mostly reverts to the strategy of trying to carve out a space where idleness might exhibit some measure of immunity from the laziness lie. To make her point, Price goes on to showcase a particular example, that of "cyberloafing at work." Employers are quick to point out the estimated annual cost of lost productivity (more than $50 billion), and these estimates, she says, make a big assumption, namely, that the time spent cyberloafing is time an employee could have spent being productive, if only they weren't so lazy. Rather than sapping productivity, taking a moment to cyberloaf helps employees hit the mental refresh button, and "can actually help you be creative and reflective."[42]

---

40 Ibid.
41 Ibid., 47.
42 Ibid., 53.

Laziness "can give the gift of insight."[43] When we consciously make room for idleness, "we can learn what matters to us."[44]

Work and Leisure in Pieper and Veblen

Praising idleness and leisure in *In Praise of Idleness* (1932) from between the wars, as previously described, Russell had sought to defend what he considered to be a higher form of leisure, one different than the sort generally recognizable under conditions of capitalism's wage-based society. In the immediate post–World War II period, the Catholic philosopher Josef Pieper also attempted a defense of a higher form of leisure (in this case, as something distinct from idleness) in his *Leisure: The Basis of Culture* (1947).[45] Despite the apparent incongruity of mounting a defense of leisure during a period of postwar reconstruction, as an academic philosopher Pieper saw his effort as also reconstructive, that is, as a call for a major reset of the foundations of Western culture. By making the case for leisure, as antithetical to the demand of modern, utilitarian society for what he called "total labor," Pieper hoped to contribute to a revalorization of the medieval *vita contemplativa,* which in the end amounted to nothing less than an audacious return of philosophy to its premodern status as "queen of the sciences."[46]

Pieper begins by invoking Aristotle's *Metaphysics,* book 1, and says that Aristotle's use of the word σχολή (*scholē*), which has come down to us as "school," literally means "leisure," and that to understand the original conception, we need to set aside the prejudice that comes from overvaluing the sphere of work.

---

43 Ibid., 58.

44 Ibid., 61.

45 A somewhat parallel attempt at describing a "higher form of leisure" can also be found in Johan Huizinga's *Homo Ludens: A Study of the Play-Element in Culture* (Mansfield Centre: Martino Publishing, 2014), which posits play as an antipode to the modern age's univocal focus on work and production.

46 Josef Pieper, *Leisure: The Basis of Culture,* trans. Alexander Dru (San Francisco: Ignatius Press, 2009), 19–24.

In antiquity, he says, a receptive attitude of mind was recognized as a realm of pure intellectual contemplation, and he says that there is also a close connection between Western (Greek and medieval Christian) notion of contemplative life and the Aristotelian notion of leisure.[47] The great medieval thinkers drew a clear distinction between the understanding as *ratio* and the understanding as *intellectus*, which was regarded as a kind of seeing with the soul, an "angelic faculty" that pointed us toward our supersensible vocation[48] So although both the ancients and the medieval thinkers said that the process of knowing involves both the active and receptive parts together, after Kant, Pieper says, knowledge is exclusively considered to be an activity, and philosophizing becomes a "herculean labor" rather than contemplation.[49] Once knowledge becomes exclusively something rational and discursive, leaving no place for intellectual intuition, "leisure" in turn becomes, from the modern point of view, just another word for laziness, idleness, and sloth.[50]

From here, Pieper makes his major set of distinctions among idleness, *acedia,* work, and leisure. He starts by distinguishing between idleness and *acedia,* saying that for the medievals, idleness means "a renunciation of one's human dignity," and acedia refers to the despair that follows from "this stubborn refusal to be oneself as God intended."[51] Pieper calls out *acedia* in this way in order to make it stand out as something separate from the opposition of idleness to work. The contrary of *acedia* is not the spirit of work, he says, but, rather, the love of God.[52] Since the love of God is found by way of worshipful contemplation, Pieper wants us to understand, the opposite of *acedia* actually involves leisure, because "leisure is only possible when a man is at one with himself."[53] Leisure, therefore, is a receptive and contempla-

47 Ibid., 21.
48 Ibid., 28–29.
49 Ibid., 33.
50 Ibid., 43.
51 Ibid., 43–44.
52 Ibid., 45.
53 Ibid., 46.

tive attitude of mind. Thinking against the modern grain, Pieper says that leisure is not, as it is popularly understood, something that is the result of "spare time, a holiday, a weekend, or a vacation."[54] For Pieper, leisure has the characteristics that we have elsewhere been describing as idleness: leisure "implies an attitude of nonactivity, or inward calm, of silence [...] it means not being busy, and letting things happen. Leisure is a form of silence."[55] Leisure as popularly understood in the modern age refers to a "break in one's work, whether for an hour, a day, or a week," but this is not really leisure, because the pause is made "for the sake of work, and in order to work."[56] Instead, in leisure properly understood, one "celebrates the end of his work by allowing his inner eye to dwell for a while upon the reality of the creation. He looks and he affirms: it is good."[57] The point of leisure is actually not to be restorative. Leisure, like contemplation, is of a higher order than the *vita activa*. Like Russell, Pieper says that there is thus a higher form of leisure, but one that is separate from idleness (which is vice) and one that is not properly opposed to modern work.

All of this, as Pieper well knows, is antithetical to the modern mind. By way of acknowledgment, he asks, "Is it possible, from now on, to maintain and defend [...] the claims of leisure in the face of the claims of total labor that are invading every sphere of life?"[58] The attempt to answer this question leads him into what he calls an "excursus on the proletariat and deproletarianization."[59] Since to be proletarian is to be fettered to the process of work, and everyone without property owns only his own labor power, the entirety of the community of wage earners are in fact proletarian. Deproletarianization, therefore, would mean enlarging the scope of life beyond utilitarian concerns, so that the "real sphere of leisure" would be available to

54 Ibid.
55 Ibid.
56 Ibid., 49.
57 Ibid.
58 Ibid., 53.
59 Ibid., 54.

the masses. As to how the masses should be liberated to real leisure, Pieper can only say that this "can't be done purely in the economic sphere," because the proletarian has to be made capable of it. So rather than calling for some sort of a politics of emancipation, he takes the transcendental turn, and asks what it is that makes leisure inwardly possible. Instead of making good on this, however, we get something closer to an informal Hegelianism of the Right. Pieper says that appeals to humanism can't vouchsafe the realm of leisure, and only divine worship or praise of God can suffice, because worship involves making sacrifice, has to do with offerings freely given, in a manner antithetical to utility.[60]

Cut off from divine worship, Pieper says, leisure becomes laziness.[61] The origin of all sham forms of leisure, with their strong family resemblance to sloth, is found in the vacancy left by the absence of worship. Pieper thus contends that leisure so understood is not the result of a capitalist culture that insists on reducing all salutary forms of idleness to mere laziness. But it is not very easy to see how Pieper can get a true handle on leisure, when his understanding of it revolves around the medieval university's ideal of the *vita contemplativa,* rather than from the way leisure is formulated in modern, work-based society. Despite his protestations to the contrary, it is necessary to insist that leisure is precisely the result of "spare time, a holiday, a weekend, or a vacation." Putting it another way, leisure's intelligibility can't be disassociated from "work/leisure," and idleness, in its turn, can't be properly specified without separating it out from the work/leisure doublet.

In Thorstein Veblen's *The Theory of the Leisure Class* (1899), we find a useful corrective to Pieper's approach to the problem at hand. Right out of the gate, Veblen makes the following point completely clear: attaining a proper understanding of leisure has everything to do with identifying the social dynamics surrounding work *and the leisure class* in societies where social relations

60 Ibid., 65.
61 Ibid., 68.

are determined in large part by the ownership of private property. Specifying the significance of leisure, Veblen implicitly suggests, begins with a background understanding of sociopolitical and economic arrangements. Nonhierarchical, subsistence-based societies lack a leisure class. Whereas, in aristocratic societies, such as those of feudal Europe and Japan, we find upper classes and their retinue exempt from productive occupations as a matter of rank, with elites (to the extent to which they participate in visible employment) largely engaging instead in things such as (the business of) warfare and priestly service.[62]

The second major point that Veblen makes distinguishes "the leisure" of the leisure class from laziness or idleness. A habitual neglect of work "does not constitute a leisure class. The present inquiry, therefore, is not concerned with the beginning of indolence."[63] A basic misunderstanding about the true nature of leisure arises from economic theory, specifically from the idea that "the struggle for wealth under condition of the institution of private property [is] [...] substantially a struggle for subsistence."[64] This idea, when applied to societies that are "beyond mere subsistence," leads to the further notion that the struggle for wealth in industrial societies is, in turn, a competition for "increase in the comforts of life," such that the end of acquisition is the "consumption of the goods accumulated."[65] In contrast with these ideas, Veblen says that "ownership began and grew into an institution on grounds unrelated to the subsistence minimum."[66] He asserts instead that "the motive that lies at the root of ownership is emulation," and that "the end sought by accumulation is to rank high in comparison with the rest of the community in point of pecuniary strength."[67]

62 Thorstein Veblen, *The Theory of the Leisure Class,* ed. Martha Banta (New York: Oxford University Press, 2009), 7–11.

63 Ibid., 20.

64 Ibid., 21.

65 Ibid., 22.

66 Ibid., 23.

67 Ibid., 26.

We begin to understand leisure, therefore, when we recognize that conspicuous leisure, as the "non-productive consumption of time," is the "readiest and most conclusive evidence of pecuniary strength."[68] The mere possession of wealth or power, Veblen says, lacks social significance "unless it is put into evidence, for esteem is awarded only on evidence." What, then, is this specific nature of this conspicuous leisure? He says that leisure, as a kind of an employment, is closely allied with what he refers to as the "life of exploit": "quasi-scholarly or academic accomplishments, knowledge of dead languages, occult sciences, correct spelling, syntax and prosody, various forms of domestic music and household art, the latest dress, furniture, equipage, games, sports, and fancy-bred animals, such as dogs and race horses."[69] Since the award of reputability also depends on the "canons of taste under the law of conspicuous consumption," the gentleman of leisure also becomes a connoisseur of such things as "manly beverages and trinkets, seemly apparel and architecture, in weapons, games, dancers, and narcotics."[70]

Veblen then tells us how to understand the sort of leisure we generally recognize today, the kind that Pieper said has to do with "spare time, a holiday, a weekend, or a vacation." Since the leisure class "stands at the head of the social structure in point of reputability," he writes, "its manner of life and standards of worth [...] afford the norm of reputability" for the community at large.[71] The "conspicuous leisure" of the leisure class thus "serves as a canon of conduct for the classes beneath."[72] There is in fact a line of constraint, therefore, connecting the conspicuous leisure of the leisure class and the sort of conspicuous consumption that has come to be the hallmark of much of contemporary society, as the sort of leisure available to the nonleisure class. As a form of class emulation, therefore, leisure (as mostly

68 Ibid., 33.
69 Ibid., 34.
70 Ibid., 53.
71 Ibid., 59.
72 Ibid., 39.

conspicuous consumption) is definitely something separate and distinct from idleness.

Idleness and Some Enlightenment Theories of Freedom

What then of idleness? In relation to what I am calling "the work-laziness-leisure nexus," which is a circuit that pervades work-based society's capitalist culture, idleness can be shown to stand outside, as something distinct and separate. But a straightforward account of idleness in its distinctiveness remains somewhat elusive. Nevertheless, the various treatments of it recounted here have yielded some important bits and pieces. Idleness is not identical to leisure, especially the conspicuous leisure of the leisure class and/or its emulation by lower classes, but idleness may indeed have some close connection to a certain higher form of leisure. Despite attempts to charge idleness with laziness, making it out to be essentially a form of vice that must be overcome in order for comportment to have moral worth, idleness has some salutary dimensions that render it something "to aspire to, rather than reject," as Hodgkinson says. From Čapek, for example, we discern that idleness is not wasting time, nor is it the mother of sin. And from Pieper, we register that it is a receptive and contemplative attitude of mind, that it promotes creativity and self-reflection and it gives the gift of insight. Creative people require it in order for imaginative processes to function at the highest level. As an intentless, "lack-purpose," idleness supports a conduct of life as a succession of experiences whose order is not always immediately apparent. It is an experience of time according to a different rhythm than the one that the avatars of work-oriented productivity would seek to everywhere impose. As such, it is an implicit form of resistance to homogeneous, abstract time, part of a process to reclaim our right to inhabit time, to assert its noncommercial, nonproductive use in the name of autonomy.

With this last aspect, we arrive at the main question still outstanding, that of the precise relationship, if any, between idleness and freedom. In *Idleness: A Philosophical Essay* (2018), Brian

O'Connor, professor at University College, Dublin, attempts to make a case for what he calls "idle freedom," in order to prevent the modern, philosophical case against idleness from "having the last word."[73] What is there that can be said about idleness per se, as a positive determination, if we have already recognized it to be inherently a negation? How can we get to an account of idleness as something worthy, as something Čapek calls "perfect and rare"? Opening with some significant audacity, O'Connor says, "I will eventually contend that idleness may, in certain respects, be considered closer to the ideals of freedom than the most prestigious conception of self-determination found in philosophy."[74] He says that his impulse to criticize the wholesale modern critique of idleness is sustained by a sense of "the harm that our idleness-excluding world does to human beings."[75]

O'Connor's book starts with a kind of a phenomenology of the experience of idleness. Idleness, he says, is experienced activity that operates according to no guiding purpose; he also identifies it as a feeling, a feeling of noncompulsion and drift. Idleness is something we come to experience by slipping into it. In terms of structure, it lacks the intentionality we associate with grand projects of self-realization, with their disciplined self-monitoring, internal struggles, and self-overcoming. When we idle, we know what we are doing, even if we have no idea of an overall end or purpose in what we do.[76] In this sense, O'Connor makes clear, it would be incorrect to say that idleness is irrational, even if it doesn't fit the pattern of self-mastering, rule-guided action.

As for what he calls its "effective content," O'Connor says that the activities that fill an idle period are not essentially geared toward any sort of productivity. If something of value to some present or future projects arises, it is a serendipitous outcome. As a result of all of this, he signals his broad agreement with the

73 Brian O'Connor, *Idleness: A Philosophical Essay* (Princeton: Princeton University Press, 2018), 4.

74 Ibid., 2.

75 Ibid.

76 Ibid., 5–6.

ways that idleness and leisure have been differentiated in this chapter thus far. Since idleness has nothing to do with performance, with work, social standing, or gaining prestige, he writes, it should be clear that idleness is not leisure.[77] The boundaries of leisure "are to be found in the degree to which leisure can be incorporated into the general model of the modern social actor [...] within a system of work."[78] Whereas idleness is an experiential state, leisure is a socially defined practice. Idleness "cannot be incorporated into the productivity model."[79] He also distinguishes idleness from laziness, mentioning that the work/leisure balance narrative is designed to exclude idleness because it is thought that idleness must lead to laziness.[80]

O'Connor does not pursue this unpacking of the phenomenology of idleness beyond this point. If his intention had been to produce a genealogy of moral concepts, he would have gone on to explore idleness versus sloth/laziness and acedia.[81] The balance of O'Connor's book, however, is taken up with an exploration of idleness in relation to epoch-defining notions of autonomy found within the German Enlightenment understood broadly, as seen in Schiller and Kant, Schlegel, Hegel, and Marx, among others. Despite the diversity of ideas and projects within modern philosophy, "there is a kind of a master narrative that necessitates arguments against idleness, despite the diversity of conceptions of freedom, society, and individuality."[82] As all stamped from this same template, the arguments of the philosophers "devalue idleness."[83]

Across these various reconstructions, O'Connor's focus is on what he considers to be an essential thesis (i.e., Kant's ideal of enlightenment), which amounts to the idea that "we must build and perfect the self as an autonomous moral entity if we are

77 Ibid., 7.
78 Ibid., 7–8.
79 Ibid., 8.
80 Ibid., 9.
81 Ibid.
82 Ibid., 10.
83 Ibid., 169.

to become properly human."[84] Drawing upon Kant's *Groundwork, Universal History with Cosmopolitan Intent,* and *What Is Enlightenment?,* O'Connor says that this Enlightenment thesis results in what he calls "the worthiness myth," which is used to deprive idleness of merit.[85] In the first instance, rationality in the realm of morality means taking possession of ourselves and giving ourselves the moral law, and then acting on principle to realize freedom as autonomy, which must stand in stark opposition to idleness, as mere inclination, which is simply incompatible with the various formulations of the categorical imperative. Similarly, the task of finding solutions for our unsociable sociability also meant that the worthiness thesis must also be seen to apply in the social realm, by way of our imperfect duties to ourselves and others.

O'Connor goes on to highlight how the so-called worthiness myth is still functioning, alive and well in both Hegel and Marx. In Hegel's account of the master/slave dialectic, for example, where Spirit is realized in and for itself on the terrain of history through the dynamic of social recognition, we see social development, propelled by skilled work, as something representing a "partial reconciliation of the slave's unfreedom, and his master's idleness."[86] When Hegel elaborates on this again in the "Ethical Life" section of the *Philosophy of Right,*[87] O'Connor says, we find the same dynamic in modern impulses to work and service, where the objectivity of what we take ourselves to be is established in patterns of social interaction," interactions aimed at recognition.[88] Work, on this telling, is not just the imposition of a natural necessity, O'Connor says, but rather something that places us in a social world, such that it is the basic dimension of human beings as social actors. It is through this conception of

84 Ibid., 28.

85 Ibid.

86 Ibid., 67.

87 See G.W.F. Hegel, *Hegel's Philosophy of Right,* trans. T.M. Knox (Oxford: Oxford University Press, 1967), "The Family Capital," 116, par. 170, and "The System of Needs," 126–34, pars. 189–208.

88 Ibid., 75.

the dynamic of social recognition, different from Veblen's, that the experience of idleness must be seen to be completely at odds with freedom, via the dialectic of human-needs satisfaction as part of the history of Spirit.

The idler, in his rebellion, is essentially an "unhappy consciousness," and represents a social form of what Hegel called "the bad infinity," because his attempt to step out and return to a simpler form of life represents a dead end, a step into a form of existence that, as Hegel would say, has gone entirely positive. Marx's position is a bit more equivocal, but the valorization of idleness nonetheless ends up represented as little more than a form of false consciousness that emerges in response to the experience of alienation that comes with the institution of abstract labor. The desire for idleness, on this telling, though understandable, is something analogous to religion as an "opiate of the masses," and so something to be replaced by a higher form of work in the utopia of the classless society.

Idle Freedom as Autonomy and/or Emancipation

In the final section of his book, O'Connor attempts to challenge the Enlightenment's "master narrative" on its own terms, making a philosophically unprecedented case for what he calls "idle freedom," and he says that "idleness may, in certain respects, be considered closer to the ideals of freedom than the most prestigious conception of self-determination found in philosophy."[89] O'Connor is at his best when he appears to argue for an enlarged and more holistic notion of autonomy, as when he says that "the notion of idleness as *implicit resistance* rather than vegetating can be set against a number of philosophical assumptions about a theory of freedom."[90] Less so, however, when he appears to drift away from his stated intention of "criticizing the wholesale critique of idleness," and instead seeks to do battle with deontological ethics per se. This he sometimes does by embracing

89 Ibid., 2.
90 Ibid., 172. My emphasis.

various arguments that have been raised against Kantian moral rigorism. But one doesn't need to overshoot the mark and make the case that a life of idleness is actually some sort of alternative to moral autonomy. O'Connor himself writes at one point that "we need not reduce the options for human action to the categories of wantonness or full, rational self-determination."[91]

In the closing pages of *Idleness,* O'Connor suggests that between these two poles, there is potentially another term, which he calls "autarchy," leveraging certain ideas promulgated by the Australian philosopher Stanley Benn. Eschewing the rigorous requirements of formal, rational autonomy "to regulate our desires under principles [...] that serve as general rules and give coherence across our actions," O'Connor says, autarchic actors live their lives as they see fit. A life of idleness on this basis would be one where we act "in accordance with values which we take to be our own, meeting our personal understanding of what we prefer to do."[92] O'Connor wants us to recognize the importance of wrestling the notion of self-governance "away from the exclusive ownership that autonomy claims over it." Per this conception, he says idleness can be seen as "freedom in a context," "a knowing indifference," and "an implicit resistance to specific recommendations about how one ought to live." Idleness as freedom "might be construed as an attitude that, in the style of the Cynics, declines to be moved by those ideals that bear down on us all," a refusal made "regardless of whether that formation has disadvantageous or even advantageous ends to our lives as social agents."[93]

The case for autarchy (autarky?) here is certainly interesting, despite the fact that it is far from being fully fleshed out. For example, it's hard not to think of an autarchic individual functioning in the style of Salieri from the movie *Amadeus,* with his monstrous confessions about how, having early on made music his God and his *raison d'être,* he therefore believed that he had

91 Ibid., 184.
92 Ibid., 184–85.
93 Ibid., 183.

no choice but to commit various immoral actions. It isn't clear that autarchy and autonomy can comfortably coexist. But if we allow the overall perspective to shift somewhat, to become less about challenging the ideals of moral autonomy, and more about social and political emancipation and related strategies of resistance, the case becomes rather more compelling. To assert idle freedom, on this view, means to recognize that, under contemporary, advanced capitalist conditions, it has now become meaningful to ask whether "all work and no idleness" is something that constrains our humanity. It is to recognize that although it is at least partially true that human beings realize their full potential through significant effort, it may also be the case that "our best effort" also requires periods of idleness. Per this way of thinking, where we make a renewed demand for the right to be useful to ourselves and others today (as something separate from our immersion in exchange values), idleness stands out as an essential element in our process of being useful to ourselves.

5

Global Pandemic and the Rhythmic Spiral of Jubilee

> The principle of political action that I am suggesting is that the rhythmic and spiral nature of time should be affirmed.
>
> — Rabbi Arthur Waskow, "Toward a Jubilee Economy & Ecology in the Modern World"

Capitalism never misses an opportunity to tell us that the functioning of the free market is the very *sine qua non* of human freedom. So what happens when the entire human race needs to pause and rest, to stay home and be quiet, shattering our monomaniacal focus on work and economic growth? Of course, we don't really know. But for a brief moment in 2020, it seemed like we were actually going to find out. When I laid out my plan for this series of chapters on refusing work-as-we-know-it, I wanted to explore the contradictions that are currently "widening the cracks" in the edifice of our pervasive capitalist realism. I wanted to see if the paradoxical lived experience of work might soon present a serious challenge to neoliberalism's TINA ("there is no alternative"). Midway through the realization of the project, the global economy, along with its work machine, appeared to be shutting down, and 2020 itself was on the way to being canceled by the COVID-19 pandemic.

As the weeks and months went by, we began to get a deeper understanding of what this actually meant, since nobody could really grasp the vast web of economic activity in its totality (certainly not Wilbur Ross). What was happening was not something captured well by looking at the usual leading economic indicators, but after a quarter or two, the GDP, CPI and PPI, money supply, housing starts, and the like all certainly had their story to tell. For many of us, before the vaccine, it went something like this: Oh. No sitting in cafes and restaurants as the weather turns warm. No Wimbledon. No going here and there for budget summer vacay. Possibly no NBA. Possibly no Tour de France. No Olympic games. No business travels. For millions of people, lost jobs, no paychecks, and so no consumer spending. No elective or minor medical procedures. No visiting nursing homes. No gym. And on and on.

Like everyone else contemplating their near-term economic and social prospects before the onset of the mask and vaccination culture wars, I had absolutely no idea what it would mean to try to "cold start" the entire global economy if we had actually taken the collective decision to shut it down on purpose. What aspects of the previous normal would return, and when? Going to the movies? Eating in restaurants? Attending sporting events? Air travel? Obviously, for many people, these things did not cease; for others, they are still yet to resume. In lieu of prognostication, however, I became very interested in what it felt like for people that this diverse activity was not happening, and I was especially interested in the sorts of things that appeared to be happening instead. At the highest level of generality, therefore, the following points seemed significant. Along with the cessation of large swathes of economic activity, at a subjective level — Everything. Was. Slowing. Down. People were checking in with family and friends, cooking almost every meal at home, spending lots of time with pets, and hanging out in the backyard (weather and living situation permitting). Second, along with the anxiety, fear, and uncertainty, a lot of people were grieving. They were grieving their previous sense of security, and their future plans. They were grieving the fact that the country was so screwed up, and they were trying to find ways to describe the novel experience of grief that was unfolding for pretty much the entire human race, all at once.

The Whole *King Lear* Thing

Did you know that Shakespeare wrote *King Lear* while under quarantine from the plague? In "Against Productivity in a Pandemic," Nick Martin pointed to this annoying factoid as a prime example of the lame sort of self-optimization and productivity messages people were encountering, once they had been told to work from home.[1] Echoing this in "Stop Trying to Be Productive," Taylor Lorenz said that "many people are feeling pressure to organize every room in their homes, become expert home chefs or bakers [...] and take part in a peloton challenge," even though people were finding it much harder to get things done because we were "living through so much."[2] Per Martin, we were everywhere being encouraged to ask ourselves, "How can you continue to improve yourself with all this solitude? How can you continue to prove your worth as a hard worker?" On the work front, people encountered even greater accountability and surveillance. New mandates, such as daily activity reports, explicit guidance on "answering chat messages within a few minutes," and "demands to leave video cameras on," among other things, became ubiquitous. The good worker during a pandemic "is the good worker at any other time: always available to management." In response to these developments, Martin concluded that "maybe more work, more mindless productivity, just isn't the answer," and he called out what he described as "the obscenity of pretending that work and the self are the only things that matter." Lorenz suggested that instead of taking on new chal-

1 Nick Martin, "Against Productivity in a Pandemic," *New Republic,* March 17, 2020, https://newrepublic.com/article/156929/work-home-productivity-coronavirus-pandemic.

2 Taylor Lorenz, "Stop Trying to Be Productive," *The New York Times,* April 1, 2020, https://www.nytimes.com/2020/04/01/style/productivity-coronavirus.html.

lenges, maybe it's better at this time "to do things like keep a gratitude journal, and work on practicing acceptance." As should be clear, these articles were describing another thing that was clearly happening out there, along with staying home, slowing down and being still, and grieving: self-optimization and productivity messages were largely falling flat. The need to slow way down, to focus on daily problem-solving to meet a threat to basic survival, and to be supportive of family and friends caused people to confront the degree to which, as Martin quotes from Jenny Odell, "we inhabit a culture that privileges novelty and growth over the cyclical and the regenerative."

Shit's Gettin' Biblical

Confronting the possibility of a collective decision to shut it all down and then to pause tends to evoke all sorts of biblical resonances. For even the most secular of Jews such as I, the experience of ceasing all inessential activity, in order to reflect and atone, calls forth the rhythm of *Shabbat* (the Sabbath). I must say that in thinking this way, I greatly surprise myself. In years past, when people asked me whether I was familiar with Jewish thought, I'd laughingly reply, "What, you mean like Spinoza and Maimonides?" Since my interest always drifted to the role of Jewish identity in the shaping of the modern experience and the Enlightenment, I was always more "Stephan Zweig than Theodore Herzl," more "Walter Benjamin than Gershom Scholem," if you catch my drift. I don't know, maybe it all has something to do with sitting at home, hoping the plague will pass over the house. Or maybe it's that mental image from the film *Ten Commandments*—you know the one, the sickly green smoke winding its way through the narrow streets, accompanied by screams inside the houses. Maybe it's the fact that the US peak of new infections was slated to occur that first year on or around *Pesach*. As I write this, I flash back, and watch myself float through Passover seders over the years in lazy indifference. After the story of the Hebrew exodus (*Magid*), we spill wine by dipping a finger or a spoon ten times, once for each plague visited upon Egypt. I hear the intoning voice, reciting as I dip and spill the drops upon my plate: *Dam* (blood). Sigh. *Tzfardeiya* (frogs). Yawn. *Kinim* (lice). Zzz. Etc. Whatever happens from here, I don't suppose I will ever snooze my way through the ten plagues again. Well, maybe just the gnats.

If all this weren't enough to establish a biblical resonance, consider this. Before my local state park was closed as part of the initial lockdown, I would meet up with my running buddy at the crack of dawn for our two-hour trail run in the woods (this was before there was good information about low outdoor transmission risk). By the time we got back to the parking lot, we became uncomfortable, because there were just too many people milling around for our comfort, so we considered the option of coming out to run even earlier the next time. In the end, however, we decided against it. Since the order to shelter in place had reduced human traffic overall, there were now just too many mountain lions around in the woods, especially in the wee hours. Is there anything more biblical than avoiding the plague only to be eaten by a lion?

Arthur Waskow and the Meaning of Shabbat

Reflecting on the decision about whether to cancel 2020 and how it resulted in a renewed appreciation for non-market-based sources of value, I've found myself thinking about the "big idea" of Rabbi Arthur Waskow, whom I met in 1988 while working as a publishing assistant for *Tikkun* magazine. At that time, Michael Lerner, Waskow, and legal scholar Peter Gabel were widely recognized as the "three horsemen" of the *Tikkun olam* arm of Jewish Renewal. Waskow (eighty-nine years old at the time of this writing) had been an antiwar activist in the 1960s, and then a leader of the Jewish Renewal movement starting in the 1970s, writing passionately about the intertwining of the Torah, social justice and human rights, and ecology, among other things. Since the day that he first saw the Mosaic injunction from Leviticus 25 on the Liberty Bell during the US Bicentennial of 1976 ("Proclaim liberty throughout the land, to all the inhabitants thereof"), Waskow has been writing and teaching about the relationship between Shabbat and release from debt peonage and the extended Jubilee cycle described in the Torah, and he has been dreaming about what it might mean to realize Jubilee in the modern world.[3]

For Waskow, if Shabbat is understood in an enlarged way that is also inclusive of the year of Sabbatical (every seventh year) and the year of Jubilee (seven times seven years), the meaning of Shabbat is extended to include also the ecological imperative to allow the land to rest, and the sociopolitical imperative for redistribution of wealth and debt forgiveness. Likewise, Waskow says, these worldly practices themselves also reflect back, and deepen the understanding of Shabbat.[4] For nonobservant people like me (and even some observant ones), Shabbat is thought of, first and foremost, in terms of its prohibitions. To this day, I can vividly recall my time in the dorms at Brandeis, where some of the secular kids would run around after sunset on Friday turning off all the light switches in the rooms of the observant. But as Waskow writes, the sabbath is "not just a set of rules about what you can't do, or even just a chance to sleep late and rest from work."[5] Rather, it is a way of understanding work, even good work, in relationship to totality.

To understand the meaning of the seventh day, Waskow says, is to reflect on what the Torah teaches about God and creation. On the seventh day, as we all know, he rested. In Hebrew, Waskow writes, "*shavat va yinafash*." That is, he paused and took a breath. To pause, to rest upon the Sabbath, therefore, is certainly "to affirm the worth of one's efforts," but also to point beyond them. When "God saw that it was good," he saw creation (in the renewal of its natural and societal cycles) as a total accomplishment, *sub specie aeternitatis*. When we rest upon the Sabbath, Waskow says, it's important recognize that "even the

---

3 Arthur Waskow, *Godwrestling—Round 2: Ancient Wisdom, Future Paths* (Woodstock: Jewish Lights Publishing, 1995), 245–58.

4 Ibid., 252–54.

5 Ibid., 250.

best acts of creation and production and accumulation are not the single goal of human effort."[6]

In shifting attention away from the action, so to speak, and more toward the contemplation, Waskow here reminds me a bit of Joseph Pieper in *Leisure: The Basis of Culture,* where he points out how the modern conception of "total work" breaks with the medieval and ancient notion of leisure that was closely tied to those ages' shared appreciation for the contemplative life. Pieper recounts the familiar Kantian narrative: to avoid the dogmatism of claims to intellectual intuition, the modern age rejects the knowledge claims of both religious metaphysics and Romantic enthusiasm, privileging *ratio* as activity to the total exclusion of *intellectus* as a kind of passion and receptivity. In so doing, Pieper says, modern thought breaks apart what premodern knowledge insisted on holding together. Doing so may make the world safe for science and technology, but it so thoroughly banishes humanity's "supersensible vocation" that it gives birth to the monstrous creature called "the intellectual worker" and thereby more or less throws out the baby with the bathwater. Pieper is at his most polemical here, calling out the "intellectual sclerosis that comes from not being able to receive or accept, of that hardening of the heart that refuses to suffer anything."[7] To bring the point home, Pieper actually goes on to quote from Rauschning's *Gespräche mit Hitler,* where in the 1920s Hitler purportedly told the author that Germans need "to be brought back to the great truth that only deeds and perpetual activity give meaning to life. Every deed has its place, even crime" and that "all passivity, all inertia [...] is senseless."[8] For his part, Waskow intends to make a similar point rather less polemically than Pieper: "The age we

6 Arthur Waskow, "Toward a Jubilee Economy & Ecology in the Modern World," *Shalom Center Legacy,* May 12, 2008, https://legacy4now.theshalomcenter.org/node/1396.

7 Josef Pieper, *Leisure: The Basis of Culture* (San Francisco: Ignatius Press, 2009), 28–31.

8 Ibid., 31. The language quoted here is taken directly from Rauschning's translated text: Hermann Rauschning, *The Voice of Destruction* (New York: G.P. Putnam and Sons, 1940), 138.

live in is essentially without Sabbath. We need more mystery and less mastery."[9]

Shabbat and the Rhythmic Spiral of Jubilee

In Leviticus 25 and 26, Waskow sees a breathing, regenerative system of seven spirals of Shabbat, a system that connects the transcendent God, the cycles of nature, and human justice:

— Seven sunsets, and then Shabbat in order to pause, contemplate one's works, and take a breath.
— Seven months of Shabbats, and the festivals of the moon (Rosh Hashanah, the new moon; Yom Kippur, the waxing moon; Sukkot, the full moon).
— Seven equinoxes, and the Sabbatical year of Shabbat, where the land is allowed to rest, and debts are forgiven.
— Then a whirl up to the final spiral, seventh seven-year cycle, and Jubilee, where in addition to everything else, land is to be redistributed.[10]

For Waskow, the entire Jubilee cycle grows from the kernel that is Shabbat, and the intrinsic recognition and insistence that nobody owns the wealth of the earth, "not the boss, not the proletariat, not even the people as a whole. Only God who is beyond." But the encompassing aspect of the entire cycle also means that "the spiritual, the political, and the practical are fused," and that the sacred and the profane are related in "such a way that our greatest social illnesses must be seen to be intertwined," such as worsening inequality, climate crisis, and a collapse of social solidarity, compassion, and love. Given its unique structure, the Jubilee cycle amounts to a distinctive ideal of Jewish socialism, even if it was likely never fully instituted in practice. Waskow says that the Jubilee speaks to a rhythm, a cycle of change and renewal, and "not to static equality." For six years of every seven,

9 Waskow, "Toward a Jubilee Economy & Ecology in the Modern World."
10 Waskow, *Godwrestling*, 252.

Waskow explains, "it is all right for someone to accumulate wealth and some to lose it, and for the earth to be forced to work under human command." Every seventh year, "loans must be forgiven, and the land must be allowed to rest." But once every generation, there must be a great transformation. In the fiftieth year, "the land must be shared, and the poor get their share." Per Waskow, the Torah represents Sabbatical and Jubilee as years of release. This means that Jubilee "does not ask for the rich to give their land away in fear or guilt, or for the wretched to rise in rage and take it." Rather, it proclaims a release, "Shabbat for everyone. The rich are released from working, bossing, production, and being envied. The poor are released from working, hunger, humiliation and despair — and others' pity of them."[11]

Jubilee for the Modern World

The basic lesson for us here, Waskow says, is that "once every fifty years or so, if there is no redistribution of wealth and power, there is a great depression. The rich get stuck in their ways, and the poor get stuck with the bill, and the society gets stuck in its tracks."[12] This seems still acutely relevant for our own time. But as he admits that "we have not yet found a way to sound the ram's horn that will call forth liberty throughout the land." For people such as Rabbi Waskow, for whom "god wrestling" apparently comes naturally (i.e., somebody actually answers back when you argue), the holism of a religious communitarian response seems like something tantalizingly within reach. All that has to happen is that each one of us, recognizing that "nobody owns the wealth of the earth, only God who is beyond," needs to affirm the rhythmic and spiral nature of time as a political principle. In this premodern holism (the fusion of spiritual, political, and practical), Waskow also sees a kind of an antidote to the stalemate of the Left versus the Right. For half a century, he's been speaking up in political meetings, both in the United

11 Ibid., 254.
12 Waskow, "Toward a Jubilee Economy & Ecology in the Modern World."

States and in Israel, and saying, "But what about the Jubilee?" The conservatives "who demand that the family be strengthened turn furious at the idea of abolishing all wealth and privilege." Whereas "the radicals who demand that the rich be expropriated" are baffled by the ideas that "the land be left unproductive, or the regressive institutions of the family be celebrated."[13] To those of us who simply cannot take the necessary step beyond, Waskow says that the Jubilee could be for us "not quite a model, but a pointer, a hint."[14] What then does the Torah and the Jubilee have to say to us, when applied to contemporary society? To begin with, the Torah envisions an economy profoundly different from the one we are used to. We live in an economy that is based on constant, explosive growth. If we want to use the Jubilee as a kind of a pointer, we need to recognize that "individual rest is not enough [...] communal rest is necessary for the renewal of work."[15]

In *Godwrestling—Round 2* (1995), Waskow turns to "scientists, business people, and economists," asking them to suspend their own skepticism about what is possible, and instead just to "imagine what might be a modern way of carrying out the Sabbatical year or the Jubilee."[16] The practical proposals Waskow receives back about what various sectors might do in the service of renewal (if given a chance to pause and reflect upon their works) are both consistent with his holistic approach to the ills of society and very much fit the pattern of the emerging domain of degrowth economics. In *Godwrestling*, Waskow wants us to recognize that there is at least some value in "Jubilee dreaming," even though the wish that society should take time to pause and reflect, to breathe, and to contemplate cycles of renewal is mostly without an object, because the possibility of such a thing occurring is exceedingly hard to imagine. Or so it was, at least until the COVID-19 pandemic nearly canceled 2020.

13 Waskow, *Godwrestling*, 253.
14 Ibid., 254.
15 Ibid., 255.
16 Ibid.

Michael Hudson and Debt Jubilee

In his history of Bronze Age debt amnesties, *And Forgive Them Their Debts* (2018), Michael Hudson situates the Mosaic injunction of Leviticus 25 within the broader sweep of ancient Assyrian and Babylonian economic practices, dating all the way back to the earliest Sumerian inscriptions from the third millennium BC: "Judaism took the practice out of the hands of kings and placed it at the center of Mosaic law."[17] Hudson makes the case that debt Jubilee wasn't just some sort of a utopian ideal, but in practice represented a sensible response to a set of universal and perennial economic challenges that we would do well to find relevant to our own present circumstances.

Under admonition from modern economics, society at large employs an imperative voice, asserting that "all debts must be repaid," even though doing so stands counterfactually opposed to a basic maxim that Hudson says actually applies in *all* epochs — "Debts that can't be paid, won't be."[18] The real question concerns the way in which they won't be paid. For two thousand years before the time of Jesus, the tradition in the ancient Near East was to declare clean slates in order to write down unpayable debts, so that debtors would not be forced into bankruptcy and stripped of their land rights and their means of subsistence. Subsequent Western civilizations, under the sway of what he refers to as "Rome's pro-creditor legal principles," have instead mostly upheld the sanctity of debt. In doing so, they have helped their respective oligarchies to replace the customary right of citizens to self-support with "the right of creditors to foreclose on the property and means of livelihood pledged as collateral, and to make these transfers irreversible." They use debts, Hudson says, "as a lever for creditors to pry away property and income [...] from the economy and the community at large."[19]

17 Michael Hudson, *And Forgive Them Their Debts: Lending, Foreclosure, and Redemption from Bronze Age Finance to the Jubilee Year* (Dresden: ISLET-Verlag, 2018), ix.

18 Ibid., xxiv.

19 Ibid.

Since economic history has been largely written from the vantage point of "the creditors and the privatizers," Hudson says, today's "free enterprise model builders" assume that calamitous financial trends self-correct to restore balance, and they deny that debt write-offs are ever needed.[20] The protection of creditors from loss is assumed to be the prerequisite for stability and growth, and turning financial wealth into land ownership and control of labor has been seen as progressive ever since capitalist enclosure drove rural labor off the land in the sixteenth to the and eighteenth centuries and privatized the commons.

Hudson thinks that "the origin myths" about antique lending told by market-oriented financial historians have simply assumed it to have been an individualistic, modern affair. Under this rubric, the tendency has been to regard "the palaces and temples of Sumer and Babylonia" as just some sort of burdensome and unproductive overhead, rather than as "the initial innovators of commercial enterprise and accounting, money and interest, standardized pricing, and weights and measures."[21] This has led to the conclusion, Hudson writes, that debt Jubilees were an exercise in "oriental despotism," because curbs on creditors, seen anachronistically, are regarded as an assault upon individual property rights. But to explain how debt originated, and what kinds of debts were canceled regularly, it is necessary to discuss the social and anthropological context in which debt and credit, and money and interest were innovated. For example, Hudson says that money did not arise out of "individuals bartering goods to set prices," but, rather, "money originated as a price schedule to denominate payments of grain debts for sharecroppers on temple or palace lands, and for free citizens owing payments for water transport, draught animals, consumer goods [...], or emergency borrowing."[22]

20 Ibid.
21 Ibid., xx.
22 Ibid., xxii.

To insist, therefore (as most modern economists still do), that the prospect of a debt Jubilee and the return of property rights could have only served to discourage future lending, Hudson says, is to misunderstand the real conditions on the ground. Near Eastern debt amnesties concerned the cancellation of specifically agrarian debts, along with the liberation of bondservants, and the return of crop rights that debtors had pledged to creditors. So-called silver, or commercial, debts reciprocally owed among traders were not subject to write-down.[23] It needs to be understood that most agrarian debts, Hudson explains, did not stem from actual loans. Early economies operated on credit, not "cash on the barrelhead."[24] Debts mounted up as unpaid bills, starting with fees and taxes owed to the palace for such things as barley for ale houses, irrigation water, and seeds and other inputs needed in the gap time from planting to harvest. Such debts were generally expected to be paid "on the threshing floor" at harvesting time. The time gap between planting and harvesting simply required agriculture and mercantile debt.[25]

When harvests failed, and there was not enough surplus to pay the debts, "the palace" had little interest in seeing debtors lose their livelihoods and be forced into bondage. This position did not stem from some sort of an egalitarian impulse per se, Hudson says.[26] Rulers canceled agrarian-related debts owed to the palace and the temple (and also personal debts owed to local headmen, merchants, and creditors) because they needed a free population to field an army and provide corvée labor to build such things as city walls and temples and to dig irrigation ditches, and other works.[27] The debt forgiveness was in the interest of preserving "an economy in which citizens could provide for their basic needs on their own, while paying taxes, performing labor duties, and serving in the army."[28] The situation with

23 Ibid., ix.
24 Ibid., xv.
25 Ibid., xv, 267.
26 Ibid., xi.
27 Ibid., xvi.
28 Ibid., x.

rights of land tenure was similar. Hudson says that "self-support land was not like townhouses."[29] Land tenure was granted so that Bronze Age families could support themselves. The return of bondservants to their traditional land tenure via amnesty, therefore, derived from the fact that arable land, as the cornerstone of societal functioning, was simply not widely recognized as a market commodity.[30]

In uncovering and then describing the long sweep of this forgotten Bronze Age history, in which populist rulers intermittently but regularly proclaimed clean slates, Hudson wants us to discern a universal principle at work: the burden of debt in agrarian society tends to expand to the point where it exceeds the ability of debtors to pay. Also, in the light of this principle, he believes we can further recognize that a major driver of human history has been the political dynamic of economic polarization in which oligarchic creditors have always sought to overthrow state power capable of enforcing debt amnesties and of reversing foreclosures on homesteads and subsistence land. Modern economists "shy away from discussing the ancient Near East because its institutions are so at odds with modern theories and assumptions."[31] Their historical legitimation narratives thus generally begin with classical antiquity, because what made classical, Greco-Roman antiquity distinctly "Western" in the minds of many historians, Hudson says, was "the privatization of credit, land ownership, and political power," all "without clean slates."[32]

Under modern conditions, where the state has become a vehicle to protect the property rights of a financial oligarchy, and the interests of creditors are everywhere seen to take priority over the indebted economy at large, Hudson says, it isn't hard to understand why our civilization insists on calling itself Judeo-Christian while nonetheless abhorring the admonition to cancel debts placed at the core of Mosaic law and the sermons of

29 Ibid., xvi.
30 Ibid.
31 Ibid., xx.
32 Ibid., xxiii.

Jesus. Despite the sincere effort of Jesus to rescind Hillel's waiver of rights to Jubilee debt cancellation in his early sermons, it's worth remembering that subsequent Christianity opted to give the ideal of debt amnesty an otherworldly, eschatological meaning (things will be better in the next life). The conflict between "social constraints upon predatory finance, and the attempt by the rentier class to gain control, has characterized all subsequent economies."[33]

A Pandemic-Depression Debt Jubilee?

At one level, it would be quite inappropriate to say that there is "anything good" about the global COVID-19 health emergency, or to go looking for silver linings and hidden opportunities that might be found in the ongoing calamity. Still, conceptual historians often talk about "complex histories of effects," because events on a global scale send out ripples in all directions, resulting in diverse unforeseen consequences. It is thus useful to ponder these emerging consequences, and to think about them "not as good or bad" but instead as "just dangerous," as Michel Foucault was fond of saying. For example, we are all aware that reduction in global economic activity resulted in some positive short-term effect on climate. And there was widespread speculation that dramatic changes in patterns of consumption and behavior that emerged to combat the spread of the virus could end up pointing the way to changes in mass behavior that are needed to fight the climate crisis. Needless to say, there are also those among us who hoped that facing a common existential threat could lead to increased intergroup solidarity (one world, one love — minus Trump and the radical Right, of course).

It is interesting to note that Hudson thinks the time is actually ripe, under conditions of pandemic depression, for a debt Jubilee. In a *Washington Post* op-ed, Hudson writes that although a US debt crisis was inevitable, COVID-19 had made it immediate, and that it is now time to abandon the ironclad logic of

33 Ibid.

capitalism that all debts must be repaid, in order to write down massive amounts of bad debt.[34] In saying that "it doesn't have to be this way," Hudson makes his argument for a bold change in economic policy by making explicit reference to the Jubilee. "Jubilee," he writes, as a "slate-cleaning, balance restoring step," recognizes the fundamental truth that "when debts grow too large to be paid without reducing debtors to poverty, the way to hold society together and restore balance is simply to cancel the bad debts." You know shit's getting' biblical when even the economists are talking about Jubilee.

34 Michael Hudson, "A Debt Jubilee Is the Only Way to Avoid a Depression," *The Washington Post,* March 21, 2020, https://www.washingtonpost.com/opinions/2020/03/21/debt-jubilee-is-only-way-avoid-depression/.

6

Millennials' Prospects for Refusing Work-as-We-Know-It

> If millennials are different, it's because [our parents and grandparents] have changed the world in ways that have produced people like us.
>
> —Malcolm Harris, *Kids These Days*

In this series of chapter-essays on the future of work, I have been thinking about what it might mean for us to find ways to refuse work-as-we-know-it and to begin to imagine "work-as-it-could-be." Social and political imaginings of this sort tend to leave the reader hanging in the perilous gap between hope and despair. This is why it's especially important to reflect upon the situation of millennials—for all practical purposes having to do with the future of work, they (along with Gen Z) are the ones who are actually hanging between an increasingly intolerable present and the possibility of a radically different future.

A lot of really crappy things have been written about millennials. In the introduction to *Kids These Days* (2017), Malcolm Harris writes that major works on millennials before his own book have been about "their intellectual degradation or how to manage them in the workplace."[1] Shorter pieces, he continues, tend to obsess on their romantic/sex lives (presumably stunted), their work ethic (presumably lacking), and the ways that their use of technology is changing culture (presumably for the worse). In "How Millennials Became the Burnout Generation," Anne Helen Petersen points out that for the last decade, the term "millennial" has been used almost exclusively to describe "what's wrong with young people."[2] Given that they were born between 1981 and 1996 (and at the time of her article's publication they were between twenty-three and thirty-eight years old), she thinks it's high time that we try to get to a deeper understanding of things millennial.

To this end, Petersen starts by turning inward and interrogates her own case of what she calls "errand paralysis" and "decision fatigue" — something she also identifies as a species of her generation's overall "inability to complete seemingly basic tasks." Understanding this is important, she says, because this characteristic is actually at the core of the millennial reputation for "being spoiled, lazy, and failures at adulting." As the millennials have grown up, the passage of time has borne witness to a rather startling truth, namely, that relentless efforts at directed self-optimization, beginning in early childhood, have given rise to a generation with the kind of symptoms that accompany acute burnout in older workers: "Why can't I get this mundane stuff done? Because I'm burned out. Why am I burned out? Because I've internalized the idea that I should be working all the time."

Along with the seeming inability to do a range of tasks that are "high-effort, low-reward," Petersen adds, there is a pervasive mindset among millennials that has also developed, one that has serious ramifications. The mindset has to do with the "psychological toll of realizing that something you'd been told, and came to believe yourself would be worth it, worth the loans,

1 Malcolm Harris, *Kids These Days: Human Capital and the Making of Millennials* (New York: Little, Brown and Co., 2017), 4.

2 Anne Helen Petersen, "How Millennials Became the Burnout Generation," *Buzzfeed News*, January 5, 2019, https://www.buzzfeednews.com/article/annehelenpetersen/millennials-burnout-generation-debt-work.

the labor, all that self-optimization — isn't." What, then, is to be done? More self-optimization can't be the answer, and you can't fix burnout, Petersen rightly points out, "by going on vacation. You don't fix it through life hacks [...] there's no solution to it." "Until or in lieu of a revolutionary overthrow of the capitalist system," Petersen jokingly concludes, there doesn't seem to be much to do to lessen or prevent millennial burnout: "Individual action isn't enough. Personal choices alone won't keep the planet from dying or get Facebook to stop violating our privacy." In the end, she confesses, "I don't have a plan of action other than to be more honest with myself about what I am and am not doing, and why."

Millennials and the Cultivation of Human Capital

In *Kids These Days,* Harris had himself already thrown down a somewhat similar gauntlet: "We need more than just proximate causes of new culture and behavior." If millennials are different, "it's because [our parents and grandparents] have changed the world in ways that have produced people like us."[3] So, by investigating the historical circumstances out of which millennials have emerged, he wrote, we can start to understand "not only why we are the way we are," but also "in whose interest it is that we exist this way."[4]

As one might easily guess, the main driver here turns out to be the cultural logic of neoliberal or late capitalism. "Capitalism changes lives for the same reason people breathe: it has to in order to survive [...] it's desperate to find anything that hasn't yet been re-engineered to maximize profit," Harris says. And lately, "this system has begun to hyperventilate."[5] To understand the millennial condition, therefore, one must follow the line of constraint that connects how the imperatives of neoliberal capital have altered the experience of work, and how this in its turn

3 Harris, *Kids These Days,* 4.
4 Ibid., 5.
5 Ibid., 4.

has raised stakes of child-rearing in the interest of maximizing human capital for success in the changing labor market.

With this in mind, Harris sets out in *Kids These Days* to follow this very line of constraint as it wends its way through the institutions of parenting, schools, the criminal justice system, higher education, and the job market in order to sketch a sort of an intellectual biography of his generation. The imperative to reach a deeper understanding of the millennial condition really comes into view, Harris says, when we "examine the major trends in the lives of American young people," and we "recognize that the quantitative changes constitute a qualitative rupture with repercussions we've yet to fully appreciate."[6] Coming to better understand millennials just now really matters, therefore, because of the present unfolding of their own self-understanding—and because of what that might mean for the rest of us. Millennials "represent the demographic territory where a serious confrontation has already begun." The battle he refers to is nothing other than that of whether "a tiny elite will maintain the social control they require to remain on their perch." If the United Stated is headed for a full-fledged dystopia, "it will have gone through us millennials first." Either millennials will have become the first generation of true American fascists, or millennials will be the ones to push the oligarchy off its ledge, "and we will have become the first generation of successful American revolutionaries."[7]

Before taking a quick tour through some key aspects of Harris's account, it is important for me to confess at the outset that over a number of years, I myself have aggressively noncomprehended the millennials, and not in the kindest of ways—where I have had close personal dealings with millennials, I have found them to be on the whole brittle, self-focused, incurious, and really poor communicators. Observing them in the workplace, I have considered them to be entitled, unwilling or unable to improvise, and generally a bunch of humorless grinds. I say

6 Ibid., 11.
7 Ibid., 12.

all this just now out of a profound sense of repentance — whatever hopes I may have concerning prospects for refusing work-as-we-know-it, I now recognize that these hopes are pinned on them. Petersen is thus absolutely right when she indicates that it's time to stop taking easy shots, punching down, and perpetrating generational character assassination. It may be the case that millennials have difficulty with certain kinds of decision-making (managing the small stuff). But if Harris is right, and this generation is a kind of a pivot point, then it makes sense to focus instead on what they might yet do about "the big stuff"; one way or another, a set of sweeping historical decisions are going to be made on their watch.

Beneath the "Pedagogical" Masking of Children's Work

If you've been around parents and kids to any degree in recent years, then you appreciate how staggering the burden of homework has become for many schoolchildren, especially for what remains of the middle class, and especially for the offspring of the PMC (professional-managerial class), whether in public or private schools. Think really little kids with ginormous backpacks, teetering stiffly down the street like Apollo astronauts on the surface of the moon. Drawing on the social science research of Sandra Hofferth, Harris says that between 1981 and 1997, elementary school children between the ages of six and eight recorded a whopping 146 percent gain in time spent studying, and another 32 percent between 1997 and 2003, along with a 19 percent increase in time spent in school.[8] In reaction to these and other statistics, Harris asks, "Why and how are twenty-first century kids required to undergo more training than their predecessors […] [and] what are the consequences for a generation raised on problem solving to the exclusion of play?"[9]

If we want to understand why American kids "find themselves overworked, underplayed, gold-starred and tired," Har-

8 Ibid., 20.
9 Ibid., 14.

ris says, we need only ask virtually any parent or teacher to get the answer. The United States is trying to engineer a generation of "hyper-enriched readers, writers, co-workers and problem-solvers," anyone will tell you, in order to "meet the demands of a changing world."[10] But what does it really mean to say this? What precisely lurks beneath this reference to "demands of a changing world"? To really understand why "the intensity and duration of this work have accelerated out of control," Harris says, we actually need to peel back what he calls the "pedagogical mask" and "look at children's work in order to grasp the reach of changes that have occurred." This is necessary, because unlike the situation with wage labor, where the whole point is to produce additional value above wages such that one can more or less follow where the surplus value goes, in the case of kid's school work, "we don't measure school children's output and wages, but rather grades, standardized tests, and school awards."[11] We know that the output has grown steeply, but if nobody is profiting, then where does this enhanced production go? Put another way, What are these blessed little workers working on with their efficient little hands? The answer is found in what we mean when we say that "going to school is your job right now." When working, what the kids are working on is of course their ability to work.

Perhaps, you will say, it has always been thus. Wage earners make money, students get a grade, and eventually grades turn into money, or if not money, choices or better life outcomes. To some extent, this is quite true. But what has changed is the extent to which "the development of human capital is the sink for student's hidden labor,"[12] and the profound sense in which "the logic of human capital is now the basis for the American educational system."[13] So the acceleration we are seeing, the "educational arms race," if you will, is the result of increasing

10 Ibid.
11 Ibid., 20.
12 Ibid., 21.
13 Ibid., 25.

economic polarization under conditions of neoliberal or late capitalism. When parents come to believe on the whole that "the best way to manifest care" is to treat their kids like "appreciating assets," a number of consequences are seen to follow.

Since the consequences of ending up on "the wrong side" of the economic and social inequality divide have been growing larger, parents adopt a pattern of extremely risk-averse child-rearing — kids are exposed only to "screened peers, vetted activities, and even approved snacks."[14] Since playdates are selected based on "potential social and cultural capital," they too have become akin to work, and the "ambient nervousness around safety," not well founded in real danger, Harris says, sinks into their young brains. The consequence of "applying risk management to people rather than to piles of money,"[15] Harris concludes, is the raising of bored children and young adults who have trouble controlling their emotions. Kids today, Harris says flatly, "are demonstrably more miserable than they used to be."[16] The other set of consequences revolve around what happens when all of this effort fails to produce the intended results. Under condition of an overall increase in ability, individual bargaining positions within the overall structure only get weaker. In short, the extra work doesn't result in the promised higher standard of living (millennials are the first generation to be worse off than their parents and grandparents and even great-grandparents).

The reality of the logic of human capital is that in the end it mostly serves the corporations and their incentive to shift the burden of training costs to trainees. The more capital new employees have already built up when they enter the labor market, Harris reminds us, the less risk they are for their employer. The direction of US capitalism has been to shift the overall burden, first to the state, then to the families, and finally to the kids themselves. As for the kids, despite their tender years, they end up living out what I have previously called "social paradoxes" of

14 Ibid., 27.
15 Ibid., 31.
16 Ibid., 39.

capitalist ideology that threaten the placid surface of capitalist realism. They are told that their work is not work, but rather learning. But they are also told that school is their job, at least until something comes up about organizing, at which point they go back to being students rather than workers.[17] They are taught to use tools that will reduce work time, without actually doing so (since these markers of efficiency are really all about making them effective workers in the neoliberal economy). Most importantly, they are told that they are doing all of this in order to ensure a better life, but that is also not the case. If they didn't do it for ensuring the good life, Harris asks, "then what was it for?"[18] To complete our understanding, we have to look at what happens when millennials start to grow up.

College Lending and Millennial Human Capital

To recognize what happens next, one must keep in mind the outline of what has just been described. For millennial school kids, increasing income polarization drives ever-greater and more intensive focus on the cultivation of childhood human capital, in order to meet the challenge of a set of greatly raised economic and cultural stakes. When millennials get to college, an effective doubling down of this overall equation occurs, albeit with some changed players and circumstances. As with the story of millennial childhood, the ultimate driver of the "social paradoxes" afflicting college-age millennials is late capitalist disinvestment in education as a public good (and the concomitant burden-shifting that follows from falling tax rates). The faith of students (and their parents) in the value of higher education, Harris says, has been largely undiminished across the maturation of millennials. If willingness to take on debt is an indicator, then one can safely say that, if anything, this faith has increased. And yet, real wages continue to go down, and underemployment continues to

17 Ibid., 16.
18 Ibid., 41.

go up. The result "is that the most indebted generation in history is without dependable jobs it needs to escape."[19]

In his chapter on college, Harris is dismissive of what he calls "the standard narrative," namely, that "cuts in government spending are making higher ed worse and more expensive." He says that the decreases in state funding don't show a withdrawal commensurate with the rise in costs to students:[20] "Between 1979 and 2014 [...] tuition and fees at four-year colleges [...] has jumped 197 percent at private schools and 280 percent at public ones, accelerating faster than housing prices or the cost of medical care, or really anything [...] except maybe oil."[21] For their part, and contra Harris, public colleges and universities defend the steep increases by pointing out that generations of students actually had a really good deal for many years, and that the depth of the cuts in public funding they have recently received (while state compliance mandates of all kinds have continued to grow) are what have set in motion the frenzied investments in things other than instructional quality in order to find new sources of cash now that "schools have hit the ceiling for charging families for higher education."[22]

About this set of effects, I believe that Harris is largely correct. It is true that the "race for tuition dollars and grants and private partnerships" has become a driving objective of contemporary university administration. It is also true that the race for "high-value customers," such as out-of-state and international students, has pressured schools to invest in all manner of things, especially expensive capital projects, and that the money hunt has led them to hire expensive professionals, including supporting business analysts, IT people, and HR. But there is really no need to quibble further over the causes and motives of steeply rising educational costs, since this is not the focus of this chapter. Whatever may be the fair balance with respect to causation, the

19 Ibid., 43.
20 Ibid., 54.
21 Ibid., 42.
22 Ibid., 55.

net result is the same. Educators and administrators, much like the parents of millennial children in the previous section, enable the burden shift to students, since they share the persistent assumption that getting a superior college education remains "a good investment" that will surely pay dividends down the line.

Here at last we get to the main difference between the directed childhood millennial investment in one's human capital and college investment in the same. In order to make these good investments, *the student needs access to cash,* and, Harris writes, "debt is the bridge over the gap."[23] The solution to this cash crunch is not to make college more affordable, or to change the conditions leading colleges down rat holes in search of uncapped revenue. Instead, under the Obama administration, the mantra became "universal accessibility." College should be available to everyone, in the form of what are essentially subprime loans. The result of all of this fabulous lending designed to cover steeply increasing college costs is twofold: conditions of borrowing that have actually made a good deal of revenue for the US government year over year, and a national student loan debt crisis ($1.4 trillion outstanding). The big difference between the loan crisis and the housing debt bubble, as Harris does not fail to point out, however, is that during the mortgage crisis, homeowners could walk away.[24] But since a college degree has value only as human capital, you can't walk away from a degree the way you abandon a house to the bank, and student loans "have no expiration date, collectors can garnish wages, social security payments, and even unemployment benefits."[25]

Millennials at Work: "We are become precarity"

As our gaily painted boat ride through the formation of millennial character silently glides out of collegeland and into the world of work, it's useful to pause briefly and consider once

---

23 Ibid., 45.
24 Ibid., 62.
25 Ibid.

again the basic outline of Harris's biography of his generation thus far. Remember the tender young millennials, having been raised like little growing assets and directed to cultivate their human capital in ways that make them different from previous generations. Then recall them when they go to college, where (under the sway of the same prevailing logic) they are induced to take out risky mortgages on their future selves. Harris writes, "Higher education, in addition to other things," is now "an economic regime that extracts increasingly absurd amounts of money from millions of young people's as-yet-unperformed labor."[26]

Perhaps you are now asking, Okay, but how does this all turn out? Before we can get off this ride, we still need to look at the stage of work, and consider what the future may hold for this generation that is so soon to eclipse the boomers (poor Gen X never had a chance). In this final foray through Harris's *Kids These Days,* the aim is not simply to revisit an overall set of conditions that justify a general effort to refuse work-as-we-know-it. These conditions have already been described elsewhere. What we want to try to capture here, specifically, is something of what the experience of work-as-we-know-it is like for the millennials. To do this, we need to understand "work" as another of the millennial "stages on life's way," along with "childhood" and "college," and in relation to the overarching imperative for them to maximize their human capital that runs through millennial experience like Ariadne's thread.

To begin with, it's important to recognize that the same forces that created distinctly millennial childhoods, optimized to ensure "the best chances for good career outcomes," and that led millennial college students to take out risky mortgages against their future labor, are also responsible for an overall intensification of work across the board. Just as private equity firms "twisted and cut companies into desired shapes, making billions by lowering labor costs, outsourcing, and increasing workloads," so too, Harris writes, "they are also molding

26 Ibid., 49.

young people into the shape that owners and investors want."[27] Whether it be through the embrace of new technologies that erase the distinction between work time and the rest of life, or by intrusive management of everything from bathroom breaks to sleep schedules to emotional availability, millennials have grown up "highly attuned to the needs of capital markets."[28]

To explain what has allowed market logic to force itself into the whole of workers' daily lives, Harris appropriately foregrounds the notion of *precarity*. For millennials in particular, employment has become less secure. It is based on at-will and limited duration contracts, the very notion of working hours has become increasingly meaningless, and job responsibility is typically incommensurate with compensation and recognition. In general, to be a millennial worker means "doing more with less, and employers getting more for less."[29] Also, since there has "ceased to be any internal necessity for having rest and recuperation as components of economic growth and profitability," millennials "are on, 24/7"; not only is this a lifestyle that is unappealing, but it can't but have serious psycho-social effects.[30] This is one of the main things Harris wants us to understand about millennials and the experience of work — inasmuch as precarity sums up the changed nature of jobs in the United States, "young people curl around this changed labor structure like vines on a trellis. We are become precarity."[31]

All of this means that once millennials enter the adult workforce, what I have called the "lived experience of advanced capitalist social paradoxes" continues. All their lives they have been told to invest in their human capital; after taking on the burden of steep college debt in order to be well prepared for a changing world, they find out that their high productivity in the skills-based information economy only helps the corporate sector to reduce its labor costs. Harris: "The better workers get, and the

27 Ibid., 76.
28 Ibid.
29 Ibid., 82.
30 Ibid., 83.
31 Ibid., 82.

more money and time we put into building up our human capital, the worse the jobs get."[32]

Raised on a Diet of Gold Stars

If you think for some reason that the millennial experience of precarity is really nothing that novel, consider for a moment the recent history of the college internship. If you are old enough, you will probably recall that back some years ago, most such internships used to be paid, pretty much at the level of an entry-level job. Then, under cover of pedagogical masking, they became mostly unpaid (thereby undermining entry-level jobs across the board). In the years since the publication of Harris's book, it has now become commonplace to see internships where the intern must pay the company for the privilege of gaining valuable human capital. Think it's not true? Check out the job sites. All of this, even though there isn't much evidence that unpaid internships per se lead to more favorable job outcomes, especially for the lower-income students who tend to fill them. It's a sign of devastated expectations, Harris writes, "that entry level workers believe they only have the leverage to ask the powers that be to confirm their labor for the record" rather than "negotiating for wages [...] *Only a generation raised on a diet of gold stars could think that way.*"[33]

Here we see Harris beginning the much-needed work of "millennial self-criticism," something necessary if there is going to be movement from documenting the millennial condition (how we became the way that we are) to forecasting a possibly different future. This wouldn't be possible "without a generation of young Americans who are willing to take the cost of training upon themselves." The basic problem here is that the ingrained instinct to reach for any individual advantage turns out to be great for producing high achievers, but not so good for putting a generation of workers into a good bargaining position. A

32 Ibid., 66.
33 Ibid., 94. My emphasis.

competitive childhood environment that "encourages each kid to be all that they can be," he says, "undermines the possibility of solidarity."[34] Kids "trained from infancy to excel and compete to their fullest potential" are ill-suited for such things as traditional union tactics. The problem with millennials is that "we're perfect scabs."[35]

Harris and the Politics of Refusal

I must say that, speaking for myself, "perfect scab" is certainly not the way I would want to be remembered. Must it play out this way? Is the millennial condition a kind of a manifest destiny? As part of the mature labor force, and as Harris has made abundantly clear, millennials have been "structurally, legally, emotionally, culturally, and intellectually dissuaded from organizing in their own collective interest as workers."[36] Nevertheless, as he has also pointed out, solidarity can actually be learned through practice. If young people "refused to pay the time, effort, and debt for our own job preparation, employers would be forced to shell out a portion of their profits to train workers in the particular skills that companies require."[37]

Between the present millennial condition, the reality of work-as-we-know-it, and the embrace of some sort of a politics of refusal, therefore, there lies the dystopian prospects found when one projects out along the present trend line. In his concluding section, "Seven Signs of a Bad Future," Harris offers some snapshots of where he thinks things are headed if nothing much changes. Since I'm trying to get on the hope train, I'm not going to enumerate them. Suffice it to say that Harris is for the most part on point, even though his analysis throughout lacks some needed sensitivity to differences based on class and race (there is a good section on gender differences and the millennial

34 Ibid., 86.
35 Ibid., 90.
36 Ibid., 91.
37 Ibid., 86.

experience of work). *Kids These Days* ends with a kind of a plea for a politics of refusal: "If we're lucky and brave, the generation of American millennials will be characterized by a choice. Either we will continue the trends we've been given and enact a bad future, or we refuse it, and cut the knot of trend lines that define our collectivity. It is up to the Millennial cohort to make something else of what has been made of us."[38]

The Case for a Generational Politics of Refusal Today

Kids These Days makes the case that the millennial generation (along with Zoomers now coming of age) should be recognized as a kind of a pivot point. One way or another, Harris says, a sweeping set of historical decisions are going to get made on their watch. As a generational biography of PMC millennials, Harris's book lays out the set of experiences that would appear to make this group ready, at least in principle, for a radical, cross-class politics of refusal. In doing so, however, he leaves open the question of the viability of a generational politics per se, over and against the traditional politics of class struggle, and/or the various intonations of the intersectional politics of identity. Is a generational politics something viable? Or should we regard generational politics, as Andrew Hart has written in *Jacobin* (which I discuss in a section below), as nothing more than a distracting "socialism of fools?"[39]

One doesn't have to search very far to find a basis for skepticism about generational politics. Generations are fleeting. Their sense of themselves as special or unique rests upon proclamations made in their collective youth, before socioeconomic forces that have shaped previous generations have had the chance to leave their mark. The counterassertion, therefore, is that although generational politics is "full of sound and fury,"

38 Ibid., 277–78.

39 Andrew Hart, "Against Generational Politics," *Jacobin*, February 28, 2018, https://jacobin.com/2018/02/generational-theory-millennials-boomers-age-history.

it tends to blow itself out, and so ultimately "signify nothing." Thinking about it in this way, I am reminded of the theme song to the mid-1960s TV show *The Monkees,* where the young pranksters, melodically announcing themselves, suddenly sound serious, singing, "We're the young generation, and we've got something to say." Watching it in syndication in the late 1970s, without the original social context in the background, I recall being perplexed. This is all well and good, I thought to myself, but what exactly is it that you have to say? Is there a message to be found in all this madcap horsing around?

This kind of skepticism also brings to mind the "set speech" at the end of Charlie Chaplin's *The Great Dictator.* The Jewish barber, having masqueraded as the dictator Adenoid Hynkel, seizes his chance, and makes a passionate speech in defense of democracy before the assembled crowds of Tomania. He says that he doesn't want to rule or conquer anyone, and that he believes that life can be free and beautiful. The root of the problem, he says, is greed, and "knowledge that has made us cynical, and cleverness that has made us hard and unkind, poisoning the world with hate." So, what then is to be done? Don't despair, he says, "because the hate of men will pass, and dictators die, and the power they took from the people will return to the people." "So long as men die, liberty will not perish."[40] There is always hope, therefore, in natural, generational cycles of death, rebirth, and renewal. As a result of mortality, and the renewing spring of our natality, there is no need for a politics of generations, because, as a point of fact, each generation *must* replace the previous one. The work of generations is, just so, to strut and fret their hour upon the stage, and then, mercifully, to be heard no more.

---

40 Charlie Chaplin, "Final Speech from the Great Dictator," *charliechaplin.com,* 2018, https://www.charliechaplin.com/en/films/7-The-Great-Dictator/articles/29-The-Final-Speech-from-The-Great-Dictator.

Hart: Against Generational Politics

Andrew Hart lays out a more specific case against generational politics. The problem with such politics, he says, is that the "generational fables" on which such a politics must be seen to rely are actually "unsubstantiated tropes," stories that amount to little more than "oafish stereotypes in a *commedia dell'arte*."[41] Hart goes on to make two main arguments against generational politics. The first is a methodological objection; the second is a moral one. In the first case, he says that what goes by the name of "generational politics" today, and which regularly appears in online discussions of the millennial condition, originated in an informal theory of historical explanation promulgated by Bill Strauss and Neil Howe of *The Capitol Steps* fame, in a series of thirteen books beginning in the early 1990s. Strauss and Howe's books have titles such as *Millennials Rising, Millennials Go to College, Millennials in Pop Culture,* and *Millennials Go to Work,* and so on. In these works, Hart says, Strauss and Howe elaborate "a cycle of generational change as a theory of history," a kind of a "generational theory of birth order," with four distinct generational personalities whose supposed pattern of succession allows for some level of prognostication concerning future events. Hart thus criticizes generational politics because the underlying theory of history relies on the assertion of recurring historical patterns and a concept of generations that he says lacks coherence, and so cannot be substantiated.

Hart wants to know why proponents of such a politics think we can fix a "consensus personality" for a generation, where we otherwise balk at making such generalizations about other groups, such as "women, Hispanics and Californians." He writes that it is "ludicrous to think that a poor person born in 1950 has more in common with a billionaire born the same year than a poor person born in 1995." But it isn't clear that this is as ludicrous as Hart suggests, especially when one considers the powerful role of predictive analytics in today's society. Self-reported

41 Hart, "Against Generational Politics."

generational attitudes actually have a high level of predictive power for modeling consumer and citizen behavior patterns. In the early 1960s, the working-class preteen with a ducktail and dungarees, and the hereditary billionaire of the same vintage could probably both do the Peppermint Twist. As for the duo from 1995, each would likely require some sort of a twist demonstration. Since not all generalizations are groundless, generalizing about generations can't just be dismissed as harmful essentializing or stereotyping. Commonly held generational attitudes derive from common experiences, and these experiences can actually be represented analytically in datasets. Here I have in mind "declining rates of home ownership over time," for example. Also, what Hart somewhat derisively calls "consensus personality" is not that far removed from familiar forms of sociological analysis, that is, studies of the changing nature of social character over the course of the twentieth century, or other instances of social ontology.

Hart's second argument against this generational politics is that it's inherently antisolidaristic. Such a politics "seeks to divide people in relation to things like war, austerity, climate change, movements of capital, and other things that threaten to pull society apart." As with the first objection, this one also appears to resolve to the assertion of generational politics as an unhelpful distraction from the effort to build class consciousness in the service of class struggle. This sort of thinking "threatens any alliance that could break the stronghold of rapacious political and economic elites. We have no place in our politics for the bad story of generations." Setting aside the issue of just what class struggle means today in a society with almost no remaining industrial working class, it is interesting to note that there may also be a "generation gap" when it comes to generational thinking. Boomers often tend to reject it as divisive, whereas millennials and Zoomers are likely to find it uncontroversial.

The line of demarcation here seems to have something to do with the extent to which generations born into the digital age, and living with the effects of climate catastrophe and pandemics, now view historical experience as what sci-fi writers Vernor

Vinge and Charles Stross, and the philosopher Bifo Berardi, for example, have referred to as a "singularity."[42] I'd like to try to offer support for the idea that a generational politics today is actually warranted, because this growing experience of "historical singularity" disarms the understanding of generational change as a continuous cycle of death and rebirth that binds together the generations. The meaning of historical singularity must thus be recognized as something more than just an accelerated pace of change, widening the generation gaps. It involves the happening of events that radically change the world in ways that would be incomprehensible to those who lived in presingularity times. "Historical singularization" means the experience of change as a radical *epoché*, a one-way trip that leaves the sorts of expressions of hope found in the speech of Chaplin's barber/Hynkel largely bereft of their prior resonance.

Rawls on Justice between Generations

To get a better sense of this "before and after" the event of historical singularization, consider the treatment of "Justice between Generations" offered in John Rawls's *A Theory of Justice* (1999).[43] Recall that in Rawls's thought experiment, the first principles of a theory of social contract are derived in a manner designed to conform to and reconstruct the needs and expectations of a modern, liberal society where "justice is fairness." Rawls shows how procedural justice demands the priority of the right over the good, and depends on a thin theory of the good for the selection of primary goods "in the original position,"[44] and behind the veil

42 Vernor Vinge, "The Coming Technological Singularity: How to Survive in the Post-Human Era," *Whole Earth Review*, Winter 1993, https://ntrs.nasa.gov/citations/19940022856, and Charles Stross, *Singularity Sky* (New York: Ace Books, 2003); Franco "Bifo" Berardi, *Breathing: Chaos and Poetry* (Los Angeles: Semiotext(e), 2018); and Franco "Bifo" Berardi, *Futurability: The Age of Impotence and the Horizon of Possibility* (London: Verso, 2017).

43 John Rawls, *A Theory of Justice* (Cambridge: Harvard University Press, 1999), 251.

44 Ibid., 348.

of ignorance. "In a well-ordered society," Rawls writes, "citizens' conception of the good conform to the principles of right publicly recognized, and include an appropriate place for the various primary goods."[45] Something is good "only if it fits into ways of life consistent with the principle of right already on hand."[46] A bit later on, Rawls also goes on to elucidate his full theory of the good, which concerns the set of rational, individual plans for the good life consistent with principles of justice.[47]

What, then, does Rawls say about the problem of justice between generations? Along with maintaining the conditions for just institutions for the next generation to inherit, it is incumbent upon each generation to "put aside a suitable amount of real capital accumulation."[48] Not an inhabitable planet, mind you, but rather a set-aside of accumulated wealth, presumably for things at the societal level that are analogous to the individual middle-class earner's college fund, or nice wedding, or down payment on a starter house. He goes on to say that the reasonable amount of this generational, societal set-aside is determined by the ability to provide for the least advantaged, here and now, and that the savings principle can be established from the standpoint of his "original position" thought experiment, despite the fact that "there is no way for later generations to help the situation of the least fortunate earlier generation."[49]

Rawls thus solves his problem concerning principles of social contract between generations by way of a new wrinkle on his own version of universalizability testing. Across generations, the parties must agree to a savings principle that ensures that each generation receives its due from its predecessor, and does its fair share for those to come. Assuming the veil of ignorance, therefore, the thing is to assume a principle of savings that one wishes that previous generations would have followed also: "We suppose the parties to ask what is reasonable for members of

45 Ibid., 347.
46 Ibid., 348.
47 Ibid., 358.
48 Ibid., 252.
49 Ibid., 252–54.

adjacent generations to expect of each other, at each level of advance."[50] What is important to recognize here, in relation to the matter at hand, is the remarkable fact that Rawls tackles the searingly relevant problem of mutual accountability among generations, first and foremost in terms of what philosophers of science refer to as "a limiting case." That is, he elaborates his "just savings principle," which he freely admits is "but one aspect of the problem of justice between generations,"[51] not because he thinks justice between generations is among the most pressing issues of our time, but in order to show that his account of the original position has an answer for the thorny problem that justice between generations poses for contemporary theories of social contract.

This same sort of continental divide separating Rawls from our own deepening experience of historical exigency also appears where he goes on to describe his fuller theory of the good. By this I mean, consistent with principles of justice, his account of the priority of the right over the good, and his further account of the good as *the rational choice of specific life plans.* What is meant by a rational life plan? Rawls says that a life plan is rational if, and only if, "it is one of the plans that is consistent with principles of rational choice," in full knowledge of one's situation, "and after a careful consideration of the consequences."[52] He reiterates his contention that a rational life plan is fundamental to the definition of the good because it "establishes the basic point of view from which judgments of value [...] are to be made."[53] Choosing from among the many possible rational life plans, therefore, is a necessary part of adopting a moral/rational point of view, something that the theory of justice generally requires.

But the extensive discussion of *the rationality* of life plans still leaves open the question of what is meant by a "life plan"

50 Ibid., 255.
51 Ibid., 252.
52 Ibid., 359.
53 Ibid.

per se. By way of an answer, Rawls says that a life plan "is not a detailed blueprint for action stretching across an entire life."[54] Describing something similar to Maslow's hierarchy of needs, he says "it consists of a hierarchy of plans, with the more specific ones being filled in at the appropriate time."[55] Rawls recognizes that such a notion requires confidence in some degree of good fortune and/or moral luck, a confidence that is not so abundant today as it might have been previously, during liberalism's heyday. Also, the idea of choosing between rational life plans raises many issues, of which Rawls is quite aware. For example, as he himself points out, there is the fact that in making such a choice, "one is choosing today which desires we will have at a later time, or at least deciding now to do something that will affect the desires we will have in the future," because we are choosing who we want to be in the future, including the all-important desire (from the standpoint of a just society) to be someone who acts on rational principles. As far as it goes, this is of course all well and good. But the "authority of the present" that this encodes, along with quiet confidence in the rational ordering of existence (because the future is something that can be expected to provide for us) starts to look dubious once the authentic substance of everyday life begins to disappear, and our biopower is harvested by work, and our subjective experience is marked by what Berardi calls "digital fractalization."

It is worth noting that John Larmore also takes Rawls to task for the account of moral personality implied by his political theory's account of the good life.[56] Larmore thinks the idea that "a life well-lived is one lived in accord with a rational plan" [57] is manifestly wrong, because "life is too unruly to be the subject of a plan," and "the happiness that life affords is less often the good we have reason to pursue than the good that befalls us

54 Ibid., 360.
55 Ibid.
56 Charles Larmore, "The Idea of a Life Plan," *Social Philosophy and Policy Foundation Journal* 16, no. 1 (1999): 96–112.
57 Ibid., 111.

unexpectedly."[58] If we are properly concerned to register the role of moral luck, and the unexpected good, Larmore thinks, then we have to recognize that "the good lies between the extremes of living life according to a plan and letting life happen to us."[59] Rejecting the "presentism" implied in the Rawlsian account, Larmore says that our present conception of the good, "drawing as it does on our previous experience, is bound to fall short of the forms of value which life has yet to show us."[60] Larmore's major claim, namely, that in our haste to vouchsafe the right over the good, we still need to leave room for chance and moral luck in our conception of the good life, is a reasonable Rawlsian corrective. But the bigger question today is not whether Rawls's present-oriented prudence or Larmore's embrace of the unexpected future-to-come should predominate, its whether we can even say that we even have such purposes anymore in the dystopia of the actual present, with its uncertain and unpredictable horizon of futurability.

Historical Singularization and the Millennial Experience

In *Breathing: Chaos and Poetry* (2018), Franco "Bifo" Berardi writes that "the digital intensification of the semiotic flow has broken the rhythm we have inherited from the modern age," and that "labor time as the source of value is now dissolving in the chaotic dimension of semio-capitalism." Whereas previously we accepted salaried labor, and the daily war of competition, "now the order based on salaried labor is crumbling." The loss of our ability to distinguish "what is relevant from what is not," he says, has left us "baroquely searching" for a new rhythm at the most general level of society.[61]

To make sense of where we have been headed, Berardi goes on to make the provocative claim that we have now come under

58 Ibid., 96.
59 Ibid., 103.
60 Ibid., 99.
61 Berardi, *Breathing*, 41, 37.

the sway of modernity's "second panlogical project," which he calls "Leibnizian" to distinguish it from the panlogism of the Hegelian *Aufhebung,* which is characterized by the "will to totality on the terrain of history."[62] Leibnizian panlogism, he says, "perfectly prefigures the late modern dynamics of digital concatenation and financial capitalism."[63] In this new reality, Berardi says, the overarching logic does not deal with the physical and historical existence of bodies, but with "the virtual condition of computational monads, to which bodies are obliged to conform."[64] Leibniz's generative panlogism is epitomized by the digital principle of recombination, and thus only recognizes "the flow of data that give artificial life to the informational units that are working, producing value, and interacting [....] It does not recognize the suffering of living bodies, does not perceive the chaos of exploitation, corruption, and war."[65]

Berardi says that the creation of digital networks and the proliferation of connected devices has accelerated the mutation of the anthropo-sphere that has been happening over the last fifty years, and that interaction with this grid has allowed the mutation to pervade our daily life and to reformat cognitive activity through the pressure of increasing compliance between the mind and the digital network. But because there are aspects of embodied life that cannot be assimilated, we end up with a space that is simultaneously one of both virtual order and chaos. Increasingly today, Berardi says, we must recognize that we have "order in the sphere of connection, and chaos in the interaction of the connected sphere with the space of bodies."[66] Taking his departure from Bergson's remark that "society is breathing together in a shared timeframe,"[67] Berardi describes the socio-political, economic, and even sexual horizon of our time as the search for a way to resist and challenge the established order that

62 Ibid., 57.
63 Ibid., 60.
64 Ibid., 58.
65 Ibid., 59.
66 Ibid., 65.
67 Ibid., 25.

aims to stiffen vibrant bodies, resulting in a kind of a spasm that provokes suffering and breathlessness in the social organism.[68]

It is at this point that Berardi's treatment of our epochal interregnum gets its distinctly millennial twist. In the section "Purity," Berardi comes down out of the philosophico-poetical clouds and makes use of Jonathan Franzen's three novels (*The Corrections, Freedom,* and *Purity*) in order to dramatize what I am calling here "the historical singularization of millennial experience." *Purity,* Berardi writes, "describes the painful process of the connective reformatting of the mind that has enabled the neoliberal disintegration of social solidarity."[69] The migration of social energies from the space of "bodily conspiration" (breathing together) to the space of disembodied communication, and from "conjunctive forms of communication to the digital purity of connectivity," Berardi writes, was inaugurated by the AIDS crisis, which, having forced the identification of pleasure with disease, "slowly turned social life into a desert. At this point, sadness settled into the social soul."[70] It's probably safe to add that this process has seen an acceleration and completion by the societal effects of COVID-19 contagion, which has wiped out any remnants of the social body left over from HIV's "mere infectiousness."

Enter Franzen, with *The Corrections, Freedom,* and *Purity.* Whereas Don DeLillo had described the dissolution of modern rationality and the expansion of postmodern meaninglessness with irony and excitement, "Franzen expresses the mood of a subsequent generation, where the loss of shared meaning is not a scandal, an affliction, or an adventure, but rather dystopia as an insuperable norm."[71] Per Berardi, therefore, it makes sense to describe Franzen as a "Cormac McCarthy for the digital age."[72]

Berardi picks up the thread of the dissolution of our social psychology in *The Corrections,* via the story of the three Lam-

68 Ibid., 23–34.
69 Ibid., 86.
70 Ibid., 71.
71 Ibid., 76.
72 Ibid., 84.

bert sons, whose lives are seen to oscillate back and forth, like so many of us today, between the poles of panic and depression.[73] From there, in *Freedom,* we witness the character Joey, eager to erase the memory of 9/11 because he finds it too disturbing to his preset expectations about the world. Nothing prepared him "to internalize an event that so disrupts the chain of predictability, and ruptures the smooth order of a coded life," so he has no option but to experience 9/11 as an "unthinkable glitch."[74] In the digital mind, Berardi explains, "events don't exist. Only infoneural stimuli register."[75]

Finally, in the third installment, *Purity,* the novel revolves around the life choices of "Pip" (Purity) Taylor, a twenty-something IT professional looking for a precarious job. Quoting from Franzen's text, he describes the experience of millennials finding themselves living in a woeful reality that they experience as unreal, because it is opposed to their birthright of good luck. They vainly hope for some sort of a *deus ex machina* to come and set things right.[76]

As a result of what Berardi calls "the digital mutation," which has thrown individuals into radical contingency and singularized the experience of history, "individuals increasingly no longer see themselves as able to pursue autonomous life projects."[77] As such, they no longer conform to Rawls's thin theory of the good, because they are "fragments of precarious time, ceaselessly recombined fractals" conforming only to competition, and effective only under "the rule of rentability."[78] As for the meaning of justice between generations, and the relevance of generational politics, if Berardi is right, and the meaning of generational politics today is that for younger generations history has become a singularity, then the sorts of narratives previ-

73 Ibid., 75.
74 Ibid., 78.
75 Ibid.
76 Ibid.
77 Ibid., 87.
78 Ibid.

ously employed to describe relations between generations may be the thing that no longer has much relevance.

Indications that this may be the case are plentiful. Consider Noam Chomsky's recent interviews, in which he tells us, in his usual deadpan, that we have arrived at the most dangerous moment in all of human history.[79] Or consider CNN chief climate correspondent Bill Weir's recent "letter to his infant son," where he says, for example, "On the day you learned to open kitchen cabinets, 15 giant sequoia trees that had been swaying with the California winds for 2,000 years, couldn't survive 2021."[80] Or finally, consider the repeating chorus from Harry Styles's recent hit song, "As It Was": "In this world, it's just us / You know it's not the same as it was / In this world, it's just us / You know it's not the same as it was / As it was, as it was / You know it's not the same."[81]

It appears that we have arrived at a point where we can no longer take solace when Chaplin/barber/Hynkel says, "Don't despair, because the hate of men will pass, and dictators die [...] and so long as men die, liberty will not perish." On this side of the divide, after the event, after the singularization of historical experience, the renewing spring of our natality no longer guarantees us the capacity for futurability, and so no longer serves to bind together the generations. Hart may be right when he says that generational politics are antisolidaristic, because they "seek to divide people in relation to things like war, austerity, climate change, movements of capital, and other things that threaten to pull society apart." But maybe that's not a bad thing. And Harris is certainly right when he says that millennials (and Zoomers)

---

79 George Eaton, "Noam Chomsky: 'We're Approaching the Most Dangerous Point in Human History,'" *The New Statesman*, April 6, 2022, https://www.newstatesman.com/encounter/2022/04/noam-chomsky-were-approaching-the-most-dangerous-point-in-human-history.

80 Bill Weir, "To My Son, Born during the Climate Crisis: Get Mad and Get Ready," *CNN Travel*, April 22, 2022, https://www.cnn.com/travel/article/climate-change-bill-weir-letter-to-son-wt-scn/index.html.

81 Harry Styles, "As It Was," track 4 from *Harry's House* (Columbia Records, 2022).

will be the pivot point. The only hope of the world at this point lies in the possibility that they might make a radical break from the assumptions, life patterns, and expectations of past generations.

Part II

To Decommodify Labor and Reweave the Social

7

Labor versus Work: A Philosophical Ramble

> The old hierarchies that defined "skilled" and "unskilled" seem to be dissolving. Some hold out for further changes, anticipating the introduction of low-carbon jobs to replace those lost, or a universal basic income, or rethinking the value of labour altogether.
>
> —Nesrine Malik, *The Guardian,* May 18, 2020

Is it even possible to have a clear understanding of the difference between labor and work? In *The Human Condition,* Hannah Arendt tells us that every European language, ancient and modern, "contains two etymologically unrelated words for what we have come to think of as the same activity, and retains them in the face of their persistent synonymous usage."[1] Arendt is clearly suspicious. Why have two words if they really just mean the same thing? There must be at least something going on here, since modern languages stubbornly retain both of these terms. If we look instead to our contemporary everyday usage, we can hear echoes of a whole range of distinctions passed down to

1 Hannah Arendt, *The Human Condition* (Chicago: University of Chicago Press, 1998), 80.

us from diverse contexts with radically different assumptions. Consider the following made-up example: *As a white-collar professional, I go off to work, and once there, I sit in my office (I am an office worker). When I look out the window, I see some laborers, digging a ditch. At lunchtime, I am delayed returning to the office, because protesting employees who are union members (and thus part of the larger, organized labor movement) block the road with their picketing.*

What exactly is happening here? Why is it that what I do is called "work," and what the ditchdigger does is called "labor"? Is it because what one does involves transforming nature? Or is it because the work is considered unskilled? Or is it mostly because one is a so-called day laborer? Also, why is it that some employees (generally referred to as "workers") are represented by collective bargaining, but others have their salaries and benefits determined by a market valuation? Aren't both groups trading their labor for a wage? Is it because these other workers are considered more skilled? Or because, as salaried employees, they are considered to be "in management" at least to some degree?

Beyond our vague, everyday sense that there are differences in the way that we think about such things as subsistence labor, wage work, salaried employment, and unpaid work, there is a complex history of other considerations that also may come into play depending on the circumstances. For example, where skilled work is at issue, there is the difference between the making of things for their use value (largely a premodern activity) and making things for their exchange value (modern, market-based money economy). There are early modern ideas about the division of labor into productive and unproductive, skilled and unskilled, and manual and intellectual, and there are contrasting ancient and modern ideas about work versus leisure and/or contemplation. Finally, there is also the continuing influence of traditional Marxism on the movements of the Left. Here I mean specifically Marx's primary distinction between "labor" and "labor power," and his identification of the industrial proletariat (the working class) as the agent of revolutionary change from the condition of alienated wage labor to nonalienated labor in the utopia of the classless society.

Let me be clear that I am not suggesting that the identities and experiences of people generally performing various types of work (including various cultural markers of class) have little or nothing to do with why—as farm workers, machine operators, cabinetmakers, financial analysts, engineers, nurses, and homemakers—we tend to stand separately from one another. For example, there are all kinds of reasons why members of the PMC have lives that revolve around work, work, and more work, and yet simply assume that something like labor organizing is very remote from them, even if the reasons are not at all as compelling as they once were. Nevertheless, it remains true that in the present epoch of capitalist exchange, virtually everybody eats because someone exchanged their labor for a wage in the labor market. If all work is wage labor in this broad sense, then why do we continue to make a series of conflicting distinctions about differences between labor and work?

Labor versus Work? Or Work-as-We-Know-It?

Heretofore, I have largely avoided delving into "labor versus work"; instead I have stubbornly employed a neologism, the hyphenated noun phrase "work-as-we-know-it." I have done so, in large part, in the hope that I might somehow sidestep the sort of confusions just described. After all, why get bogged down in a complex conceptual dispute with a legacy that spans millennia, when nearly everybody in the contemporary neoliberal work machine is experiencing the same set of increasingly miserable conditions? "Work-as-we-know-it" stands for the new reality of work in the United States: an increasingly universal cocktail of post-Fordist precarity, highly financialized enterprises, bullshit jobs, neorentier debt peonage, authoritarian employment contracts, blurry barriers between work and private life, and more than just a small dose of stress, anxiety, depression, and despair.

By focusing on the experience of work in this way, I've been free to explore Peter Fleming's question: "Can the impossibility at the heart of contemporary capitalism be politically activated to oppose and escape work?" To this point, I've mostly maintained that it is only the pervasive ideology of capitalist realism that now stands in the way of the postwork political imaginary and a broad-based refusal of neoliberal capitalism and its harsh terms and conditions. But if we are to have any hope for identifying a new, nontraditional form of solidarity, one capable of enacting a cultural refusal of work-as-we-know-it, then it's also necessary to make some progress in overcoming the raft of confusions surrounding labor versus work. To achieve this, there needs to be a shift in focus. We need to be able to say precisely what is meant by work in the modern period, as a baseline for assessing the significance of its boundaries and exclusions, and in order to understand how contemporary changes in technology and socioeconomic conditions are calling forth new dynamics of political and social resistance. The situation is rendered even more acute under conditions of pandemic, where designation of "essential workers," for example, is upending contemporary hierarchies of so-called human capital.

Rethinking Work to Overcome Laborism

To get a sense of a recent play of ideas concerning labor versus work, consider British economist Guy Standing's "The Left Should Stop Equating Labour with Work."[2] As part of a general critique of British laborism (the decades-long project of trying to win specific concessions from management), Standing calls for an end to what he regards as the "systematic distortion of work as labour" and argues that social democrats need to adopt a more progressive and/or more radical posture concerning work if they want to stop losing elections. He wants to see an enlarged definition of work, one that counts all the various ways that people are productive in the commons, and not just their

2 Guy Standing, "The Left Should Stop Equating Labor with Work," *SocialEurope*, March 23, 2018, https://www.socialeurope.eu/why-work-not-labour-is-ecological-imperative.

productivity under conditions of wage labor. It's absurd, Standing says, that taking care of someone else's relative for a wage for three hours a day is work, but the six hours a day you spend taking care of your own relative isn't. And yet the real scandal in all of this, he says, is not that this work-as-wage-labor is predominant under contemporary neoliberalism, rather, it's that the social democrats have largely shared this basic viewpoint with parties of the center-right.

The Left fell into a political trap "by putting the notion of full employment on a pedestal," since doing so meant little more than "maximizing the number of people in labour, in positions subordinate to bosses." For Standing, the notion that "being in a job gives someone dignity, status, and the means of social integration or a sense of belonging in society" is a pernicious form of false consciousness. For most people, since jobs are instrumental, "there is no justifiable reason for elevating them above other forms of work." Besides, the conditions under which the laborist project made strategic sense have now broken down, as more work is being performed away from formal workplaces and outside of labor time, and continued prioritization of job creation over environment places the labor movement often on the wrong side of the climate issue. Standing calls for a new, nonlaborist approach, one "where the value of work that is not labour — commonly called use-value — would be given at least equal weight to the value of labor — exchange value."

Overall, there is much to admire in Standing's impassioned plea. But there are some things that remain rather puzzling, at least on the face of it. For example, it's hard to understand how we renew the general critique of all wage labor as alienated (as he also wishes to do contra laborism) by so thoroughly disassociating labor and work. Standing's baseline assumption is that "labor equals wage labor under capitalism," and that work, by contrast, is something more general, more expansive, and thus more comprehensive, and more transhistorical in its significance. This is fine, as far as it goes. Work *should* be recognized as more than just wage labor. And yet, this unjust reduction of work to wage labor, which is actually decisive for our age, cannot be simply wished away. After all, it was precisely Marx's specific intention to frame the reduction of all work to wage labor as a structural problem to be solved through political action. So there needs to be a way to valorize the use value in socially necessary yet unpaid work without also losing sight of this as a political problem. Surely, if unpaid labor is work, then wage labor, as alienated, is also work. We need to worry about both the baby and the bathwater. All of which brings us back to the central perplexity that needs to be addressed, that of labor versus work.

Arendt and the Pyrrhic Victory of *animal laborans*

A strikingly different (and alas infinitely more complex) treatment of the problem of labor versus work emerges through a close reading of Arendt's highly influential *The Human Condition* (1958). In the most straightforward sense, her project in the book is to show how "the most elementary articulations of the human condition" (which she identifies as labor, work, and action) come to expression differently in the ancient world, the Middle Ages, and then in the modern age.[3] But it's important to recognize that Arendt's interest in these "general human capacities" actually serves a very specific purpose. To really understand what Arendt has to say, one almost has to read the book in reverse, since its overarching logic is essentially retrospective. In surveying this terrain, she wants to explain how it is that "the distinction between labor and work is abandoned in favor of labor" in the modern age, and thus how it came to pass that the whole modern age ultimately agreed that "labor (and not reason) distinguished man from the other animals."[4]

The modern age "has carried with it a theoretical glorification of labor and has resulted in a factual transformation of the whole of society into a laboring society."[5] By charting the rise

3 Arendt, *The Human Condition*, 5.

4 Ibid., 86.

5 Ibid., 4.

in prestige of what she calls the *vita activa* ("active life," understood as labor, work, and action) relative to the *vita contemplativa* ("life of contemplation"), Arendt sets the stage for her attempt to account for the unexpected victory of human being as *animal laborans* ("laboring animal") over human being as *homo faber* (human being as fabricator, toolmaker, and world-builder).[6] In trying to follow this extremely complex history of concepts throughout the book, it is helpful to think of Arendt as the caller of a square dance. For a while, on the modern dance stage, Arendt calls out *homo faber,* and the dancers do their do-si-dos. Then, like poor *contemplativa* (who became winded earlier in the dance and had to sit down), *faber,* too, returns to his or her original position. But this isn't even the end of it. Her ultimate purpose in doing so is to understand the origins and significance of something she calls "modern world alienation" or "inter-worldly asceticism," which she considers to be the defining characteristic of the modern age.[7] I told you it was complicated.

Here and in the next two chapters, I consider labor versus work by comparing the arguments found in Arendt's *The Human Condition* with the perspective of the mature Karl Marx, as found in *Capital.* For both Arendt and Marx, as will be made clear, the modern age has effectively reduced the concept of work to that of labor (wage labor). Yet despite this broad agreement, they curiously disagree quite deeply about what it all means. In seeking to clarify the basis of this agreement/disagreement, I also hope to cover most of the significant permutations in the labor versus work conceptual dynamic. This chapter mostly lays out the argument made by Arendt; chapter 8 focuses on Marx's

---

6 Arendt's use of the term *homo faber* is elastic. Repeatedly, Arendt says that *homo faber* is a fabricator (ibid., 139, 140, 149, 151, 155). She also says, *homo faber* instrumentalizes (156); and she says *homo faber* is a toolmaker (151); beyond this, however, as fabricator, she repeatedly tells us that *homo faber* creates the human artifice, and in so doing is a world-builder; *homo faber* erects a world of things (144, 151); *homo faber* encompasses the human faculties that are directed to the building of a world (307).

7 Ibid., 251, 254.

concept of abstract labor. I approach this matter in the form of a philosophical ramble. I am certainly not a labor economist. But I believe that there are substantial grounds for defending a "post-Marxist" labor theory of value in the face of marginalist economic assumptions.[8] However, setting out to defend the continued relevance of value theory per se would be an entirely different project.

Arendt 1: On Premodern Labor and Work

What most people tend to remember from reading *The Human Condition* is Arendt's striking account of the difference between labor and work. The descriptions she offers outline the basic story of labor versus work from the time of the ancient Greek *polis,* up until the early modern period, with only the status of the activity of contemplation changing somewhat in the Middle Ages. The first thing to understand is that to begin with, labor and work denote the difference between "the laboring body and the work of the hands."[9] Whereas, in the case of *animal laborans* (human being qua "laboring animal") one "mixes one's labor with natural products" in order to secure necessities of life, *homo faber* (human being qua maker/worker) "makes and works upon, as opposed to mixes with."[10]

Admittedly, labor can sometimes look like work. For example, tilling the land transforms the landscape, and in this sense, it leaves behind a product of a kind. But cultivated land is not a "use object per se, because it needs to be labored upon time and time again."[11] It's this aspect of a particular sort of repetition that is here decisive. The potential multiplication inherent in work, Arendt says, "is different in principle from the repetition that is the mark of labor." Whereas a craftsman's impulse

8 See Maurice Dobb, *Theories of Value and Distribution since Adam Smith* (London: Cambridge University Press, 1973), and Mariana Mazzucato, *The Value of Everything* (New York: Public Affairs, 2018).

9 Arendt, *The Human Condition,* 85.

10 Ibid., 136.

11 Ibid., 139.

toward repetition comes from the need to earn the means of subsistence, the process of crafting is thus repeated for reasons that are really "outside itself," something different than "the compulsory repetition that is inherent in laboring."[12] It is this closeness to the cyclic necessity of nature that give us the sense of labor's repetition as toil. To be governed entirely by necessity (subject only to natural laws and processes) was understood by the ancients as contrary to functioning as a human being, since such an existence was lacking the spontaneity of the products of human freedom.[13]

The premodern distinction between labor and work is initially disorienting for us because of its stark clarity, and because Arendt's methods of analysis are quite idiosyncratic, but that's another story. In the modern age, by contrast, everything has been thoroughly muddled—we exchange both natural products and useful crafted things in the marketplace, and also our labor power—all as commodities in exchange for money, and we purchase nearly everything we need to satisfy both our needs and our wants. But in Greek antiquity, which admittedly also had a money economy and a barter system, and both slave and subsistence labor, the sense of *laborans* "as a servant of nature, of the earth"[14] had still not yet receded to the extent that it has today.

Arendt goes out of her way to try to make it clear that the use of the Latin *animal laborans* as a term to describe this funda-

---

12 Ibid., 142.

13 A number of historians have argued that this assertion of Greek antiquity's disdain for labor and work is likely overstated; for example, see Catharina Lis, "Perceptions of Work in Classical Antiquity," in *The Idea of Work in Europe from Antiquity to Modern Times,* eds. Joseph Ehmer and Catharina Lis (New York: Routledge, 2009), 33–68. Lis writes, "Only in the self-serving language of an elite was 'being liberated from work' associated with happiness and wealth" (35). Lis argues that there is actually an audible polyphony concerning labor and work to be heard if we look beyond the testimony of philosophers and statesmen, one where the notion of pónos as productive virtue is foregrounded, as in Hesiod's *Works and Days,* and also in the plays of Euripides and Aristophanes.

14 Arendt, *The Human Condition,* 139.

mental human persona recognizable in antiquity is not meant in a strictly pejorative sense. To identify human beings performing certain activities as *animal laborans* is no more prejudicial than referring to human beings, engaged in other sets of activities, as rational animals, as Aristotle famously did. Also, Arendt does not mean to suggest that labor, in its bodily movements, or in the products that it creates through the admixture with labor, and even in its repetition, does not have its satisfactions. The issue is simply that being completely tied to such cycles of natural necessity leaves no time or space for doing things that are distinctly and spontaneously human (action in the political realm, and the contemplation of the beautiful, the good, and the true).

As for work, the persona of *homo faber* that Arendt describes also cuts an equally striking figure in her social ontology of the premodern world. Whereas the activity of *animal laborans* is guided by "bodily sensations, pleasure or pain, desires and satisfactions," fabrication is performed "under the guidance of a model in accordance with which the object is constructed."[15] In this sense, what guides the fabricator (whether before the mind's eye or via blueprint) precedes the actual work processes in "much the same way as the urgencies of the life process within the laborer precede the actual labor process."[16] But once again, the big difference is that *homo faber* produces all manner of things for use, whereas *animal laborans*'s products lack what she calls "true reification" where the produced thing is durable, and so "in its existence is secured once and for all."[17] Whereas the products of *animal laborans* are fit for consumption, she says, the products of *homo faber* are fit for use. *Homo faber* "fabricates the sheer unending variety of things,"[18] and so literally makes the human world in which we live together out of all of its durable goods as building blocks. Along with the stable

15 Ibid., 140.
16 Ibid.
17 Ibid., 139.
18 Ibid., 136.

objects from which we fix our general concept of objectivity (I see before me this chair …), Arendt wants us to recognize that the durability of these goods also becomes the foundation for the modern concept of property, and the value with which they become imbued is the basis for the commodity exchange market as a dominant component of modern life.

If you stop reading *The Human Condition* at this point, you do indeed walk away with a kind of an answer to the question of labor versus work. But even if Arendt turns out to be correct about this set of ancient world distinctions, it isn't yet clear what it is that this has to do with us, gazing into this distant mirror. After all, we are not simple craftsmen fabricating objects for their usefulness, like hobbits in the Shire. Why then does Arendt go to the trouble to distinguish these sociohistorical personae (*Homo laborans, homo faber*), especially since they coexisted together in a shared premodern world, and even in the Greek city-state, the distinction between them was not all that terribly pronounced?

Recall that for Arendt, the *vita activa,* when taken as a whole (i.e., as a complex that includes the meeting of basic needs, living in a constructed world, and having relations with others) represents ancient political life and its supporting conditions. What Arendt actually wants to foreground here, in the portrait of human capacities and their related activities in the ancient city-state and beyond, is thus not at all a contrast between labor and work per se. Rather, it is the contrast between the *vita activa* (including labor, work, and action) with the *vita contemplativa,* the activity of *theoria,* which the ancient and medieval world of letters recognized as the highest level of functioning for a human qua human. The initial demarcation between labor and work thus functions as a kind of a baseline, as just the first step in an attempt to explain how the lowly *animal laborans* ends up "on top" in the modern age, having vanquished figures such as *animal rationale, homo politicus, and homo faber,* eventually standing alone as the defining characteristic of human being.

Arendt 2: On Distinctly Modern Labor and Work

What then, per Arendt, are the dramatic changes that so transform labor and work with the coming of the modern age? So far, we only know this much: that the path of the modern transformation of labor and work, in some way still not very clear, involves a wholesale reversal of the ancient/medieval hierarchical order between the *vita contemplativa* and the *vita activa.* Writ large, the causes of this reversal that she goes on to identify are the things most often cited as the threshold events leading to the modern age as such—the Protestant Reformation, the discovery of the New World, and the rise of modern sciences:[19]

- In the case of the new science, it seems that Arendt wants to show how its rise led to a new preeminence for our friend *homo faber,* and, in so doing, contributed to the great reversal: Man's thirst for knowledge could be assuaged only after he had put his trust into the ingenuity of his hands. Increasing reliance on instruments and tools,[20] and with it the preoccupation with process and method over pregiven ends;[21] mathematization of natural knowledge[22]; the prioritization of utility over meaningfulness.[23] These all become hallmarks of the modern age, so it can't be a surprise that a society of such craftspeople in the early Enlightenment would promote Deism's "God the watchmaker."[24]
- Arendt's paragraphs on the age of discovery are among the strangest things in the book. How does the discovery of America support the trend under discussion? Shrinkage, she says. The mapping of the entire world reduced it all down to a determinate quantum, disenchanting it in some way that

19 Ibid., 248.
20 Ibid., 261.
21 Ibid., 296.
22 Ibid., 264–65.
23 Ibid., 156–57.
24 Ibid., 297.

dovetailed with the other elements bringing *homo faber* to the fore.[25]

— Her ideas on the Reformation's role mostly concern the rise of a universal, modern laboring class. The Reformation disrupts traditional patterns of economic life in the northern countries, with implications that end up spreading everywhere. It begins with the expropriation of ecclesiastical possessions and peasant labor. The expropriation and secularization of group identities is what transforms labor, creating the first general working class, a necessary condition for widespread capitalist accumulation.[26]

Most of the rest of what she has to say about the eventual "victory of *animal laborans*" has to do with much more immediate causes of both the rise and the fall of *homo faber* within the newly preeminent *vita activa.* It seems plausible that the new prestige of the *vita activa* should have elevated *homo faber* rather than the *animal laborans,* Arendt argues, but the relegation of the *vita contemplativa* to the sidelines actually contained within it the seeds of *faber's* demise,[27] ultimately explaining why he only gets to strut around for a little while, like some doomed *Australopithecus afarensis.*

The subtle transition from world-builder to primarily toolmaker, she writes, includes also the reversal of means over ends, so that "the end product" of *homo faber's* works "is no longer the true end."[28] Usefulness becomes the end of fabrication, displacing the guiding model understood as object of contemplation. Finally, "the turning point in the history of the modern age came," she says, "when the image of organic life development appeared in the place of the watchmaker who must be superior to all watches whose cause he is."[29] This second major reversal thus concerns the evolution of the concept of process, "whose

25 Ibid., 250–51.
26 Ibid., 252–55.
27 Ibid., 307.
28 Ibid., 308.
29 Ibid., 312.

concepts and categories are altogether alien to the needs and ideals of *homo faber*." The set of key paragraphs on "the rise and fall of *homo faber*" go by rather quickly, and are rather hard to make out. For present purposes, it's enough to say that per Arendt, "the defeat of *homo faber* may be explainable in terms of the march of modern sciences."[30] There is no need to spend more time unpacking this, since, as she herself indicates, the cause of the demise of *homo faber* is not the most important thing: "What still remains to be explained is why this defeat ended with a victory of the *animal laborans*."[31]

If one doesn't read *The Human Condition* extremely carefully, one might get the idea that human being as "laboring animal" finally becomes ubiquitous because there are no other contenders left standing. Sort of like how small mammals take over the earth because tyrannosaurs lie fossilizing in the marshy ground. But if one looks very closely, along with her wide-ranging account of the various threshold events that lead to a distinctly modern consciousness, Arendt also lends support to the notion that *labor and work are primarily transformed by capitalism.*

Arendt and the Modern Discovery of Labor Power

Initially, in the early modern age, labor versus work looks a lot like the ancient conception. In Adam Smith and John Locke, for example, you see work described as being productive or unproductive, conforming to previous distinctions, and other writers on political economy from the period talk about skilled and unskilled, and so on. However, it is also possible to see that some significant changes are taking place, as identified by Arendt:

— Recall how *homo faber*, in constructing the entire human artifice, the world in which we live socially, thereby provided Locke with the durable objects he needed for elaborating the modern concept of private property.

30 Ibid., 313.
31 Ibid.

— Also recall that *homo faber,* in producing things fit for use, also comes to exchange them for money in the marketplace, providing Smith with "the value he needed for the exchange market."
— Finally, recall also, that after the Reformation, and as a result of its complex history of effects, we see for the first time the transformation of labor through the emergence of a universal working class, a necessary condition for the capitalist accumulation of wealth.

With these dots connected, we can see that Arendt is describing how the world-building, toolmaking *homo faber,* with his or her fabrication of all manner of objects of use value, set in motion a chain of events that decisively transformed labor. For *homo faber,* "labor power is only the means to produce the necessary higher end, that is, either a use object, or an object for exchange."[32] But once we step firmly out of what I like to call "the Shire" (the mythical premodern world of use value fabrication) and into the exchange market, something happens. For one thing, the semiskilled activity of tending machines for a wage transforms previous work into labor, and the stage of automation "characterized by electricity" intensifies the trend. At this stage, per Arendt, what we see is "not a gigantic enlargement and continuation of the old arts and crafts" and "the categories of *homo faber* [...] no longer apply."[33] Once *homo faber* is making things repetitively in order to earn money for subsistence, she or he becomes a laborer: "In a society where exchange is pre-eminent, laborers become proprietors, owners of their labor power."[34]

From this we can see that where "the distinction between labor and work is abandoned in favor of labor," the transformation in question clearly involves not just work, but labor also. Where ancient labor "leaves nothing behind," in the modern

32 Ibid., 162.
33 Ibid., 148.
34 Ibid., 162.

age, Arendt says, "labor has a productivity even if its products are not durable."[35] Labor is seen to eclipse work because something else is liberated along with Church property and feudal tenants. Whereas the modern age produces the "first free laboring class in history,"[36] the *force inherent in labor power per se* is liberated (my emphasis).[37] Workers and laborers of all kinds "become equally proprietors," precisely because they have something to exchange in the market other than produced useful objects—they have the surplus value contained in their labor power, such that, in contracting with an employer to do work over time, they provide the abstract labor needed for the capitalist enterprise.

In seeming complete agreement with Marx, Arendt writes that market capitalism marks the transition from *homo faber* understood in terms of use value to alienated wage labor under conditions of exchange value.[38] However, what she doesn't seem to want to say, along with Marx, is that this transition is really the critical development for explaining how "the distinction between labor and work is abandoned in favor of labor" in the modern age. If the advent of capitalist society is what fundamentally transforms both labor and work, effectively reducing all manner of work to wage labor, then why does she relegate it to the status of merely a cofactor, along with a variety of other transformations of modern consciousness? The key statement relating to this in *The Human Condition* turns out to be the following: "World alienation, not self-alienation, as Marx thought, has been the hallmark of the modern age."[39] In making this statement, I explain in chapter 8, Arendt clearly chooses Max Weber as the "regnant genius" of her book, rather than Marx, despite the fact that modern laboring society is her topic, and not "the spirit of capitalism" per se.

35 Ibid., 88.
36 Ibid., 255.
37 Ibid.
38 Ibid., 163.
39 Ibid., 254.

Formally, Arendt's highly complex narrative relies on effective history—on showing how various events and trends explain major conceptual shifts through unanticipated causal lines of descent. Her preference for this sort of transhistorical critique has to do with her admiration for ancient Greek politics and also with its flipside, namely, her wholesale refusal of the methods and intentions of modern social science. This admiration for the *polis* (and her related lack of a functional concept of modern society) helps to explain why she feels free to appreciate Marx and integrate his thinking into her narrative, on the one hand, but why she nonetheless declines to follow his lead, on the other.

Marx on Abstract Labor and Social Domination

Arendt, along with Marx, says that the modern age reduces work to labor, and Arendt says that Marx's account of labor power is "the most original and revolutionary element in his whole system."[40] Also, she recognizes that the rise of a manufacturing society brings with it a laboring society, one that judges people not as persons, but "according to the function they perform in the labor process,"[41] that is, as commodities. So how to understand the apparent similarities between Arendt and Marx on labor and work in the modern age, given that there is ultimately such divergence? To get at this, it is useful to provide a rejoinder to Arendt by describing some key aspects of Marx's mature labor theory. In doing so, in these three chapters, I follow the insights of notable critics who tend to read Marx as a whole through the prism of the later works, including Louis Althusser, Leszek Kolakowski, Harry Braverman, Michael Hudson, and, especially, Moishe Postone.[42] In the end, it appears that

40 Ibid., 88.

41 Ibid.., 162.

42 However, as Søren Mau has recently asserted, Marx is polyphonic. There doesn't have to be a serious contradiction between early and late, *Grundrisse* and *Capital*. Nor is it simply a question of preference or emphasis. The critique of capital adequate to a politics of refusal requires a compati-

Arendt parts company with Marx primarily because she fails to grasp the full significance of his account of labor power, what Marx in *Capital* calls "that very peculiar commodity."[43]

bilism — accounts of both horizontal and vertical domination, of fetishism as both something constitutive of modern social existence, and fetishism as a ruling class ideology. See Søren Mau, *Mute Compulsion: A Marxist Theory of the Economic Power of Capital* (London: Verso, 2023).

43 "A commodity whose use-value has the peculiar property of being a source of value"; Karl Marx, *Capital,* Vol. 1 (London: Penguin, 1990), 270, 274.

8

Arendt and Marx on Modern Wage Labor

> The bourgeoisie has stripped of its halo every occupation hitherto honored and looked up to with reverent awe. It has converted the physician, the lawyer, the priest, the poet, the man of science, into its paid laborers.
>
> — Karl Marx and Frederick Engels, *The Communist Manifesto* (1848)

In chapter 7, I tried to address ongoing confusions over labor versus work by exploring the history of these concepts, as described by Hannah Arendt in *The Human Condition*. I was quite surprised to discover the apparent convergence of Arendt's position (after all was said and done) with that of Marx, namely, that the modern age has effectively reduced the concept of work to wage labor, and that work—so understood—is essentially labor power sold to an employer as a commodity in the labor market.[1]

1 It is certainly true that in the modern age, work becomes, first and foremost, wage labor, but it is also true that the story is quite a bit more complex. Jürgen Kocka points out that capitalism has always depended on various elements of unfree labor, in both the colonial and postcolonial period, at home in the developed countries and abroad. See Jürgen Kocka,

Among the virtues of Arendt's book is the constant reminder that things have not always been this way. For most of recorded history, human beings (albeit in comparatively tiny populations) performed subsistence labor and fabricated useful objects without anybody paying them an actual wage to spend their time in these pursuits. Of course, some people were actual slaves. Others worked hereditary lands or Church properties, or they were free men living in towns, and in each case they and "their women and children" disposed of any surpluses in a variety of ways mandated by their specific cultural, socioeconomic, and political circumstances. Even up through the early modern mercantile era, however, *nobody worked according to employment contracts in a modern capitalist enterprise designed specifically to generate commodities to be sold for a profit and to expand capital.* This is why it is so surprising that *The Human Condition,* ostensibly about the political meaning and significance of modern labor, forgoes any substantive analysis of industrial capitalism, seemingly just deferring to Marx when she indicates that market capitalism marks the transition from *homo faber,* understood in terms of use value, to alienated wage labor under conditions of exchange value.[2]

Despite this nod to alienated wage labor, however, her analysis of labor and work strangely stops with market exchange under mercantilism: "The public realm of *homo faber* is the exchange market."[3] When fabricators met there, "they did not meet as persons, but as owners of commodities and exchange values." In a society where exchange is preeminent, "laborers become proprietors, owners of their labor power."[4] From here, despite the apparent agreement with Marx, Arendt omits analysis of the rise of a manufacturing class and critique of political economy, and instead heads off in other directions. But why? Why stop here?

Capitalism: A Short History, trans. Jeremiah Riemer (Princeton: Princeton University Press, 2016), 124–45.

2 Hannah Arendt, *The Human Condition* (Chicago: University of Chicago Press, 1998), 162–63.

3 Ibid., 160.

4 Ibid., 162.

Especially since a key maneuver of Marx's *Capital* is precisely to try to get us to leave the level of exchange (where the worker's goal of income and the capitalist's demand for surplus value are treated as equivalents) and to focus instead at the level of wage-based production, that is, on the labor process itself.

Should we continue, even now, to regard our labor power, as capitalists everywhere still invite us to do, as so much human capital? Or is it rather more compelling, following Marx, to recognize it instead as a commodity, and then embrace all the consequences that this understanding might entail? The dystopian US response to the COVID-19 pandemic provides us with ringing testimony about how utterly pernicious it is to simply trust in the logic of the market to provide us with our true north in all things, so that some people are literally willing to die for it, as if the market were something other than an abstraction. In light of this current societal provocation, I'd like to try to re-enliven for myself the singular weirdness of the nexus "labor power-commodity-monetary exchange-capital," and how it fundamentally structures our social relations.

Doing this is hard. After more than a 150 years of living out the possibilities and consequences of the bourgeois-democratic state, pretty much everything has been thoroughly naturalized. Getting a feel for what was truly revolutionary in the bourgeois revolution has to be wrested from our pervasive experience of capitalist realism with significant effort. But the effort is worth it, because this is capitalist realism's citadel, its innermost sanctum. Of course, it would be a waste of time to try to argue that the bourgeois revolution and the liberal state are simply lacking in material accomplishments, or that this phase of modern social and political development was actually a terrible mistake. But given the intensifying cultural logic of advanced technological capitalism, not to mention its unsustainability, the full implication of abstract labor needs to be much more widely recognized and foregrounded. Maybe it's now time, once again, to dare to take seriously the far-reaching implications of having a society where *value is expressed exclusively through the commodity form*, and all of social reality is tied to the fundamental decision that (so that we may live) nearly everyone must sell their labor time in the market for a wage. In this chapter, my objective is thus to try to refresh my understanding of Marx's view of labor power in relation to capital, taken from *Capital,* Volume 1. My aim in doing so is to set the stage for chapter 9, where I compare what Arendt and Marx say about the primary meaning and significance of this fateful, world-historical development concerning labor and work.

9-9-6: Jack Ma and the Sign of the Beast

If you've ever had any business dealings with the Chinese tech sector, then perhaps you are also familiar with the practice that has come to be known as "9-9-6." If you are not so familiar (and also slightly dyslexic) you can be forgiven for thinking this must refer to "the sign of the beast," especially since this turns out not to be too far from the truth. This 9-9-6 is the general expectation of some Chinese companies that their employees should work from 9 am to 9 pm, and 6 days per week, as a matter of course. In the spring of 2019, 9-9-6 became rather more famous when Alibaba founder Jack Ma actively defended it in a series of comments posted to the company's Weibo account, and the ensuing controversy went global. "I personally think that 996 is a huge blessing," the fifty-four-year-old entrepreneur wrote. For his part, Ma said, he "never regretted working 12-hour days," and then went on to say that "prospective employees of Alibaba should be prepared to work 12 hours a day if they want to succeed." It really shouldn't be a problem, Ma added, if you like your work.[5]

The pushback Ma received on Chinese social media (and even from Chinese state media) serves as an indicator that the standard capitalist gambit — that of insisting upon an equiva-

5 Serenitie Wang and Daniel Shane, "Jack Ma Endorses China's Controversial 12 Hours a Day, 6 Days a Week Work Culture," *CNN Business,* April 15, 2019, https://www.cnn.com/2019/04/15/business/jack-ma-996-china/index.html.

lence between the capitalist with his or her accumulating profits and the worker with his or her wage income — is apparently no more convincing today in state-capitalist China than it was in the Central Europe and Britain of Marx's day. Leszek Kolakowski has written that in the modern age, a universal laboring class is made "free to sell their labor power for a fixed time — and free from ownership of means of production, i.e., possessing nothing but their labor power, [they are] thus consequently obliged to sell it."[6]

Thinking about Jack Ma and 9-9-6 leads me to reflect more deeply on my own experiences with maniacal CEOs and with what unreflectively and euphemistically is called "overwork." For example, I vividly recall a certain lunchtime Christmas party from more than fifteen years ago, where staff and management were celebrating a remarkable year of bringing new customer products to market and increasing revenues. Since the insane hours and stressful conditions endured by the team had brought the private company within range of the earnings needed for a lucrative acquisition, we were all expecting some level of graciousness from the boss, especially since he clearly had the most to gain when the company went over the top. We all understood that he was the controlling shareholder among the Series-A founders, and the rest of us were looking at a small one-time windfall, followed by a likely layoff in the postsale consolidation. The holiday gathering started out fine, with the lifting of glasses and so on. But just a few minutes into the CEO's speech, his mood darkened, his eyes grew hard, and our boss began warning the assembled team that we were actually going to have to work even harder in the new year, or else he really couldn't guarantee what was going to happen, and there might have to be some big changes — oh, and Merry Christmas!

Our society is generally very quick to dismiss the sort of attitude and behavior exhibited by Jack Ma and my former CEO, to see it as just typical of a certain type of player. These people, so

6 Leszek Kolakowski, *Main Currents of Marxism,* vol. 1 (Oxford: Oxford University Press, 1992), 279.

the story goes, have type-A personalities and exhibit the drive and will to succeed that announces their readiness to assume business leadership roles. It's just who they are, and, anyway, the economy needs rainmakers. But what if the attitudes and behavior described here have to do with something more than just personality types? We generally call it "overwork" in order to make it seem the result of a set of local and one-off conditions, but maybe it's more about fundamental structural relationships instead. Maybe, even within the privileged domain of the US tech sector, words such as "exploitation" and "alienation" are now becoming less antiquated than they once were. With respect to these maniacal, rainmaking CEOs, maybe Harry Braverman had it just right: "Only one who is the master of the labor of others will confuse labor power with any other agency for performing a task, because to him, steam, horse, water, or human muscle which turns his mill are viewed as equivalents, as factors of production."[7]

Labor Power, That Peculiar Commodity

To try to unpack what might be going on in this gap between Arendt and Marx, I think we should accept Marx's invitation to leave what he calls "the noisy sphere of the exchange market," where we find the "Free-Trader Vulgaris" with his predictably tiresome views and ideas. Accompanied by "Mr. Moneybags," as Marx writes, we should head down to the scene of production and instead look at the set of relations that constitute the actual labor process.[8] It's helpful to first grasp what is truly innovative in Marx's labor theory, and how it relates to his account of value in a capitalist society and the commodity form. Long before Marx, classical economists understood that the value of produced commodities came from labor time. Adam Smith

7 Harry Braverman, *Labor and Monopoly Capital: The Degradation of Work in the 20th Century* (New York: Monthly Review Press, 1974), 35.

8 Karl Marx, *Capital,* vol. 1, trans. Ben Fowkes (London: Penguin Books, 1990), 280.

said that "labor, therefore, is the real measure of the exchange value of commodities."[9] And up until Marx, it was also believed (following Ricardo) that the quantity of labor time determined "the natural price" or real measure of the exchange value of all commodities, an approach that still begged the question of the source of the value of labor, and so could not explain where profit came from. Marx's first innovation was to take the long-known distinction between labor and labor power (actual work versus capacity to do work) and give it a crucial twist. Marx recognizes that before industrial capitalism, the distinction between labor and labor power is not a particularly fateful one — it looks a lot like the way Arendt describes it. In premodern labor, one engages in a process of appropriating nature's products and adapting them to human needs and wants. Labor power is harnessed in work to produce use values and for exchanging these in the market, where individuals meet each other, Arendt writes, as proprietors, owners of their labor power.

Before modern capitalism, labor power, as an attribute of living persons, is a possession lacking in specific significance. Either one is effectively disposed of it permanently (by becoming an actual slave) or one produces use values with it. It cannot be leased, since one cannot receive it back like rental equipment — once labor is expended, it's gone. But with the appearance of ubiquitous capitalist production, the thing that workers sell to capitalists in exchange for wages is not their labor, their actual work, but, per an employment contract, their willingness to work for a certain period of time.[10] They sell their labor power, not their labor. This sea change (the reduction of work to labor power in wage labor) itself depends on a monumental discovery — labor power, once put to work, is transformed into capital. When labor power is transformed into a day's work, it produces more exchange value than what the worker receives in return to provide the means for his or her subsistence (as determined

9 Adam Smith, *The Wealth of Nations* (New York: Bantam Classics, 2003), 43.

10 Marx, *Capital,* 271.

socially). Somewhere between the happy "use value days in the Shire" (the world of *homo faber* in Arendt's social ontology) and the world of today, capital found for itself in the market a very peculiar commodity—a commodity whose use value is that it is a source of exchange values. As such, a commodity different from all other commodities, because it is a value-generating commodity: use values, new value, and surplus value.

The Valorization of Capital and Abstract Labor

The making use of this "peculiar commodity" in capitalist production is what Marx calls *Kapitalverwertung*. English translations generally employ the French term *valorisation* in order to make it stand out as a novel concept with specific characteristics. Where the worker increases the value of capital along with creating use values, there is *valorisation*.[11] *Valorisation* is thus the scheme whereby concrete labor power becomes abstracted, and thus is yoked, becoming a reliable cog in a production or enterprise process designed to increase capital. Doing this involves an extremely weird "double movement" of commodification within the purview of abstract labor.[12] In the first instance, the ability to abstract from particular characteristics of concrete labor (use values) to harness labor power (as labor time) becomes the basis for all commodity exchange value. That there are commodities at all (which as such can be exchanged using money) comes about because abstracted labor becomes a value instituted as the standard for their convertibility. In the second place, labor power then becomes just another commodity rather than the source of commodity value per se. Units of labor power can be harnessed in employment once their value has been established

11 Ibid., 252.

12 Søren Mau writes that fetishism is "an ideological inversion of a real inversion." By this he means that capitalism gives rise to new, fetishized social forms, which in turn serve as the basis for the ideological inversions that render fetishism's mediations invisible; Søren Mau, *Mute Compulsion: A Marxist Theory of the Economic Power of Capital* (London: Verso, 2023), 191–95.

according to a preexisting fabric of universal exchange values or, to use the correct term, when it has been "abstracted."

The baseline value of labor itself as a commodity is the exchange value of goods and services needed for the subsistence and reproduction of workers at a socially determined standard, variant by time and place. A day's work (creating use values and new value, and maintaining and transferring asset value) becomes a job when it is given a price/wage/salary that ensures the regular and reliable creation of surplus value. A job can exist wherever and whenever it's safe to say that the worker has "earned one's wage" by 11 am each and every day, and is thereby enabled to show up dressed and fed after having had somewhere to sleep, ready to do it all over again tomorrow.[13]

To repeat: first, abstract labor as such gives rise to the commodity form, that is, monetary exchange value. Then this set of conditions is applied to labor power itself, so that abstracted labor becomes just another commodity within the overall nexus of exchange. When productive labor becomes organized and managed in relation to a set of exchange values (such that a quantity of labor time is equal to a quantity of money) and the labor process is folded into considerations of commodity input costs and sales revenues, and so on, then the *valorisation* process turns what was concrete labor and labor power into the commodity "abstract labor" needed for capitalist enterprises. Under capitalism, labor always appears first and foremost as the creative power of capital. Labor power "at work" becomes a component of capital, functioning as working capital, with workers as an abstract labor force, something that then gives rise to "the problem of management."[14] In this way, distinctions that previously determined the difference between labor and work must be seen to recede—subsistence labor versus crafting useful things, manual versus intellectual, productive versus unproductive—none of it really matters, if in each case the surplus can be taken in a way that increases the value of capital.

13 Marx, *Capital,* 272–75.

14 Braverman, *Labor and Monopoly Capital,* 40.

It should be noted that the full realization of abstract labor in practice is a characteristic of modern bourgeois society alone.[15] Only here do we see the uniform reduction of the value of all forms and quantities of labor to sums of money. The *valorisation* of capital requires that labor be abstracted—but the *valorisation* of capital in any one enterprise is dependent on the entire web of *valorisation*, since each element influences all the others with respect to costs, values, and prices. All of this tells us two important things. First, that when all is said and done, the value of commodities in general, and each commodity in particular, is an inherently social phenomenon, one that doesn't have all that much to do with concrete labor as a physiological activity per se. Second, that the provision of abstract labor for the *valorisation* of capital as a total system of social value must also be a total (albeit abstract) system of social domination.

Braverman reminds us that capitalist production as a system depends on three conditions that must be generalized throughout society:

— Workers are separated from the means of production, and can gain access to them only by selling their labor power.
— Workers are freed from any legal constraints that prevent them from disposing of their labor power.
— And the conditions of employment, via standard terms and conditions, become explicitly tailored to the expansion of the capitalist's units of capital.[16]

Abstract Labor and Self-Alienation

Marx's analysis of labor power harnessed as abstract labor, and giving rise to monetary exchange value, sets the stage for his nuanced account of the relationship between abstract labor and alienation. In wage labor, a worker submits to the authority of

15 Karl Marx, *Grundrisse*, trans. Martin Nicolaus (London: Penguin Books, 1973), 103–8.
16 Braverman, *Labor and Monopoly Capital*, 36.

the capitalist, per contract, producing goods and services that the capitalist enterprise can then sell to obtain surplus value. But what Marx means by "alienation" is something deeper and more profound than just the sense of exploitation one first grasps from this wage labor process (alienation is not some mere sulking about being exploited). In fact, the "later Marx" rarely uses the term "exploitation" precisely because he wants to try to express the sense of abstract structural social domination that this system implies rather than just its underlying and concrete class-based antagonism (i.e., per my employment contract, I have to do what Mr. Moneybags says, and he keeps the profits). Marx tells us that workers as wage laborers are alienated by the form of social organization that reduces them to the commodity of abstract labor in order to extract surplus value. This is the meaning of the expression "alienated from the means of production."

This alienation from products has two aspects, which we have already made clear. There is the aspect of wage compulsion (one really has no other option), and there is the imposition of an alien content—to be directed in one's work in a fashion where one's actions are not the result of the spontaneous determination of one's own will. The sense of alienation from the content also contains within it an additional fourfold aspect. With the commodification of labor in the capitalist enterprise, the worker becomes alienated from his or her products, from their acts of production, from other workers, and, in the last analysis, from their own species-essence.[17] This last aspect is the broadest and most significant consequence of these different elements of alienation in the aggregate. Self-alienation, or estrangement (*Entfremdung*) from the species-essence (*Gattungswesen*) or one's common humanity, is what can be said to occur when the individual, within the limitations of one's historical circumstances, is not free to subordinate one's will to the dictates of their own imagination, but rather must always respond, in one's willing, to external demands imposed by others.

17 Karl Marx, *Economic and Philosophical Manuscripts of 1844*, trans. Martin Milligan (New York: Prometheus Books, 1988), 75–80.

The theory of alienation thus explores the human and social implications of the abstraction of labor. Kolakowski writes that "the whole edifice of capitalist production is based in the commodity character of labor power. The fact that labor power functions as a commodity means that man functions as a thing."[18] And to be turned into a thing, he adds, has the ultimate implication that in exchanging labor power for variable capital, human beings as producers are "prevented from forming a human community," because having sold their labor power, which is now no longer their property, they enter into communities of what are essentially forced cooperation.[19] Marx invites us to try to recover (from beneath the dull throb) the original sting of coercion at the heart of our fundamental social arrangements. I have used terms such as "yoked" and "harnessed" in this same spirit. Your labor power is your own, a seemingly inalienable possession. In and through it, you quite literally have the time of your life. Then you are presented with the Faustian bargain: sign here, and you can have a reliable income, with which you can purchase the necessities of life. All you have to do is take up this yoke, whereby your labor power becomes abstracted, becomes a commodity like everything else, whereby you are engulfed in busyness, part of a larger process to produce exchange values for a profit, rather than use values.

There's a good reason why we are disquieted, for example, by seeing factory farming operations up close, even if we believe that eating other animals and their products is natural, or that our making use of nature in whatever way we require is "what God intended." It's because we don't like to see "nature denatured." It's why, even though we may not think much of chickens per se, we still like them to be free-range, if at all possible. Or why we hope that the ox, walking in a circle to turn the grindstone, should only be made to do this for so many hours a day, and then otherwise be left to his pasture. Since Marx was very

18 Leszek Kolakowski, *Main Currents of Marxism,* vol. 1: *The Founders,* trans. P.S. Falla (Oxford: Oxford University Press, 1978), 281.

19 Ibid., 285.

much a creature of the Enlightenment, he had the audacity to believe that human beings are born to be free, in the sense of rationally self-determined, both in the moral practical sense and in the prudential sense. He wanted us to recognize that an equally dismaying sort of denaturing can also be seen when we lose our autonomy through the commodification of our labor power.

Abstract Labor and Commodity Fetishism

In resistance to such assertions, something like the following has often been said: "Wow, you are really being idealistic. Realism requires just this — that everyone has to work to live — that's just the way things are. Sure, one must suffer one's job, even while being grateful to have it. But, hey, all life is suffering." A good reply to this "but don't you need to be realistic?" reaction comes from John Holloway in *Crack Capitalism* (2010). In his chapter on the dual nature of labor as concrete and abstract, Holloway points out that there is a sense in which such refrains are surely true. But they are only true, he says, with respect to concrete labor that produces use values, which is a transhistorical constant because it is intrinsic to our relationship with nature. Only this nonalienated form of labor, because free, "conscious-life activity" is an expression of our species-essence.[20] Yes, it is true that we must work to live, and that in confronting nature and finitude we suffer all sorts of limitations upon our individual wills. But it is most definitely not true with respect to the historically specific form of social totality in which this "concrete doing" is expressed, via capitalism, as abstract and thus alienated labor. We do not need to live to work.

Recognizing the difference between the set of transhistorical limit conditions on human existence (such as needing to struggle to carve out a human life through fabrication and artifice) and what are otherwise historically specific social forms of alienation, brings us to the final major term in our brief tour

20 John Holloway, *Crack Capitalism* (London: Pluto Press, 2010), 89–90.

of Marx's theory: "commodity fetishism." Commodity fetishism provides a kind of an explanation for why recognition of the fundamentally alienated character of labor power as commodity (abstract labor) generally meets with this sort of resistance and denial. In the first instance, commodity fetishism refers to the very coming-into-being of the commodity itself, in the depersonalizing of what is essentially a social relationship, the valuing and exchanging of goods and services.[21] The fetishizing of the commodity is the transformation of an economic abstraction (exchange value) into objects that people believe have intrinsic value. The object, seen as commodity, and thought to have intrinsic value, is as such fetishized. So just as alienation doesn't refer merely to a psychological state (sulking because the capitalist keeps the profits garnered by the worker's surplus value), so, too, commodity fetishism also has a deeper sense, in that it refers to a fundamental truth about the meaning and place of value in our society, and how the coming-to-be of this form of value fundamentally structures all our social relations.

The especially mournful consequence of this investment of the "commodity idol" with these "magical powers" is that all our human social relations are henceforth continually mediated and expressed by means of commodities — by means of things and money, and this abstract mediation masks the extent to which our fundamental relationships are alienated, and characterized by structures of abstract social domination. Moishe Postone points out that this is why Marx begins *Capital* not with labor,

21 Mau, *Mute Compulsion*, 194–99. Mau writes that Marx's remarks on fetishism can be put into two groups, those that identify fetishism as the naturalization of a social form (i.e., as ideology), and those that posit it as the social form itself. He goes on to say that this second set of remarks has led a number of scholars, including Moishe Postone, to downplay the significance of class domination and conclude that "the domination of everyone by the value form is the most fundamental form of power in capitalism" (195). Since there can be no value without class, however, Mau opts for a unified field theory of horizontal and vertical capitalist domination, which he says is necessary in order to grasp the power of capitalism.

but with the commodity.[22] If we are to understand what it means for human beings, in their labor power, to become just another commodity, one has to first recognize how it is that the value of commodities, in the first instance, already represents the masking of a set of social relations by means of the abstraction of labor. The commodity, Postone writes, "seems not to *be* a value, a social mediation, but rather a use value that *has* exchange value."[23] As a use value, the commodity is particular, the objectification of a particular concrete labor. As an exchange value, the commodity in general is the objectification of abstract labor. It does not appear so, in large part, because money stands in for it as such. The commodity appears as a good that is mediated by money, and money appears external to social relations, rather than as the materialized externalization of commodity and abstract labor.

If you have trouble grasping all of this, it is quite understandable. For example, you might say something like this, "But doesn't the cost of various commodities used in production determine exchange value as much as labor?" The answer would be, "Yes, of course!" But then you have to ask where the value of those input commodities comes from too — the answer is that their price/value is also based in exchange, which is ultimately based on social value derived from the commodity of abstract labor. The manner in which a historically specific set of labor arrangements has fundamentally determined the meaning of value in our society, and done so in a way that is perpetually obscured, because its false appearing is something integral to it, is no easy pill to swallow. It's like finding out you've been plugged into the Matrix.

22 Moishe Postone, *Time, Labor, and Social Domination: A Reinterpretation of Marx's Critical Theory* (Cambridge: Cambridge University Press, 1993), 168.

23 Ibid., 169.

Arendt on Labor and World-Alienation

In presenting this restatement rocket tour through *labor power, valorisation, abstract labor* and the *commodity form,* and *commodity fetishism,* I suppose I was torn between wanting to make it all easier to understand and making it harder, and I don't doubt that it shows. If I have in some ways made it harder, it's only because I wanted to give an accounting of Marx's labor theory that doesn't just reduce it down to an everyday understanding of class antagonisms, not because antagonism should be downplayed, but rather because a certain "capitalist realism" clings to this sort of reduction. Modern industrial capitalism, as a historically specific event, gives rise to abstract labor, which becomes the source of all social value. This value is such that social domination becomes abstract and diffuse, centerless and without author, and continually masks its social origins in fetishizing objectifications.

Employing Postone's lingo, to capture capitalism's abstract form of social domination, we need "a critique of labor in capitalism rather than a critique of capitalism from the standpoint of labor."[24] But this doesn't mean that this critique ceases to be political (nor does it forget that class antagonism is still very much at the root of things). Kathi Weeks says that Marx, in descending from the market to the scene of productive labor, as he asks us to do in *Capital,* sought precisely to politicize "what is otherwise an abstract mode of domination.[25] At the very least, I hope it's clear that Marx considered the modern reduction of all forms of labor and work to wage labor as something of the most profound, world-historical importance, something that, because of its nature, also required an explicit political project oriented to human emancipation. From the standpoint of these reflections on modern work as wage labor, this is important,

---

24 Ibid., 5.

25 Kathi Weeks, "Karl Marx and the Problem with Work," in *De Gruyter Conversations,* May 15, 2018, https://blog.degruyter.com/marx-and-the-problem-with-work/.

because despite her apparent agreement with Marx about modern wage labor as alienated, Arendt says that "in a society where exchange is pre-eminent, laborers become proprietors, owners of their labor power." And she says that "world-alienation, and not self-alienation, as Marx thought, has been the hallmark of the modern age."[26] In chapter 9, I will try to show, following Postone, that Marx's labor theory and critique of capital directly undercuts the sort of transhistorical social ontology that Arendt marshals in support of her account of modern labor as "world-alienation."

26 Arendt, *The Human Condition*, 254.

9

Arendt and Marx on Labor and Emancipation

> Marx's analysis does not refer to labor as it is generally and transhistorically conceived [...] but to a peculiar role that labor plays in capitalist society alone.
>
> —Moishe Postone, *Time, Labor, and Social Domination*

Perhaps we are prepared to follow both Marx and Arendt and accept that in the modern age, the meaning of work has been effectively reduced to wage labor—to labor power sold to an employer as a commodity in the labor market. If we are also prepared to accept that wage labor, in its abstractness, is essentially "labor in an alienated form" (as both of them recommend), then the need to embrace some version of an emancipatory project would seem rather difficult to deny. Kathi Weeks, says Marx seeks "to publicize the true nature of work in order to politicize it, to show how work as wage labor is an abstract mode of domination."[1] It's primarily for this reason (to develop his pointed critique of political economy) that Marx intentionally

1 Kathi Weeks, "Karl Marx and the Problem with Work," *De Gruyter Conversations,* May 16, 2018, https://blog.degruyter.com/marx-and-the-problem-with-work/.

decenters the terms of market exchange in favor of the labor process, the conditions of wage-based production.

With Arendt, however, something else is going on. She agrees that the modern age "produces the first free laboring class in history," and that what is liberated in this development is "the force inherent in labor power per se."[2] She agrees with Marx that market capitalism marks the transition from *homo faber* understood in terms of use value to alienated wage labor under conditions of exchange value. But rather than looking to describe the scene of alienation and domination, Arendt instead effectively depoliticizes it, saying instead that the modern age has carried with it "a glorification of labor" and that this glorification has resulted in "a factual transformation of the whole of society into a laboring society."[3] Apparently, we are to understand, it is this "capitalist spirit of the age" in which "workers and laborers of all kinds become equally proprietors" that explains the transformation, and not the abstract social domination inherent in the modern labor process.

What then is this new spirit that glorifies labor? Arendt gives it to us in bits and pieces. She makes it clear that it is through capitalism that man is created, first and foremost, as *laborans*. But by capitalism, she does not mean here the labor process per se. She means the driving force of capitalist accumulation itself. Early modern expropriation (of lands, possessions, and laborers into a universal working class) led to accumulation, and "thus the possibility of transforming wealth into capital through labor." It is this endless looping of capital through the production labor/process that she finds decisive, and not the specific nature of the labor process.[4]

Under the terms of what I have been calling her "transhistorical social ontology," with its distinctive historical personae, such as the ideal social types *animal laborans* and *homo faber,*

2 Hannah Arendt, *The Human Condition* (Chicago: University of Chicago Press, 1998), 255.

3 Ibid., 4.

4 Ibid., 255.

what matters here are the conditions of possibility for this endless drive to accumulate. Arendt finds these conditions in something she calls "modern world-alienation": "This process of capitalist accumulation is only possible if the world, and the very worldliness of man, are sacrificed."[5] This shift in focus, from labor process to process of accumulation, comprehends what she means when she says "world-alienation, and not self-alienation, as Marx thought, has been the hallmark of the modern age."[6] Per Arendt then, the long-held distinction between labor and work is "abandoned in favor of labor" because capitalist accumulation (as the pursuit of wealth for its own sake) infuses both the capitalist and the worker alike, and thus becomes the spirit of the age. It is principally for this the reason, she thinks, that work is reduced to wage labor, and not because labor power is coercively harnessed as abstract labor to valorize capital, thereby turning everyone's labor power into a commodity used to generate accumulated wealth.

But to indicate that one's topic is "the laboring society" along with Marx and then change the topic to what Max Weber called "the spirit of capitalism" is really something of a bait and switch. Effectively, it is also to refuse Marx's invitation, as seen in *Capital*, to leave "the noisy sphere of the market" and travel into the domain of capitalist production itself, in order to understand what goes on there. This maneuver is tantamount to accepting the testimony of what Marx calls the *free trader vulgaris* that we are all equally "human capitals," both the wage laborer and the capitalist, one with labor power, the other with his money bags. Of course, this is not to say that trying to understand why there are a class of people who "live to work" is a valueless endeavor. It is only to say that living to work is not the same thing as having to work to live.

5 Ibid., 256.
6 Ibid., 254.

Arendt and the Oracle of Omaha

Sometime in 1958, at virtually the same time that Arendt and her publisher were putting the final touches on *The Human Condition,* a young investor named Warren Buffet bought a fairly modest house on Farnham Street in Omaha, Nebraska, for $31,000. Now in his nineties, Buffet was the third richest man in the world in 2020, with total assets of around $70 billion. Despite his immense wealth and power, he still lives in the house on Farnham Street, and every day, so the story goes, he drives to McDonald's for his breakfast, with a precalculated cost not to exceed $3.17.[7] At dinner time, he is often seen at the local, nothing-special steakhouse, Gorats.[8] His Berkshire Hathaway salary is $100,000 per year.[9] Until recently, he actually had a second home in Laguna Beach, California, one he purchased back in the 1970s for around $150,000, because his wife insisted.[10] In an interview with CNBC, Buffet said that he "never had any great desire to have multiple houses and all kinds of things and multiple cars."[11]

At the heart of the legend of the Oracle of Omaha, therefore, there is the riddle of Buffet's thriftiness: Why would a man who made $37 million per day in 2013 from his Berkshire Hathaway

7 Cheyenne Devon, "Billionaire Warren Buffett Still Lives in the Same Home He Bought for $31,500 More Than 60 Years Ago," *CNBC,* March 3, 2023, https://www.cnbc.com/2023/03/03/warren-buffett-lives-in-the-same-home-he-bought-in-1958.html.

8 Fred Imbert, "Warren Buffett's Favorite Steakhouse Fits His Modest Style," *CNBC,* May 19, 2018, https://www.cnbc.com/2018/05/19/gorats-warren-buffetts-favorite-steakhouse-fits-his-modest-style.html.

9 Jeannine Mancini, "Warren Buffett's Salary Is $100,000 Per Year — He Hasn't Had A Raise in 40 Years, And He Gives Half of It Back to Berkshire Hathaway," *Yahoo Finance,* July 13, 2013, https://finance.yahoo.com/news/warren-buffetts-salary-100-000-150916458.html.

10 Noah Buhayar, "Buffett's $11 Million Beach House Is Still on the Market," *Bloomberg,* February 27, 2018, https://www.bloomberg.com/news/articles/2018-02-27/buffett-s-11-million-beach-house-is-still-on-the-market.

11 Alex Crippen, "Warren Buffett Buys This with His Billions … And It Makes Him Happy," *CNBC,* November 12, 2012, https://www.cnbc.com/id/49787452.

investments in companies such as Geico, Disney, American Express, and JP Morgan Chase live in this fashion? How should we understand the wolfish hunger for accumulation, married to this extreme thriftiness? We can be almost certain that Arendt was never aware of Warren Buffet. She died in 1975, and the glory days of Berkshire Hathaway were yet to come, such that the legend and riddle were not yet born. But if she had seen Buffett's combination of wealth and thriftiness, she would have said that she and Weber knew the answer to this riddle. She would go on to describe Buffet's strange existence in terms of the "inter-worldly asceticism," or world-alienation that, following Weber, she considered to be the hallmark of the modern age.

On the Spirit of Capitalism: Weber and Arendt

It has often been said that Marx and Weber are largely compatible, even complementary, and this is no doubt true. Most of the disputes between Marxist theorists and Weberians (both community studies and sociological types) are long-running family arguments. For example, both Marx and Weber (and later Arendt) agree that the emergence of distinctly capitalist enterprises is something new, something different than the basic desire for gain expressed in mercantile operations that has existed in various forms in every society. Only in the West, and in relatively recent times, do we see the first appearance of what Weber called the "rational organization of free labor" (routinized, calculated administration within continuously functioning enterprises). Weber also rightly points out that such a rationalistic capitalist enterprise requires two basic things: a "disciplined" labor force and the regularized investment of capital.[12]

Where Marx prioritizes the first element (with his analysis of abstract labor harnessed as a commodity), the critical pro-

12 Anthony Giddens, "Introduction," in Max Weber, *The Protestant Ethic and the Spirit of Capitalism*, trans. Talcott Parsons (New York: Charles Scribner's Sons, 1976), 3.

ject becomes an expressly political/emancipatory one. Where Weber focuses on the second element (the continual accumulation of wealth for its own sake), the investigation quickly gives rise to what, in my discussion of Warren Buffet, I have referred to as the "riddle of the Oracle of Omaha." Anthony Giddens says that Weber's question in *The Protestant Ethic and the Spirit of Capitalism* was just this: What explains this historically specific circumstance of a drive to the accumulation of wealth conjoined to an absence of the worldly pleasures it can purchase? What explains the spirit of modern capitalism?[13] Weber thought he must be on the right track when he noticed that the outlook in question was a distinctly moral one, requiring high levels of self-discipline, even though the sense of an otherworldly calling as a motive for this comportment was largely missing. He thought he found the source of this new spirit of worldly asceticism in Puritan Calvinism, as seen in the concept of "the calling," or the obligation to fulfill one's worldly duties in the context of the general doctrine of predestination. Since it was all but obligatory to behave as if one were among "the elect," success at one's worldly calling came to be associated with having been so selected. In this way, Weber thought, Calvinism supplied the passion and drive of the capitalist entrepreneur.[14]

Although there is an enduring ring of truth in Weber's thesis, the controversies surrounding it began immediately and have never really died down. Per Giddens, it turns out that there was something in it for almost everyone to hate: the claim that religious ideas had this level of historical effectiveness challenged vulgar Marxist economic determinism; Catholics reacted to the suggestion that their traditions lacked a solid work ethic; Protestants thought Weber was trying to say that Puritan Calvinism literally and univocally caused the rise of capitalism. It has also been consistently argued that Weber misinterpreted and overstated "the calling," that he relied too heavily on Anglo-Saxon sources over Germanic ones, and that his take on the Ameri-

13 Ibid., 4.
14 Ibid., 5.

can Puritan scene was equally off the mark.[15] This set of specific objections aside, *The Protestant Ethic* has remained alive because of the continued relevance of Weber's doctrine of "the iron cage" of modern, instrumentalizing rationality, to which he says Puritan asceticism significantly contributed.[16] As Weber tells it, the Puritan was motivated to work in his worldly calling, but increasingly we are all actually forced to do so, to live in a thoroughly impoverished, bureaucratized world where the spontaneous enjoyment of life is ruthlessly expunged.

In *The Human Condition,* Arendt takes a different path to what is ultimately the same destination—the despairing critique of instrumental reason in the modern age as a kind of an iron cage from which there is no apparent escape. Arendt's version of the devolution of work and rationality, leading to the rise of the iron cage, begins with the loss of the "higher ends" that guided the fabrication of *homo faber* in his "world-building," which I described in chapter 7.

In crafting all manner of useful things, *homo faber*'s world comes to be permeated with a principle of utility, one that displaces the previous "for the sake of."[17] *Homo faber*'s instrumentalization (in the service of various ends) leads to a degradation of all things into means, an environment where all ends are of short duration, and become means for other ends, in an endless circle. This circle of utility is in its turn rapidly eclipsed, Arendt says, by eudaimonic utilitarianism, by the principle of the greatest happiness for the greatest number, which for a time provided the jumble of means and ends with a kind of a logic, if not a *telos*. But then even this gives way, so that we end up with just "bare life" as a guiding principle, to the hedonic promotion of individual life as a general value.[18]

It is in this fashion that Arendt brings us to her grand thesis of "world-alienation." When we think of the loss of transcend-

15 Ibid., 12.
16 Ibid., 8.
17 Arendt, *The Human Condition,* 154.
18 Ibid., 311–13.

ence that accompanies the modern age, we tend to think of the loss of focus upon "the hereafter" as a sign of "worldliness." But, Arendt says, this is not so. With the loss of the world above, "man was thrown back upon himself, and not upon the world."[19] Where the new focus becomes the worry and care about the self, "the only contents were appetites and desires [...] and to labor, to assure the continuity of one's own life and of his own family."[20] The inwardness of the modern subject bereft of higher ends is thus the condition for the interworldly asceticism that fuels the drive for capital accumulation on the part of the capitalist. "The greatness of Weber's discovery about the origins of capitalism," Arendt writes, "lay in his demonstration that an enormous, strictly mundane activity is possible without any care for or enjoyment of the world whatever."[21]

Arendt and the Emancipation of Labor

Arendt's skepticism about the prospects for freedom as emancipation on the part of the laboring classes is found in her subsection on the consumer society.[22] The first thing to recognize about these paragraphs is that they contain her thoughts on the consequences of the emancipation *of* labor (through the establishment of a universal laboring class, free for waged activity) and are not primarily concerned with the prospects for emancipation *from* labor, as one might expect from someone supposedly in broad agreement with Marx.

Given that the ideals of *homo faber* (which are permanence, stability, and durability) have been sacrificed to abundance, to the ideal of *animal laborans,* we now live in a laboring society. A society of laborers, it turns out, is first and foremost a consumer society. The emancipation of labor — of humanity *to* labor, to the pursuit of abundant life as the individual and collective goal

19 Ibid., 254.
20 Ibid., 320–21.
21 Ibid., 254.
22 Ibid., 130–31.

and purpose of existence — is fateful. But this is not because, she observes, "for the first time in history laborers were admitted and given equal rights in the public realm," but rather because in doing so we have almost succeeded in "leveling all human activities to the common denominator of securing the necessities of life."[23] The major problem with the emancipation to labor turns out to be that it leads to the ubiquity of instrumentalism and the iron cage. As such, it is thus utterly destructive of the public realm, to the space of political action in which people such as Arendt, who long for the ancient Greek *polis,* look to find the highest realization of common humanity. The *polis,* understood as a public realm, as the space of human appearance par excellence, is one unavailable to the slave, the foreigner (and women) in antiquity, and the "jobholder or businessman in our world," she says, also "do not live in it."[24] Reflecting on the laboring and mass consumer society, Arendt says that "whatever we do, we are supposed to do for the sake of making a living, such is the verdict of society."[25]

The classical political economists (who channeled the spirit of the age in claiming that the point of the *vita activa* is to grow wealth, abundance, and the happiness of the greatest number) also hoped, Arendt says, "that free time eventually will liberate *laborans* from necessity, and make the *animal laborans* productive."[26] This assumption in turn rested upon the notion that "labor power not spent and exhausted in the drudgery of life will automatically nourish other, higher activities." The emancipation of labor does indeed result in *animal laborans* occupying the public realm. But this society no longer knows of the other higher and more meaningful activities" for the sake of which this freedom "would deserve to be won in the first place. "A hundred years after Marx," Arendt says, we know that the spare time of the *animal laborans* "is never spent in anything but

23 Ibid., 126.
24 Ibid., 199.
25 Ibid., 127.
26 Ibid., 133.

consumption, and the more time left to him, the greedier and more craven his appetites."[27]

As a result, as long as *animal laborans* remains in possession of it, Arendt says, there really can be no public realm, "but only private activities displayed in the open."[28] What then of emancipation *from* labor? She does not fail to mention it, after a fashion. The danger is not only that the modern age's emancipation of labor will fail to usher in an age of freedom, but that it will actually result in forcing all mankind under the yoke of necessity. And this was already perceived by Marx, she says, when he insisted that the aim of revolution could not be the already accomplished emancipation of the laboring classes, "but must consist in the emancipation of man from labor."[29] And yet, when Arendt does write specifically about emancipation from labor, her musings are invariably only about "the end of labor" through capitalist innovation and automation, and not about some articulation of modern political action. What happens when *animal laborans* will have nothing to do? We have already arrived at a moment where we do more consuming than producing, she mused in the 1950s. The last stage of the laboring society, the society of jobholders, "demands of its members sheer automatic functioning," and thus "the modern age may end in the deadliest, most sterile passivity history has ever known."[30]

The Problem with Transhistorical Accounts of Modern Labor

The main point here, again, is that Arendt's account of the meaning and significance of modern work as wage labor largely follows Weber rather than Marx. Modern labor is to be understood as part and parcel of a general capitalist "spirit of the age," in which instrumentalizing reason has eclipsed all other forms of rationalization, thereby destroying the possibility of the pub-

27 Ibid.
28 Ibid., 134.
29 Ibid., 130.
30 Ibid., 322.

lic realm and politics proper, at least as she understands it. In focusing on the driving force of capitalist accumulation rather than on the labor process, I have argued, Weber and Arendt effectively depoliticize the Marxian critique of capital, ending (for Arendt) in a yearning after the bygone days of the ancient Greek *polis,* and in a totalizing pessimism concerning prospects for freedom as emancipation under modern conditions.

In *Time, Labor, and Social Domination* (1993), Moishe Postone lays out the definitive case for the centrality of alienated labor and abstract social domination for the Marxian critique of capitalism. In recognizing the "peculiar nature of labor" in the modern age, Postone says, one also must recognize, along with Marx, that "the labor that constitutes value should not be identified with labor as it may exist transhistorically."[31] Marx's analysis refers to "a peculiar role that labor plays in capitalist society alone."[32] Postone does not discuss Arendt in his magnum opus, and I am unaware of such consideration elsewhere. But in a key chapter, Postone addresses the role of Weber in the critical theory of Jürgen Habermas, and does so in a way that allows us to pinpoint, in a much more formal way, what is problematic about Arendt's account of modern labor, and why it is that the Marxian and the Weberian accounts of labor are not as compatible as it might first appear.[33]

In his chapter "Habermas' Reading of Marx," Postone enacts what we might refer to as a "double reading" of Habermas's encounter with "Marx on labor" and Weber's theory of societal rationalization. In the first reading, he describes Haber-

31 Moishe Postone, *Time, Labor, and Social Domination* (Cambridge: Cambridge University Press, 2003), 29.

32 Ibid., 5.

33 I employ Postone's arguments against "transhistorical accounts of labor" in two different ways in this book. First, I use the critique of Habermasian critical theory as a way to settle the argument I have constructed between Arendt and Marx, since I regard these criticisms as fully applicable to Arendt's account of the meaning of modern wage labor. Second, in chapters 10 and 11, I use the broader arguments about the error of ontologizing labor—and the need to confront abstract social domination—as a backdrop for consideration of the trajectory of wage labor in the digital age.

mas's take on labor in Marx as found his early writings (*Theory and Practice, Knowledge and Human Interests*), where, Postone says, Habermas was still writing in the shadow of the Frankfurt School and its dialectic of the confrontation between consciousness and nature. In these writings, Habermas is seeking a way to get beyond the Frankfurt School's near totalizing view of modern instrumental reason as an iron cage, looking to find a basis for critical reason from which to resist technocratic control, bureaucratization, and the like, in the service of emancipation.[34] In doing so, Habermas actually locates the source of the critical theorists' pessimism about modern rationality in their reliance on labor (productive activity) as the basis for world constitution or social synthesis.

"But instead of abandoning the Frankfurt School's traditionalist Marxist account of labor, where social practice is reduced to labor-as-production, for Habermas, the way out was thought to be an account of self-constitution of the human species through both labor *and* interaction."[35] The basic maneuver here, in finding another, coeval source of social synthesis, is to relocate emancipatory potential to this separate sphere, as an antipode to instrumental reason that supposedly derives from labor.

Postone says that Habermas decides that the problem with Weber's theory of societal rationalization is that it is too narrow, collapsing interaction into labor.[36] But all is not lost, Habermas says, because Weber's account of the differentiation of value spheres in the modern age points the way to a theory of historical development recognizing two distinct processes of rationalization, the purposive rational or instrumental and the action-theoretic, corresponding to two dimensions of social existence, which, following Talcott Parsons, Habermas calls "system and lifeworld."[37] Postone's objection is that Habermas's approach proceeds on the basis of a "transhistorical notion of labor" (what

34 Postone, *Time, Labor and Social Domination,* 229.

35 Ibid. My emphasis.

36 Ibid., 230.

37 Ibid., 243–44, 250.

Arendt would call "labor as a general human capacity"), which he says "does not register the Marxian analysis of the double character of labor," and so overlooks "Marx's conception of the historical specificity of forms of wealth, production, and social relations" in capitalist society.[38] Habermas does this, Postone writes, despite the fact that "Marx spends the better part of *Capital*, vol. 1 demonstrating that production in capitalist society cannot be understood simply in transhistorical terms" because the labor process is shaped by abstract labor, by the process of creating surplus value. Marx's mature critique is not that of labor in a transhistorical sense, "but of the commodity, abstract labor, value and so on — that is, forms of social relations mediated by labor."[39] To project this mode of transhistorical constitution of society through labor, Postone contends, or to replace it with an equally transhistorical scheme of the existence of two independent spheres (labor and interaction), is to obscure the historical specificity of commodity-determined labor in capitalism.[40]

As to Postone's second reading, he says that in the later *Theory of Communicative Action* (1981), Habermas opts for a full-blown transhistorical social ontology of communicative competence, a process where, Postone writes, "linguistically mediated communication increasingly realizes itself like Hegel's *Geist* [...] via social evolution."[41] In doing so, he again "hypostatizes transhistorically the alienated character of capitalism as an attribute of labor per se" (i.e., instrumental reason). But this time, from the viewpoint of a critique of capitalism oriented toward emancipation, he makes the situation even worse, Postone says, by attempting to locate the standpoint of critique in the pragmatic function of language as communicative action. The resulting critical opposition of system and lifeworld, like the earlier recourse to labor and interaction, Postone says, dissolves capitalist social relations into material and symbolic spheres[42] and

38 Ibid., 231.
39 Ibid., 230.
40 Ibid., 241.
41 Ibid., 249.
42 Ibid., 259.

offers an immanent logic of human history as yet another projection onto history in general of capitalist society's conditions. To attribute instrumentality to labor as such, Postone says, is to understand labor as material production, and thus "to naturalize that which is socially constituted and to project transhistorically what is historically determinate."[43]

Arendt's Transhistorical Social Ontology of Labor

Where, then, does all of this leave the transhistorical social ontology of Arendt? After all, there really is nothing wrong with a bit of social ontology, now and again. According to the *Stanford Encyclopedia of Philosophy*, "social ontology" can mean "analyzing the various entities in the world that arise from social interaction," such as the various properties of things like "money, corporations, institutions, property, social classes, races, genders, artifacts, artworks, language, and law," to name just a few. It can also mean a set of questions that pertain to "the constituents or building blocks of social things in general."[44] Arendt's concern to show "how the most elementary articulations of the human condition" (which she identifies as labor, work, and action) come to expression differently in the ancient world and the modern age appears to be of this type. It's also important to note that Marx, too, does not lack a social ontology. Where Marx tells us, in the section of *Capital* titled "The Fetishism of Commodities and the Secret Thereof," that various social categories that might appear to be natural are products of social and economic relations,[45] he gives an answer to the question of the origins of the social world, namely, that, borrowing from Lukács, social entities in the modern age are reified by capitalism.

---

43 Ibid., 238.

44 See Brian Epstein, "Social Ontology," *Stanford Encyclopedia of Philosophy*, eds. Edward N. Zalta and Uri Nodelman, March 21, 2018, https://plato.stanford.edu/entries/social-ontology/.

45 Karl Marx, *Capital*, vol. 1, trans. Ben Fowkes (London: Penguin, 1990), 163–66.

I should also say at this point that, along with social ontology in general, there isn't a big problem about *transhistorical* social ontology either. Where Arendt engages in transhistorical social ontology, as she does throughout *The Human Condition*, and uses an effective history of concepts to trace back modern world alienation to its origins, there really is no reason to object. I also think there needn't be an immediately negative reaction to transhistorical accounts of labor as such either. Recognizing the *differentia species* of labor in different periods, contexts, even epochs can be interesting and informative, as long as the focus, where it comes to modern labor, is on the difference, and thus does not include overarching claims of transhistorical continuity and evolution.[46] The problem, at least from the point of a Marxian critique interested in emancipation, arises in a very specific circumstance: that of the *transhistorical* social ontology of *labor*.

In closing, let me offer a brief example. There is a moment in the chapter on labor from *The Human Condition* where we can see how the effective history of concepts, in the framework of a transhistorical social ontology, can cause a spot of trouble. Arendt writes in a footnote that "the creation of man through human labor was one of the most persistent ideas of Marx since his youth," and she goes on to say that it is manifest from these

46 It is worth noting that Andrea Komlosy, *Work: The Last 1,000 Years*, trans. Jacob K. Watson and Loren Balhorn (London: Verso, 2018), makes a very compelling case that there is an underpinning of Eurocentric, universal history in such accounts that renders them historiographically problematic. Such grand narrative accounts, which she says are nearly ubiquitous after Weber, provide cross-sectional insights into various epochs, progressing teleologically from Greek distain for *ponos, oikos,* and *ergon* relative to *praxis,* to the Roman shift from public life to the worthiness of private activities, to early Judeo-Christian equivocalness, to monastic work ethic and contemplation in the Middle Ages, to Reformation, and then to Enlightenment and capitalist transition via utilitarianism and mercantilism, and so on. Komlosy rightly points out that these accounts are vulnerable to challenges by historical studies that undermine their generalizations, and by points of view that explore their failures to integrate spatial and temporal dimensions inconsistent with their teleology, and also feminist and postcolonial experience and perspectives on labor and work.

early writings that Marx meant to replace the traditional definition of man as *animal rationale* "by defining him as an *animal laborans*."[47] It is no doubt true, as she writes just before the footnote, that Marx's notion that labor (and not God) created man "was only the most radical and consistent formulation of something upon which the whole modern age was agreed."[48] But it is decidedly less helpful to say, as Arendt also does here, that Marx was actually *seeking to replace* the previous determinations with labor. This is because to do so is to lapse into an excessive kind of formalism, and thereby to miss something absolutely critical. With all the pageantry of a transhistorical social ontology's succession of concepts, one must not lose the understanding that Marx, unlike Adam Smith and the other representatives of the age, was in no way seeking to *replace* previous conceptions of work with wage labor. Marx's overarching concern was *criticizing* the reduction of work to waged labor. One really needs to be clear about this from the outset if there is going to be any hope that a compelling emancipatory project could yet emerge from the critique of capitalism.

47 Arendt, *The Human Condition*, 86.
48 Ibid.

10

The Struggle against Labor in the Digital Age

> The method of the cracks [...] is negative dialectics [...] we think the world from misfitting.
>
> —John Holloway, *Crack Capitalism*

> The concept of a double bind has nothing to do with dialectics.
>
> —Franco "Bifo" Berardi, *The Soul at Work*

Borrowing an approach from Moishe Postone, I have argued that the transhistorical social ontology of labor in Arendt's *The Human Condition* effectively depoliticizes Marx's critique of capitalism, blunting its force as an emancipatory project. The mature Marx insists that we foreground the relationship between distinctly modern abstract labor processes and the weaving and maintenance of the dominant capitalist system of social relations. In this light, Arendt's primary focus upon "the spirit of capitalist accumulation," coupled with her inattention to modern industrial labor processes and commodity markets, appears stubbornly fetishized.

Kolakowski once again reminds us that the whole edifice of capitalist production is based in "the commodity character of labor power. The fact that labor power functions as a commodity means that man functions as a thing."[1] Nonetheless, it must be admitted that Postone does not go terribly far in showing us how the abstract structural social domination that the capitalist system creates and maintains is to be overcome. In part, this is because his book, *Time, Labor, and Social Domination,* is primarily theoretical in orientation, concerned with describing social constitution by labor in capitalism, and leaving it to others to cast this understanding into the terms of social and political struggle. But it's also because he has set the bar pretty high, by rejecting the claim of orthodox Marxism that the struggle should be understood as merely "labor against capitalism," as something like class-based antagonism over ownership of the means of production, or control of the state, and so on. Basically, Postone's critique is designed to tell us something that we also learn from Elvis Costello: When it comes to capitalist social domination, "every day, every day, every day we write the book." Clearly, then, given a fulsome appreciation for what John Holloway has pithily called "the gelatinous suction of the capitalist social synthesis,"[2] the project of finding a determinate locus for social and political emancipation remains an open question.

The Capitalist Nonsociety of Post-Fordism

But the problem deepens even further when we recognize, as does André Gorz, that today "we are living through the extinction of a specific mode of social belonging and a specific type of society, the society [...] Hannah Arendt called work-based."[3] It bears repeating here that the running dispute between Marx and Arendt that was built up in chapters 7, 8, and 9 concerned *the modern reduction of work to wage labor under conditions of Fordist, industrial capitalism.* Since its inception at the end of the eighteenth century when commodity labor was imposed

1 Leszek Kolakowski, *Main Currents of Marxism,* vol. 1: *The Founders,* trans. P.S. Falla (Oxford: Oxford University Press, 1978), 281.

2 John Holloway, *Crack Capitalism* (London: Pluto Press, 2010), 51.

3 André Gorz, *Reclaiming Work: Beyond the Wage-Based Society* (Cambridge: Polity Press, 1999), 55.

to meet the needs of the new manufacturing class, to its high-water mark in the Fordist period after World War II, the pattern of work and commodity exchange structured a certain kind of society. Gorz also reminds us that abstract labor itself had its own emancipatory moment, in that it put an end to precapitalist relations of personal submission.[4] Instead of work being understood as service owed to a master, work becomes universally supplied as contract labor that is measurable, quantifiable, and detachable from the person who provides it, and it can be bought and sold in the labor market. For a time, despite the profound "psychic wages" of abstract labor that came with the ubiquitous valorization of capital (myriad forms of personal and social alienation), Fordist capitalism also brought relatively high wages, robust trade union movement protections, and welfare state social benefits.

Under these conditions, which explicitly recognized the basic antagonism between living labor and capital, what was owed to employers was laid out in contracts, such that subjects reserved their sense of belonging "to themselves, their own trade unions, their class, their society,"[5] says Gorz. As a result, everyone was recognized by their wages and social benefits as useful in an objective, impersonal, and anonymous way: "The essential ideological message of the wage-based society was what counts is having a job."[6] If we say that this modern, wage-based society as such was defined by the asserted universality of these economic and social conditions, then it is also fair to say that *this society has now vanished,* since today, under post-Fordist conditions, it is simply manifest that only a minority of workers can claim full membership in such a society. But if abstract labor, as it was understood under Fordist industrial capitalism, is in the process of disappearing, how should we understand work today, in the post-Fordist, digital age? Are the subjects of this new configuration of work alienated individually and socially in more or less

---

4 Gorz, *Reclaiming Work,* 38.
5 Ibid., 37.
6 Ibid., 56.

the same way? Or are there new forms of alienation emerging? Does this new post-Fordist pattern and expectation of work point to new opportunities for increased autonomy, or does it instead herald an even greater degree of subjection? Finally, in what direction do we find prospects for autonomy and emancipation under these conditions? How should we attempt to reweave the social to strengthen social relations in a way that breaks with, and is incompatible with, capitalism?

In Holloway (*Crack Capitalism*), Berardi (*The Soul at Work*), and Gorz (*Reclaiming Work*), we find some of the building blocks needed to begin to answer these questions (I discuss Gorz in greater detail in chapter 11). Holloway sets the stage by taking Postone's insights about how abstract labor continually constitutes capitalist society, and he makes the case for a permanent crisis of capitalism. Basically, he takes Postone's theoretical ideas and then casts them into the terms of political struggle.[7] Berardi and Gorz, by contrast, describe the post-Fordist digital age as a time in which capitalism has effectively overcome its crisis (and we're the worse for it). Berardi has penetrating insights about digital age alienation per se; Gorz, with his more traditional narrative about post-Fordism, comes closest to having practical ideas about transformation, about how to encourage what he calls a "multi-activity society."

Post-Fordist Labor and the Crisis of Capitalism

In all three of these works just mentioned, however, we find strikingly similar views on *the crisis of Fordist capitalism,* offered up by each as a necessary prerequisite to their respective answers to the above-stated questions. The parallels in the three books on this topic are striking, especially given that they each have different sources of inspiration — Holloway looks to Adorno, Gorz to Althusser and Touraine, and Berardi to Tronti, Virno, and Deleuze and Guattari. However, after this initial stage of agree-

7 Holloway, *Crack Capitalism,* 187.

ment, the three diverge over whether and in what way "crisis theory" even remains something relevant.

Holloway

Holloway characterizes the crisis of capitalism in terms of what he calls "the double flight from labor," something he considers to be the basic instability at the heart of the generalized social arrangement.[8] On the one hand, capital depends upon living labor for production, and for providing the yardstick for the value of everything in capitalist society, but it also constantly flees from this dependency, by replacing labor with machines, software, and digital devices, that is, dead labor. On the other hand, workers, who are otherwise compelled to sell their labor power, are constantly attempting to flee from the alienation of abstract labor and exchange value into concrete doing and use value.[9]

Holloway identifies the social upheavals of the 1960s as an explicit revolt against the society of abstract labor, and says that post-Fordism "is the pattern of life that reflects the failed revolution against Fordism," and "the surpassing of the society of labor within capitalism itself."[10] Holloway does not deny that today we have arrived at Tony Negri's "social factory," where "there is now no difference between labor time and non-labor time and place,"[11] but he still believes that even under these conditions there is a permanent crisis of capitalism, such that various efforts to stabilize it, such as the massive expansion of credit, serve only to conceal its essential fragility.[12]

8 Ibid., 179.
9 Ibid., 180.
10 Ibid., 191.
11 Ibid., 192–93.
12 Ibid., 184.

Berardi

By comparison, in *The Soul at Work,* Berardi identifies something that sounds similar, which he calls "the double bind of capital."[13] On the one hand, he says, capital seeks to reduce labor time to a minimum; on the other hand, however, it insists on "positing labor time as the sole source of and measure of wealth." Berardi makes it clear that he does not see this as a contradiction to be overcome in the dialectical sense. He refers to the inherent contradiction as a double bind, which he describes as a "paradoxical communication" or a "contradictory injunction."[14] The social content of capitalist production is contradicted by its own semiotic framework, and functions as a "pathogenic mechanism" for which there should be no expectation of a dialectical overturning, since "there is no positive or negative totality in the social history of capitalism."[15] Berardi thus locates the crisis of capitalism in the Fordist prehistory of the present, and says that in post-Fordism there is no crisis, but rather that "abstraction reaches its perfection in the digital era."[16] Today the centrality of intellectual labor and digital technology instead gives rise to the panlogism of a self-mediating system, one where the individual subject with its "species-essence" disappears in favor of total subjection. From here, Berardi finds inspiration in his experience of Italian Workerism (*Operaismo*) for the elements of a politics of refusal, of a struggle against wage labor as such. It is necessary to "study the constitution of autonomous collective activity starting from the subtraction of lived time from labor, the refusal to work, and the project of its extinction."[17]

13 Franco "Bifo" Berardi, *The Soul at Work: From Alienation to Autonomy,* trans. Francesca Cadel and Giuseppina Mecchia (Los Angeles: Semiotext(e), 2009), 65.

14 Ibid.

15 Ibid., 66.

16 Ibid., 61.

17 Ibid., 59.

Gorz

Gorz, in his *Reclaiming Work,* is in agreement with Berardi that there is no longer any crisis, since Fordism itself was the crisis of capitalism.[18] Under post-Fordist conditions, by contrast, capital uses the collapsing wage-based society itself as a tool of domination. He writes about an "exodus of capital" from society into a supranational state of capital.[19] Money and capital have cut themselves off from states and societies, substituting an absolute nonsociety and a virtual state that has no territory, distances, or citizens.[20] In response to this, Gorz calls for a doubling of this exodus, a flight of workers from labor to multiactive society to match the flight of capital from society.[21]

Whether one prefers "double flight," "double bind," or "double exodus," the initial message, at least, is more or less the same. Capitalist society is inherently contradictory, and thus is ultimately unsustainable, even if it is also inventively durable. The crisis, however, is in some sense behind us (either as a past event or as a perennial one), and we are now living in a time in which capitalism has (unsurprisingly) developed strategies to capitalize even upon the collapsing of its own type of society. Acknowledging this means rethinking the terms of social and political struggle in relation to work. It means refocusing it as struggle against labor per se under contemporary conditions.

Abstract Labor and the Weaving of the Social Synthesis

Holloway's *Crack Capitalism* is included in this discussion because he takes all of the most important theoretical insights about abstract labor and social relations from Postone's *Time, Labor and Social Domination,* and then manages to cast them into the action-oriented terms of political struggle, at least to

18 Gorz, *Reclaiming Work,* 1, 14.
19 Ibid., 14–15.
20 Ibid.
21 Ibid., 74, 76.

some degree. Holloway lays out an elaborate, sevenfold classification of the primary ways that abstract labor "weaves" the capitalist social nexus or synthesis.[22] In doing so, he makes abstract labor decidedly "less abstract," by showing how it continually gives rise to living forms of social antagonism.

It is useful to provide the barest sketch:

— Abstract labor encloses minds along with bodies in the process of industrial labor. Money interrupts the social relation, so that the valuation of things predominates. This is what Marx called "fetishism." The breaking of social cooperation into a system of commodity exchange is also distinctive in the way that it creates the individuals that exchange those commodities, everywhere disclosing reality on an identitarian basis.[23]

— Beyond mere identity, "the abstraction of concrete doing into labor" is also a process of personification. Individuals become laborers and capitalists, for example, roles that are imposed by the structure of social relations. Just as commodity exchange becomes something that comes to be regarded as simply factual, so too these roles: Holloway writes, "How can we think about changing the world radically where people are personifications of their social function?"[24]

— The abstraction of doing into labor is also "the creation of the male laborer," and as such wage labor institutes a new hierarchy between men and women, since in the money economy, the man's wage defines the *paterfamilias*.[25]

---

22 Holloway, *Crack Capitalism*, 109.

23 Ibid., 109–13.

24 Ibid., 116.

25 Ibid., 119–24. The critique of wage-based society's reliance upon a naturalized system of gender roles should certainly be considered an important element of the postwork political imaginary. Since this book is principally concerned with the possibility of a radical politics of refusal of capitalism's (collapsing) wage-based society, I haven't attempted to support the case for gender-based equity in the existing system of work-as-we-know-it today. To the extent that representations concerning gender are provided here,

— The abstraction of doing into labor separates people into town and country, leading to an unprecedented alienation of humans from nature, constituting nature as a domain of objects.[26]
— Further, the abstraction of doing into labor creates the citizen, politics, and the state, since capitalist social relations imply a web of obligation, compulsion, and domination—they give rise to class conflict, which in turn calls forth the state in order to secure the social order necessary for the rule of abstract labor.[27]
— Abstract labor also calls forth the homogenization of time, since there is no concrete doing in clock time, only the duration of time imposed to ensure production. When the doing is for someone else, when it becomes labor, the activity is external to the doer, such that time itself is an essential part of the weave of capitalist society.[28]
— Finally, abstract labor creates a new form of social totality. Whereas in precapitalist societies things as a whole are knit together by custom, or command, or communal decision, abstract labor constitutes a totality that is independent of anyone's conscious determination, through monetary exchange and the circulation of commodities.[29]

Taken as a whole, then, abstract labor structures every aspect of capitalist society, weaving a complex prison of fetishism, identity, role personification, dimorphous sexual identity, separation from nature, clock time, and exchange-based social totality (social cohesion and coherence). With all this in mind, Holloway says, "the movement against abstract labor cannot be reduced to struggles over work in any narrow sense,"[30] either

therefore, they touch upon the role of gender in the modern division of labor, or gendered notions of productive and unproductive labor.

26 Ibid., 125–29.

27 Ibid., 130–34.

28 Ibid., 135–40.

29 Ibid., 141–44.

30 Ibid., 197.

via trade union movement gains or via a revolutionary aspiration to seize the means of production. We need to find a way to break with the existing totality without creating an alternative one. Instead of labor against capital, we need to find ways to split doing from labor.[31]

How, therefore, to break the logic of capital? Holloway believes that we need to start by recognizing that the weave actually has gashes, which he goes on to call "cracks." *Crack Capitalism* gets its name from his specific articulation of a politics of refusal as the means for escaping the capitalist social synthesis, what he calls, once again, "the weave of capitalist domination."[32] What, then, are these cracks? A crack can be any effort to decommodify a type of activity, and to subject it to popular control. The cracks, as gashes in the weave of capitalist domination, are found wherever there are important struggles going on all over the world to remove such things as water, natural resources, education, health care, communication, software, and music from the workings of capitalism. Basically, any struggle against capitalist enclosure, and in favor of some sort of a commons (i.e., ecological, social, networked) fits the bill.[33] Cracks can also have an event-like character, for example, temporary community activities that obey their own rules, such as the pre-Lent celebration of carnival. Even the eruption of ad hoc community solidarity in disaster zones has the character of cracks in the capitalist social synthesis.[34]

But how is all of this supposed to work, Holloway rhetorically asks, given that the cohesion of the capitalist social synthesis always draws us back into itself in myriad ways? At the level of the state, for example, there are always the asymmetric threats of violence and repression in the name of property, and of law and order.[35] Also, we are trapped, individually and collectively, by commodity and labor markets, and gestures toward form-

---

31 Ibid., 180.
32 Ibid., 197.
33 Ibid., 28.
34 Ibid., 31.
35 Ibid., 54.

ing an alternative economy all too easily end up becoming just a complement to the dominant capitalist production. Finally, even within our alternative councils and assemblies, capitalist contradictions tend to reproduce themselves. If we want to understand the cracks as something more than just a series of endless hit-and-run attacks upon the rationality of capitalism, Holloway says, we have to be able to understand the cracks in some way as the crisis of this social synthesis, as something offering a path to a radical reorganization of our daily life. To find this understanding, Holloway returns to Marx, to the dual theory of labor found in *Capital*. The totality of social relations woven by abstract labor is a process that nobody controls, he writes, but the dual character of labor (concrete labor/use value vs. abstract labor/exchange value) "is the pivot, because we are the pivot — we make it so we can break it."[36]

Holloway and the Ecstasy of Doing into Labor

Consistent with Postone's rereading of the later Marx, Holloway characterizes "abstraction" as simultaneously an alienation of our activity and the constitution of the social nexus, the weaving of capitalist society.[37] Capitalist society everywhere wants to present concrete doing in the form of abstract labor, but, Holloway says, the dominance of this abstract labor continues to conceal the dual nature of labor, and the basic situation is one of tension and instability. "The double flight from labor" that characterizes the society as a whole causes the asserted unitary character of labor to be continually split open. Abstract labor's internal drive is for the valorization of capital, or the creation of surplus value/profit. At the same time, the drive of concrete labor is toward doing the activity well. The need of capital for "undifferentiated socially necessary labor time" thus inbuilds conflict with concrete doing. In every refusal of authority, Holloway says, and "in every attempt to gain control of the work process, in every

36 Ibid., 95.
37 Ibid., 97.

attempt to develop meaningful activities inside or outside the hours of employment," there is some measure of revolt against abstract labor.[38]

The tension is also manifest in the "neuroses and frustrations and struggles of creative workers who try to do things well against the constraint of time and money," and yet our "other doings," Holloway says, exist despite the claims of money, that is, the demand that all human activity should be converted into abstract labor.[39] They exist individually and socially as "the cracks" in the capitalist social nexus. Concrete labor, or use value, or what Holloway calls "concrete doing" can and must be seen to continually overflow abstract labor, because—in the manner of negative dialectics—it cannot be totally subordinated to it without some remainder. It is for this reason that Holloway says that the relation between concrete doing and abstract labor can be characterized as "ecstatic": concrete doing exists embedded within abstract labor while also at the same time standing outside of it.[40] Per Holloway, then, the struggles that make up the cracks in the capitalist social synthesis or nexus illuminate concrete doing *as a permanent crisis of capitalism.*[41]

Since concrete labor is not completely absorbed within abstract labor under the present, post-Fordist paradigm of domination, which has rendered capitalism increasingly fragile, Holloway says that we are called upon to rethink the meaning of struggle. Contrary to traditional Marxism, which asks us to adopt the standpoint of an "alternative totality" in a way that requires the vanguardism of the party, he says that we are called upon instead to recognize a confluence of struggles from below, and to recognize them as a constellation in a way that somehow teaches us a new language of anticapitalism. The new politics of refusal waiting to be born should thus not be mistaken for a politics of difference (which would deny the movement of the

38 Ibid., 175.
39 Ibid.
40 Ibid, 99.
41 Ibid., 178.

dialectic), nor is it merely a micropolitics. Instead, Holloway refers to it as a critical and practical movement of antifetishism, the "recovery of our power to do."[42]

The "No" as a Constant Weaving of a "We"

Early on in *Crack Capitalism,* Holloway says that "the cracks begin with a No."[43] In a very real sense, his analysis ends here also. Revolution is not about destroying capitalism, but about refusing to create it. In the concluding section, he admits that "rephrasing the question of revolution as 'stop making capitalism'" does not really give us any answers. Even if we see all the forms of social relations "as form-processes [...] swollen ecstatically with their own negation," he admits, "we do not know how to stop making capitalism."[44] All that we do know is that the shared "No" is a practical connection, "the constant weaving of a We."[45] Our struggle, therefore, is to "open every moment and fill it with an activity that does not contribute to the reproduction of capital,"[46] and to strengthen, expand, and multiply all the little rebellions. He describes the movement "against and beyond" as a kind of a thawing, and as a flowing, while acknowledging that we are all contradictory, all involved in the daily recreation of the social relations we are trying to overcome. There is no purity here, so there should be no purity tests.[47] In the end, he says, the relation between our concrete doing and abstract labor is to be understood as one of repression. He concludes (rather wanly in my view) by characterizing the work to be done as a form of collective self-therapy in the service of the return of the repressed.[48]

42 Ibid., 209.
43 Ibid., 17.
44 Ibid., 255.
45 Ibid., 257.
46 Ibid., 254.
47 Ibid., 257.
48 Ibid., 224–25.

Berardi on the Workflows of Semiocapitalism

In *Crack Capitalism,* Holloway doesn't really have that much to say about the meaning of abstract labor in the digital age per se. For him, it is enough that current conditions "widen the cracks" that define the permanent crisis of capitalist society. But what if abstract labor itself is in the process of evolving? If so, what might this portend? And what if the crisis of capitalism is not, in fact, permanent, and so not pregnant with the seeds of its own demise? Berardi's *The Soul at Work* places these questions at the center of concern. With Berardi, we move from a consideration of how abstract labor constitutes capitalist social relations to a discussion of how technology has increasingly enabled capitalism to harness mental labor itself as production. The entire problematic is captured well by the book's title. When we see the words "the soul at work," Berardi does not want us to think about how "work can crush the soul," for example. Instead of invoking alienation in this traditional sense, the phrase is meant to refer to the manner in which contemporary capitalism, in the digital age, "extends work beyond the traditional domain of wage labor" to include mind/language/creativity as primary elements of the production of value.[49] The book's subtitle, *From Alienation to Autonomy,* completes the basic thought problem: What is the potential vector from alienation to autonomy, Berardi is asking, given that work now harnesses the parts of ourselves that in the past were left to us, once the workday was over?

Recall that for Marx, "abstract labor" means the distribution of value-producing time without regard to quality or relation to any use value that the objects might have, in order to valorize capital. Under Fordist industrialization, activity loses its concrete character, becoming purely rented out time, per contract, and objectified in products designed for enabling exchange, and the accumulation of surplus value. And though capitalism employs the many advances in techno-science to eliminate human labor to the greatest extent possible, creating successive

49 Berardi, *The Soul at Work,* 21.

waves in the crisis of its system of social relations, the conditions thereby also emerge for reducing our mental labor to an abstracted activity. In the digital age, Berardi says, everyone does the same thing with their bodies, sitting in front of the computer screen. But what does it mean to sell one's time for a wage when the content of what everyone is doing is so diverse and cognitively complex that nobody thinks these jobs are interchangeable, as was the case under Fordism?[50] The meaning of productive labor itself becomes uncertain if the relationship between time and quantity of produced value is rendered effectively indeterminate. Capital's solution to the problem of fixing the value of abstract labor over recent decades is at once inventive and grotesque — it is simply to swallow the person whole, to claim the balance of what Peter Fleming calls our "biopower." Wage labor, once mentalized, has no set hours, and no set place, because it is the very soul, the aspects of the person that Marx called "the species essence," mind/language/creativity, that have been abstracted.

The Equivocal Condition of the New Cognitariat

And yet Berardi knows that something more has to be said about this new kind of worker, which he calls "a virtual class of those who do not identify with any class," a class whose structuration is neither material nor social, because their identity "depends upon the removal of their own social corporeality."[51] This is necessary because, at least from a certain angle, it appears as if the mentalization of labor is actually rather less alienated than the Fordist, disciplined body. Does not the investment of tech workers' specific competencies, and their creative, innovative, and communication energies in the labor process, point to a reduction of alienation? It appears to be the case that since the work is more personalized, tech workers are more identified with it, explaining things such as voluntary increases in the

50 Ibid., 74–75.
51 Ibid., 104.

length of the working day, and lower levels of absenteeism and disaffection reported in some segments over recent decades.[52]

How then did we go from widespread alienation from capitalist production processes to the situation today, Jason Smith asks in the preface to *The Soul at Work*, "in which work has become the central locus of psychic and emotional investment?"[53] Wither this huge investment of desire in work? Berardi does not fail to mention all the traditionally skeptical explanations: the "irrational exuberance about work," at least in some sectors, can be partially explained by the political defeat of the working class in the 1970s.[54] The apparent exuberance, therefore, masks the success of capital in terrorizing people through precarity, increased workplace authoritarianism, for example. He also mentions the "rarefaction of community ties."[55] Where less and less pleasure and reassurance can be found in everyday life, a greater investment of desire in one's work can provide the needed narcissistic reinforcement. Finally, and perhaps most compellingly, Berardi describes some pervasive zones of apparent empowerment: cognitive labor is heavy on communication, which can be seen as a certain kind of enrichment. Also, cognitive labor "in the network" is nonhierarchical and deterritorialized, leading to an increase in the experience of independence, at least at the nodal, team level.[56]

But both of these have a downside, too. Where communication becomes an economic necessity, Berardi says, it loses its spontaneous (gratuitous, pleasurable, erotic) character and is thus ultimately a kind of impoverishment.[57] So too with the new workplace independence. It ultimately masks a new form of dependency, that of the process itself, which regulates "a constant flow that cannot be interrupted and from which one

52 Ibid., 78.

53 Jason Smith, "Preface: Soul Strike," in Berardi, *The Soul at Work*, 12.

54 Berardi, *The Soul at Work*, 79.

55 Ibid., 80.

56 Ibid., 86.

57 Ibid., 87.

cannot step back, save at the price of being marginalized."[58] It is this experience of post-Taylorist, infocentric, networked mental labor that Berardi refers to throughout as "semiocapitalism." Whatever the set of contributing reasons, Berardi's emphasis on the desiring aspect of cognitive labor describes a contemporary society caught in the firm grip of the economistic ideology of what one might call "eudaimonic hedonism." The focus of life is accumulating wealth, which translates to purchasing power, such that loving your job means money and money buys happiness. Berardi goes on to explore the flipside of this for the desiring subjects of semiocapitalism, specifically, intensified competition, widespread anxiety and panic, and an experience of depression so widespread that it becomes almost completely normalized.[59]

The expansion of abstract labor to our mental activity, so that, increasingly, mental time serves in the production of exchange value, has significant consequences for capitalist social relations. In high-tech production, cognitive faculties are literally put to work, and "personal peculiarities seem to be valorized, opening new perspectives for self-realization," but it is also true that all of this "opens up a field of completely new energies for the valorization of capital."[60] "Abstraction," Berardi says, "reaches its perfection in the digital era."[61] Where productive labor consists in "enacting simulations later transferred to actual matter by computerized machines"[62] and "information [...] subsumes every space of the human habitat,"[63] the historical perception of time is replaced with the digital one. "The matrix is replacing the event," Berardi says. "To be recognized in the networked universe, one must become compatible with the generative logic of the matrix. What does not belong to a codified domain is

58 Ibid., 89.
59 Ibid., 100.
60 Ibid., 96.
61 Ibid., 61.
62 Ibid., 75.
63 Ibid., 73.

not socially recognizable or relevant."[64] Computerized society becomes the realization of a kind of panlogism,[65] in which we may see the total subjection of human beings by semiocapitalism.

Berardi on Rethinking Alienation and Autonomy

Berardi's prescription for overcoming these new forms of alienation, as it turns out, is pegged to what he calls the cognitariat's "investment of desire" in work and the dynamics of market capitalism. He wants to see politics transformed into something like a social therapy of desire. But for this idea to make sense, it first needs to be situated within a particular intellectual history and milieu of political struggle. The relevant backstory begins with the atmosphere of Marxist-humanism that permeated leftist intellectual circles in Italy in the 1960s, and the understanding of alienated subjectivity found in the young Marx of the *1844 Manuscripts* that supported it. In this Hegelian-idealist conception, the working class, as the bearer of universal reason in history, is generally regarded as a passive object, split between life and labor, lost in the historical process, and waiting to be restored to its essential self-identity.[66]

For Berardi, as with Holloway and Gorz, two interrelated factors are simultaneously decisive. The first is the Italian *Operaismo* (Workerist) focus on the relation between working-class struggles and technological transformations. Once intellectual labor had become part of the autonomous process of capital, Berardi says, it became impossible to maintain the role of the intellectual as it was described by critical theory still under the sway of the philosophy of consciousness: "neither the presuppositions of a humanity needing to be redeemed, nor the analysis of capital are sufficient to understand what happens [...] on the

64 Ibid.
65 Ibid.
66 Ibid., 40.

stage of working-class struggles."[67] Instead, the working class must be seen as an active subject of refusal, one capable of building a community starting from its fundamental and collective estrangement from capitalist society.

The second major factor is a new and rather explosive reading of Marx, once the *Grundrisse* became widely available for the first time beginning in the late 1960s.[68] As part of the reception of the *Grundrisse, Operaismo* theorists actively oppose the Marxist-humanist description of alienation (*Veräußerung*) and the associated role of the intellectual vanguard, in favor of a new understanding of estrangement (*Entfremdung*) and "the general intellect" centered on the social function of cognitive labor. The workers' fundamental situation, Berardi says, is one of estrangement.[69] The term is somewhat suggestive of what Adorno/Holloway mean by "negative dialectics"—workers occupy a position of exteriority, of nonintegration, a position that is unsustainable and not amenable to laborist, incremental relief. Estrangement is at once the feeling of alienation and its refusal. In *Operaismo,* therefore, contrary to trade unionism, which seeks concessions, wage struggle is valorized specifically as a political fight to destabilize the equilibrium of capital. Berardi explains that the *Operaismo* vision is founded on the idea that in the social process, what comes first is the workers' resistance to capital and the refusal of work, where this refusal means "the valorization of human activities which have escaped from labor's domination."[70] This position, which ultimately follows from an understanding of wage labor as a specific, historical condition needing to undergo a political critique, leads to a conception of struggle that involves intentionally turning passive alienation into active estrangement, and, as such, into a mass politics of refusal. It is necessary "to study the constitution

67 Ibid., 59.
68 Ibid.
69 Ibid., 43–45, 51.
70 Ibid., 60.

of autonomous collective activity, [...] the refusal of work, and the project of its extinction."[71]

Berardi on Reweaving the Social Relation

What, then, per Berardi, are the prospects for reweaving the social, especially since he believes there no longer is a crisis of capitalism, and we are on a path toward total subjection under the terms of post-Fordist abstract labor? Holloway, we recall, tries to make a case for a permanent crisis of capitalism via the dual theory of labor, insisting that if "concrete labor is totally absorbed within abstract labor, and there is no question of an against and beyond [...], then the cracks get lost."[72] On what basis are we to find our way to a mass politics of refusal, if it is indeed the case, as Berardi argues, that abstract labor reaches its perfection in the digital age? Berardi's thought process toward a prescription goes something like this: In the new economy, many are called, but few are chosen. Among the cognitariat, those who can, try to isolate themselves from others in a pressurized and hyperconnected capsule,[73] but the dark side of the soul at work (fear, anxiety, panic, depression) still surfaces,[74] disturbing the normal flow of capitalist validation.[75] In fact, ever since its mutation into semiocapitalism, the "exchange value machine" has swallowed not only all the various forms of life, but also thought, imagination, and hope. By emancipating itself from its heritage of humanistic values and enlightenment, hypercapitalism is now revealing a regime of pure, endless, and inhuman violence[76] — a new system of production in which solidarity has vanished, working-class community has been eliminated by technology, and labor is precarious.

71 Ibid., 59.
72 Ibid., 193.
73 Ibid., 104.
74 Ibid., 207
75 Ibid., 208.
76 Ibid., 132.

Despite all of this, we are not, in fact, experiencing a crisis[77] — so we must be careful to reject the dominant discourse that says that overcoming is to be had by means of some sort of a recovery, a return to the dynamics of growth and consumption. In point of fact, society does not need more work, more jobs, more competition, Berardi says. Rather "we need a massive reduction in work time, a prodigious liberation of life from the social factory in order re-weave the fabric of the social relation."[78] What we need instead are things such as degrowth, deprivatization of goods and services, an end to the domination of the wage, and an economy based on sharing common things and the liberation of time. To get there, Berardi says, will take nothing less than a profound "anthropological shift," a significant change in human being.[79] "There is a truth" within depression.[80] Today, old age is becoming the average social condition of the human race. Libidinal energy is declining. The social brain is decomposing.[81] Submission becomes the dominant form of relation between individuals and groups. The body of the other is no longer within the reach of an empathetic perception: "One suffocates every day, and the symptoms [...] are disseminated all along the paths of daily life and the highways of planetary politics. Our chances of survival are few. We know it."[82]

At a certain moment in the *Operaismo* movement's theoretical and practical struggle, therefore, questions about "how autonomous selves are to be individualized" in relation to changing social, economic, and media conditions became most pressing (as part of the problem of class composition/recomposition). This concern with subjectivation against subjection, conducted in the absence of a crisis theory, led to an encounter with what Berardi calls "French desiring theory."[83] In order to

77 Ibid., 210, 212.
78 Ibid., 213.
79 Ibid.
80 Ibid., 129.
81 Ibid., 132.
82 Ibid., 131.
83 Ibid., 123.

explain the process of social recomposition, he says, "we need to refer to the notions of desire, machinic unconscious, and schizoanalysis."[84]

By looking to Deleuze and Guattari to analyze the process of the formation of "the social imaginary," Berardi signals his decision that henceforth, "political action needs to be conceived first of all as a shift in the social investment of desire."[85] Having thus committed to the additional premise that such political action "must happen according to modalities analogous to therapeutic intervention,"[86] Berardi traverses Deleuze and Guattari's path to reformulate the work of analysis, placing the aesthetic paradigm at the core of his therapeutic and political perspective.[87] Analysis, they argue, should not be understood as a process of recovery, of uncovering something latent in order to dispel a neurotic fixation. Instead, we need to view it as akin to a creative process: "Analysis is the creation of new centers of attention capable of producing [...] a rupture within the closed circuit of obsessive repetition."[88] There is much more than could be said, following Berardi, to continue to flesh this all out. Of special interest would be the discussion about how the aesthetic, as a discipline of attunement, can be a kind of therapy of our relation with the world, about how the creation of "psychological cores capable of transforming a certain mental cartography into livable space," and about how all this could redirect our collective investments of desiring energy to a different political reality.

But I do not choose to travel this road any further with Bifo. I don't doubt for a moment that many (if not all) of us could benefit greatly from some version of art therapy. But Berardi's path to a mass politics of refusal here, in relation to post-Fordist abstract labor, relies on what Ágnes Heller calls an "anthropological revolution." All that is necessary, he says, is that we give birth to a new humanity, that we overcome human being as it

84 Ibid.
85 Ibid., 139.
86 Ibid., 140.
87 Ibid., 135.
88 Ibid., 131.

currently exists in favor of a "new man of the future." We have seen this movie before. It feels like an unwelcome return to the Nietzsche-inspired poststructuralism of the 1990s, where the substitution of culture criticism for the theory and practice of politics was ubiquitous in France. Berardi, like Foucault, relies on what I like to call "the productive imagination gambit," something far in excess of what Jenny Odell, for example, is suggesting with respect to regaining some measure of control of our attention. He wants to give an aesthetic answer to what is essentially an ethical and political question. In reply, I will say only this: Nietzsche understood that in taking this path, he was addressing himself to "men of the future," perhaps of the distant future. But for a viable project of class recomposition, we simply don't have the luxury of time, because the arrival of the future can no longer be relied upon. It's something that has been taken from us.

11

The Exodus from Wage Labor

> We need a massive reduction in work time, a prodigious liberation of life from the social factory in order to re-weave the fabric of the social relation.
>
> —Franco "Bifo" Berardi, *The Soul at Work*

In chapter 10, I began exploring the following question: If abstract labor, as seen in Fordist, industrial capitalism, is actually in the process of disappearing, then how should we understand work today, in the post-Fordist digital age? I considered what both Holloway (*Crack Capitalism*) and Berardi (*The Soul at Work*) had to say about the changing character of work and our present prospects for increasing emancipation in light of these transformations. I then considered their various ideas about how we might attempt to "reweave the social" to strengthen social relations in a way that breaks with, and is incompatible with, the "dominant capitalist social synthesis."

Holloway's main gambit is to try to salvage the central function of crisis theory given the account of the constitution of capitalist society found in the later Marx, and most recently reconstructed by Moishe Postone. It is true that capitalist society is something we collectively remake for ourselves every day, but it's also true, he believes, that at its core, capitalism must remain in a permanent state of crisis. Our capacity and need for what he calls "concrete doing" (being primarily useful to ourselves and others) is always under some measure of repression, and remains in constant tension with the abstraction of labor, with relations of commodity exchange, accumulation, and the pursuit of surplus value. Despite this constant tension, however, Holloway freely admits, we really don't know how to "stop making capitalism."[1] As a result, he never gets very far beyond the need for resistance, for "saying no" in myriad ways in order to widen the cracks that run all through capitalist society. In the end, however, Holloway's book doesn't offer very many ideas about how we might come to realize a mass politics of refusing work-as-we-know-it.

For his part, Berardi says that abstract labor reaches a kind of perfection in the post-Fordist digital age, and thus should be recognized as a total accomplishment once capitalism morphs into what he calls "semiocapitalism" (the knowledge economy). Where post-Fordist semiocapitalism swallows the parts of the person that used to live outside the wage relation, the project of emancipation takes on a postcrisis orientation, and so becomes that of somehow culturally producing "subjects of refusal," that is, people who do not invest their desire so thoroughly into work. It's hard to be satisfied with ways of framing practical problems that result in only vague, open-ended prescriptions. I said that we need to find our way to something more concrete and substantive than having recourse to some form of collective art therapy today. This is especially true because we don't have the luxury of the timescales that might be required for bringing about a complete revolution in human nature (assuming, of course, that such a thing even exists and that it can be changed). In this chapter, I go on to sketch Gorz's account of the rise of what he calls a "supranational state of capital," where capital itself has become committed to an exodus from its own proper form of society. The main purpose here is to showcase Gorz's claim, in *Reclaiming Work,* that it's now time for a commensu-

1 John Holloway, *Crack Capitalism* (London: Pluto Books, 2010), 255.

rate exodus of labor and to highlight the specific proposals he makes for bringing about what he calls "the multiactive society."

The Rise of a Supranational State of Capital

Gorz's analysis starts with a general description of intertwined economic, social, and technological changes that created widespread post-Fordist working conditions in the 1970s. On the economic front, the period saw an end to easy Fordist growth, resulting in increasing economic stagnation. The Keynesian welfare state confronted a situation in which fiscal and monetary stimulation had reached effective limits, at the same time that the marginal productivity of capital was declining, in fact tending toward zero.[2] On the social front, the early 1970s experienced a crisis of governability, reflecting a countercultural refusal of the social terms of abstract labor, mass consumption, and the like. This was coupled with labor resistance to top-down Fordist efficiency management in the industrial sector, and with the effects of increasing automation on employment levels and working conditions. Fearing socialization, Gorz says, capital determined instead to end its wholesale symbiosis with the welfare state, substituting the anonymous laws of the market for the laws that state-societies lay down for themselves, effectively moving capital beyond the power of the political sphere. In the subsequent era of neoliberalism, therefore, states find themselves called upon, first and foremost, to serve the competitiveness of multinational companies, with things such as liberalized trade policy, support for the free flows of capital needed for investing and producing abroad, and borrowing in foreign markets.[3]

Finally, capital receives critical support in overcoming the crisis of Fordism by means of a multifaceted technological revolution that allows it to free itself from the social state, to reduce

2 André Gorz, *Reclaiming Work: Beyond the Wage-Based Society*, trans. Chris Turner (Cambridge: Polity Press, 2005), 12.

3 Ibid., 12–13.

labor and unit costs, and speed up productivity and growth via global market penetration. According to Gorz, all of this provides the background for understanding how capital managed to attain historically unprecedented rates of profit, "while consuming less and less labor, distributing less in wages, paying less in taxes," and "ceasing to finance the social and environmental costs engendered by production."[4] In the new era of the supranational state of capital (deterritorialized, unregulated, untaxed, etc.), we see what is essentially an exodus of capital, such that the market becomes largely independent of societies and the real economy. Money makes money, he says, without selling anything other than itself—financial logic wins out over economic logic, and rent wins out over profit.

Gorz on Post-Fordist Working Conditions

Gorz's specific evaluation of our post-Fordist working conditions is rooted in the organizational and management challenges that arise from both the crisis of Fordism, and from the adoption of digital age technology (both robotic automation and data/network communications). The end of reliable patterns of Fordist growth led capital to focus on increasing global market shares through foreign investments. But it also meant that a fundamental problem still needed to be addressed and at the most general level, namely, how to continue to increase production, when the quantities demanded for domestic markets were not expected to significantly increase. The solution to this basic problem certainly included greater reinvestments in R&D/innovation to lower unit costs, decrease lead times, and such. But Gorz points out that it also included "an increased focus on image, novelty, and symbolic value" in order to create an "intentional volatility of fashion and consumer desires."[5] The maintenance of profits thus also required both built-in obsolescence and lean manufacturing to meet the fast renewal

4 Ibid., 5.
5 Ibid., 27–28.

of product demand. Per Gorz, because all of this turns out to be largely incompatible with traditional Fordist/Taylorist principles of organization, it caused what he calls a "cultural revolution in the history of industrialization,"[6] one complete with new approaches to management and production, which he describes broadly speaking as the progression from "Taylorism" to "Toyotism."

Since the scene of production called forth a premium on greater speed and flexibility, and the harnessing of intellectual labor for innovation, continual improvement, and enhanced novelty, we see the emergence of a new constellation of post-Fordist production processes and management techniques. Along with just-in-time, lean manufacturing, a certain degree of entrepreneurialism is newly encouraged. Taylorist management, Gorz says, consistent with modern abstract labor, had sought efficiency by means of highly formalized tasks to be achieved in procedures that were largely independent of the intentions, personalities, or good will of the operators. Under Toyotism, by contrast, "the total and entirely repressive domination of workers' personality was to be replaced by the total mobilization of that personality."[7]

With these new approaches to management (later to be called "agile"), traditional organization is replaced by that of "the network of interconnected flows," one in which workers interface with other members of their group, which is then coordinated at the nodes with others down the line. The net result is the creation of largely self-organizing collectives that perform intellectual labor, consultation, and information exchange, becoming essentially the "collective manager of a common endeavor."[8] Gorz is also explicit in saying that this "cultural revolution in industrialization" is made possible by the transformation of abstract labor in the digital age. In the information age, he says, the crisis of Fordism is overcome by means of the dematerali-

6 Ibid., 30.
7 Ibid.
8 Ibid., 31.

zation of both labor and fixed capital, since "the most important kind of fixed capital is now the knowledge stored in, and instantly available from, information technologies [...], and the most important kind of labor is brain power."[9] Because there is now no fixed boundary between living knowledge and machine knowledge, the difference between living labor and dead labor (as captured in technological products) is effectively erased, and human labor can now be seamlessly subsumed within the production process. The changes in workplace social relations that follow from the post-Fordist situation give rise to what is essentially a new (monstrous) category—where human being can be so subsumed, as both human resource and as human capital, we get "fixed human capital."[10] Gorz's analysis here largely parallels the one offered by Luc Boltanski and Ève Chiapello in *The New Spirit of Capitalism,* written around the same time.[11] What then is the bottom line, with respect to prospects for worker emancipation, under these new post-Fordist conditions? Gorz rhetorically asks, Does this Toyotist conception open up an unprecedented scope for workers' power, heralding a possible liberation both within work, and from work? Or does it rather carry the subjugation of workers to even greater heights?

The False Emancipation of Post-Fordism and Post-Taylorism

Gorz references three basic conditions necessary for transcending the alienation of labor, and says that various specific cases of digital age labor can be seen to be "on the way" to meeting them:

— Self-organization by workers, who become active subjects
— A mode of cooperation that is fulfilling, and the development of faculties and skills by each person

9 Ibid., 6.
10 Ibid.
11 Luc Boltanski and Ève Chiapello, *The New Spirit of Capitalism,* trans. Gregory Elliot (London: Verso, 2018).

— The materialization of work in a product recognizable by workers as the meaning and goal of their own activity[12]

For the most part, Gorz says, post-Taylorist working conditions fail to meet the total criteria because of intractable problems with the third point. Despite increases in autonomy, and engagement with more aspects of the total person in the performance of work, the goal of work still remains, as ever, the valorization of capital. As a result, where something like "product quality" is certainly considered an appropriate matter of concern for the community of workers, decisions about what is to be produced still remains in the hands of capital. Workers everywhere continue to experience the goal of the work as something imposed, in that it is everywhere generically reducible to *serving users of commodities designed for individual use by those who can pay for them.* This certainly does indeed cover a great many cases, but it can't be seen to cover much of anything that might be found under the rubric of *the noncommodity satisfaction of collective needs by collective means.*

What then, per Gorz, should we think about the broad measure of self-management that Toyotism encourages, in order to achieve maximum flexibility, productivity, and speed? At best, Gorz says, we see here a measure of autonomy against a backdrop of pervasive heteronomy. To what purposes and to whose ends, Gorz asks, are the products of workers' labor put? And where do the needs come from which their products are supposed to meet? Post-Fordist capital enjoins workers to consult and reflect, to plan and discuss (in short, to be the autonomous subjects of production), but it enjoins them to do so "within pre-set limits, and directed to pre-set aims."[13] In the end, he says, capitalism applies certain post-Taylorist principles only where it can be sure that doing so does not threaten the capitalist order.

The basic post-Fordist approach for ensuring this outcome turns out to be fully consistent with the transformation

12 Gorz, *Reclaiming Work,* 34.
13 Ibid., 39.

of abstract labor in the digital age. How then is capitalism to function, "if the most important types of capital (data and brain power) cannot be owned?"[14] Gorz says that Toyotism provides two related answers that taken together represent an explicit strategy:

— First, it seeks to motivate elite knowledge workers, a high-tech, nomadic tribe who valorize themselves as human capitals.
— Second, it seeks to take possession of most other workers by means of the imposition of neofeudalist conditions that leverage increasing job scarcity.[15] Toyotist post-Fordism, Gorz writes, "eliminates the antagonism between capital and labor for the stable core of its elite workers," and "shifts those antagonisms […] to the peripheral, insecure or unemployed workers."[16]

Autonomy in work is ultimately of little significance, Gorz says, when it is not carried into the cultural, moral, and political spheres. Political autonomy does not come from "productive cooperation," from what is only a virtual emancipation of post-Fordist workers within their work.[17] It comes from cooperation in the properly public sphere. Also, the extensive precariat (e.g., nonelites, subcontractors) have to bear the burden of the social implications and consequences of increasing levels of subjection that the elite knowledge workers are largely spared (even if capital insists on absorbing all of their biopower). In this way, Toyotism replaces modern social relations with premodern ones (relations of personal subjection and vassalage). Only this time around, everything is also imbued with big doses of distinctly modern alienation.

---

14 Ibid., 6. Since it is prima facie obvious that companies can own datasets, presumably Gorz means data specifically as a product of brain power per se.

15 Ibid., 7.

16 Ibid., 45.

17 Ibid., 40.

Exodus from Labor and Transition to a Multiactive Society

"This is how the new era began," Gorz writes, "in which changes that could have served to liberate men and women from needs and servitude were turned round against them."[18] The massive abolition of work that transpires in the era of post-Fordism could and should have opened up "the social space for all manner of activities aimed at satisfying self-defined needs."[19] But it didn't happen, because capitalism only applies post-Taylorist principles where it can be sure that it has "forearmed itself against the autonomous use by workers of the limited power conceded to them."[20] In the most general sense, the liberatory potential of the post-Fordist era did not materialize, therefore, because for it to do so, it would have required "an end to the power of capital over labor." In short, it would have required the birth of a different type of society. Instead, he says, everyone has been made to fight for a share of the work capital is abolishing, and despite these precarious conditions, "one's 'right to have rights' is still dependent upon accomplishment of some measurable, classifiable, saleable work." Every banner declaring "we want work," Gorz says, "proclaims the victory of capital over a subjugated humanity who can no longer be workers, but are denied the chance to be anything else."[21]

Where industrial capitalism's wage-based society offered ubiquitous full-time employment as the foundation of its particular sort of social contract, under the new reality, work becomes "an asset for which one must make sacrifices [...] work is now a commodity, employment a privilege."[22] In this way, capital brings rebellious working classes into line, by "abolishing work while continuing to make work the basis of social belonging and rights."[23] Instead, our aim must now be "to disconnect

18 Ibid., 5.

19 Ibid.

20 Ibid., 36.

21 Ibid., 53.

22 Ibid., 57.

23 Ibid., 5.

the right to have rights from work."[24] As long as our primary mode of socialization remains "social integration through employment, to the exclusion of all else," socialization "will continue to produce frustrated, ill-adapted, mutilated, disoriented individuals."[25] Perhaps, he concludes, it's time to seriously entertain a revolutionary proposal: maybe we should meet the exodus of capital with an exodus from work-based society.[26]

The reality of our situation today, Gorz wants us to recognize, is that since production demands less and less work, and thus distributes less and less in wages, it is becoming increasingly difficult for a majority of people to find a sufficient income via traditional waged work. But the problem is not, as capital would like us to think, a shortage of work (or better yet, a lack of competitive job applicants). Rather, it's a "failure to distribute the wealth which is now produced by capital employing fewer and fewer workers."[27] When we begin to talk seriously about the remedy, Gorz tells us, we also begin to imagine a certain kind of society. It is one where "people will be able to divide their lives between a wide range of activities which will have neither payment nor profitability as their necessary condition or goal."[28] Such changes correspond to the aspiration of what he calls a "multiactive life" (where life is not limited to the time allowed for it by the constraints of work), but its realization presupposes nothing less than the "optimal distribution of all socially necessary work, along with all the socially produced wealth."[29]

Gorz does not fail to see the full implication of this particular thought experiment. He recognizes that it presupposes nothing less than a "political break" for it to become reality, because for it to be so, "work must free itself from the domination of capital."[30] Here we come at last to the tipping point, the point where both

24 Ibid., 53.
25 Ibid., 69.
26 Ibid., 7.
27 Ibid., 72.
28 Ibid., 73.
29 Ibid., 72.
30 Ibid., 73.

Holloway and Berardi deny the relevance of the crisis of capital, and go down the road of proposing what I have called (following Ágnes Heller) an "anthropological revolution," or the invention of a new kind of human being.[31] Holloway, it's true, does claim that there is a crisis of capitalism. But he says that the crisis is something "perpetual," and in the last analysis, it's hard to see how a perpetual crisis is really a crisis. What distinguishes Gorz from Holloway and Berardi is that he wants to show, in the absence of a theory of crisis, how we might transform our work-based, post-Fordist "nonsociety" into a postwork society, and do so by some sort of a break with the existing capitalist hegemony. His approach starts with the formulation of what Kierkegaard famously called an either/or.[32] Either we can subordinate the apparatus and the social process of production to the power of living activities, or we can enslave those activities even more completely to that apparatus and that process.[33]

How then to push through this problem, since it becomes even more acute under post-Fordist conditions, where the human capacity for autonomy itself has lately been harnessed in the drive to valorize capital? Gorz is worried about what Holloway calls "the gelatinous suction of the capitalist social synthesis." The encouragement of autonomy, he says, has to be about being useful to ourselves and others (to society) and not about being useful to corporate overlords. Given the paradoxical "heteronomous autonomy" we see under post-Fordism, he says that we need to find a way to vouchsafe the "autonomy of autonomy," to show how we might develop people's autonomy irrespective of companies' need for it, so that autonomy's rights over itself are not effectively hijacked.[34]

To highlight this distinction, Gorz goes on to review various proposals that were being floated in France at the time he was writing, ideas that seemed to be headed in the right direction,

31 Ágnes Heller, *Beyond Justice* (Cambridge: Basil Blackwell, 1987), 103.

32 See Søren Kierkegaard, *Either/Or*, trans. Howard V. Hong and Edna H. Hong, 2 vols. (Princeton: Princeton University Press, 1978).

33 Gorz, *Reclaiming Work*, 73.

34 Ibid., 74.

especially since the dream of full employment had largely gone by the wayside. He considers so-called activity contracts, under which companies might loan out employees during periods of low demand, so as to make employment more discontinuous, without it becoming either insecure or temporary. Under this scenario, it was even proposed that companies might lend their temporary surplus labor to public bodies, such as communities, schools, or associations, or that workers be allowed to take "social utility leave" for such purposes. But Gorz is flatly dismissive of these proposals, since under this framework, staff on temporary social utility leave would be constrained to perform voluntary work or cultural activity consonant with the wishes and interests of the contracting companies. Such activity contracts, Gorz writes, extend "the domination of productivist logic and subordination to company interests" to activities that otherwise might have been truly self-directed during gaps in employment.[35]

Instead, Gorz embraces a much more radical framework, one where companies (in the ultimate interest of all) should be somehow called upon to maintain the right of employees to a continuous income despite discontinuous working,[36] where the (reduced) working hours and the nonwork activities may be organized on a basis that they themselves select. Insisting upon this right to choose is essential, Gorz says, because it will necessarily lead to a new approach to work, one that will "set each of us on the way to other modes of participation in collective life, in society."[37] The company, it's true, will have to do without the excessive importance waged work has given it, because the work-based society must give way to a society based on "multiactivity" with a concomitant "diversification of social allegiances."[38] Given where we have arrived (exodus of capital from the work-based society, with resulting social disintegra-

35 Ibid., 75.
36 Ibid., 96.
37 Ibid., 76.
38 Ibid.

tion), Gorz believes that this dramatic alteration in the place, role, and function of work in human experience is now necessary for the survival or reconstitution of a society in which both persons and companies can flourish. Society must be constituted so that flexible, discontinuous, and evolutionary forms of working, far from leading to accelerated disintegration, can give rise instead to new forms of "sociality and cohesion".[39]

Exit Routes: From Crisis to Transformation

Embedded in Gorz's argument is the claim that under the right conditions (nothing short of the reorganization of social time and space) society as such can be seen to regenerate. If we put an end to "subjection in the economic sphere, the work-based society will have to give way to a society based on multi-activity."[40] Under this new, overarching form of social organization, the norm will be for everyone to belong or be able to belong (for example) to a self-providing cooperative, or a service exchange network, a science research experiment group, an orchestra or a choir, a drama, dance, or painting workshop, and/or a sports club.[41] How, then, to cross the bridge into this future world, in which society is able to assert the priority of individual and collective human needs? Where, precisely, do we find the meaning and significance of the "political break" that the coming-to-be of such a society would require?

For multiactivity to develop, Gorz writes, *"society will have to organize itself to achieve it through a range of specific policies."*[42] At first glance, the turn to "specific policies" at this juncture is rather surprising. How does the recommending of a set of specific policies deliver on a needed "political break," one where work somehow frees itself from the domination of capital? Surely, the lengths that capital is willing to go to ensure that

39 Ibid., 77.
40 Ibid., 76.
41 Ibid., 78.
42 Ibid. My emphasis.

there should be "no free anything" can never be underestimated. Invoking an implicit developmentalist logic, Gorz appears to be making a case for how a culture change can lead to a change in politics, and thus to political action. It is important to show "that the possibility of transcending capitalist society is inherent in the evolution of capitalist society itself."[43] For example, it is not that farfetched to anticipate widespread acceptance of the idea that people, on balance, ought to be able to work less, both today and in the future. If we also insist that the new social time should not be dominated by capital and market-based activity, then it also becomes possible, Gorz believes, to imagine taking steps to enact policies that protect the new fields of activity that are opened up, to decisively withdraw them from the power of capital. "All we can ask of politics" is "to create the spaces in which the alternative social practices can develop."[44] And yet, it remains a very tall ask, just the same.

The politics of multiactivity must thus be seen as an engine of the exodus and as prefiguring its final goal. Enacting policies that change the social environment hasten the change in mentalities, Gorz says, generating what, following systems theory, he calls a "positive feedback loop."[45] As a result, the kinds of policies that he has in mind (in anticipation of the required political break) are of a particular type. They are what, following Anthony Giddens, he calls "generative policies."[46] Such policies are those that are aimed at the individual and collective reappropriation of time and its organization. They are prioritized because of their ability to generate "new social relations lying beyond the logic of the market, money, and the sexual division of labor," new "areas of time outside the wage relation," and "new production techniques, and relations to the environment."[47]

For purposes of illustration, Gorz selects three interrelated types of policies to showcase, because they are aimed at the indi-

43 Ibid.
44 Ibid., 79.
45 Ibid.
46 Ibid., 83.
47 Ibid., 80.

vidual and collective reappropriation of time and its organization:

— Guaranteed basic income
— Redistribution of work and the liberation of free time
— Encouraging new modes of socialization beyond the wage-relation[48]

In what remains of this chapter, it is useful to consider Gorz's account of these interrelated policy prescriptions, with emphasis placed on the ways in which he believes they encourage a positive feedback loop of the sort he would like to see. In doing so, it is important to continue to recall assumptions that are always in the background so that Gorz gets a fair hearing. Recall that under post-Fordist conditions, working time is ceasing to be the measure of labor, because, increasingly, it is becoming impossible to define an irreducible quantity of work to be performed over a determinate period. The more the quantity of socially necessary labor time diminishes, the more work will become necessarily discontinuous. In the future, Gorz says, there will be less employment, less selling of labor and services, and a concomitant growth in collective facilities and services and nonmonetary exchange and self-providing.

Gorz's first major skirmish is over whether guaranteed basic income should be either sufficient or insufficient and conditional (i.e., workfare). Gorz has a whole host of complaints to raise against the idea of a guarantee being set at less than subsistence, and thus linked to some sort of concrete obligation. His basic objection to workfare-type approaches is that they turn out to be a subsidy for employers rather than for citizens. Workfare forces the unemployed, or discontinuously employed to accept "dirty, low status jobs on the cheap,"[49] creating what is essentially a secondary labor market, one protected from both low-wage foreign competition and labor laws. And workfare

48 Ibid., 80.
49 Ibid., 81.

stigmatizes the unemployed as "incompetents and scroungers" whom society is entitled to force to work, because they are the ones at fault.[50]

But the point of providing this income, Gorz says, is not just to dovetail with the most unfortunate aspects of post-Fordism, by incentivizing people to accept part-time work with variable wages and hours under precarious conditions. Rather than subsidizing low-skilled work, the focus should be on the equitable redistribution of skilled work instead.[51] The increasing discontinuity of work, Gorz insists, need not reflect capital's discretionary power over labor. Instead, it could be made to reflect the individual and collective right of those performing work to control how they manage their own time. Gorz asks us to consider the idea that the purpose of granting social income isn't to provide assistance or even social protection. What if the purpose, he asks, is rather to enable a genuine "right to work" where this right refers to the concrete labor one does without being paid for it, without its profitability or exchange value figuring into the equation? As hard as it may be for many us to recognize, presumably because we are held in the thrall of capitalist realism, the granting of a *sufficient* social income isn't about enabling people "not to work." Instead, Gorz contends, "it's about enabling all citizens to decide, on an ongoing basis, between the use value of their time and its exchange value."[52]

To try to drive the point home, Gorz asks us to consider the viability of the alternative conceptions. Let's say for a moment that we agree that nonconditional, universal basic income would disincentivize people from working, so we insist that people must work to get the allowance. What will be the content of the compulsory work? And how is it to be defined, measured, and distributed? How can we avoid having this work compete with and/or eliminate regular jobs? Now consider the other alternative where what must be done in exchange should

50 Ibid., 85.
51 Ibid., 84.
52 Ibid., 83.

be conducted in the realm of volunteer work. This would have the effect of making voluntary work compulsory throughout the society, turning spontaneous social obligations into something under public administrative control. In the end, Gorz writes, if we want the grant to be linked to performance of equivalent work, two conditions have to be met. The work to be done must be in the public sphere, and thus of benefit to everyone, and the work has to have payment as its aim in such a way that the payment doesn't corrupt the meaning of the work. If these conditions can't be met, then the grant should be sufficient, universal, and unconditional.[53]

Generative Policies, Transitional Forms

Gorz's *Reclaiming Work* offers a reasonably detailed account of both guaranteed social income and redistribution of skilled work among flexible employees who are otherwise made free to create use value as they see fit. For example, Gorz describes experiments undertaken by the Dutch and the Danes (see, e.g., his account of successful job sharing on the part of the Aarhus refuse collectors).[54] It is interesting, but some of what he offers is highly specific to the European context, and some of it feels somewhat out of date at this point. Various ideas he has about the costs associated with work redistribution, for example, appear to assume some version of national health care. Also, it's hard to see how something like a government-run "environmental corps," as has been considered here in the United States, wouldn't meet the standard he sets for linking a grant of income to the performance of work.

So rather than getting bogged down in even more detailed policy discussions about how these things might work, it makes more sense instead to move on to consider Gorz's third type of generative policies, namely, those that encourage new modes of socialization "beyond the wage relation," especially since these

53 Ibid., 87.
54 Ibid., 95.

things are intended as the telos for the basic income and discontinuous working scenarios. The so-called generative policies matter, Gorz wants us to recognize, precisely because they are designed to yield various, new transitional social forms: "The granting of a sufficient basic income must be inseparable from developing and making accessible the resources which enable and encourage self-activity to take place."[55] It is in this spirit that we should also understand his remark that the policy of reduction of working time can be effective only if it is *an evolving measure*.[56] Or when he says that the "continuous income for discontinuous working formula," where the discontinuity can be managed by work collectives, "is particularly interesting as a *transitional policy*."[57]

To see where this goes, consider what he says near the end of the main part of the book, where he turns to "cooperative circles," or what in England came to be called LETS (Local Exchange Trading Systems). Gorz is interested in these arrangements because he sees them as both a "crisis measure" and a "source of new subjectivity."[58] LETS represent an "exodus from present social arrangements," he writes, and thus are "a potentially radical response to the impossibility of large masses of workers selling their labor power." Why, he asks, "must workers require an employer capable of paying them" in order to sell their labor power for money to a customer?[59]

LETS are designed to allow members of a community to exchange their work without intermediaries, without resorting to just barter or in-kind, because they innovate "work-money or time-money" so that exchange doesn't have to be done "on the spot" as a determinate exchange between two individuals. In the LETS scenario, members are granted credit to call on the services of other members, and every hour of work or equivalent they receive represents a debt they have pay to with an hour

55 Ibid., 83.
56 Ibid., 94.
57 Ibid., 98. My emphasis.
58 Ibid., 102.
59 Ibid., 103.

of work for any other member within a predetermined time period. Under such a system, you get "time-money" that cannot be hoarded and cannot be desired for its own sake, going some distance toward abolishing commodity fetishism, and strengthening local mutualism and thus greater individual and collective autonomy.[60]

Consistent with his belief that "the possibility of transcending capitalist society is inherent in the evolution of capitalist society itself," Gorz explains that LETS should not be seen as an attempt to take us "back to the village economy."[61] The expectation is still that everyone will work discontinuously in the macro-social system of exchange, and that there will still be money, accumulation and surplus, and the state. Gorz thus recognizes that the self-managed collective cannot be extended to planetary scale, and that, following Habermas, "the system cannot dissolve [...] entirely into the lifeworld."[62] Instead, Gorz thinks we can at least create a feedback loop connecting the evolution of the system back to that of the lifeworld.

Discontinuous Working and Multiactive Life

Today, Gorz writes, we are confronted with a reality in which there is a surplus of both labor and capital, while unemployment, poverty, and destitution continue to spread. Capital, he says, wants to continue to expand without passing through the mediation of productive work, but rather via investments in financial markets and in low-wage countries. With wages contracting, and massive tax breaks afforded to capital to prevent its flight, long-term social investments, including in education, research, public services, and environmental protection, cannot be financed, and we see the increasing privatization of all public goods. All of this leads to another twenty-first-century inconvenient truth: given where things are headed, the distribution

60 Ibid., 103–5.
61 Ibid., 106.
62 Ibid., 110.

of means of payment "must correspond to the volume of wealth socially produced, and not the volume of work performed."[63] It is for this reason that he thinks that a universal, unconditional grant of basic income is the best instrument for redistributing paid work and unpaid activities as widely as possible. The grant of basic income, or what we lately call UBI (universal basic income), Gorz says, "shows up the nonsensical nature of a system which makes unprecedented savings of working time, but turns that time into a disaster for those who save it, because the system can neither share it out, nor recognize the intrinsic value of leisure time."[64]

The multiactive society is thus intended as the seedbed for growing widespread acceptance of this inconvenient truth, "behind the back" of our politics, which otherwise will surely prevent such a rupture or break with capitalist society, even though capital itself has already taken flight. As Gorz sees it, the first and most crucial step is that "work must be made more discontinuous" in a way that allows workers to choose "form a wide range of forms of discontinuity."[65] This is Gorz's exit route—if we encourage policies that support a right to work intermittently and to lead a multiactive life, we might yet arrive at a form of social and economic reality in which the distribution of means of payment, in the broadest sense, "no longer reflects the value of the labor done" (since this is collapsing in any case), but rather reflects "the needs, desires, and aspirations that the society chooses to meet."[66] Social policies, Gorz proposes, could perhaps support a significant cultural shift from crisis to transformation, maximizing the paths out of capitalism—think of it as sort of a biblical exodus, one that "invents its own promised land as it goes along."[67]

63 Ibid., 90.
64 Ibid., 91.
65 Ibid., 94.
66 Ibid., 90.
67 Ibid., 79.

The Double Bind of Capital

By invoking the idea of an exodus to somewhere, but we know not where, Gorz is perhaps telling us something about how the social is woven (mythico-historically) in the first instance. Or in a more modern vein, it tells us something about how utopias function, as regulative ideas, giving direction to our political *praxis*. But there is something else going on here, too, something having to do with the "double binds" described by Berardi in *The Soul at Work*. Animating Gorz's entire discourse is belief in the impossibility that capitalist society should continue to insist, foundationally, upon *both a thesis and its antithesis*. Increasingly, and by design, there are no jobs (you cannot have a job), but to enjoy any social benefits, you must have a job. Gorz writes in his introduction, "A new system has been established which is abolishing work on a massive scale." But it's "not this abolition we should object to." Rather, what is objectionable is claiming to perpetuate the work that is being abolished as "an obligation and a norm, and as the irreplaceable foundation of the rights and dignity of all."[68]

Gorz embraces the possibility that "transcending capitalist society is inherent in the evolution of capitalist society," even while anticipating some sort of a political break that would allow generative social policies to be widely implemented. In this respect, he appears to be slipping in some version of crisis theory, in the form of a kind of a gravediggers of capitalism thesis. At the most generic level, one must hear a certain sort of a rational appeal in his assertion of the double bind. It is not reasonable, Gorz seems to be saying, that a political order can long rest upon a destabilizing order of being, one that insists upon declaring its law, its thesis, and its antithesis. Surely, he implicitly argues, a time will come when leaders of industry and politicians will stop gaslighting us, and recognize that it is not rational to continue to insist upon this fundamental "double bind." Instead, the system as such will have no choice but to

68 Ibid., 1.

begin to address our individual and collective needs by instituting policies to ensure the "optimal distribution of all socially necessary work, along with all the socially produced wealth."[69] He doesn't want to entertain the possibility that such an unstable social foundation could actually be made to endure, and that there is actually a historical precedent for establishing a regime of tragic suffering.

Recall from chapter 10 that Berardi also discussed what he referred to as "the double bind of capital." Capital seeks to reduce labor time to a minimum, but at the same time insists on "positing labor time as the sole source of and measure of wealth." But Berardi sees the contradictions of capitalism, understood as a double bind, rather differently. He refers to it as a "paradoxical communication" or a "contradictory injunction," and says that it functions as a "pathogenic mechanism" for which there should be no expectation of a dialectical overturning.[70] Presumably, he thinks that there can also be no return to a simple assertion, either as support for the demand of capitalist society under Fordism that everyone must have a job, or else the recognition that in the absence of a wage-based society, social wealth must be shared out. If the basic contradiction cannot be overcome dialectically, and it cannot be dissolved by returning to an originary simple admonition (by either reasserting the original "law" of capitalist society or denying the antithesis as Gorz intends), then what options remain? How are we supposed to continue to live with the consequences of an incoherent social and political foundation?

Tragic Double Binds

In his "Ultimate Double Binds," which has haunted me for close to three decades, my old advisor, Reiner Schürmann, reminds

69 Ibid., 72.

70 Franco "Bifo" Berardi, *The Soul at Work: From Alienation to Autonomy,* trans. Francesca Cadel and Giuseppina Mecchia (Los Angeles: Semiotext(e), 2009), 65.

us that "the heroes of Attic tragedy" lived under just such a complex injunction or double bind.[71] Referencing Martha Nussbaum's close reading of *Agamemnon,* where the hero famously must sacrifice his daughter, Iphigenia, under the demands of the city, but must not do so, under the law of the family, Schürmann actually takes seriously the idea of a tragic social order. It is one, following Gregory Bateson, in which there is a primary injunction declaring the law, a secondary injunction declaring a counter-law (and thus conflicting with the first), and a tertiary injunction "prohibiting the victim from escaping from the field constituted by the first two."[72]

Schürmann thinks that *knowledge* of tragic differing (of the ineluctability of the two opposing demands) in the end *singularizes* Agamemnon, making him tragic, and, as such, something highly disruptive of any hegemonic social order.[73] By pointing beyond an established order in this way, Schürmann says, singularization shows us that "what is possible" stands higher than what is actual, because it calls forth an as yet indeterminate "what is to come," freeing the possible from the tyranny of some fixed regime of phenomenal actuality. In this respect, he sounds a lot like Holloway taking inspiration from Adorno's negative dialectics,[74] and finding a ray of hope in the ecstatic, in the residual and supplemental use value that always remains even in the harnessing of labor power as abstract labor. Of course, it's important to remember that once the die is cast, and Agamemnon must stand outside the complex tissue of social obligation, the situation demands nothing less than his total ruination. Needless to say, Oedipus fares no better.

71 Reiner Schürmann, "Ultimate Double Binds," *Graduate Faculty Philosophy Journal* 14, no. 2/1 (1991): 213–36.

72 Ibid., 234.

73 Ibid., 217.

74 See Theodor Adorno, *Negative Dialectics,* trans. E.B. Ashton (New York: Continuum, 2007).

Part III

From Privatized Stress to the Politics of Refusal

12

On the Seducements of Capitalist Spirituality

Affective disorders are a kind of captured discontent.

—Marc Fisher, *Capitalist Realism*

Politics as therapy, changing the world one individual at a time, doesn't make the world less brutally competitive and unequal, it helps people cope with these conditions.

— Ronald Purser, *McMindfulness*

Self-Optimization and the Politics of Refusal

If work today has really gotten you down, you are not alone. In the United States, lots of boomers, well past working age, chase seasonal retail, and wonder how they could have worked so hard and still have so little to show. Much of Gen X's PMC is already suffering from serious burnout, and will be exiting, voluntarily or not, long before the age of sixty-five. Among millennials, who invested heavily in college, there is a strong feeling of having been shafted by the disappearing "social contract" of US capitalism. As for Gen Z, the bulk of whom are now approaching college age, there is a lot of uncertainty; nobody really knows what the landscape of postpandemic higher ed looks like, much less what sort of economy they will be entering.

Throughout this book, I have been probing the possibility (however dim it may be) that the conditions of work-as-we-know-it today might be challenged by forms of collective action, something that implies the thorny prerequisite of increased solidarity across traditional social divisions. The logic has gone something like this: If we come to recognize the pervasive exodus of capital from its own, work-based society, and see the abandonment of things such as full employment, social benefits, and public goods as a defining characteristic of late capitalism, then we also must recognize the need for an updated concept of political struggle.

Given the increasing imposition of a post-Fordist, neoliberal capitalist "nonsociety," the updated concept of struggle thus involves the liberation of *work itself* from what Holloway has called the "gelatinous suction of the capitalist social synthesis." The struggle today is not so much about winning concessions from capital, as in traditional trade unionism, but rather turns out to be a struggle against the continued preeminence of wage labor per se, under post-Fordist conditions, where it is in fact steadily disappearing. The recognized need to break with the overarching logic of capital in order to escape the fabric of capitalist social domination, therefore, calls forth what one might refer to as a "politics of refusal." But this immediately raises the question of precisely how we want to specify this kind of politics. For his part, Holloway has stated, for example, that the constant assertion of our "concrete doing" over and against abstract labor should be understood as a form of "collective self-therapy." Open every moment "and fill it with activity that does not contribute to the reproduction of capital,"[1] and then multiply all the little rebellions. From there, the task is apparently to stitch together these "thousand points of light," presumably under the banner of what, in the Francophone world, is called the international *mouvement altermondialiste*.

1 John Holloway, *Crack Capitalism* (London: Pluto Press, 2010), 254.

I tend to be skeptical of critical theories that characterize a sought-after politics as a kind of collective self-therapy, presumably as a way to fill the hole that remains once revolutionary zeal has waned, both practically and theoretically. This is because much of what goes by the name of "self-help," "self-care," "self-optimization," and so on, has already been thoroughly co-opted and enlisted to meet the needs of capital. Berardi points out that digital technology has now enabled capitalism to harness mental labor as production, and to extend work beyond traditional wage labor to include mind-language-creativity as elements of the production process.[2] For aspects of mental labor to become stable elements of production, all that is needed is that the person as a whole has to be swallowed up by their work. This is what Berardi means by "the soul at work."

If today we are seeing "an epidemic of fear, anxiety, and depression," Berardi writes, it's important to remember that these things "continually disturb the normal flow of capitalist validation in the new economy" as a consequence of these very working conditions.[3] What then is the potential vector from alienation to autonomy now that work harnesses the parts of ourselves that in the past were left to us when the work day was over? Like Holloway, Berardi thinks that we require a shift in the social investment of desire away from work, with the prescription to transform politics into a social therapy of that desire. But it seems like this characterization of modes of refusal as collective self-therapy hits a major snag if capital has thoroughly co-opted the parts of the self that are supposed to be the seat of this resistance.

This whole line of reasoning brings up a number of disquieting questions. Can something like an aesthetics of existence really be marshaled as a politics of refusal today, when projects of self-optimization, recovery, wellness, and personal happiness

2 Franco "Bifo" Berardi, *The Soul at Work: From Alienation to Autonomy*, trans. Francesca Cadel and Giuseppina Mecchia (Los Angeles: Semiotext(e), 2009), 21.

3 Ibid., 207–8.

are actually what capital most fervently recommends? Also, how should one orient oneself, with respect to personal projects of healing and recovery, of mindfulness, wellness, and happiness, if the things one wishes to recover from are all ills arising in relation to hegemonic neoliberal capitalism? Is there, or should there be, a connection between our diverse projects of personal recovery and social/political movements of resistance and refusal? Certainly, millions of people make good use of self-help instruction to embark upon personal journeys of recovery and self-optimization, and obtain real, and even lasting, therapeutic benefit. And one can easily argue that well-considered programs of intentional self-care are a universal precondition for just about any other sorts of projects. As RuPaul says, "If you can't love yourself, how you gonna love somebody else?" But maybe there are still some good reasons to retain a healthy skepticism toward hyperindividualist programs for changing the world "one individual at a time," even if leading gurus from RuPaul to Jon Kabat- Zinn have things of value to offer us. Ronald Purser has written that "mindfulness is therapy for [capitalist] realists who have swallowed the idea that 'there is no alternative' to the market logic of Margaret Thatcher."[4] What if, as Slavoj Žižek has also pointed out, mindfulness (as a set of practices that encourage a particular kind of self-knowledge and self-care) is actually "establishing itself as the hegemonic ideology of global capitalism?"[5]

The Bricolage of Capitalist Spirituality

Perhaps, like millions of other people (including a great many born into advantages of race, gender, and class), you suffer from PTSD/anxiety or depression caused by long-term job precariousness. Or maybe you also exhibit some combination of real or psychosomatic illnesses, attributable (at least in part) to the effects

4 Ronald Purser, *McMindfulness: How Mindfulness Became the New Capitalist Spirituality* (London: Repeater Books, 2019), 245.

5 Ibid., 29.

of workplace powerlessness or toxicity, or the "bullshitification" of work. Maybe you are feeling really burned out, because your job makes increasing demands upon your personal "biopower" —you work massive overtime, and you are always on call and monitoring communications. If you work in media-oriented parts of the services sector, perhaps your employer seeks to leverage various aspects of your personality or talents or interests, and even seeks to dictate aspects of your lifestyle. For those afflicted by some combination of work-related maladies—PTSD/anxiety, depression, despair, eating disorders, other neuroses, sleep problems, burnout, boreout—it's only natural to want to try to save oneself from a life cut short. It makes sense to look for recovery, for healing, for a new way of managing one's life energies, a new life path. Recovering a sense of well-being in the face of these conditions can take many months or even years of patient and determined effort, even assuming the most ideal conditions.

If you are someone who is an active participant in an organized religion, then you probably reach out to a pastor, rabbi, or imam for guidance, and in response to your concerns, you are encouraged to deepen your expression of devotion and your commitment to your family and faith community. I'm told that for the faithful, this sort of guidance offers at least a "quantum of solace," even if one still must "render unto Caesar" and/or "bow before Mammon." But if you belong to the PMC or if you find your direction rather osmotically, via popular culture and advertising messages, then it's likely that you frame your problem in spiritual terms, and seek help with self-help, via offerings available in the spiritual/wellness marketplace. What does one find there? Almost without exception, if one cares to look closely enough, one finds a rather improbable amalgam, a strange stew of loosely combined elements. William Davies says that "the psychology of motivation blends into the physiology of health, drawing insights from sports coaches and nutritionists, to which is added a cocktail of neuroscience and Buddhist meditation. Various notions of fitness, happiness, positivity, and success blend into one another with little explanation of how or why."[6]

In a similar vein, Purser has called this sort of self-help material spiritual practice "junk food," and has given it the derisive label "McMindfulness."[7] He takes a dim view of its breezy claim to have captured the essence of Buddhism without the mumbo jumbo of beliefs, rituals, institutions, and cultural baggage,[8] because everything important is now "based on the latest neuroscience."[9] And yet, one must assume that the majority of those who consume this motivational self-help literature find it to be essentially coherent. What then is the underlying (but otherwise invisible) substrate that supports all these disparate elements, what Nicolas Rose calls this "bricolage"?[10] For critics such as Davies (*The Happiness Industry*), Purser (*McMindfulness*), Carrette and King (*Selling Spirituality*), and Ehrenreich (*Natural Causes*), the essential connective tissue is *nothing other than capitalist spirituality.*[11] What brings together "sportsmen, business gurus, and statisticians, to extend lessons from sport into politics, from warfare into business strategy, and from life-coaching into schools," Davies says, is a "science of winning to entrench neoliberal competitiveness as the defining culture of business, cities, schools, and nations."[12]

The Meaning of Capitalist Spirituality

But what precisely is meant by the term "capitalist spirituality"? In *Selling Spirituality: The Silent Takeover of Religion*, Jeremy Carrette and Richard King explain that this term refers to a self-

6 William Davies, *The Happiness Industry: How the Government and Big Business Sold Us Well-Being* (London: Verso, 2015), 112.
7 Purser, *McMindfulness*, 15.
8 Ibid., 14.
9 Ibid., 13.
10 Nikolas Rose, *Governing the Soul: The Shaping of the Private Self* (London: Free Association Books, 1999), 265.
11 The term was introduced by Purser, *McMindfulness*, 18.
12 Davies, *The Happiness Industry*, 141.

focused, individual human potential orientation, where we find "productivity, work-efficiency, and accumulation instead of an emphasis on self-sacrifice, the disciplining of desire, and recognition of community."[13] Capitalist spirituality thus devolves, as Purser further explains, "upon the notion of freedom embraced by neoliberal *homo economicus,* "the idea that we must maximize our welfare and happiness by managing our internal resources in a way that increases our human capital." Mindfulness "is capitalist spirituality attuned to maintaining the neoliberal self."[14]

If we then ask what this is really all about, that is, what this specific, historically conditioned notion of the self is actually for, and why it must be maintained, the answer these writers give is more or less univocal: Capitalist spirituality is designed to help people to better "adjust" to their present working conditions, to accept them as a given, as a way to address the growing problem of workforce disengagement. Where mental labor is a commodity, "managing emotions generates surplus value equivalent to the acquisition of capital," Purser points out.[15] Davies says that "unions may be weakened or crushed, but managers must deal with employees that are absent, unmotivated, or suffering from mental health problems." Since resistance manifests first and foremost as absenteeism, sickness, and presentism, burnout must be addressed in order for employers to maintain profits. Disengagement thus calls forth new ways of "intervening in the minds, bodies, and behavior of the workforce"; instead of social and economic reforms, we get "'the hard science of workplace happiness.'"[16]

In a similar vein, Carrette and King add that capitalist spirituality offers a "sedative of inner explanation," one that satisfies capitalism's need to stabilize the self in a way that is accommodationist and supports manufactured consent, thus meeting the demands of the corporate sector for a compliant workforce. The

13 Jeremy Carrette and Richard King, *Selling Spirituality: The Silent Takeover of Religion* (London: Routledge, 2005), 23.

14 Purser, *McMindfulness,* 29.

15 Ibid., 44.

16 Davies, *The Happiness Industry,* 108–9.

new gospel of psychological individualism is thus everywhere promoted in order to develop resiliency for productivity under stressful and demoralizing conditions, and to reinforce responsibilization (individuals are solely responsible for their own suffering). Well-being, once it is seen as the product of individual effort, reframes problems as outcomes of choices rather than socioeconomic conditions.[17] In relation to the workplace, Davies says that "instead of dialogue and empowerment, we get performance management and healthcare fused into a science of well-being and self-optimization."[18]

Further, according to Carrette and King, the very term "spirituality" has now thus become "the brand label for the search for meaning, values, transcendence, hope, and connectedness in advanced capitalist societies."[19] Capitalist spirituality is in fact nothing other than this new "spirit of capitalism" in the Weberian sense. And Nicole Aschoff says, "If you acquire enough cultural capital (skills, education) and social capital (connections, access to networks), you will be able to translate that capital into economic capital (cash money) and happiness." The "work of a life" for the self so conceived, is to clear and otherwise remove any and all impediments, found within oneself, to realizing this "virtuous circle."[20]

But even with these troubling connections out on the table, can there really be anything to gain by taking a firm stand against the pursuit of happiness? Putting aside the matter of the necessary personality traits (curmudgeon, iconoclast, crank), the question is a serious one. Davies actually asks himself this question in the introduction to *The Happiness Industry,* and not long after asking it, provides a qualified answer in chapter 1, if only between the lines: one can be against happiness, he indicates, if it turns out that happiness management, rather than being offered as a kind of resolution of a moral and philo-

17 Carrette and King, *Selling Spirituality,* 62.
18 Davies, *The Happiness Industry,* 136.
19 Ibid., 32.
20 Nicole Aschoff, *The New Prophets of Capital* (London: Verso, 2015), 93–94.

sophical debate, is actually a way of silencing it.[21] In this chapter and chapter 13, I explore this question and related concerns by sketching the ideas of a group of authors who dare, from a critical sociopolitical perspective, to question the value of our corporate-sponsored search for mindfulness-wellness-happiness.

Mindfulness as a Neoliberal "Technology of the Self"

In *McMindfulness,* Purser sets his critical sights upon the mindfulness-based stress-reduction movement (MBSR) launched by Jon Kabat-Zinn. Purser does not deny that there are useful dimensions of mindfulness practice for the reduction of stress, chronic anxiety, and the general alleviation of emotional suffering. MBSR and Kabat-Zinn end up in Purser's crosshairs, he says, mainly because MBSR has allowed itself to become complicit with the wholesale pathologization, privatization, and depoliticization of stress: "Guided by a therapeutic ethos aimed at enhancing mental and emotional resilience, MBSR endorses neoliberal assumptions that everyone is free to choose their responses, manage negative emotions, and flourish through various modes of self-care."[22] The problem with this, Purser says, is that where the burden of managing stress is completely shifted to the individual, the name of the game becomes self-optimization. I want to reduce *my* stress. I want to enhance *my* concentration.[23] But stress, he counters, also has societal causes, and we urgently need to find ways to address the causes of our collective suffering.[24]

Once Buddhist mindfulness is stripped of its cultural teachings (minor details such as overcoming attachment to a false sense of self, striving for universal compassion, etc.), it becomes only technique, merely concentration training. In so doing, Purser says, it also becomes void of moral compass or ethical

21 Davies, *The Happiness Industry,* 38.

22 Purser, *McMindfulness,* 11.

23 Ibid., 11–12.

24 Ibid., 9.

commitments, and as such unmoored from the common good. In assuming that ethical behavior will somehow arise naturally from practice, MBSR actually leaves the question of the good firmly anchored in the ethos of the market. Where mindfulness is commodified, it becomes "McMindfulness," or spiritual junk food. Effectively fetishized, mindfulness becomes just another link in the chain of commodities that includes the neoliberal self that functions as a human capital.

Purser's major point is just this: where mindfulness practice is packaged as something more ambitious than just stress management, as a way to help people cope, it must be unmasked as simply a new form of capitalist spirituality.[25] Purser's use of this term is decisive, because the characterization of mindfulness as capitalist spirituality provides him with an opening onto Foucault's famous fourfold conception of technology (technologies of production, technologies of sign systems, technologies of power, technologies of the self).[26] It thus allows Purser to identify this sort of mindfulness as what Foucault calls "a form of governmentality," as comprising a set of practices (technologies for the care of the self) that ultimately must be seen to resolve to technologies of power/domination.[27]

The problem with mindfulness-as-commodity is not just that it's spiritual junk food. The problem is that mindfulness, as complicit with the privatization of stress, depoliticizes it, and helps to harness the psyche as a productive force under neoliberal social and economic conditions. In so doing, it stands revealed as part of the hegemonic ideology of neoliberal capitalism. Purser says that mindfulness functions as a neoliberal technology of the self, therefore, in demanding that each individual must act entrepreneurially, and develop skills to actively manage their self-care in order to remain employable, as a condition for

25 Ibid., 18. "Mindfulness is the latest iteration of capitalist spirituality whose lineage goes back to the privatization of religion in Western societies."

26 Michel Foucault, "Technologies of the Self," in *Technologies of the Self: A Seminar with Michel Foucault,* eds. Luther H. Martin, Huck Gutman, and Patrick H. Hutton (Amherst: University of Massachusetts Press, 1988), 18.

27 Purser, *McMindfulness,* 30.

thriving.[28] It encourages individuals to make a project of their own identities, to constantly monitor their personal conduct, and to embrace neuroplasticity's dream of unfettered agency. As part of an ongoing effort to optimize oneself through personal life hacks, mindfulness-as-capitalist-spirituality serves as a major conduit by which neoliberal disciplinary power reaches into people's psyches to create sought-after subjectivation effects (for an example, Purser points to the wellness-related funding priorities of the right-wing Templeton Foundation).[29]

Ehrenreich and the "Epidemic of Wellness"

But perhaps we still need a less theoretical *casus belli* for being against mindfulness/wellness/happiness. To this end, it may be helpful to take a half step back and consider Barbara Ehrenreich's *Natural Causes* (2018), which offers more of an organic critique of the wellness industry. The book defies easy description, but it's at least fair to characterize it as a cancer survivor's rather somber, late middle-age reflection on successful aging, and on agency in relation to life and mortality. For our purposes here, what matters most is its curmudgeonly and effective assertion of a compelling set of grounds for being against wellness/happiness. Ehrenreich's various arguments throughout the book are all inscribed in the space of what she considers to be a fundamental conflict of interpretations. On the one hand, there is the neuroplasticity concept, by which "contemplative neuroscience" supports all manner of projects of "personal control over your body and mind." On the other hand, there is an emerging scientific case for a view of the body as a site of ongoing conflict at the cellular level, where life processes play themselves out through disharmony and even self-sabotage.[30]

Calling the neuroplasticity concept into question, Ehrenreich goes on to describe what she refers to as the "societal epi-

28 Ibid., 30–31.

29 Ibid., 33.

30 Barbara Ehrenreich, *Natural Causes* (New York: Twelve, 2018), xiii–xv.

demic of wellness," saying that it is "acted out through medical care, lifestyle adjustments [...] and a nebulous but ever-growing wellness industry that embraces both body and mind."[31] She does not deny that we would all like to live longer and healthier lives, but she still thinks that these "forms of intervention invite questions about the limits of human control."[32] The real question, she says, is how much of our lives should be devoted to it, given the relative costs, tradeoffs, and diminishing returns of doing so. With Gilbert Welch's *Over-Diagnosed: Making People Sick in the Pursuit of Health* (2011) as a touchstone, Ehrenreich goes on, in the opening chapters, to explain how she decided to largely abandon preventative medical care in middle age, having decided that she had arrived at an age where it was not inappropriate to die, all other things being equal. The time remaining to her is "too precious to spend in windowless waiting rooms and under the cold scrutiny of machines. Being old enough to die is an achievement, not a defeat, and the freedom it brings is worth celebrating."[33] Ehrenreich's personal courage and independence is on display in this section of the book, so there is much to find admirable in it, but her indifference to health screenings, *even where heredity indicates heightened risk,* does seem somewhat reckless. How then, do we account for the prevalence of so much apparently questionable preventative medicine? Her answer is that "the compulsive urge to test and screen and monitor is profit,"[34] and "a cynic might conclude that preventative medicine exists to transform people into raw material for a profit-hungry medical industrial complex."[35]

Along with this account of "a pound of prevention for a pinch of cure," Ehrenreich goes on to offer criticisms of medical procedures that amount to nothing more than rituals, and charts how the medical establishment, in recent years, came to accept much of alternative medicine as complementary. She says that

---

31 Ibid., xiv.

32 Ibid.

33 Ibid., 13.

34 Ibid., 9.

35 Ibid., 4.

the rise of the new integrative/holistic medicine is also reflective of a larger trend, the project of the self in the late twentieth century, which also includes the surge of interest in physical fitness. Beneath these workout/fitness imperatives, Ehrenreich sees Christopher Lasch's "culture of narcissism." All the myriad ways of getting healthy and happy are actually reflective of a broader "withdrawal into individual concerns" on the part of elites and the PMC, who have taken up the challenge of the project of *themselves*.[36]

It's important to mention here, along with Aschoff (*The New Prophets of Capital*), that this project could not have succeeded to such a great extent without an elite group of gurus, people such as Oprah Winfrey, whom Aschoff calls "the storytellers of capitalism." By emphasizing individual strategies for success, "Oprah and the other prophets downplay the real structures of power and inequality in our society,"[37] papering over the ongoing crises of capital by promulgating a configuration of the self that is compatible with the world as it is. Through their charisma and inspirational stories, they shift the burden to solutions within the existing economic and social logic, because, as we are supposed to recognize, cultural and social capital are actually just there for the taking, assuming one has the necessary pluck, passion, and persistence.[38] Per Ehrenreich, all of this tracks with the manner in which the political radicalism of the late 1960s is transformed into Silicon Valley tech entrepreneurialism. Tech solutionism innovates all manner of "self-hacks," which then spreads "it's deranged syndrome of inattentiveness and self-involvement to everyone else" through Silicon Valley's corporate culture and products.[39]

36 Ibid., 54.
37 Aschoff, *New Prophets of Capital*, 14.
38 Ibid., 104.
39 Ehrenreich, *Natural Causes*, 76.

Disciplining the Body, Controlling the Mind

Ehrenreich acknowledges the increasing intensity with which the body must be trained and disciplined, and put to evermore daunting tests, and evaluated by the conscious mind in contemporary society. But why "should the mind want to subdue the body, day after day?"[40] She says that this turn to self-optimization is also explicable in terms of the unfolding story of deindustrialization and diminishing expectations taking place at the same time—if you can't change the world, or even chart your own career, she writes, at least you could "control your own body." For the PMC, there is an even darker side, however: "There is a need to counter the widespread suspicion that if you can't control your own body, then you're not fit in any sense to control anyone else [...] and in their work lives[....] This is what gym-goers do."[41] Naturally, these subtle imperatives also dovetail nicely with the messages of employee wellness programs mandated to try to reduce employer health insurance costs with prevention and responsibilization.

On the mindfulness front, Ehrenreich identifies its origins in the perverse tech solutionist "solution" to what turns out to be the pathological effects of *solutionism* itself.[42] Something had to be done "to counter the addiction to devices—something that in no way threatened the billionaires."[43] So when Kabat-Zinn extracted the secularized core of Buddhism and called it "mindfulness," she writes, it provided the basis for the needed "neural hack," and thereby transformed the masters of the universe "from the villains in the inattentiveness epidemic into the putative saviors."[44] But Ehrenreich's most serious issue with mindfulness turns out to be the claim that it is "based firmly on science."[45] She points to a 2014 analysis of major studies

40 Ibid., 62.
41 Ibid.
42 Ibid., 77.
43 Ibid., 82.
44 Ibid., 83.
45 Ibid., 85.

that showed that "meditation programs are neither more nor less effective at treating stress symptoms than other interventions," and she suggests that the same results can be had by solving an interesting math problem or having a glass of wine with friends.[46] Also, she says there is an almost complete lack of evidence for the usefulness of mindfulness apps. Why then are these things largely ignored? Ehrenreich says it is "because of the allure of the neuroplasticity concept," which she says actually rests upon a powerful analogy operating in our culture, that of "the mind as muscle," and not upon science. The mindfulness industry, relying on the concept of wellness from holistic/integrative medicine, says that the mind can be controlled in much the same way as the body, through disciplined exercise, and "possibly conducted in a special place, like a corporate meditation room."[47]

As with her rejection of preventative medicine, Ehrenreich's dismissal of neuroplasticity appears to be something of a mixed bag. As a long-distance runner for many years, I have personal experience of the essential entwinement of physical training with learned mental discipline, and it seems pretty clear that martial arts traditions going back thousands of years cannot be easily disassociated from this sort of mind/body "spiritual training." What needs to be understood here is that Ehrenreich is reacting to how these notions have become popular articles of faith, which then come to have a certain currency in a broader social-political economy of capitalist hegemony. Whenever mindfulness is characterized predominantly as a form of fitness training, therefore, and we say we are performing "bio hacks" upon our own brains, presumably in order to control our minds, she is right to ask, "Who is the we who is doing the controlling?"[48]

Ehrenreich asks this question in two related but distinct senses. The first is at the level of the individual: What does it

46 Ibid., 87.
47 Ibid., 88.
48 Ibid., 181.

really mean to say that "we" hack our own brains? If we really mean that the brain is just a muscle, then who is the self that we are, if we are not our brains or our minds? And what, if anything, could be the nature of this higher-level agency? The implications of how we answer or don't answer this are potentially profound. The second sense of her question, "Who is doing the controlling?" closely parallels what we find in Purser and also Carrette and King. Ehrenreich is here also asking about subjectivation/subjection, that is, the way that mindfulness-as-capitalist-spirituality serves as a major conduit for neoliberal disciplinary power. The question, "Who is doing the controlling?" thus also concerns the commodification of the self, and how our most prominent "technologies of the self" also turn out in the end to be (neoliberal capitalist) technologies of domination.

Three Orders of Human Suffering

In this chapter, I have tried to step through what Purser identifies (following Kabat-Zinn) as the "ambiguities of healing,"[49] because the dominant pattern of refusing work-as-we-know-it today is found in the individual search for self-optimization, for healing and recovery in the face of widespread work-related, debilitating illnesses and conditions. Even in meditating, running, getting therapy, doing EMDR, spending more time in the garden, unplugging from the internet, and putting down my phone, I have also harbored gnawing doubts about whether the clear benefits obtained from these things really amount to anything having to do with political projects of resistance and refusal. The problem with both mindfulness and wellness programs, Purser explains, is that mindfulness only offers us palliative care for what he calls "first order suffering," things such as the distress that comes from confronting old age and death, chronic pain, psychological conflicts, relationship problems, and personal experiences of loss. This, of course, is far from trivial. But mindfulness needs to have its ambitions curbed and

49 Purser, *McMindfulness*, 244.

its wings clipped, as Kant would say, precisely because it does nothing to address second-order suffering (wars, genocide, social injustice, political oppression). It also doesn't address the amorphous, pervasive, and systemic third-order suffering that he says is caused by neoliberal hegemony (obscure power relations, class interests, social inequities, etc.).[50] Quite to the contrary, because mindfulness/wellness programs are recommended by all manner of elites and are essentially forms of capitalist spirituality, mindfulness/wellness programs, consciously or not, have become complicit with this third-order suffering.

On Resisting Capitalist Spirituality

What, then, can be the recommended prescriptions? There needs to be a way to avoid an unacceptable either/or, one where our choices are either to remain complicit with things that make us sick (such as neoliberal wage labor and consumer culture) or to withdraw instead into some personal health/wellness project, centering our life on goals of self-optimization. As it turns out, Purser, Carrette and King, and Ehrenreich converge to some extent in seeking to support alternative models of spirituality, ones that register the various lessons of social, community, and positive psychology. Purser writes that "if mindfulness were to be liberated from its neoliberal shackles[51] it could lead to the widespread realization that the self is a construction that can foster delusional self-understanding. He champions a return to explicitly Buddhist goals, such as realizing *pratitya-samutpada* ("the interconnectedness of all things").[52] In the individual self of mindful healing and recovery, he finds a "false understanding of universal dharma," as if everyone, unique in their own way, could and should see themselves as a generic (privileged, white) individual living outside of group socialization.[53] Instead, he

50 Ibid., 255.
51 Ibid., 251.
52 Ibid., 249.
53 Ibid., 256.

says that we need to build solidarity out of the ruins of McMindfulness, and he calls for a new social or civic mindfulness, without experts or gurus, that pursues a regenerative set of aims to try to repair community bonds through community action. He says that this form of mindfulness would resemble liberation theology.[54]

Similarly, Carrette and King say that resistance to the commodification of human life itself is to be found through creation and fostering of a solidaristic umbrella movement with loosely coupled and complementary elements, such as those found in the "Seattle Consensus," for example, Zapatistas, liberation theology, the Chipko and Swadhyaya movements, plus a dash of Thich Nhat Hanh for good measure.[55] For her part, Ehrenreich says that part of what it means to find a way out of our dilemma is to "confront the monstrous self that occludes our vision,"[56] and she has various things to say about ego dissolution, and the stoic consolations of "dying in a living universe," one "shot through with non-human agency."[57] These suggestions, on the whole, seem to be sensible ones. Nonetheless, "if wishes were horses," so the old saying goes, "beggars would ride." Most of us tend to recognize that things are the way that they are today not because we are somehow lacking in the requisite treasure trove of cultural wisdom. Rather, things are the way they are because we are in the grip of the seemingly inexorable economic and cultural logic of advanced capitalism, and this social order is hegemonically maintained by its major stakeholders.

To their credit, Purser, Carrette and King, and Ehrenreich each actively seeks to resist the seducements of forms of capitalist spirituality that offer healing/recovery and wellness specifically tailored for the optimization of a commodified self. They recognize that these interventions are palliative care offered in a context where capitalist society as such is disappearing, along

54 Ibid., 259–60.
55 Carrette and King, *Selling Spirituality,* 178–80.
56 Ehrenreich, *Natural Causes,* 203.
57 Ibid., 208.

with traditional wage labor benefits and protections, and where the remaining labor is increasingly disengaged and suffering from work-related illnesses. Each of them also has suggestions to make programs of mindfulness and wellness more able to resist being co-opted to meet the needs of capital, and thus more conducive to genuine, autonomous thriving.

It must be admitted, however, that nothing offered here really points the way to some purported mechanism of historical agency that could support a politics of refusal in relation to work and work-related illnesses. But as Carrette and King recognize, the ideology of privatization—the privatization of religion, spirituality, stress, and wellness—presents today's social and political projects of freedom with a new and particularly insidious challenge. Privatization "breaks the social self and conceals [. . .] the collective manipulation of isolated individuals in the language of free will and choice."[58] Purser also echoes this point. We are told "that if we practice mindfulness and get our individual lives in order, we can be happy and secure." In doing so, he adds, "it implies that all these concrete good things will follow." Where mindfulness becomes the subject of inflated promises and fetishized, it is a "cruel optimism." The cruelty lies in "supporting the status quo while using the language of transformation."[59] Under such conditions, where even our instincts for freedom and our striving have been essentially commodified and captured by the market, the value in defetishizing theory itself, as a kind of resistance, should not be completely discounted.

58 Carrette and King, *Selling Spirituality,* 80.

59 Purser, *McMindfulness,* 44–45.

13

Capitalist Spirituality and Behavioral Neuroscience

> Psychology is very often how societies avoid looking in the mirror.
>
> —William Davies, *The Happiness Industry*

Neuroscience in Contemporary Culture

I am driving on the freeway and listening to classical music on the radio. The station interrupts the playlist to do its standard membership pitch. They refer to the station as "an island of sanity in an otherwise hectic day." I'm told I should join because this music has the power to "transport me to another place" and represents "an escape from the troubles of the workaday world." At one level, I really don't have a big problem with this. After all, music soothes the savage beast. But it's also true that large parts of the orchestral repertoire (which are also played on my radio station) do not have this effect at all. Listening to a twelve-tone composition by Alban Berg or an opera by Phillip Glass doesn't exactly evoke vacations on a tropical island paradise (okay, maybe *Águas da Amazônia*). Why should serious music be sold as a source of momentary bliss, in much the same way that marketers often sell candy bars or cigarettes? Not that long ago, it was commonplace to hear people refer to serious music as a "universal language," something that overcomes our differences and thus speaks to the human condition. How is it that we've gone from saying this sort of thing to the suggestion that music has value because it functions as some sort of a brain hack?

If you think that this is just a random observation that doesn't reflect a broader change in our culture, consider also the case of the famous soprano Renée Fleming. Recently, Fleming has been crisscrossing the country giving a series of lectures — not on musicology or master classes on vocal technique or stagecraft, as one might expect. Rather, Fleming is "spearheading" (whatever that means) a collaboration between the National Institutes of Health (NIH) and the National Endowment for the Arts (NEA) to bring attention to scientific research at the intersection of music, health, and neuroscience, an effort that has yielded Fleming and her partners a $20 million grant from NIH.[1]

As a roving ambassador, Fleming is quite passionate about the importance of music and the other performing arts to our society. But this interest in what the granting world calls "broader impacts" notwithstanding, her focus here is upon "what music can teach us about the brain itself." She writes on her project webpage that "music engages many neural regions at once, and evidence suggests that it can shape and even alter our brains." Why, we must ask (other than the grant money), is Fleming so interested in what music can tell us about our brains? For example, do we really need neuroscience research to justify our calls for increased funding for the arts? What is really going on here, when everything must be backed by the latest neuroscience? Fleming's webpage goes on to add that all of this research is being done in the service of the healing potential of music therapy in a range of healthcare settings, including those that pertain to "creative aging, childhood development,

1 National Institutes of Health (NIH) News Release, "NIH Awards $20 Million over Five Years to Bring Together Music Therapy and Neuroscience," *NIH*, September 19, 2019, https://www.nih.gov/news-events/news-releases/nih-awards-20-million-over-five-years-bring-together-music-therapy-neuroscience.

and community wellness." But can the potential benefits to which Fleming points really explain why this brain research is such a high-priority area for government research grants? After all, actual social spending in these areas has been chronically underfunded by the US government for decades. Even if this sort of basic research might lead to advances that could help people in therapeutic ways, there can also be little doubt that the high level of funding for it reflects what the world of government research calls "dual-use applications."

Perhaps it is indeed the case that we, as individuals, can find some measure of empowerment by intentionally hacking our own brains with sublime music and with various other things. Instead of taking a break and having a KitKat bar, maybe in the future (if it can be monetized) I will be encouraged by advertisers to listen to an overture or a prelude. It may even be true that as a society we will also learn how to hack the brains of those recovering from traumatic head injuries, sharpen the minds of those with dementia, or make small children better prepared for school. But it is also just as likely that this basic research will lead to other applications—to soldiers able to stay awake for longer stretches, fighter pilots or drone operators more able to focus on complex instrument panels, and corporations more able to wring greater productivity out of disengaged or resistant employees.

Capitalist Spirituality and Neuroscience Research

In chapter 12, I set about to call into question the value of our corporate-sponsored search for mindfulness-wellness-happiness. The primary focus there was on mindfulness training, and the theorists I showcased (Ronald Purser, William Davies, Jeremy Carrette and Richard King, and Barbara Ehrenreich) were all in strong agreement about how stress and stress-related illness have become privatized and depoliticized in relation to the commodified self of neoliberal capitalism. Based on the mindfulness-related focus of chapter 12, if one were to ask how this capitalist spirituality came about, we might agree with Carrette and King (*Selling Spirituality*), that the major culprit behind the privatization and depoliticization of stress turns out to be the takeover of religion by capitalist ideologies across two distinct phases of *the privatization of religion.*[2] First, there was the individualization of religion, they say, which happened as part of the Enlightenment process of secularization, and which relegated religion to the private sphere. Then there is the commodification of religion that occurs in the late twentieth century, where the "cultural assets" of religious traditions are being plundered for purposes of consumption and corporate gain and rebranded as spirituality.

But Carrette and King's account of the descent of contemporary capitalist spirituality, which is conducted on the terrain of the psychology of religion, can't cover the entirety of the complex stew of mindfulness-wellness-happiness imperatives and projects that we confront today. For example, the privatization of religion narrative, though useful for understanding the descent of mindfulness, doesn't get us very far when it comes to understanding the relationship between capitalist spirituality and behavioral neuroscience. By contrast, William Davies's genealogy of modern happiness management in *The Happiness Industry* charts a course from early modern utilitarianism, to the subjectification of value and the privatization of utility as seen in neoclassical economics, to the apotheosis of privatized utility under conditions of neoliberalism. It can be somewhat difficult to follow at times. One really has to strain against our own pervasive capitalist realism in order to grasp the significance of these major distinctions. But I've become convinced that Davies's story of the "privatization of utility" in the modern age, as the condition for understanding projects of happiness management, is a serious candidate for being the master narrative for contextualizing capitalist spirituality in general, one that also encompasses "the privatization of religion," as a more

2 Jeremy Carrette and Richard King, *Selling Spirituality: The Silent Takeover of Religion* (New York: Routledge, 2005), 13–16.

regional account of how the psychology of religion is transformed by the commodified self of neoliberal capitalism.

In this chapter, I now turn to the role of neuroscience in relation to capitalist spirituality, and, following Davies, I want to situate it in relation to the long-standing, modern project of societal happiness management. From the viewpoint of this chapter, the basic questions that hover over both the mindfulness part and this part on neuroscience and happiness management are as follows: How is it that we have all become "human capitals" who are looking to hack our own brains in order to optimize ourselves in the interest of increased happiness? And how is it that so many of us have become stakeholders in organized (corporate, governmental) efforts to develop programs of happiness management, backed by the latest behavioral neuroscience research?

The Aims of Big Money Neuroscience Research

Before turning to Davies's arguments, it is worth noting here that uneasiness about the role of neuroscience research in our culture is not limited merely to classical music lovers, such as I. A sense of disquiet about the aims of contemporary neuroscience has also made it into the pages of the *New York Times.* In his farewell to the mental health/biosciences-behavior beat, Benedict Carey offers up a remarkable summation of his nearly two-decade career as a *New York Times* columnist.[3] For years, Carey writes, "I covered psychiatry, psychology, brain biology, and big data social science, as if they were somehow related." Apparently caught up in the hype, he says that he had hoped "to cover something big, something that would shake up our understanding of mental health problems." At a minimum, "I expected research that would help people in distress improve their lives." "But during my tenure, the science informing men-

3 Benedict Carey, "Science Plays the Long Game: But People Have Mental Health Issues Now," *The New York Times,* April 1, 2021, https://www.nytimes.com/2021/04/01/health/mental-health-treatments.html.

tal health care did not proceed smoothly along any trajectory," and despite attracting enormous talent, and making significant discoveries, "almost every measure of our collective mental health — suicide rate, anxiety, depression, addiction — went in the wrong direction." In short, the science "did little to improve the lives of the millions living with persistent mental distress."

Carey thinks that this disappointing outcome has at least something to do with the influence of the great swells of money continually washing over biopharmaceutical research, making it "virtually impossible to interpret psychiatric drug studies" because much of what is produced amounts to "drug ads dressed up as research." As for government-sponsored research, he says that he had hoped to find easier answers to such questions as, "Could this work potentially be useful to someone, at some point in their lifetime?" But here too, despite uncontestable advances in the tools and technical understanding of brain biology, the answer was generally no. Government agencies "continue to double down, sinking enormous sums of taxpayer money into biological research to try to find a neural signature or blood test for psychiatric diagnoses that could, maybe, one day in the future, be useful — all while people are in crisis now."

Nonetheless, Carey looks at the $300 million NIH Brain Imaging Study (10,000 children, with too many variables of development and experience) and the $50 million project to understand neural development (comprising myriad, cascading, and random processes) and still regards them as "well-intentioned." For Carey, the direction and shape of brain and behavior research priorities over the last couple of decades clearly reflect overfunding, a misdirected lack of urgency, and some measure of self-dealing. He even goes so far as to characterize neuroscience research as "gravy train science," as being on "fishing expeditions" and as throwing "Hail Mary passes." And yet, he still doesn't really want to question the overarching aims of neuroscience per se, and won't challenge the unreflective faith that led him to cover "psychiatry, psychology, brain biology, and big data social science, as if they were all somehow related." He ends his farewell with the statement that contemporary brain and behavioral science funding is in need of serious review, a process that should result in cuts, with spending redirected toward things that are relevant to people's lives. For this to happen, he says, "researchers need to speak out and funders need to listen" about the need for treatment, supports, and innovations "that could be implemented in the near future."

What sense should we make of this? The ease with which we now recognize a compelling need to hack our own brains so that we can be okay (as individuals, and collectively, as a matter of health policy) belies the fact that today's neuroscience research is taking place against a backdrop of what I am describing as "capitalist spirituality." By this I mean a complex bricolage of mindfulness/wellness/happiness projects and imperatives that have now permeated our culture and that take the painful contradictions of capitalism as simply a given, thereby aligning with the objectives of the elite, capitalist class.

I would like to suggest that this cultural context also helps to explain why a brain and behavior beat columnist would admit to having covered advances in various research disciplines for almost two decades "as if they were all somehow related," apparently without a very clear understanding of how or why. Like many of us, Carey has trouble seeing the darker side of the neuroscience of happiness management. He doesn't recognize how such a massive commitment of research spending might be considered worthwhile by its sponsors on what are essentially behaviorist grounds, independent of the relatively thin track record of significant therapeutic advances being deployed in clinical practice to improve people's lives.

Neuroscience and the History of Happiness Management

In the preface to *The Happiness Industry,* Davies expresses his own doubts and concerns about the scope and direction of contemporary neuroscience research. Over the last decade, global elites have become increasingly preoccupied with "mindfulness, re-wiring the brain, and devices for monitoring well-being."[4] Davies charts the rise of this phenomenon to sometime between the Davos Economic Forum of 2008, where everyone was fixated on global economic recovery from the crash, and the forum of 2014, where everyone was obsessed instead with the latest wellness apps. He says that this change, which correlates quite well with the neoliberal abandonment of responsibility for the putative society of capitalism, reflects a collective resolve on the part of elites to paper over major structural contradictions, having decided that the future success of capitalism now depends "on our ability to combat stress and misery" and "put relaxation, happiness, and wellness in their place."[5] Much of contemporary neuroscience research (both privately and publicly funded), he thinks, is designed to generate rapid advances in support of this agenda: "Neuroscientists identify how happiness and unhappiness are physically inscribed in the brain," and they seek out "neural explanations" for why certain things improve our well-being.[6] And technological monitoring and data science, he adds, accumulate statistical evidence, feeding the growing field of "happiness economics" that is increasingly leveraging all this new data.

As happiness studies become more interdisciplinary, Davies says, "claims about minds, brains, bodies, and economic activity" morph into one another without much attention to the philosophical problems involved.[7] Instead, "happiness science presents itself as a hard science of subjective affect,"[8] and under the banner of positive psychology, a "single index of general human optimization looms into view."[9] But what if it is the case that the emerging science of happiness today turns out to be "simply

4 William Davies, *The Happiness Industry: How the Government and Big Business Sold Us Well-Being* (London: Verso, 2015), 2–3.
5 Ibid., 4.
6 Ibid.
7 Ibid., 5.
8 Ibid., 6.
9 Ibid., 5.

the latest iteration of an ongoing project?"[10] What if this project is none other than "happiness management as an alternative to politics" that has been asserted repeatedly since the birth of the modern age? To make this argument, Davies goes on to survey the troubling history of happiness management, touching on many of the figures (both major and minor) implicated in the complex entanglement of psychology and economics with capitalism in order to ferret out its intriguing modern genealogy.

Benthamite Roots of the Neuroscience of Happiness

For those who have spent any significant time sitting in classes on modern moral philosophy (we are legion!), the immediate tendency, when invoking Jeremy Bentham, is to try to perform the hedonistic calculus, and to then consider arguments for and against its coherence, its sufficiency, and its practicality. To recognize what Davies is driving at with Bentham, however, one has to leave behind this set of practical, "philosophy as a way of life" assumptions. Davies's Bentham is first and foremost a political theorist, offering up a novel psychological theory of politics and statecraft. Per Bentham, the subject of politics is not abstruse philosophical problems, such as justice or natural rights, something he famously considered "nonsense upon stilts." Politics should instead be concerned with the question of happiness.[11]

Per Davies, Bentham's politics turns psychological when it is framed as the question of how we should "divert human activity toward the greatest happiness of all."[12] As a psychological political theory, therefore, it is thus also statecraft, because it's concerned with intervention, using both carrots and sticks, to alter the psychological calculation of individuals, all other things being equal. Such a project, Davies explains, immediately opens up a whole new horizon, because unless utility

10 Ibid., 7.
11 Ibid., 17–18.
12 Ibid., 19.

could somehow be grasped by measurement,[13] "unless a set of instruments, techniques, and methods could be designed,"[14] this ambition to recast politics and law could not be realized. As it turns out, two proxy answers to the question, "How shall we measure the intensity of the pleasant and the unpleasant?" are offered by Bentham. Taken together they opened up "vast zones of enquiry" later to be explored by psychologists, economists, and neuroscientists, along with marketers, human resources experts, and policymakers, among others.[15]

The two happiness proxies that Bentham identifies are human pulse rate (i.e., body measurements) and *money* (we can measure quanta of utility in the rational choices of buyers and consumers). In the interest of happiness management, Davies says, there is a direct line of descent from early ideas about body measurements to contemporary neuroscience, one that consummates a reduction of psychological to biological processes.[16] As for the second proxy, the idea that "money might have some privileged relationship to our inner experience" sets the stage for "the entanglement of psychological research and capitalism" that plays itself out across the nineteenth and twentieth centuries.[17] In both of these vectors, Davies sees a drive to largely bypass language/speech as a medium of representations about people's inner states. Whether the technology involves money and prices or measurements targeted at the human body, what Bentham unleashed is extended by sciences to the point where we have largely arrived today at the society of bodies, a society in which "experts and authorities are able to divine what is good for us without our voices being heard."[18] Having set this initial Benthamite baseline, *The Happiness Industry* then unfolds by following the intertwined, uneven, and sometimes subterranean

13 Ibid., 24.
14 Ibid., 14.
15 Ibid., 24.
16 Ibid., 20.
17 Ibid., 25.
18 Ibid., 33.

parallel progress of these two approaches to happiness management since the late nineteenth century.

Neoclassical Economics and the Subjectification of Value

Since the scientific and technical advances necessary for the "direct measurement of subjective affect" don't actually appear until the late twentieth century, the next major moment in the history of happiness management that Davies explores has to do with the money side of this equation, and the rapid entanglement of economics and psychology under mature, nineteenth-century capitalism. Initially, Bentham's utilitarian "psychological politics" has little or no connection with economics (i.e., the political economy of Smith, Ricardo, Malthus, and Mill). The classical economists "had no discernable concern with psychological questions of feelings or happiness."[19]

Where these so-called worldly philosophers were generally concerned with the question of how to increase the wealth of nations, the analysis was largely a macroeconomic one, concerned with productive industrial capacity, the division of labor, land ownership, the meaning of productive versus unproductive (i.e., critique of monopoly rents), and the reinvestment of surplus profits, among other indicators. The classical economists generally sought to bolster the prestige of industrial capitalism, and to criticize aristocratic landowners with their unproductive, unearned income, and to make a case for reinvestment, for wealth distribution through wages, and other means. For each of them, some version of the labor theory of value (LTV) was also operative, along with supply-and-demand considerations to account for fluctuations in prices. Mariana Mazzucato says that "until the mid-nineteenth century, almost all economists assumed that in order to understand the prices of goods and services, it was first necessary to have an objective theory of value, a theory tied to the conditions in which those goods and

19 Ibid., 50.

services were produced [...] and the determinants of value actually shaped the price of goods and services."[20]

But once Marx exposed how profits resulted from the exploitation of labor power, decisively radicalizing what was always implicit in the LTV, something arguably even more revolutionary happened in the history of ideas—something, ironically enough, that is materially traceable to the rise of a mass consumer culture in the counterrevolutionary, bourgeois world after 1848. Davies says that "the first department store opened in 1852, introducing the experience we now recognize as shopping. Never before had products simply appeared on display, magically separated from their producers, with nothing but a price tag [...]."[21] As late as the 1830s, most goods and services were locally sourced, so much so that fixed prices were actually uncommon. Merchants kept ledgers of who owed what to whom at what price, based on special considerations, such as price offsets from seasonal barter, and so on. But with the advent of nationwide rail networks, so that goods could move around farther and faster than most people, we see the rapid rise of commodity capitalism, and with it, a universal market that increasingly came to be viewed as "an arena of psychological experiences."[22]

It's against the new reality of this socioeconomic backdrop that we can start to make sense of how classical political economy's macroeconomic concern with the wealth of nations is replaced by the microeconomic analysis characteristic of neoclassical marginalism. Marx had resolved Smith's and Ricardo's "price/value transformation problem" by means of a theory of exploitation (a critique of capitalist society). In response to the extreme social and political challenge to the existing order that this represented, the marginalists (Jevons, Walras, and Menger, and later Marshall and Pareto) developed an alternative theory

20 Mariana Mazzucato, *The Value of Everything* (New York: Hatchette, 2018), 7.

21 Davies, *The Happiness Industry*, 58.

22 Ibid.

that actually rested on the de facto "capitalist realist truth" found in commodity capitalism's own market experiences.

Whereas all the representatives of the classical tradition saw value as equal to a quantity of labor time, at least in some way, "Jevons, Menger, and Walras," Davies writes, "wondered whether the mentality of consumers might actually be decisive in determining the price of things." The novelty "was to conceive of value from the perspective of the person spending the money, rather than the person producing the goods."[23] In order to find a way to restore the pre-Marxian, legitimation concept of price/value equilibrium to the functioning of capitalism, therefore, marginalism declares (rather breathtakingly) that *value is something subjective.*[24] Or put another way, whereas it was always assumed that value was at least some sort of quantum, they decided that it was, in fact, not a thing. In doing so, Mazzucato says, they also rather conveniently swept away most of the concerns that lay at the heart of critiques of capitalism. They denied the difference between productive and unproductive work, and they reaffirmed that prices are only grounded in supply and demand. They said that rents are earned income, and that the rate of profit is exclusively the reward for the productive contribution of capital. Under this economic theory, "what you get is what you are worth," she writes, and "there are no classes, only individuals, and there is no objective measure of value."[25]

The Marginalist Revolution and the Privatization of Utility

The basic innovation of marginalism is often illustrated by means of the example commonly called "the paradox of water and diamonds."[26] Why is it that the price of water is cheap, and diamonds expensive, when water is a necessity for life, and diamonds, which are an ornament, and which we can therefore do

23 Ibid., 54.
24 Ibid., 55. See also Mazzucato, *The Value of Everything,* 62.
25 Mazzucato, *The Value of Everything,* 68.
26 Ibid., 64.

without, are expensive? The price of diamonds is higher, so the theory goes, because of the critical role of scarcity in rational, economic decision-making, in relation to what is called "the law of diminishing marginal utility." For most people, the marginalists say, water is sufficiently abundant that the loss or gain of a gallon wouldn't matter that much, whereas diamonds are much rarer, so that the loss or gain of one diamond would be much more impactful. It is helpful, therefore, to think of constraints affecting decisions as a border or margin. A value that holds true only given particular marginal constraints is thus a marginal value, and a change that would come about as a result of a specific loosening or tightening of those constraints is a marginal change.

Taking insights from gambling-related decision theory, marginalism seeks to explain unit prices and their perturbations in terms of these relative values. It assumes that for any given set of constraints, a rational agent will first satisfy wants of highest possible priority, so that no higher-priority want will be sacrificed to satisfy a want of lower priority, if it can be avoided. This is also illustrated by what is called "the example of the parrots." Someone has a limited number of sacks of grain, and various settled uses for each (including feeding himself, feeding chickens, making whisky, and, famously, feeding his pet parrots). If the number of sacks becomes constrained, rather than reduce the amount of grain for all the uses, he will continue making biscuits, eating eggs and chickens, and drinking whiskey, and he will starve the parrots. The example is meant to illustrate that, all other things being equal, individuals are willing to trade, the marginalists contended, based on the respective marginal utilities of the goods that they have or desire, so that prices develop accordingly.

There is much more that can and should be said in order to arrive at a critical understanding of the meaning of neoclassical economics per se. Of special interest here, for example, is Maurice Dobb's amplification of Marx's rejection of a value theory grounded only in individualist responses to supply and demand.[27] Dobb argues that the marginalist approach to the derivation of prices smuggles in preexisting social contents, because the ability of consumers to "express their preferences" is actually dependent on their spending power, thus implicating the whole business in a vicious circularity that simply assumes capitalist society as a privileged given. But further elaboration of both the details of marginalism, along with its notable critical challenges, have to be parked, so that we don't lose the forest for the trees. For purposes of getting at the critical history of happiness management, there are a few significant developments that Davies thinks need to be drawn out and highlighted. First, there is the sense in which the marginalist revolution, with its subjectification of value, transforms utilitarianism from a project oriented around statecraft "into a theory of rational consumer choice."[28] Looking initially only at Jevons, for whom marginalism is built directly upon the psychology of pleasure and pain, we can see quite clearly (following Mazzucato) that marginalism "is a spillover from utilitarian ethics — the value of a commodity resides in its utility to a buyer."[29]

Second, Davies's great insight is that the subjectification/privatization of utility continues to reign uncontested, even after marginal utility was in eclipse, even after it was argued by Marshall and Pareto that indifference curves could be taken as a given without bothering with psychological notions of utility. Davies makes just this point when he says that where Bentham was looking primarily at the reform of government, "Jevon's contribution was to plant the vision of a calculating hedonist firmly in the marketplace."[30] When Marshall and Pareto update Jevons, and say that "the way I spend my money is determined by my preferences, and not by my actual subjective sensations,"[31] nothing much really changes with respect to the privatization of

27 Maurice Dobb, *Theories of Value and Distribution Since Adam Smith* (London: Cambridge University Press, 1973).

28 Davies, *The Happiness Industry,* 56.

29 Mazzucato, *The Value of Everything,* 61.

30 Davies, *The Happiness Industry,* 56.

31 Ibid., 61.

utility. Whereas Jevons was trying to show a kind of coordination between the mechanics of the mind (where value resided) and the mechanics of the market, after marginalism the market itself is simply regarded as a "giant mind-reading device" with prices (money) as the condition of possibility, a vast psychological audit that unswervingly discovers and represents the desires of society.[32] Finally, Davies also wants us to recognize that it's the establishment of a widespread normalization of "privatized utility," as part of the universal experience of market capitalism, that sets the stage for what he refers to as a index of general human optimization, the project of happiness management in which neuroscience research will ultimately assume a leading role.

Neoliberalism and the "Iron Cage" of Privatized Utility

The next major moment in Davies's narrative has to do with how the marginalist model of rational decision-making and its associated analytical techniques, which had been developed to "help understand markets," and so was useful to explain why people buy and sell things, came to be applied, more and more, *outside the narrow monetary arena.*[33] As it turns out, this collective assumption of a "happy chance" isomorphism between minds and markets that first emerges in the late nineteenth century does more than just provide for market behaviors to become tools for measuring our levels of individual and collective happiness. This assumed accord also comes to function as "the manger for the virgin birth of *homo economicus,*" the sort of human beings that exist, first and foremost, as rational calculators of private gain, in every domain permeated by market logic.

In Davies account, we go on to see how this newly privatized notion of utility expands, piggybacked on the increased penetration of market logic into every aspect of life under late twentieth-century neoliberalism, like a modulated signal riding on a carrier wave. The mechanism of this transport is the

32 Ibid., 57.
33 Ibid., 62.

tandem functioning of competitiveness and happiness management under neoliberal conditions, starting in the 1960s and gathering steam thereafter. The enshrinement/entrenchment of competitiveness as "the defining culture of businesses, cities, schools, and entire nations," which becomes the mantra after Thatcher and Reagan, is intentionally designed to produce unequal outcomes.[34] It should be no surprise, Davies writes, that things such as "spiraling executive pay together with unprecedented levels of unemployment, and the growing dominance of the global finance sector" would also generate a host of social consequences, especially the growth of widespread psychological depression, stress, and burnout.

The appearance of these consequences in the workplace, becoming increasingly acute by the 1990s, Davies says, leads to a "reunion of economics and psychology," which had parted company, at least on the surface, with the rise of midcentury marginalist microeconomic analysis.[35] Happiness science "emerges because of burnout as a form of resistance."[36] Occupational health and stress management also appear as disciplines during this time, because increasing numbers of people start to exhibit a form of "psychosomatic collapse that we have come to identify with the concept of stress."[37] It is a newly minted concern over the mental happiness of employees, therefore, as a means to combat stress-related illnesses and passive resistance, that becomes one of the avenues whereby private utility exceeds narrow market relations, seeping into everyday life under the guise of self-optimization for increased productivity. Corporate rationality, now quite concerned with how we are feeling, starts to tell us that there is "an optimal way of taking a break from work, and even going for a walk can be viewed as a calculated act of productivity management."[38]

34 Ibid., 141.
35 Ibid., 64.
36 Ibid., 127–28.
37 Ibid., 133.
38 Ibid., 115.

According to Davies, it must be remembered, this is all traceable back to Bentham, but with a new wrinkle. To the extent that we now live in the age of neoliberal *homo economicus,* Davies says, happiness itself now becomes *a form of capital.* For Bentham, happiness was a result of activities and choices. But today, happiness is represented as an input to our various projects, as a resource to be drawn upon which will generate a return. "Bentham and Jevons' premise that money yields a proportionate quantity of happiness is turned on its head, suggesting instead that a quantity of happiness will yield a certain amount of money."[39] Where happiness comes to be conceived in this way, as a form of capital attaching to a *homo economicus* (i.e., to someone who is regarded as a human capital), economic and political elites magically start to become very interested in promoting projects of individual self-optimization. Davies says that the privatization of utility in the modern age reaches a kind of apotheosis where we see such things as calculations of private utility being used to determine the ostensible value of nonmarket goods (willingness-to-pay surveys used to determine the amount of a judgment against ExxonMobil for environmental damages).[40] We also see it with the phenomenon of health-related "social prescribing," where under influence of behavioral economics and network analysis, the value of social life is reduced to the positive effects it has for the well-being of the individual. Davies says that "once social relations can be viewed as [...] properties of the human body, they can be dragged into the limitless pursuit of self-optimization that counts for happiness in the age of neoliberalism."[41]

Another vector of the advance of privatized utility even deeper into everyday life has to do with the confluence of big data analytics with personalized web behavior, social media, smartphone apps, and the internet of things (IoT). The mass monitoring of moods and feelings, Davies writes, "is becoming

39 Ibid., 114.
40 Ibid., 63.
41 Ibid., 212–13.

a function of our physical environment." And once happiness management "floods our everyday lives, other ways of quantifying feelings in real time are emerging that can extend capital even further into our lives beyond markets."[42] Given the now all-encompassing laboratory of online behavior, the "hope and promise of synthesizing neuroscience and big data," he says, is that we might dispense with separate disciplines, the science of markets (economics), a science of the workplace (management), a science of consumer choice (market research), a science of organization and association (sociology) through the discovery of hard laws of decision-making.[43]

It is here that we come at last to the related resurgence of Bentham's other "happiness proxy," the rubric of the physical science of body measurements. Once most domains of human existence become subject to market forces, and happiness becomes a kind of capital, the possibilities for behavioral analysis and experimentation multiply, and at last find their golden age. Under these conditions, Davies says, where vast resources (corporate, governmental) are marshaled for maximizing collection of large datasets, inquiry into the "conditions and nature of human welfare can swiftly mutate into new strategies for behavioral control."[44] The behavioral neuroscience of happiness we see today, Davies writes, reflect forms of knowledge "that [...] combine benign intentions (to improve health and wellbeing) with those of profit and elite political strategy."[45]

Are Our Thoughts Really Like Horses?

To see how neuroscience finds cultural significance in relation to capitalist spirituality's projects of self-optimization and happiness management, it is useful to consider one more recent example from *The New York Times*. *The Ezra Klein Show* featured

42 Ibid., 10–11.
43 Ibid., 237.
44 Ibid., 232.
45 Ibid., 225.

an interview with Jud Brewer, director of research at The Mindfulness Center.[46] As a professor of psychiatry and the author of a popular book on addiction, Brewer thinks that it is useful to look at anxiety through the lens of the addiction "dopamine reward model," and in the interview, Klein probes him to try to understand the implications of this claim.

Brewer sketches out his position by making the "argument from neuroplasticity": anxiety, he says, is actually a learned habit, and as such is made up of "a trigger, a behavior, and a result." If you think about it "from a survival brain perspective," our ancient ancestors were running around pursuing pleasure (foraging) and avoiding pain (running away from danger), and in each case were getting a dopamine reward for doing so (either a satisfied stomach or a hooray, I didn't get eaten!). On this basis, he makes the case for his claim that anxiety is a dopamine habit: "For the anxious, worry can become a mental behavior because our body can get in a loop where we think we are rewarded for it."

In response to Brewer's blithe assertion of a behaviorism of our higher-order functions (What exactly is meant here by a mental behavior?), Klein is clearly skeptical. "What you are saying is counter-intuitive," Klein says. "It doesn't feel like a reward. It doesn't feel good, I don't enjoy it." But Brewer nonetheless holds firm, and responds by insisting that we need to recognize how our ancient, survival brain "goes into problem-solving mode." Anxiety is a product of reward-based learning, he says, and anxious people are anxious, in the first instance, because they come to associate good outcomes with worrying a lot.

Klein again responds that he finds all of this to be unnerving — ostensibly because of Brewer's casual use of the language of CBT (cognitive behavioral therapy), and thus his inclusion of our higher functions, what Klein calls "the me part," in a machine-like functionalism usually reserved for the body or

46 Ezra Klein, "Anxiety Is a Habit You Can Unlearn," *The New York Times*, April 20, 2021, https://www.nytimes.com/2021/04/20/opinion/ezra-klein-podcast-judson-brewer.html.

lower mental processes. Either that, or maybe it has something to do the obvious chutzpah of someone telling us, during a pandemic, burning forests, extreme political polarization, and economic uncertainty, that anxiety is just a bad habit we've learned somewhere along the way. From here, there is a whole lot of what I call "talking brain talk." Brewer moves through a series of examples in order to explain how something that feels bad (anxiousness, worry) is actually part of a dopamine reward habit loop. "Our brains say, ooh, this is bad," or "our brains love to make causal connections." Worry itself is actually a form of excitement, and thus is something "baked right into our brains." We like to think that our minds are in control, Brewer says. But our brains are driven "based on how rewarding something is." So, if we can change our relationship to our thoughts, then we can actually get in control. Our thoughts "are like horses, and we are the riders."

Following this, Brewer cites a study on attention that shows that on average, people's minds are "wandering to the past or the future" for almost 50 percent of their waking life. Apparently, per Brewer's basic thrust, this is "just the way we are." There's no apparent need to ask, for example, why so many of us might not want to "be here, now." Instead, Brewer says, "we should be looking in the neuroscience direction [....] If we can understand how our mind works, then we can actually hack it, if you want to put it in the life hack perspective." In reply, to this rhetorical aside, Klein is emphatic: "I don't. I want to avoid that word for what you are talking about." Once again, Klein finds himself uncomfortable when Brewer tells him that "we're trained to think using our brains [...] yet that's not what really drives behavior," and he encourages him that "we should endeavor to hack our own brains," to conspire behind the back of our own thoughts, so to speak.

But who are we, it must be asked, if not our thoughts and sensations? Or put another way, where have we come to, historically speaking, when it seems plausible to apply an addiction model to all our negative thoughts and feelings? Under the addiction model, as people in recovery will tell you, willpower is a myth. We fail to meet our own expectations and those of others over and over again, because we are caught in habit loops fueled by repetitive negative thoughts and emotions. We can only free ourselves, so the story goes, if we first accept that we are powerless, if we accept that we have hit rock bottom. Recovery begins when we learn how to separate ourselves from these very thoughts and feelings, to begin to regard them with objectivity, or, put another way, to see how thoroughly subjective they are.

It cannot be denied that many people find therapeutic value in relation to addiction and certain kinds of mental illness (including anxiety) by practicing this set of techniques associated with CBT. But I'm told that the religiously inclined, for example, obtain similar benefit just by being under consistent pastoral care, and it is apparently the case that studies bear this out. Additionally, it's still hard not to wonder why neuroplasticity doesn't allow us to update our somatic reward system by strengthening the autonomous self, by encouraging the practice of decision-making according to properly moral motivations and other techniques. It is not within my purview here to revisit well-worn mid-twentieth-century debates about behaviorism (see, e.g., Noam Chomsky and B.F. Skinner). Instead, I will only say this: Brewer's horse metaphor bears more than a superficial resemblance to Plato's allegory of the charioteer from the *Phaedrus*, but with a difference. Plato wanted us to see the higher functions of the soul as guiding the harmonious movements of both our rational and animal natures. But Brewer, in saying that it is actually our own thoughts that are like horses, apparently wants to seat yet another charioteer somewhere above Plato's. In reply to this suggestion, we can only direct him to the *Parmenides*, and the problem of the third man regress.[47]

---

47 Lest this is taken too far in the opposite direction, a Buddhist friend has pointed out that the important thing here is to recognize the impermanence of specific thoughts and feelings, i.e., that they come and go, and that we need not remain attached to them, and not that as selves we are something profoundly other than the sum of our own thoughts and feelings.

It becomes clear a bit further along why Brewer is working so hard against the grain here, why he wants to apply the addiction model to generalized anxiety. By using the recommended techniques to separate ourselves from our anxious thoughts, "we can start to develop our tolerance for unpleasantness." The objective "is not to avoid anxiety, but to recognize it as just a set of physical sensations," and so not something "we need to run away from." The "survival brain says, 'Ooh, this is bad, run away.' But that's not how life works," Brewer adds. "I can be ok with unpleasantness, accepting what's happening rather than pushing it away." The question, of course, is whether, from a social and political perspective, we *should* "accept what's happening," and learn to be "ok with all manner of unpleasantness." If the answer is yes, then the Foucauldians are probably right when they identify this sort of self-optimization as a "technology of the self," one that ultimately resolves to a "technology of domination."

Pushing back, some people might still want to say that everything has its season, and that getting healthy and pressing for social and political change are actually different, even if they can be seen to be complementary. This is fair enough. But the discussion of digital detox further along in the interview tends to expose this as something of a dodge. You experience yourself as "addicted to the smart phone," Brewer says, when you are deprived of it, and feel withdrawal symptoms when you can't check the phone and various apps when the brain tells you it's time to do so. Techniques associated with the addiction model can indeed help you to manage withdrawal successfully, so that you can break this worrisome habit. This is no doubt the case, but it leaves out something critically important. We need to remember that the phone, its services, and apps have all been intentionally designed using the latest interdisciplinary research in order to create this very addictive behavior in the first place, in the name of enhanced profits. The problem with Brewer's model is that it simply reifies our contemporary anxiety, turning it into something permanent and unchanging, something transhistorical, and just "baked into our brains." It refuses to say anything about the underlying relations of power in society that lead us to obsessive loops in our dopamine systems.

The "Psy-Shaped Space" within Us

Over the course of this chapter, I have provided strong support for the claim that behavioral neuroscience is largely inseparable from capitalist spirituality's project of happiness management, and, as such, that its seducements (Who doesn't want to be happier?) also represent a form of ensnarement. For Davies (and for Purser, Carrette and King, and Ehrenreich), the dynamic of ensnarement refers to the expectation that we have of being empowered through personal projects of self-optimization, despite the evidence of the neoliberal commodification of the self. Where Davies writes that emancipatory projects "become ensnared" when unhappiness is expressed via instruments of measurement,[48] he thus has in mind the manner in which human energies and passions, and our discontent and aspirations, become effectively depoliticized, and how they also become harnessed as productive forces under neoliberal social and economic conditions.

In privatizing stress and anxiety, and "responsibilizing" individuals in relation to their unhappiness, capitalist spirituality in all its forms (mindfulness-wellness-happiness), Purser says, enacts a cruel optimism. The cruelty lies in "supporting the status quo while using the language of transformation."[49] Or as Carrette and King similarly write, privatization "breaks the social self and conceals the collective manipulation of isolated individuals in the language of free will and choice."[50] The question that can be seen to hang over much of Davies's book, therefore, is whether this ensnarement of the human feeling for freedom/autonomy is actually some new and insidious version

48 Davies, *The Happiness Industry*, 242.

49 Ronald Purser, *McMindfulness: How Mindfulness Became the New Capitalist Spirituality* (London: Repeater Books, 2019), 44–45.

50 Jeremy Carrette and Richard King, *Selling Spirituality: The Silent Takeover of Religion* (London: Routledge, 2005), 80.

of Weber's iron cage, one from which we can see no real hope of escape. In thinking about this dilemma, Davies has reminded me of some of the arguments found within the final chapter and afterword of Nikolas Rose's landmark work on technologies of subjectivity, *Governing the Soul: The Shaping of the Private Self* (1989).

Initially, Rose stakes out a very Foucault-like, "value-neutral" position with respect to what he calls "the proponents of the sciences of autonomy," those professional experts who promote "the cultivation of an individualized, secular art of lifestyle, consumption, and pleasure—as a universal solution with a scientific basis."[51] Writing in the early days of the neoliberal era, Rose says that it would be a mistake to view this responsibilization of the individual, aided by expert knowledge and the help of professionals, with a totalizing skepticism. The primary importance of the new apparatuses and techniques, which he says seek to align political, social, and institutional goals with the happiness and fulfilment of the self, flows from the increased pluralization of the mechanisms for the regulation of individual and group life. What really matters, in the intensified demand that individuals take responsibility for their own conduct in the name of self-realization, Rose says, is not that these "assemblages of power extend domination."[52] It's that it frees many questions concerning the conduct of life "from the authoritative prescriptions of political, religious, and social authorities,[...] opening up a field of diversity in which each subject is advised to locate themselves."[53]

Today it is hard to share Rose's Foucauldian "happy positivism," his willingness to applaud unreservedly whatever appears to widen the field of our cultural possibilities. In his afterword written ten years later, which is part of the second edition, Rose's enthusiasm appears somewhat chastened, although the

51 Nikolas Rose, *Governing the Soul: The Shaping of the Private Self* (London: Free Association Books, 1989), 260.

52 Ibid.

53 Ibid.

seeds of it are already there in the text prior to that. Along with this appreciation for a new field of possibilities, there is also a mood of resignation about *the way that things are*. Contemporary human beings, he says, "inhabit a network [...] which presupposes, fabricates, and stabilizes particular versions of the self."[54] In having been made increasingly responsible for their own self-governance, large numbers of people seek the guidance and assistance of "the professionals of psy" for various problems of living. Along with this expert guidance, there is also a burgeoning arena of mutual self-help that disseminates an array of nonprofessionalized techniques for acting on oneself.

This network, which should be recognized as "a complex and contradictory domain of authorized psychological knowledge distinguished by "bricolage, translation, and hybridization," Rose writes, "refers to the psy-shaped space within us," an internal zone with its own characteristics and laws, that lies "between [...] the body [...] and the moral complexity of human conduct."[55] In making this rather remarkable statement, Rose invites us to accept this status quo as simply de facto at this point. The interpenetration of science with an aesthetics of existence, he says, "has become fundamental to the ways that individuals are governed in accordance with the economic, social, and political conditions of the present."[56]

This acceptance of the status quo can also be seen where Rose writes, "It is through the promotion of lifestyle by the mass media, by advertising, and by experts through the obligation to shape a life [...] that the modern subject is governed."[57] Or finally this: "In the complex web they have traced out, the truths of science and the powers of experts act as relays that bring the values of authorities and the goals of businesses into contact with the dreams and actions of us all."[58] What then does it really mean to simply acknowledge that today, "questions of the

54 Ibid., 265.
55 Ibid.
56 Ibid., 260.
57 Ibid., 261.
58 Ibid.

conduct of life are tied to norms of truth and health," because "science today is the mode by which ethical statements come to place themselves within the true"[59]? The question becomes even more acute when one recognizes, as Rose also does, that this effectively binds us, as subjects, to a subjection that is profound because "it appears to emanate from our autonomous quest for ourselves — it appears as a matter of our freedom."[60]

In the closing paragraphs of his afterword, Rose goes on to propose a provocative thought experiment: What might an ethic of existence be that did not refer to the psy-shaped space that has been installed at the heart of each modern individual? Might there be another kind of freedom that we could imagine, one "whose vector did not run from outer to inner?" He invites us instead to imagine another kind of freedom, one that "ran across the outsides, between and among persons, where subjectivities were distributed, collective and oriented to action."[61] I'd like to end by suggesting that we really don't have to strain that hard to imagine what Rose has in mind here. Something quite similar is going on when Davies asks, "What would it mean for politics and organization to be de-psychologized?"[62] The other kind of freedom, "running across the outsides, between and among persons" starts to come into view when Davies points out that "utilitarianism in pursuit of mental optimization can be consistent with quasi-socialist forms of organization and production, if it is open-ended human flourishing that is intended."[63] It continues to come into focus when he asks, "What if a definition of optimization were offered that included control over one's time, power over decision-making — in short, a definition of autonomy not reducible to neural or psychological causality?"[64] Finally, it is also glimpsed when he says, in an adaptation of an insight of Raymond Williams's, "Teach the practice

59 Ibid., 260.
60 Ibid.
61 Ibid., 272.
62 Davies, *The Happiness Industry,* 259.
63 Ibid., 243.
64 Ibid.

of democratic dialogue rather than just resilience and mindfulness, which are silent relationships to the self."[65]

65 Ibid., 273.

14

Self-Renewal and the Collapsing Occupational "Pseudo-Public Sphere"

> Weakened social capital is manifest in the things that have vanished almost unnoticed [...] the unreflective kindness of strangers, the shared pursuit of public good rather than a solitary quest for private goods.
>
> — Robert Putnam, *Bowling Alone*

Where can we find the conditions for genuine self-renewal today? The unmasking of contemporary projects of happiness management as forms of capitalist spirituality tends to summon our experience of the collapsing public sphere. Whether we heed the imperative to lean in and optimize our work-related human capital, embracing some form of the neoliberal prosperity gospel, or instead withdraw into highly commodified personal projects of self-care and recovery, the result is the same. Our discontent and aspirations become privatized and depoliticized, and effectively harnessed as productive forces in support of the dominant neoliberal hegemony. It is precisely the absence of any readily apparent third option today that describes a certain boundary condition, and thus traces the contour of our public sphere dissolution.

Jürgen Habermas actually lays out this exact predicament in his earliest book, *The Structural Transformation of the Public Sphere* (1962). The book concerns what he calls "the functional phase" of early modern bourgeois society, in which the rise of civil society frees both commodity exchange and social labor from the state, and the public sphere is seen to take on modern political functions.[1] It then goes on to describe a follow-on set of structural and normative transformations, where the distinctions between private and public spheres from the liberal phase are shown to be progressively muddled by attempts to ward of crises of the capitalist social order. Throughout, Habermas remains focused on his major historical theme, that of the downfall of the classic bourgeois public sphere, as demonstrated by its changing political functions in the face of the increasing "societalization of the state and statification of society."[2] Nonetheless, he also ends up describing how welfare statism in the twentieth century stripped the nuclear family of its remaining social labor, turning it into mostly a site of consumption and coordination of leisure. It is in this context that he starts talking specifically about contemporary society's "world of work."

When the type of work seen in early bourgeois private occupations was replaced with employment that has significant dependencies on both the state and concentrated capital, Habermas writes, "new forms of social labor evolved," and along with this, we saw "a new attitude toward work."[3] Here we find the first emergence of what, in some quarters, is called "the company man," whose value is based in a generalized functional performance, and, reciprocally, who has a depersonalized relationship to work, a relationship to the institution per se, rather than to other persons. Under these conditions, that of advanced bourgeois public sphere transformation/dissolution, the world of work, Habermas says, came to be established as a sphere in

1 Jürgen Habermas, *The Structural Transformation of the Public Sphere,* trans. Thomas Burger and Frederick Lawrence (Cambridge: MIT Press, 1994), 73–74.

2 Ibid., 142.

3 Ibid., 152–53.

its own right between the private and public realms. Opposed to a private realm reduced to that of the nuclear family, this independent, quasi-public occupational realm in some cases takes over various social labor functions, such as company housing and organized leisure, thus trending toward a kind of industrial neofeudalism. Today, "time not spent on the job represents precisely the preserve of the private."[4] Additionally, private people today "withdraw from their [prior liberal bourgeois public/political] roles as property owners into the purely personal ones of the noncommittal use of leisure time," inasmuch as "leisure behavior supplies the key to the [...] privacy of the new sphere, to the externalization of what is declared to be the inner life."

Despite the jolt of pattern recognition that this account tends to provoke, it must be remembered that Habermas is writing about welfare state malaise and the changing character of work in northern European social democracies in the early 1960s. As a result, what is of most interest here is the extent to which this account describes how the dissolution or collapse of a set of structural social possibilities in itself can actually determine the array of choices that appear before us as individuals. With this in view, I want to suggest that the alternatives popularly available to us today (options for addressing challenges to our happiness and well-being created by work-as-we-know-it) also tend to be reflective of this sense of living in two spheres. There is a "semipublic occupational sphere" that has taken the place of the spectral, bourgeois public sphere (now crossing into true oblivion) and there is a "truncated private sphere," defined by leisure and the imperative to externalize contents of an inner life.[5]

Our Collapsing "Occupational, Pseudo-Public Sphere"

With millions working from home under pandemic conditions, we are now experiencing the collapse of even this pallid, substitute public sphere. The sense that we are entombed in our own

4 Ibid., 154.
5 Ibid., 159.

privacy is palpable. Of course, this is not to suggest that there has been an abundance of what Robert Putnam calls "bridging social capital" to be found in the world of work in recent decades. The casualness of work relationships might qualify them as "weak-tie" social bonds, the highly competitive, overmanaged, instrumentalizing, anxious, low-trust, and precarious nature of work-as-we-know-it militates against the notion that "the occupational public sphere" has ever been much of a candidate, Putnam says, for "replacing the back fence as the locus for social capital."[6]

For the most part, concern about the loss of the public sphere has been expressed through dismay over the privatization of the commons across a wide spectrum of public goods, especially the enclosure of land, and other spatialized and territorialized elements. For critics who came of age in the bubble of a largely uncontested liberal sociopolitical consensus, it was the mutability of "the goods" that was a matter of intense concern, while the notion of "a public" to which they rightly belonged was something taken for granted, even though the very notion of a commons must be seen to depend completely upon the historically specific, political assertion of a political public sphere.

In *The Fall of Public Man* (1977), for example, Richard Sennett points out how the rise of modern privacy (understood to be a domain of intimate feeling and the externalized search for authenticity) is correlated at the physical level with dead public space, with a public domain that is abandoned and empty, and thus essentially meaningless. The public square as a place for the intermix of diverse persons and activities is increasingly replaced in the twentieth century by the spaces in and around skyscrapers, for example, which is all about movement into the interior, with no tarrying purposes permitted, much less

6 Robert Putnam, *Bowling Alone: The Collapse and Revival of American Community* (New York: Simon and Schuster, 2000), 87.

encouraged. Public space thus becomes a function of motion, losing any independent experiential meaning of its own.[7]

More recently, however, a generalized anxiety about the collapse of the public sphere has also been manifesting in the form of explicit reflections on diminishing weak-tie sociability, the loss of what Blanche Dubois in Tennessee Williams's *A Street Car Named Desire* identified as the ability to "rely on the kindness of strangers." In *Talking to Strangers* (2019), for example, Malcolm Gladwell presents a collection of informal case studies highlighting what he takes to be the various kinds of "stranger danger." Taken together, these cases are meant to be a catalogue of the mistaken strategies whereby people attempt mutual translation with disastrous effects. Starting with the infamous 2015 Sandra Bland traffic stop case in Texas, which led to her jailhouse suicide, Gladwell stages a would-be intervention, insisting that the debate between those who focused on racism, "looking down from 10,000 feet," and those who instead examined every detail of conduct "with a magnifying glass" missed something important, specifically, the dynamics of an encounter between total strangers.[8] He thinks that "things going wrong between total strangers" is actually reflective of a distinctly modern pattern of interaction. Today, "we are now thrown into contact all the time with people whose assumptions, perspectives, and backgrounds differ from our own."[9]

As it turns out, Gladwell thinks that the history of "mutual mistranslation between strangers" has a pedigree that actually goes all the way back to a new type of encounter that emerged in the sixteenth century, traceable to the fateful meeting between Hernán Cortés and Montezuma II. Until that time, he claims, conflicts of all types involved people who were essentially neighbors—people who shared a border and were thus closely related,

7 Richard Sennett, *The Fall of Public Man* (New York: W.W. Norton, 2017), 14–17.

8 Malcolm Gladwell, *Talking to Strangers: What We Should Know About the People We Don't Know* (New York: Back Bay Books, 2019), 6.

9 Ibid., 11.

or else internal conflicts between related groups inside borders.[10] It is hard to know exactly what to make of this set of remarks concerning the modern history of mistranslation. There is certainly an obvious counternarrative that could be offered here in reply, one having to do with settler colonialism and structural racism, for example. There are also some rather glaring exceptions to Gladwell's breezy generalizations about the character of premodern conflicts—anybody remember Alexander crossing the Indus, imperial Rome on the Danube, Genghis Khan sweeping into eastern Europe, Viking raids on Britain? But putting this aside, it is quite surprising that Gladwell does not attempt to locate his growing unease about "stranger danger" in something more ready-to-hand, such as the experience of a collapsing modern public sphere.

Tara Menon, an English professor at Harvard, provides something of a corrective to all of this, recasting the problem of talking to strangers in terms of what the bourgeois public sphere allowed the middle-class consumer to take for granted. "When major characters communicate with unnamed strangers, we see the ways in which modern society is a collection of atomized, isolated individuals, unconnected by meaningful bonds [...] but they also show the reliability and neutrality of the public sphere."[11] In mass societies "in which most people are not connected by blood or community or religion, but rather by impersonal rational ties," Menon writes, "these anonymous interactions play a vital role[....] Interactions in the public sphere might be dispassionate and impersonal," but "there is something reassuring even comforting about this." Menon thus understands something that Gladwell appears to have missed. Since the rise of modern civil society's public sphere in the eighteenth and nineteenth centuries, most "encounters with strangers" have tended to "rely on cooperation," "they are reciprocal (you

10 Ibid., 7.

11 Tara Menon, "What Jane Eyre and Oliver Twist Tell Us about Talking to Strangers," *Psyche*, September 29, 2021, https://psyche.co/ideas/what-jane-eyre-and-oliver-twist-tell-us-about-talking-to-strangers.

pay for a coffee, you get a coffee) respectful (you ask for coffee politely) and while distant, also social (the barista asks how your day was)." If Gladwell is correct, and, as he says, "the modern world is not two brothers feuding for control of the Ottoman Empire […] it is Cortéz and Montezuma struggling to understand each other through multiple layers of translators,"[12] we would still have to ask the question, "Yes, but why now?" Why, after five hundred years of mutual mistranslations, does the stranger danger suddenly seem so acute that Gladwell needs to write a book about it? This question needs to be answered with the awareness that we live in a society where weak-tie sociability has, at least until recently, been uniquely enabled and supported as a foundational aspect of the United States understood as a civic nation.

The Public Sphere as a Condition for Self-Renewal

The collapsing occupational, "pseudo-public sphere," where the elements of wage-based society's informal social contract are seen to be in dramatic decline, should be recognized as directly related to our current epidemic of work-related physical and mental illnesses. In response, once again, the dominant capitalist hegemony supports the maximization of one's human capital and happiness management as palliative care. If we next ask what an alternative to capitalist spirituality's projects of self-optimization or personal recovery might actually look like, there are certain features that almost immediately start to come into focus. To begin with, a genuine third option would have to involve the deprivatization of stress, in favor of a much more social understanding of human striving. Community-oriented notions of self-renewal, where individuals can seek to redefine themselves in complex networks of socialization, tend to recommend themselves.

The goal orientation here isn't the optimization of one's work-related human capital in order to beat out competitors and be

12 Gladwell, *Talking to Strangers*, 11–12.

able to buy the constituents of a happy life. Nor is it to commit to merely individually expressive projects supportive of wellness and recovery. Personal projects of self-renewal conceived on this basis (which involve transforming one's social identity) involve finding new purposes together with others. These are ones that leverage capacities, skills, and experience, and holistically grow new and healthy parts of oneself in the aftermath of the immediate work of recovery from trauma. They fit Nikolas Rose's description of "another kind of freedom" (as we saw in chapter 13), one that doesn't so much address "the psy-shaped space" within each modern individual, but instead has a vector that runs "across the outsides, between and among persons," rather than "from outer to inner."[13]

It's important to recognize that calls for just such a radical departure from the dominant neobehaviorist, "diagnose and treat disease" model of mental health have a long history in the United States, going back at least as far as R. D. Laing and Thomas Szasz in the 1950s. At a disciplinary level, practitioners and advocates for community psychology models have regularly attempted to argue for the importance of life contexts, alternate settings, second-order (community-level) interventions, along with investment in planning and prevention, participatory research, consultation, and other empowerment strategies. A fairly recent example of this genre is seen in British psychologist Peter Kinderman's *A Prescription for Psychiatry: Why We Need a Whole New Approach to Mental Health and Wellbeing* (2014). Kinderman argues in his introduction that we need to move away from the disease model, "which assumes that emotional distress is merely a symptom of biological illness, and instead embrace a psychological and social approach to mental health and wellbeing."[14] Despite enormous volumes of evidence that social factors lead to mental health problems, "routine medical

---

13 Nikolas Rose, *Governing the Soul: The Shaping of the Private Self* (London: Free Association Books, 1989), 243.

14 Peter Kinderman, *A Prescription for Psychiatry: Why We Need a Whole New Approach to Mental Health and Wellbeing* (New York: Palgrave Macmillan, 2014), 1.

care in practice relies on the attempted treatment of illnesses assumed to reside physically in the body (more specifically the brain) as opposed to helping people to address these social challenges."[15]

In response, he offers what he calls his "radical prescription" for psychiatry: instead of treating mental health as a branch of medicine, with links to social care, Kinderman says, we need a model where mental health is "part of the social provision with specialist input from medical colleagues." In short, to offer "social and psychological interventions rather than treating diseases," we need nothing less than "a formal transfer of mental health care to local authorities."[16] Kinderman thus takes direct aim at the status quo disease model from the viewpoint of social psychiatry, saying that the present degree of privatization is designed to support big pharma, and to meet capitalist individualism's need to shift attention away from social causes of mental health problems. He also argues that the diagnostic criteria remain unacceptably imprecise, that the drugs provide only short-term benefits and have bad side effects, and that the overall model ends up involving coercion. To move from a disease model to a psychosocial model, Kinderman says, there also needs to be a sharp reduction in reliance on medication. Mental health services should be delivered as part of community service, provided by democratic, multidisciplinary teams that address the full range of people's social, personal, and psychological needs, and they should be focused on prevention. He also says that there should be provision for nonmedical residential care for those who need an alternative setting in order to get well.[17]

In the *Handbook of Community Psychology* (2000), which deals with prevention, the authors make the textbook case that these sorts of prevention-oriented interventions have the potential to be both more efficient and more cost-effective at a societal

15 Ibid., 15.
16 Ibid., 25.
17 Ibid., 27–29.

level than individually focused models of intervention: "There will never be adequate levels of economic or human resources to address the needs of the 35–50M people who need intensive, reconstructive or individually focused" mental health services.[18] With robust prevention, the reduced need for after-the-fact services, coupled with the gains in productivity from those who didn't end up needing services, Felner, Felner, and Silverman argue, results in either overall cost neutrality or actual cost savings.

The economic studies are pretty much univocal—and yet the persistent calls for various types of community empowerment, as necessary in order to realize broad-based prevention strategies, pretty much always "hit the wall." Community psychologists, social psychiatrists, and others thus continue to call for a dramatic shift in approach regularly at their annual meetings, yet we continue to see increasingly severe retrenchment in the current mental health system, which has been headed steadily in the other direction for decades. Also in the *Handbook of Community Psychology,* Heller and colleagues write that "the existing levels of federal spending has brought us back to the 1950s, where there was private psychotherapy for those who could afford it, and supportive care for only the most chronic mental patients."[19]

If the economic arguments are sound, why then aren't there large-scale investments in these sorts of prevention programs? Why don't we regularly see public policy modeled around the value of supporting healthy communities? Both Kinderman and Felner, Felner, and Silverman come to more or less the same conclusion. The latter write that it's hard to escape the conclusion that as a society "we operate from a core assumption that

---

18 Robert D. Felner, Tweety Yates Felner, and Morton M. Silverman, "Prevention in Mental Health and Social Intervention," in *Handbook of Community Psychology,* vol. 1, eds. Julian Rappaport and Edward Seidman (New York: Springer Science and Business Media, 2000), 9–10.

19 Kenneth Heller, Richard A. Jenkins, Ann M. Steffen, and Ralph W. Swindle, Jr., "Prospects for a Viable Community Mental Health System," in *Handbook of Community Psychology,* eds. Rappaport and Seidman, 445.

there is an acceptable or necessary level of casualties."[20] In the end, the necessary "social prescription" cannot be filled, because such prescriptions themselves also require an "alternative setting": they require a society whose primary purpose is meeting human needs, and not the valorization of capital. A society that everywhere prioritizes the valorization of capital over human needs satisfaction can't facilitate significant public ownership of mental health issues because the meaning of "public" itself is being evacuated by the dissolution of the public sphere.

On the Transformations of Modern Social Character

How then to describe something very important, yet rather intangible, something we may actually have been losing for quite some time? The literature related to the dissolution or collapse of the public sphere turns out to be diverse and complex. In lieu of further exploration of social prescriptions in support of community mental health (since the recommended social world is becoming increasingly remote in any case), it's important to try to get a clearer sense of how the dissolution of the public sphere is increasingly limiting our choices for certain kinds of social belonging. To this end, it is helpful to next consider instead a certain genre of sociological writing on disintegrating social bonds, a genre that I like to refer to as the "something is missing" literature. These works have in common a set of "ideal type" investigations into the changing nature of social character, and can be traced directly back to David Riesman's *The Lonely Crowd* (1950). Robert Bellah's *Habits of the Heart* (1985) is an example of another work that fits in this category.

Sennett has pointed out that the writers on modern society who investigate the "shifting weight between public and private life" and describe "the imbalance between psychological and social claims in modern culture" actually fall into two camps,

20 Felner, Felner, and Silverman, "Prevention in Mental Health and Social Intervention," 10.

what he calls "the moralists and the Marxists."[21] In what follows, I try to come to grips with the significance of our collapsing public sphere in relation to the challenges presented by work-as-we-know-it by stepping through a series of contrasting pairings. Starting first with examples from the "moralist group," I introduce aspects of two works from the 2000s, Ehrenreich's *Dancing in the Streets,* and Putnam's *Bowling Alone.* After that, in chapter 15, I consider Arendt's account of the public and private realms in *The Human Condition,* as contrasted with Sennett's notion of the modern *res publica* from *On the Fall of Public Man,* identifying these as representative of a second group I want to call the "historicist group." The third part, offered in chapter 16, attempts to deepen this understanding further, by considering representatives of the "Marxist camp," that is, by comparing Habermas's treatment of the bourgeois public sphere as ideology in *The Structural Transformation of the Public Sphere* with Oskar Negt and Alexander Kluge's description of possible counter-publics in *Public Sphere and Experience.*

Ehrenreich: The Lost Bonds of Seductive Wildness

In *Dancing in the Streets* (2006), the "something is missing" lamented by Ehrenreich concerns the disappearance of what she calls the "expressions of collective joy" that were once nearly ubiquitous in non-Western cultures, and seen in Dionysian rites of the ancient Greek Near East. Ehrenreich chooses these two related *mise-en-scènes* in order to demonstrate the Western mind essentially at war with itself over these expressions. She starts by describing the evolving (cultural and social-scientific) response of Western observers to encounters with group ecstasy and trance since the age of conquest, what Joseph Conrad labeled "the heart of darkness," in order to capture the way in which Westerners experienced them as abhorrent and yet some-

21 Sennett, *The Fall of Public Man,* 36.

how also strangely compelling.[22] In the second case, Ehrenreich chooses Euripides' *The Bacchae,* using the conflict between Pentheus and the Maenads to demonstrate the complex entwinement of Apollonian and Dionysian impulses in something of a restatement of Nietzsche's *The Birth of Tragedy.*[23]

The question that motivates Ehrenreich's book "originates in a wide sense of loss.[24] How can civilization be regarded as progress if it precludes something as distinctly human and deeply satisfying as […] collective joy?"[25] In the "three-thousand-year-old struggle between Pentheus and Dionysus, between popes and dancing peasants, between puritans and carnival goers, between missionaries and the practitioners of indigenous ecstatic danced religions—Pentheus and his allies seem to have finally prevailed."[26] Per Ehrenreich, all of this matters because we experience palpable consequences for the way that we live today, in a consumer culture of spectacle within "an epoch without festivals," as Guy DeBord famously said.[27] Conditions of mass society alone can't account for "the long hostility of elites" toward collective ecstasy, because modern festivals continue to build up group cohesion among subordinated groups.[28] Quoting from Jean Duvignaud, Ehrenreich says that despite this, "market economies and increasing industrialization are crystalizing the social conditions for the elimination of such manifestations."[29]

Not only has the possibility of collective joy been largely marginalized, she says, "but the very source of this joy, other people, including strangers, no longer holds much appeal." Other people "have become an obstacle to our individual pursuits. They impede progress on urban streets and highways; they compete

22 Barbara Ehrenreich, *Dancing in the Streets: A History of Collective Joy* (New York: Holt Paperbacks, 2006), 2.
23 Ibid., 32–41.
24 Ibid., 15.
25 Ibid., 250.
26 Ibid., 248.
27 Ibid., 250.
28 Ibid., 251–52.
29 Ibid., 249.

for parking spots and jobs; they drive up the price of housing and ruin our favorite vacation spots."[30]

Contemporary civilization, Ehrenreich writes, unites the members of our society with economic interdependency, "but it unites them with no strong affective ties."[31] Today we are "aware of our dependence upon Chinese factory workers, Indian tech workers, immigrant janitors," but we don't know these people, or, for the most part, "we have no interest in them." We "barely know our neighbors, and all too often, our fellow workers are competitors."[32] She adds that decades of conservative social policy have also undermined any sense of mutual responsibility or common good, and placed the burdens of need satisfaction squarely upon the individual and the family. Ehrenreich thinks we pay a very high price, in terms of isolation and depression, for what she calls "this emotional emptiness,"[33] and insists that "the compensatory pleasures of consumer society do not satisfy our longings [...] for strong bonds connecting us to those outside our families."[34]

Ehrenreich is probably not wrong when she says that there is a near universal and transhistorical human need for self-transcendence in experiences of group ecstasy (and with people who are effectively strangers) and that this need exists today under rather extreme repression—rock concerts and sporting events are the closest thing to it for most of us. But it's not entirely clear what sort of "strong bonds" she actually has in mind here, since what other sociologists call "bonding social capital," of the sort one finds in exclusive or homogeneous communities, for example, appears not to be in very short supply in our society today. What sorts of social bonds, we must ask, support reciprocal relations with people who are essentially strangers? Does the question point us to an inherent cultural conflict, one going all the way back to the dawn of Western civilization itself? Or is it,

30 Ibid.
31 Ibid., 253.
32 Ibid., 253–54.
33 Ibid., 254.
34 Ibid., 255.

as also appears to be the case with Gladwell, a matter of maybe mistaking something distal for something more proximate?

Putnam: The Lost Strength of Weak-Tie Sociability

In *Bowling Alone* (2000), which also concerns our growing, visceral sense of disintegrating social bonds, Putnam offers nearly the opposite view from that of Ehrenreich. He identifies the "something that's missing" today, not with the loss of "strong bonds," but rather with the lost strength of weaker ones, with the erosion of what he calls our "bridging social capital." Where bonding social capital "constitutes a kind of sociological superglue," it is bridging social capital that provides a "sociological WD40."[35] What then is referenced by this erosion? Weakened social capital "is manifest in the things that have vanished almost unnoticed [...] the unreflective kindness of strangers, the shared pursuit of public good rather than a solitary quest for private goods."[36]

Putnam's overall project in *Bowling Alone* is to try to understand the decline of civic engagement in the United States over the course of the last third of the twentieth century. He wants to capture the set of causes for why the boomers, unlike their "greatest generation" parents, ceased to be "joiners" of voluntary organizations (clubs and associations, religious bodies, unions, professional societies, etc.). He is therefore most interested in the kind of social capital that tends to support norms of generalized reciprocity among strangers, rather than the inward-looking, bonding social capital that is characteristic of exclusive groups, and that tends to support extreme out-group antagonisms. In his search for an adequate explanation for why we are "withdrawing from the networks of reciprocity that once constituted our communities,"[37] Putnam goes on to investigate various factors. These include lack of time/money, increasing mobility/

35 Putnam, *Bowling Alone,* 23.
36 Ibid., 403.
37 Ibid., 184.

sprawl, changes in technology and mass media, and generational change, and the result of such things as changes in family structure, race relations, and the role of government. All of them have some effect, he says, but none of them, on their own, is really decisive. For example, he acknowledges "commodity capitalism's erosion of social ties and trust," but downplays it as a background constant, despite the fact that commodification has steadily pushed ever deeper into the heretofore nonmarket relations of everyday life.[38] If anything, Putnam puts the most weight on generational change, saying that the anomaly may in fact be the high level of midcentury solidarity, rather than the subsequent steep decline.

If we want to rebuild social capital, however, what is to be done? To build social capital, Putnam writes, "requires that we transcend our social, political, and professional identities to connect with people unlike ourselves."[39] Consistent with Ehrenreich, Putnam writes, "we need to participate in (not consume or appreciate) cultural activities from group dancing to songfests, to community theater, to rap festivals."[40] But how, specifically, to go about replenishing our stock of bridging social capital? As a member of the "moralist camp," Putnam looks to the Progressive-era reforms in the early part of the twentieth century as something of a template for the revitalization of civic life. For those of us who see "the good in public goods" (sadly, only half the voting electorate), he proposes new, generative-type policies across multiple domains in order to create the conditions for renewed civic engagement. Along with other worthy prescriptions, Putnam thinks that there should be a renewed emphasis on civics education, community service programs, and extracurricular activities programming. We need less contingent working conditions and support for part-time employment to help redress unequal distribution of work and create a social dividend of more free time. We need urban revitalization

38 Ibid., 282.
39 Ibid., 411.
40 Ibid.

and transportation.[41] As a wish list, this is all well and good. But we should also add, while we are at it, that Scarecrow needs a diploma, and Tin Man needs a heart.

Members of the moralist camp of American social character analysis have tended to situate themselves within major theoretical debates that have dominated sociopolitical discourse in the last quarter of the twentieth century (whether implicitly or explicitly). Worried about consumer culture and excessive individualism, and sensing that something has gone very wrong with the demarcation between what is properly public and what is private, these critics nonetheless generally seek to find the mean between the claims of two opposing poles, whether it be liberalism versus communitarianism, proceduralism versus contextualism, or critical theory versus hermeneutics. Bellah's *Habits of the Heart,* for example, acknowledges the claims of critical rationality in the modern age as a legitimate horizon line, but then, drawing on Tocqueville, seeks to show that there are two pillars of our unique American heritage, "the republican and the biblical," that can be drawn upon to help us to repair our "damaged social ecology."[42] Recognizing that contemporary society offers two primary forms of social integration, reflecting the bourgeois/homme split at the heart of liberalism, Bellah says there is "the dream of personal success" and there is "the vivid portrayal of personal feeling."[43] Many of those with whom we talked "were locked into a split between a public world of competitive striving, and a private world supposed to provide meaning and love that make competitive striving bearable."[44] His prescriptions for "making our public and private worlds more mutually coherent" thus also fall into two groups. First, there is a cluster concerned with the concept of work, which he says should be seen "as a contribution to the good of all and not

41 Ibid., 405.

42 Robert Bellah, *Habits of the Heart: Individualism and Commitment in American Life* (Berkeley: University of California Press, 2008), 284.

43 Ibid., 281.

44 Ibid., 292.

merely as a means to one's own advancement."[45] Second, there is a set that deals with overcoming "obsessive self-manipulation," that is, the cultivation of the self through "peak experiences" and the sharing of what he calls "expressive solidarities in life-style enclaves," because these things, he says, do not result in any real and enduring civic consciousness.[46]

45 Ibid., 288.
46 Ibid., 292.

15

The Existence or Nonexistence of a Modern *res publica*

The *polis* was for the Greeks, as the *res publica* was for the Romans, first of all their guarantee against the futility of individual life.

— Hannah Arendt, *The Human Condition*

There is a rough parallel between the crisis of Roman society after the death of Augustus and present-day life […] Romans began to treat their public lives as a matter of formal obligation [….] As the Roman's public life became bloodless, he sought in private a new focus […] this private commitment was mystic, concerned with escaping the world at large and the formalities of the *res publica*.

— Richard Sennett, *The Fall of Public Man*

Modern Society's Multitude of "mute, inglorious Miltons"

A year before he was confirmed as US secretary of health, education, and welfare in the Johnson administration, where he was one of the architects of the Great Society, Republican John W. Gardner published *Self-Renewal: The Individual and the Innovative Society* (1963). Gardner, who would be completely anathema in today's GOP, later also went on to become the founder of Common Cause. Among other things, he was also a prominent critic of the Vietnam War and the father of campaign finance reform. But in 1963, Gardner was busy fretting about Spengler and Toynbee, writing that we should be more concerned about the conditions for "the ever-renewing society" than "the rise and fall of civilizations."[1]

In *Self-Renewal,* therefore, Gardner sought to describe what the self-renewing person is like, because he wanted to understand what society should do to provide the appropriate support and encouragement. Gardner believed that the individual capacity for self-renewal actually depends upon a set of generalized societal conditions. What matters "is having a system or a framework within which continuous innovation, renewal, and rebirth can occur."[2] Invoking the poet Thomas Gray, Gardner said that we have to start by recognizing that our world today, much like Gray's eighteenth-century churchyard, is full of "mute, inglorious Miltons," people whose full potentials are not "readily evoked" by what he calls "the common circumstances of life."[3] Gardner recognized that the issue runs far deeper than just talents going unnoticed. The basic challenge, he says, is compounded further by apathy, rigidity, and routine, among other ills, and because of modern conditions most of us become "accomplished fugitives from ourselves by middle age."[4]

What then are the societal supports necessary for encouraging the self-renewing person? Gardner's laundry list reads like a primer in Great Society political liberalism: the need to limit inequality arising from such things as prejudice and poverty; supporting the mobility of talent across all strata of society; the celebration of pluralism, tolerance, and the open society. Structurally this entails ensuring procedural justice, rule of law, protection of dissent, democratic checks and balances, limited

1 John W. Gardner, *Self-Renewal: The Individual and the Innovative Society* (New York: W.W. Norton, 1991), 2.

2 Ibid., 5.

3 Ibid., 11.

4 Ibid., 13.

government, and corporate power bounded by organized labor. Like old school liberals everywhere, Gardner denies that the social and political obstacles to realizing such a program of support for self-renewal have to do with "one social class dominating another."[5] Instead, they stem from a set of impersonal structural forces, which he calls "the tyranny of mass society."[6] He says that modern society comes replete with incidental causes of conformism, including market pressures that encourage common denominators, standardization, and homogenization, and also management techniques and large organization cultures that threaten innovation and creativity.

Per Gardner, there is also the problem of "bohemian nonconforming conformism," as had been described by David Riesman. Gardner's overall preoccupation with the problem of social conformism (and the related struggle to encourage innovation) thus closely mirrors Riesman's search, in his influential *The Lonely Crowd* (1961), search for "the utopia of the autonomous individual in an other-directed society." [7] As such, it does not yet register the extent to which a commodified, hyperindividualism has come to limit our choices for social belonging, and by weakening our bridging social capital, has come to threaten the public sphere as such. Were it not for the fact that the Great Society approach to reinvesting in our public (physical and social) infrastructure remains the official position of the Democrats even today, we might simply dismiss it as a laudable but naïve artifact of a previous time. By this I mean a time in which there was still a collective will to use major public investments to offset the social desert of our collapsing occupational, pseudo-public sphere, on the one hand, and its opposing pole of private intimacy and self-optimization, on the other.

In offering social policy prescriptions for how we might make our public and private worlds more mutually coherent, Gardner shows affinities for the genre of sociological writing I

5 Ibid., 55.
6 Ibid., 57.
7 Ibid., 73.

have referred to in chapter 14 to as the "moralist camp" of US social character analysis. This is the group that tends to worry about how consumer culture and excessive individualism are causing previous social bonds to disintegrate, throwing off the balance of public and private, leading to withdrawal from the networks of reciprocity that formerly constituted our communities. But does it really make sense just to search for some sort of a mean between public and private spheres as these appear to us as given under contemporary conditions? What if it turns out to be the case that these aspects of social character have actually been undergoing alterations on a continual basis, with increasing acceleration across the modern period? To come to a better understanding of what is meant by dissolution or collapse of the public sphere, its implications for work-as-we-know-it, and the prospects for realizing conditions for self-renewal, it is necessary to move beyond the moralist critique of individualism to arrive at a properly historical and then structural account of the modern transformations that have taken place in the meaning of "public" and "private." To this end, it is helpful to start with a comparison between Arendt and Sennett on the meaning and significance of the modern version of the Greco-Roman *res publica* (public realm).

Arendt's Denial of a Distinctly Modern Public Realm

The most well-known account of transformations in the meaning of public and private is undoubtedly the one found in Arendt's *The Human Condition,* where she famously rejected the entirety of the modern pattern in favor of the one supporting aristocratic, ancient Greek norms of political speech and action. For Arendt, first and foremost, the collapse or dissolution of the public sphere always refers to the way in which the "rise of the social" in the modern period came to destroy the ancient world's exemplary understanding of both the private and the public. Within the ancient Greek *polis* and the Roman *res publica,* therefore, Arendt sees what she regards to be the pure case, the one she says must serve as the yardstick for measuring what she says becomes blurred in the modern period. In antiquity, public life and private life are seen to be properly distinct and separated realms, which despite being wholly separate, nevertheless are interconnected by relations of dependency.[8]

The apparent contradiction is resolved when one comes to recognize how, for the ancients, participation in political life was thought to be the fullest flowering of what it meant to be a human being as such. The *polis* offered a life of excellence for the few, for those free to be seen and heard in public, and to contest for renown over matters of collective importance among an elite class of equals. Arendt says that the ancient notion of what we call "society" was a thoroughly political one, having the character of a temporary "alliance between people," that is, of political organization for specific purposes, and it stood in stark opposition to the private life of the household and the family, which they considered akin to that found among all forms of animal life, that is, the sociality of the flock, the herd, and the pack.[9]

However, the fundamental enabling condition for this public participation (along with that of being a male citizen head of household) was significant freedom from the yoke of necessity by means of having one's own place in the world. Arendt says that property literally placed a family on the map. To own property "meant to be master of one's necessities of life, and therefore potentially to be a free person, free to transcend his own life, and enter the world all have in common."[10] But how then to understand the Greco-Roman attitude toward the private realm if Greek *arete* and Roman *virtus* are to be assigned exclusively to the public realm? As a natural form of community rooted in biological necessity, Arendt makes clear, it was characterized first and foremost negatively, by its unfreedom in contrast to the public space of the *polis*. Arendt repeatedly uses expressions such as "deprivation" and "mere necessity," along with some-

8 Hannah Arendt, *The Human Condition* (Chicago: University of Chicago Press, 1988), 28–32.

9 Ibid., 23–34.

10 Ibid., 65.

what more positive terms, such as "sheltering and protecting" (i.e., women, children, and slaves) and even "hiding" (referring to the diverse class of things that should not be seen).[11]

Woven throughout Arendt's admiring description of the freedom of ancient Greek public political speech and action, and its enabling domain of privacy, one also finds the threads of her highly uncomplimentary characterization of modern society and its contrasting notions of public and private. Where ancient privacy is necessarily understood as a form of privation, modern privacy, by contrast, has been enriched by individualism into a sphere of intimacy that instead merits a high degree of public valorization. Arendt pinpoints this new phenomenon in the reaction to the rise of bourgeois social conformism in the eighteenth and nineteenth centuries; to the widespread desire for a space in which to retreat from the demands and pressures of market-based, mass society. The division of labor in modern capitalistic economies, buttressed by state policy supports, has the effect of relocating the diverse activity that formerly belonged to the domain of the ancient *oikos* (family property/the household) or of the medieval estates (landed nobility and the Church) to the heart of the public realm.

According to Arendt, "the rise of housekeeping from the shadowy interior of the household into the light of the public sphere"[12] has deleterious consequences for both private and public. To begin with, the functioning of a market-based economy completely transforms the meaning of private property. The dissolution of the ancient public realm can be seen in the way in which "the distinction between property and wealth loses significance […] because every tangible […] thing becomes an object of consumption; it loses its private use value." After the advent of a market-based society, she continues, a tangible thing acquires social value through its "ever-changing exchangeability," which

11 Ibid., 38, 59, 60, 62.
12 Ibid., 38.

becomes everywhere fixed "only temporarily, by relating it to the common denominator of money."[13]

The second major consequence involves the way in which the loss of the preeminence of this private use value affects the meaning of the public realm. Whereas in the ancient conception, private property was seen as the condition for entering the public realm (understood as the place where one could seek a kind of immortality via the pursuit of public displays of *arete/virtus*), under modern conditions, the public realm becomes instead something from which the owners of private property actively seek social protection.[14] What is common, in the modern period, turns out to be the commonwealth, which is nothing other than private interests in the aggregate, projected into the public realm. With this development, the permanence of renown in the public *polis* is decisively traded for the permanence of the process of accumulation, by monetary reward rather than *arete*.[15]

Finally, and perhaps most importantly for Arendt, the submersion of both the private and public in "the sphere of the social" leads to what she refers to as a generalized substitution of "behavior for action." The social realm, having "transformed all modern communities into societies of laborers and jobholders," is such that even though we have become "excellent in the laboring we perform in public, our capacity for action and speech has lost much of its former quality."[16] Modern society as such is most concerned with imposing rules that tend to normalize its members, and expects from each a certain kind of behavior, thereby excluding public political speech and action, and relegating to the private and the intimate what was once characteristic of the public realm.

In response to the question of the status of a distinctly modern public realm, therefore, Arendt's basic answer is that there

13 Ibid., 69.
14 Ibid., 72.
15 Ibid., 68.
16 Ibid., 46, 49.

can be no modern *res publica,* because such a thing would be a contradiction in terms. The public realm fell into dissolution already in the period of late antiquity. After a thousand years with no meaningful public sphere in the Middle Ages, modern society then emerged from feudalism, profoundly transforming the meaning of the private. On this basis, Arendt says, the modern age instituted a kind of a *pseudo-public* realm characterized by "the private in public," hopelessly blurring the distinctions necessary for a properly common world.[17]

Aspects of Arendt's critique of modern society are clearly still quite resonant. And yet, after almost forty years of conservative and neoliberal efforts to privatize everything common, to slash upper-income and corporate tax rates, eliminate many forms of social spending, deregulate markets, and to curtail most union activity, it has become rather difficult to affirm her glum assertion of the modern "victory of society." It would seem that her judgment may have been premature, unless of course we are willing to redefine the social world to include nothing but families and churches, bosses and co-workers, the state to protect private property and project power internationally, and the machinations and leisure activities of business/government/media elites. In lamenting the substitution of an ethic of accumulation for ancient public virtues, without then embracing a critique of capitalist society coupled with a modern emancipatory project, Arendt appears to be advocating for some sort of an exit from modernity. In her *Life of the Mind,* she specifically criticizes Nietzsche and Heidegger for wanting to follow "the rainbow bridge of concepts" back to the ancient world.[18] And though it is true that in this instance she was expressing her skepticism about a certain style of metaphysical speculations, it is still surprising that she would ignore the conditions of inequality and domination in modern mass society in order

17 Ibid., 69.
18 Hannah Arendt, *The Life of the Mind* (San Diego: Harcourt Brace Jovanovich, 1978), 151.

to focus instead upon the ancient Greek, aristocratic values of public excellence.

Sennett on the Crisis of the Modern *res publica*

Since Arendt effectively denies the existence of a distinctly modern *res publica,* recognizing it to be only a pseudo-public realm, she doesn't really have much to offer with respect to our contemporary experience of its relative dissolution or collapse. In *The Fall of Public Man* (1977), however, Richard Sennett investigates a similar terrain, but with these sorts of considerations thrust into the foreground. The major departure concerns how Arendt lumps together Greek and Roman experiences of public and private. Arendt writes, "The *polis* was for the Greeks, as the *res publica* was for the Romans, first of all their guarantee against the futility of individual life."[19] In another place, she says that "for the Greeks, "a life of privacy outside the world of the common" was idiotic by definition, and that for the Romans, "it was but a temporary refuge from the business of the *res publica.*"[20] Nothing is said about any possible differences between public and private in the *polis* of classical Greece versus Roman society, and there is certainly no comparison between contemporary society and the post-Augustan age.

At the start of his first chapter, however, Sennett writes that "there is a rough parallel between the crisis of Roman society [...] after Augustus, and the present day, concerning the balance between public and private life."[21] In the diverse society of imperial Rome, *res publica* had stood for "those bonds of association and mutual commitment which exist between people who are not joined together by ties of family or intimate association."[22] But as the Augustan age faded, Romans began to treat their public lives as a matter of "formal obligation," as duties to be enjoined

19 Arendt, *The Human Condition,* 56.
20 Ibid., 38.
21 Richard Sennett, *The Fall of Public Man* (New York: W.W. Norton, 2017), 3.
22 Ibid., 4.

"in a passive spirit, conforming to the rules of the *res publica,* but investing less and less passion in its acts of conformity."[23] Additionally, "as the Roman's public life became bloodless," Sennett writes, "he sought in private a new focus for his emotional energies [...] another principle to set against the public, a principle based on religious transcendence of the world." This commitment "was to the various Near Eastern sects, of which Christianity gradually became dominant."[24]

It is to this "later Roman" experience of privacy that Sennett then compares the modern one. Where the late Roman person sought an experience of mystical transcendence of the world, in private we moderns "seek not a principle, but a reflection [...] of what is authentic in our feelings."[25] Invoking Riesman's *The Lonely Crowd,* Sennett says that things are actually moving back from what Riesman called "an other-directed society" to becoming once again an "inner-directed" one, only this time, inner-directedness refers not to Riesman's notion of a strong ethical gyroscope, but rather to being "self-directed" or narcissistically self-absorbed.[26]

Much like Arendt, Sennett draws out implications of the changes in the meaning of privacy for the public realm. To begin with, where masses of people are concerned with "their single life histories and emotions like never before," we are led to believe that "community is primarily an act of mutual self-disclosure, and to undervalue the community relations of strangers." Sennett says that this overvaluation of individual experience is actually rooted in a kind of social anxiety that has its source in "broad changes in capitalism and religious belief,"[27] that is, what I have elsewhere referred to as the emergence of "the ideology of privatization" and of "capitalist spirituality" in chapter 12. Where social interaction is defined primarily in terms of "reciprocal revelation," or through what Sennett calls "the mar-

23 Ibid., 3.
24 Ibid.
25 Ibid., 4.
26 Ibid., 6.
27 Ibid.

ket exchange of confession," people seek to address public matters in personal terms, when they are better dealt with through codes of impersonal meaning. This obsession with the self "at the expense of more impersonal social relations," Sennett says, tends to create distortion effects, such as obscuring the "continuing importance of class in advanced industrial society."[28] The overall problem with privacy as a realm of intimate feeling is that it "tends to lose all boundaries," and once this happens, it is "no longer restrained by a public world in which people make alternative and countervailing investment of themselves,"[29] the kind of investments that conditions for self-renewal would seem to require. In the end, as Sennett recognizes, the erosion of a strong public life also ends up deforming our intimate relations.

Sennett's appreciation for the crisis of a specifically modern *res publica* clearly devolves upon his recognition of the relative achievements and trajectory of the bourgeois society of the eighteenth and nineteenth centuries: "The thesis of this book [...] is that these blatant signs of an unbalanced personal life and empty public life have been a long time in the making. They are the result of a change that began with the fall of the *ancien régime,* and the formation of a new, capitalist, secular urban culture."[30] Coextensive with the rise of a market economy and civil society, we see in the seventeenth and eighteenth century, depending upon the country and region, the emergence of what Sennett refers to as a "special region of sociability," one which begins with a self-reflexive, non-aristocratic audience or public for modern arts and letters.[31]

In Paris and London, for example, as the ranks of the bourgeoisie grew, the sense of "who the public were" and "where one was when one was out in public" grew and became increasingly enlarged, according to Sennett. It came to refer to "not only to a region of social life located apart from the realm of family and

28 Ibid., 5.
29 Ibid., 7.
30 Ibid., 19.
31 Ibid., 20.

close friends," but also that this "public realm of acquaintances and strangers included a relatively wide diversity of people," and a network of sociability and places where "strangers might regularly meet."[32] This included the development of urban parks and streets suitable for pedestrian strolling, coffee houses and cafes, inns and other public social centers. Once the cash economy expanded, and "modes of credit, accounting and investment became more rationalized," Sennett says, business was carried on in offices and shops [...] on an increasingly impersonal basis."[33] In both the realms of necessity and leisure, "patterns of social interaction grew up which were suited to exchange between strangers, and did not depend on fixed feudal privileges or monopolistic control established by royal grant."[34]

In the period of classical liberalism, therefore, one can discern what Sennett calls a certain "universe of social relations," where the bourgeois man "made himself in public," that is, in the realm of the market and its associated civil society, but "realized his nature in private," in the sphere of family, intimate relations, and feelings. By the mid-eighteenth century, "behaving with strangers in an emotionally satisfying way and yet remaining aloof from them was seen [...] as the means by which the human animal was transformed into a social being."[35] Sennett grants to this pattern of public and private life a certain coherence, but he acknowledges that it was doomed from the outset, destined to be torn apart by the "traumas of 19th-century capitalism."[36]

Sennett then goes on to describe the various ways in which the industrialization of labor and the effects of maturing capitalism across the nineteenth century transformed bourgeois society, eroding its social ties through privatization and commodity fetishism, among other things.[37] He also describes how, along

32 Ibid., 21.
33 Ibid.
34 Ibid.
35 Ibid., 22.
36 Ibid., 24.
37 Ibid., 25.

with increasing levels of inequality, worker alienation, and political foment, it also created broad patterns of status anxiety and stranger aversion. The mass production of clothing, for example, "meant that many diverse segments of the cosmopolitan public began [...] to take on similar appearance," such that "social differences [...] were becoming hidden, and the stranger more intractably a mystery."[38] Echoing Arendt, Sennett says that gradually, "as the will to control and shape the public order eroded," people responded to the traumas of capitalism "by putting more emphasis on protecting themselves from it," a circumstance in which the family then became an idealized refuge. Using family relations as a standard, "people perceived the public domain not as a limited set of social relations," but instead "saw public life as morally inferior," and the legitimacy of the public order was thrown into question.[39]

In *The Fall of Public Man,* as should be clear, Sennett uses the categories of social character analysis, welded to a historical narrative of transformations in the meaning of "public" and "private," to describe an extended crisis of the modern *res publica,* the bourgeois public sphere. Whereas in the *ancien régime* (and in the bourgeois society of classical liberalism) "public experience was connected to the formation of a social order," he writes, increasingly across the nineteenth century, "public experience came to be connected to the formation of personality."[40] The society we inhabit today, he concludes, "is burdened by [...] the effacement of the *res publica,*" i.e., the belief that "social meanings are generated by the feelings of individual human beings."[41]

Unlike Arendt, therefore, Sennett is willing to register something of the positive accomplishment of bourgeois social revolutions. On this basis, he then goes on to consider the increasingly solvent effect of "the tyranny of intimacy" on the bourgeois

38 Ibid., 24.
39 Ibid.
40 Ibid., 29.
41 Ibid., 419.

public sphere resulting from changes attributable to industrial capitalism and its effects on society. But despite the compelling historical analysis of transformations in the meaning of public and private, and his recognition of the role of underlying causes, such as privatization and commodity fetishism, Sennett's account of the effacement of the modern *res publica* remains firmly in what he himself has called the "moralist camp" of relevant social criticism. Since his focus remains primarily upon the tyranny of intimacy, that is, on the increasing absorption of society in questions of the self, his treatment of the bourgeois public sphere and its history of crisis is lacking a sufficiently nuanced account of the structure of the bourgeois public sphere and its functional political role in liberalism as ideology. Without this aspect, Sennett's critique ends up being merely prescriptive, and thus similar to the exhortations of the moralist critics we saw chapter 14. If we truly knew what is good for us, so the story goes, then we really ought to stop placing so much emphasis on the individual, and instead place a much higher premium on properly social action.

Up to this point, pursuit of an answer to the question, "What is meant by dissolution or collapse of the public sphere?," has seemed a bit like scenes from Plato's *Sophist,* where the Stranger's repeated efforts to catch the sophist in his conceptual divisions (*diaeresis*) yields dubious results. Just when he thinks he has caught him, and much to Theaetetus's consternation, the sophist breaks free of the angler's net and escapes again. In Arendt's and Sennett's accounts, we see the introduction of compelling historical snapshots of the differences between ancient and modern notions of public and private. These deepen the understanding gleaned from reading Ehrenreich and Putnam in chapter 14, but the picture of what constitutes the crisis of the public sphere today remains inhibited by the lack of a more complete account of the structure and function of the bourgeois pubic sphere, necessary for grasping the significance of its apparently long process of dissolution and collapse.

16

On the Crisis of the Public Sphere and Possible Counter-Publics

> In a post-liberal era, when the classical model of the public sphere is no longer socio-politically feasible, the question becomes: can the public sphere be effectively reconstituted under radically different socioeconomic, political, and cultural conditions?
>
> —Thomas McCarthy, introduction to Jürgen Habermas, *The Structural Transformation of the Public Sphere*

In the opening section of *The Structural Transformation of the Public Sphere,* where he reflects on transformations that have remade the categories of public and private, Jürgen Habermas makes the following key points in just a few short sentences:

- He is more or less in agreement with Hannah Arendt's account of the features of the Hellenic public sphere.
- This model has come down to us through the Middle Ages primarily in the sterile definitions of Roman law, finding a meaningful application once again only with the rise of the modern state as separate from civil society.
- In the early modern period, we see the legal institutionaliza-tion of a public sphere that was bourgeois in a specific sense.

— For about a century now, this sphere has been caught up in a process of decomposition, such that today "tendencies pointing to the collapse of the public sphere are unmistakable."[1]

There are obviously a great many details one would have to unpack to fully understand what Habermas has in mind here. But boiling things down further, there are three basic points that warrant focused attention, because together they represent his overall position. The first is that, according to Habermas (and contra Arendt), there is in fact a distinctly modern, bourgeois public sphere, one that arose out of early modern civil society. The second point is that this uniquely modern public sphere has been undergoing a long-standing process of decomposition. The third, and perhaps most important point, is that today the modern public sphere is tending toward a decisive collapse.

In chapters 14 and 15, related to this topic, I explored some prominent accounts of what is meant by the "dissolution or collapse of the public sphere," out of an urgent sense that today, the weakening of our "bridging social capital" has severely limited our overall choices for social belonging. I have further argued that the fading of our properly political public sphere tends to leave individuals with an unacceptable, binary choice between heeding the imperatives of the occupational, "pseudo-public" sphere, on the one hand, or choosing its opposing pole of private intimacy and leisure-oriented projects of self-optimization, on the other. Richard Sennett's *The Fall of Public Man* describes the crisis of the modern public sphere in relation to society's increasing absorption in questions of the self, which then throws off the balance of public and private, resulting in what he refers to as the "tyranny of intimacy."[2]

Sennett's account, however, proceeds primarily *by analogy*, that is, according to the assertion of a historical parallel between

1 Jürgen Habermas, *The Structural Transformation of the Public Sphere: An Inquiry into a Category of Bourgeois Society*, trans. Thomas Burger (Cambridge: MIT Press, 1994), 4.

2 Richard Sennett, *The Fall of Public Man* (New York: W.W. Norton, 2017), 417.

the *decline* of the Roman *res publica* after Augustus and the *decline* of the modern public sphere, beginning in the period of high modernism in the nineteenth century. As a result, the public realm in itself tends to be described by him in rather similar terms in both periods. In imperial Rome, he sys, the *res publica* "stood for those bonds of association and mutual commitment which exist between people who are not joined together by ties of family or intimate association."[3] In the seventeenth and eighteenth centuries, we also see the emergence of what Sennett calls a "network of sociability" along with "places where strangers might regularly meet" and then carry on business "on an impersonal basis," in patterns of social interaction "suited to exchange between strangers."[4]

Despite Sennett's clear understanding that the pattern of private and public found in early modern, liberal society is effectively dissolved by "the traumas of 19th-century capitalism," that is, via the erosion of social ties by such things as commodity fetishism, privatization, and class anxiety, we end up with an account that concerns only what he calls a certain "universe of social relations,"[5] without any specific understanding of the bourgeois public sphere's explicitly political task and functioning. Sennett's basic approach, that of simply comparing two periods in which a retreat into privacy devalued the public order, leaves us without a full consideration of the modern public sphere in its distinctiveness. As a result, the picture of what constitutes the crisis of the public sphere today remains inhibited by the lack of a more complete account of its overall structure and function, something that also turns out to be necessary for grasping the significance of its apparently long process of dissolution and collapse.

For as long the modern public sphere has been in a state of crisis, and whatever the process of its unwinding might be, anxiety over its impending collapse has reached enough of a high-

3 Ibid., 4.

4 Ibid., 21.

5 Ibid., 23.

water mark today that it has actually broken through into popular awareness. Consider, for example, the language of NBC News anchor Brian Williams's final broadcast signoff in December 2021.[6] Along with uttering the usual broadcaster thank-yous and platitudes ("what a ride it's been"), Williams used the balance of his final three minutes to say things such as this: "The darkness at the edge of town has spread to the main roads and highways and neighborhoods. It is now at the local bar, and the bowling alley, at the school board and grocery store." Just a few weeks later, in January 2022, US attorney general Merrick Garland, in an address to the assembled staff of the Department of Justice in which his voice thickened with emotion, also addressed the rising tide of social and political violence in our communities: "Across the country, election officials and election workers; airline flight crews; school personnel; journalists; local elected officials; US Senators and Representatives; and judges, prosecutors, and police officers have been threatened and/or attacked.[7] These are our fellow citizens […] these acts and threats of violence […] are permeating so many parts of our national life that they risk becoming normalized and routine if we do not stop them."

What can be happening here, it must be asked, when leading public persons, without much reflection, lamely attempt to address "the public" with urgent concerns about the crisis of modern publicity itself? To arrive at such an understanding, there has to be greater clarity about the structure and function of the public sphere. It is therefore useful, as a springboard, to consider Habermas's answers to the following questions: What is the nature of our distinctly modern public sphere? What is its connection to modern civil society? What has been its process

6 Brian Williams, "Until We Meet Again,", *American Rhetoric Online Speech Bank,* December 9, 2021, https://www.americanrhetoric.com/speeches/brianwilliamsmsnbcnewssignoff.htm.

7 Merrick Garland, "Attorney General Merrick B. Garland Delivers Remarks on the First Anniversary of the Attack on the Capitol," *U.S. Department of Justice,* January 5, 2022, https://www.justice.gov/opa/speech/attorney-general-merrick-b-garland-delivers-remarks-first-anniversary-attack-capitol.

of decomposition? What is the specific nature of its present crisis?

Emergence of the Bourgeois Public Sphere

Habermas signals his broad agreement with Arendt concerning the constituent features of public and private in the classical Greek *polis* and in the ancient *res publica*. The *polis,* he says, was strictly separated from the *oikos,* and public life, comprising debate (*lexis*), courts of law, and common action (*praxis*), went on in the *agora*. It was a contestation carried out among male citizens, who were largely free from productive labor, and whose participation was conditional upon their status as the unlimited master of an *oikos*. As for the *oikos*, it was an umbrella for all aspects of necessity—economic activity, the lives and work of women, the labor of slaves, and, of course, birth and death.[8] But where he departs from Arendt's position, the separation is swift and sharp, even if rather subtle. The Hellenic public sphere, understood as a realm of freedom and permanence, he remarks, has been handed down to us since the Renaissance in the stylized form of Greek self-interpretation, and, as with everything classical, it has been "imbued with a peculiarly normative power."[9] With this one comment, Habermas lets us know that the ancient Greek public sphere should be treated with some skepticism. If we keep in mind that it reflects the ideology of a ruling class, and therefore masks various things about its underlying social and economic relations, then it can no longer function as an ideal, and therefore should not be accepted as a yardstick against which the modern public sphere should be exclusively measured.

Unlike Arendt and Sennett, whose analyses are anchored in historical comparisons with Greek and Roman antiquity, Habermas turns instead to an in-depth consideration of the meaning of public and private in the Middle Ages in order to arrive at

8 Habermas, *The Structural Transformation of the Public Sphere*, 3.

9 Ibid., 4.

an account of the emergence of the modern public sphere in its structural and functional distinctiveness. On the Middle Ages, Arendt only says in *The Human Condition* that in the Christian era, "the common good" came to refer only to Christendom's universal interest in salvation and the hereafter, and that the ancient public *arete/virtus* was replaced decisively by charity/brotherhood in the Christian philosophy of Augustine.[10] This is all well and good, but Habermas thinks that *the specific manner of the public sphere's nonexistence* in feudal society, and also under early modern absolutism, is highly relevant to our understanding of what comes after. In the Middle Ages, there is no opposition between the public and private spheres corresponding to either the ancient or the modern model, Habermas says, because "a public sphere, in the sense of a separate realm" cannot be shown to have existed in the feudal society of the high Middle Ages.[11]

To begin with, despite the superficial resemblance based in similar "relations of domination," the feudal lord's position, Habermas says, "was not comparable to the private authority of the *oikodespotes*," the ancient "master of the household."[12] Because medieval society was strictly hierarchical, any relative sovereignty or prerogatives always resolved upward, to still higher sovereignties: The elements of hierarchical political life," of "lordship, caste, and guilds" determined the relationship of individuals to the state, and "his political situation via his separation and exclusion from the other elements. In such a society, "there was no status that [...] defined in some fashion the capacity in which private people could step forward into a public sphere."[13] In the Middle Ages, "lordly and *publicus* were used synonymously," and "the common man became the private

10 Hannah Arendt, *The Human Condition* (Chicago: University of Chicago Press, 1998), 53–55.

11 Habermas, *The Structural Transformation of the Public Sphere*, 7.

12 Ibid., 5.

13 Ibid.

man," reversing the Roman inheritance, where special privileges were deemed to be private.[14]

As hard as it may be for modern persons to grasp, despite our great familiarity with medieval times via various modern revivals, beginning with nineteenth-century Romanticism, the publicness of medieval public representation in no way involved what we think of today as the public sphere. The attributes of lordship in themselves were considered public, because lordship was represented "before the people" and not "for the people." The staging of publicity, Habermas explains, involved the representation of things wedded to personal attributes, things such as the ducal seal, insignias, dress, demeanor, and even rhetoric, which were all part of the system of courtly virtues that persisted into the period of the Renaissance. They communicated an economy of legitimacy, authority, and power.[15] As long as the prince and the estates of his realm "were the country," as in, "I am France," and not just its representatives, Habermas says, representation and publicity had nothing to do with "representation in the sense in which members of a national assembly represents a nation, or a lawyer represents his clients."[16]

In describing the absence of any sort of a public sphere in feudal society, Habermas's intention is to set the stage for an understanding of the emergence of the modern public sphere grasped in terms of its *structure and function*. The story of this emergence, for Habermas as with Arendt and Sennett, begins with the birth of a civil society as such in the eighteenth century as a new framework of sociability. With the growth of early finance and trade capitalism, Habermas writes, "a far-reaching network of horizontal economic dependencies emerged that in principle could no longer be accommodated by the vertical relationships of dependence characterizing the organization of domination in an estate system."[17]

14 Ibid., 6.
15 Ibid., 7–8.
16 Ibid., 7.
17 Ibid., 15.

Structure of the Bourgeois Public Sphere

Initially, Habermas says, modern state functions arose within the context of the traditional, hereditary absolutism, as something necessary to accommodate the exploding traffic in commodities and the needs of maturing national economies. We see the development of efficient systems of taxation to meet the demands of capital, and a public, administrative class as part of the state that now had an objective existence over and against the person of the ruler. He also points to things such as the proliferation of mercantilist stock companies, and as industrial production replaced trade as the leading source of wealth, the increasing nationalization of town-based economies.[18] The first major implication of this new "sphere of public authority" was the rapid diminishment of publicity of the type involved in the representation of the traditional, estate-based authorities. The advent of the national and territorial power states that came about on the basis of the early capitalist commercial economy "shattered the feudal foundations of power,"[19] with Church, prince, and nobility each having to give way before various dimensions of private autonomy.

In parallel with this, Habermas also wants us to see that "civil society came into existence as the corollary of a de-personalized state authority."[20] Once commodity exchange and social labor become emancipated from government directives, and commodity owners gained private autonomy, the capitalist division of labor led to a transformation in previous social relationships resulting in a new, overall *status naturalis* centered around relations of exchange.[21] Here we see, for the first time, such things as the legal equality of commodity owners freely disposing of their property in the market, and also the freedom to specify heirs, to choose one's line of work, to train for and freely exercise a trade,

18 Ibid., 17.
19 Ibid., 10.
20 Ibid., 19.
21 Ibid., 75.

and to receive a wage as determined by a free contract between an employer and an employee, among other things.

Following the growth in dense, horizontal networks of commercial activity and new types of social labor, the new civil society, as a realm of "private activity in public" separate from state functions, also led to the appearance of an array of public (or quasi-public) spaces: strolling boulevards and arcades, coffee houses, and salons and table societies, for example.[22] Where Sennett quite rightly describes the appearance of these spaces as "networks of sociability where strangers might regularly meet," and as such integral to the civil society's pattern of impersonal exchange, Habermas discerns something more, namely, the extent to which "the public sphere *in the political realm* evolved from this public sphere in the world of letters."[23]

The "world of letters" "was of course not autochthonously bourgeois," Habermas says, nonetheless, the "bourgeois avant-garde of the educated middle class" learned the art of critical-rational debate from the men of letters/philosophes who formed a kind of a *protopublic* sphere, or a "training ground for a critical public."[24] In this way, private individuals came together in these spaces, without regard to preexisting social status or rank,[25] to compare ideas and positions, and to reflectively form a reading public composed of all manner of people, including jurists, doctors, pastors, officers, professors, journalists, merchants, bankers, entrepreneurs, and manufacturers.[26]

By coming together in this fashion, Habermas says, t*he public of the now-emerging public sphere of civil society,* whether they grasped it or not, "readied themselves" to take up a properly political task, namely, "to compel public authority to legitimate itself before public opinion."[27] The distinctiveness of the bourgeois public sphere, therefore, as a part of the private realm

22 Ibid., 30.
23 Ibid., 30–31. My emphasis.
24 Ibid., 29.
25 Ibid., 36, 54.
26 Ibid., 23.
27 Ibid., 25.

between civil society (commodity exchange, social labor, and the family) and public authority, is thus found in its embrace of this new sort of publicity, one oriented to the exercise of a principle of control that was opposed to the traditional concentrations of power, and thus directed as a check on prior patterns of domination. Above all, Habermas writes, "the bourgeois public sphere may be conceived "as the sphere of private people coming together as a public" to engage public authorities "in a debate over the general rules governing relations in the [...] sphere of commodity exchange and social labor."[28] Having come to "think their own thoughts," he writes, "this counterpart of public authority [...] was led into an awareness of itself as the latter's opponent."[29] The authorities, for their part, for the first time "came to address their promulgations to the public," which of course meant primarily the educated classes and the owners of commodities.[30]

It is worth noting here that in *On Revolution,* published just four years after *The Human Condition,* Arendt shows that she understands and appreciates all this quite well, notwithstanding her extreme dread at "the rise of the social." Reflecting on the importance of the eighteenth-century philosophes, Arendt writes that their greatness is found not in their philosophical originality, but rather that "they used the term freedom with a hitherto new, almost unknown emphasis on public freedom," something distinct from either Augustinian free will or the freedom of choice (*liberum arbitrium*) between alternatives.[31] For them, she says, "freedom [...] was a tangible, worldly reality, something created by men to be enjoyed by men rather than a gift or a capacity."[32] She says that what the philosophes shared with the poor, apart from any compassion for their suffering, was "their obscurity, namely that the public realm was invisible to them, and that they lacked the public space where they

28 Ibid., 27.
29 Ibid., 23.
30 Ibid., 22.
31 Hannah Arendt, *On Revolution* (London: Penguin Books, 1977), 115.
32 Ibid.

themselves could become visible and be of significance."[33] What distinguished them, along with the emergent bourgeoisie after them, was not so much the "hatred of masters," since this can be seen anywhere. What was distinctive was their recognition that the possibility of freedom is found in "the foundation of a body politic which guarantees the space in which freedom can appear."[34]

Task and Function of the Bourgeois Public Sphere

After having characterized the bourgeois public sphere's emergence and structure, Habermas turns to the matter of its task and functioning. Insofar as civil society's bourgeois public sphere understood itself as a check on arbitrary authority and domination, he wants us to see that it functions in what is essentially a normative dimension, and that it does so in the contradictory manner of the ideology of classical liberalism. Like all intellectuals of the Left, Habermas can only show his appreciation for bourgeois revolutions for just so long, and then the appreciation must give way to a more equivocal and thus more ambivalent evaluation. On the one hand, the achievement of this new principle of publicity was located in the reality of the nineteenth-century bourgeois constitutional state, which established the bourgeois public sphere as an institution, formally linking it to the rule of law as its preeminent mechanism for the legitimation of rightful authority. Under the *Rechtsstaat*, so the story went, where the government derived its authority from laws ratified by a popularly elected parliament, citizens of the constitutional state were made equal under the abstract, universal protections of the rule of law, and as such would no longer be subject to arbitrary and capricious acts of domination.

On the other hand, Habermas says, "the fully developed bourgeois public sphere was based on the fictitious identity of the two roles assumed by the privatized individuals who came

33 Ibid.
34 Ibid., 116.

together to form a public: the role of property owners, and the role of human beings pure and simple."[35] By fictitious identity, Habermas here refers to the optimistic belief, which is a hallmark of liberalism, that one can go about one's business in the market as an acquisitive bourgeois and simultaneously express the values of a human being nurtured in the realm of the intimate, and do so publicly without significant contradiction, that is, without thereby reflecting an overall order of domination. For the private person, Habermas says, "there was no break between *homme* and *citoyen*, as long as the homme was simultaneously an owner of property who, as a *citoyen*, was to protect the stability of the property order as a private one."[36] The society solely governed by the laws of the free market presented itself "not only as a sphere free from domination, but as one free from any kind of coercion." This was certainly far from true, even during the liberal phase, but Habermas contends that it was not entirely false either — as long as the presuppositions of the bourgeois public sphere "could be assumed as given," that is, "as long as publicity existed as a sphere and functioned as a principle, what the public itself believed to be, and to be doing was ideology and simultaneously more than mere ideology."[37]

Dialectic and Crisis of the Bourgeois Public Sphere

During what he calls the initial, laissez-faire or liberal phase of the bourgeois public sphere, where it is seen to function as "both idea and as ideology," Habermas says, it nonetheless still retained at least some measure of credibility. But once the presuppositions changed, "a new kind of society of domination came to the fore."[38] By "changed presuppositions," Habermas means the manner in which the contradictions of capital result in social power becoming concentrated instead in private hands,

35 Habermas, *The Structural Transformation of the Public Sphere,* 56.
36 Ibid., 87.
37 Ibid., 88.
38 Ibid., 87–88.

creating a crisis of inequality that "pulled the veil of an exchange of equivalents off the antagonistic structure of society."[39] These changes, along with the state welfare interventions that come to be implemented to counter the oligarchic tendency, and to stabilize the capitalist order, are identified by Habermas according to the label "the dialectic of societalization."[40]

Despite some valid reasons to think that Habermas might be describing a dialectic in the Hegelian or Marxian sense, that is, as a change in historical forms brought about by a movement of determinate negation, his use of the term "dialectic" to describe the postliberal period's public sphere should be taken primarily in the unfavorable, Kantian sense of that term, as a logic of mere appearance and, as such, something illusory and false. To understand this "further career of the bourgeois public sphere" under conditions of its distressing dialectic, it is useful to locate what he is saying with reference, once again, to the position of Arendt. Habermas agrees with Arendt that, with the rise of civil society's public realm, "the private sphere of society becomes publicly relevant."[41] But the relevance of the private in public, at least in this initial phase, Habermas contends, was based on a strict separation of the two, inasmuch as "production was disengaged from functions of public authority, and political authority was released from production tasks."[42]

The dialectic of the bourgeois public sphere, therefore, describes what happens once the underlying crisis of capitalism leads to "public functions transferred to corporate bodies, and state interventions in society," and the demarcation between private and public becomes muddled.[43] It results in a social sphere in which "state and societal institutions fused into a single functional complex that could no longer be differentiated according to public and private."[44] We end up with a kind of industrial

39 Ibid., 144.
40 Ibid., 142.
41 Ibid., 19.
42 Ibid., 141.
43 Ibid., 142.
44 Ibid., 148.

feudalism, on the one hand, and a disassociation of the family from the work of social reproduction, on the other. Despite our remoteness today from the welfare statism of the mid-twentieth century through the 1970s, it's not hard to see the resemblance of this pattern to our present condition of occupational, pseudo-public sphere standing opposed to the private realm of leisure and self-optimization.

Finally, Habermas is also at pains to show how this progressive dialectic of societalization leads to a specific *crisis* of the public sphere also, with respect to its distinctive task and function. Since this emerging configuration does not support "either a spatially protected private sphere, or free space for public contacts and communications that could bring people together to form a public," he says, "the public, rational-critical debate also became a victim."[45] The intermeshing of society with various sectors of the state leads to wholesale administrative decision-making "without involving any rational critical political debate on the part of private people."[46] Increasingly, under this form of the bourgeois society, the political task and function of the public sphere is superseded by organized associations of private interest intent on shaping public policy, and by bureaucratic interests fused with the organs of public authority that attempt to establish themselves above the public. The political exercise and equilibration of power, Habermas writes, "now takes place directly between private bureaucracies, special interests, and public administration. The public is only included sporadically, and brought in only to contribute its acclamation."[47] Today, the consensus developed in rational-critical public debate has yielded to compromises either fought out or simply imposed nonpublicly, so much so that even the parliamentary public sphere has all but collapsed. The speeches made in parliament, he says, are no longer meant to convince delegates whose opinions differ "the task of providing a rational justification for polit-

45 Ibid., 158.
46 Ibid., 176.
47 Ibid.

ical domination can no longer be expected from the principle of publicity."[48]

The sense of crisis also bursts forth in and through the wholesale appearance of what he refers to as "manipulative publicity." With mass media and the public sphere now functioning primarily as a platform for advertising, warping politics and voting patterns, publicity loses its critical function in favor of a staged display, where "arguments are transmuted into symbols to which [...] one cannot respond by arguing, but only by identifying with them."[49] Where publicity goes from being "a critical principle wielded by the public [...] into a principle of managed integration wielded by [...] special interest groups,"[50] we get a public sphere that operates primarily as a field of manipulation via "social-psychologically calculated offers that appeal to unconscious inclinations," and "an acclamation prone mood comes to predominate."[51]

Bourgeois Publicity as Ideology and as False Consciousness

Given Habermas's assertion that the bourgeois public sphere is seen to function as "simultaneously ideology and more than ideology" in its initial liberal phase, the question of just what it means to function as *both* idea *and* ideology presents itself for further consideration. This turns out to be highly significant, because recognizing how the idea of the bourgeois public sphere itself continues to function today as an *ideology*, despite its decomposition, and despite its crisis, is a critical aspect of thinking through how the public sphere might yet be reconstituted. Put another way, it's not enough to say, as Miriam Hansen has written, that Habermas's concept of the public sphere "oscillates between the empirical and a normative pole"[52] because the

48 Ibid., 180.
49 Ibid., 206.
50 Ibid., 206–7.
51 Ibid., 217.
52 Miriam Hansen, "Foreword," in Oskar Negt and Alexander Kluge, *Public Sphere and Experience: Analysis of the Bourgeois and Proletarian Public*

relationship between these elements is even more complex than this would lead one to suppose.

In his earlier discussion of the bourgeois public sphere's emergence, structure, and function, Habermas seems to want to establish a hard line of demarcation between the concrete achievements of civil society's principle of publicity and its class-based self-delusions. To the extent that the new publicity results in civil society as a sphere of private autonomy characterized by the generality and abstractness of legal norms, and this framework of formal equality rests on legislation traceable back to a popular will, it functions as an *idea*. To the extent that it then represents liberal, market-based society as the foundation of a just order, as somehow free from coercion and from outright domination, it functions as a class-based *ideology*.

But in chapter 4, "The Bourgeois Public Sphere: Idea and Ideology," Habermas also acknowledges that the constitutional state, as the empirical achievement of the civil society's bourgeois public sphere, actually owes its existence, at least in part, to a set of strong liberal idealizations "concerned with rationalizing politics in the name of morality" that get explicitly addressed to its reading public.[53] Per Habermas, Kant's theoretical elaboration of the principle of publicity in his philosophy of right and in his philosophy of history provides the mature articulation of what he calls "the moral self-interpretation of the bourgeois public sphere," which ultimately undergirded the bourgeois constitutional state. Market-based civil society's new principle of publicity had held out the promise of human liberation through the foundation of a just order, free from domination and coercion. But how could the order of coercion imposed by bourgeois civil society somehow lead to a just society? If, as Rousseau suggested, "men must be forced to be free," then how is it that sociopolitical legitimation can lead to a general will that is also a good will? Per Habermas, Kant resolved the problem of how *res publica phaenomenon* could actualize *res publica noumenon*

Sphere (London: Verso, 2016), xxvii.

53 Habermas, *The Structural Transformation of the Public Sphere*, 102.

by means of an equivocation between two versions of his political philosophy, reflecting a liberal optimism that permitted the conflation of *citoyen* and *homme,* the "self-interested property owner" and the morally "autonomous individual."[54]

According to Habermas, in Kant's philosophy of right, he proposed the establishment of a cosmopolitan order arising out of natural necessity alone, seemingly in and through society's natural antagonisms, such that a "moral politics amounted to nothing more than legal conduct out of duty under positive laws." In the other version, as found in Kant's philosophy of history, he argued that the function of politics was to push for the actualization of the system of laws regulating civil society, and that through the political workings of *the public sphere itself,* society would see a progressive realization of an "intelligible unity of the ends of everyone."[55] At some point (i.e., in utopian fashion) human beings would emerge from the immaturity of their self-incurred tutelage, and perpetual peace would reign, because legality would then somehow issue from morality.

But this philosophy of history, with bourgeois publicity at its theoretical center, Habermas indicates, can only appear to function as a regulative ideal for as long as a certain set of social conditions prevailed, that is, where it was still believable that civil society was actually a "natural order for converting private vices into public virtues." This "fiction of a justice immanent in free commerce" could only be maintained for as long as the gap between the two sorts of legislation (acquisitive bourgeois and moral exister) remained narrow, keeping alive the ruse that everyone had equal chances to become enfranchised citizens via the market. "By the mid-19th century," Habermas writes, "the public sphere no longer sufficed as a principle for the linking of politics and morality."[56] Where proletarians were making demands for political rights and a new social order, the claim that the liberal order led to a just society had lost all credibility.

54 Ibid., 111–12.

55 Ibid., 115.

56 Ibid., 117.

In simply recognizing the civil society as primarily (i.e., as nothing more than) an antagonistic system of needs, Hegel was actually first, Habermas writes, to simply demote public opinion.[57] By the time of Hegel's maturity, it was possible to label the liberal, moral self-interpretation of the public sphere as nothing more than mere ideology. Since Hegel had identified the goal of civil society as such to be the protection of property and the freedoms of the propertied classes, it couldn't be seen to rise to the level of "reason in history," and so had no claim upon centrality to the being of the state.[58] For his part, and in predictable conservative fashion, Hegel asserts that the being or actuality of the state is found in and through its unity with the subjectivity of the monarch, as an ethical substance unique to each nation. Habermas says that Hegel "rejects the problem of the congruence of morality and politics as a false question," advocating instead for a return to the traditional estates system.[59]

Where Hegel internalizes the mature insight that civil society cannot ultimately be construed as a zone of rationality, and, in response, moves to the political right, Marx saw through Hegel's attempt to "rescind the factually completed separation of state and society,"[60] Habermas says, and thus elects to tack to the left instead. Wherever the private sphere is seen to achieve an independent existence, Marx indicates, a republic in the form of the constitutional state predicated on civil rights must be seen to emerge. Nevertheless, Habermas says, Marx denounced public opinion as false consciousness, inasmuch as it "hid before itself its own true character as a mask of bourgeois class interests."[61] Here we can see Marx making the last available move on the modern public sphere game board: recognizing the progressive achievement of bourgeois revolution while also denouncing its

57 Ibid., 118.
58 Ibid., 120.
59 Ibid., 122–23.
60 Ibid., 123.
61 Ibid., 124.

enabling idea as nonetheless a form of false consciousness, as pure ideology.[62]

Because the bourgeois public sphere could not reproduce its underlying social and economic order without continual crises, the critique of political economy thus takes specific aim at its self-interpretation as a natural order of things. The emancipation of civil society from the state led to capital valorization based on the appropriation of labor power and the extraction of surplus value, rather than to a new dispensation of freedom from domination and coercion. Instead, new relations of power were created, Habermas says, and so "control over private property could not be transposed into the freedom of autonomous human beings." The bourgeois did not in fact develop into the *homme/citoyen,* but he remained an agent in the process of the valorization of capital. As long as power relationships were not effectively neutralized in the reproduction of social life, "no juridical condition which replaced political authority with rational authority could be erected on its basis."[63]

Once the reproduction of social life took on private forms, the private realm, as Arendt pointed out, "took on public relevance." "The general rules that governed interaction among private people became a matter of public concern," Habermas says.[64] But the punctual and deepening crisis of the public sphere actually produced a revolutionary consciousness and politics, changing the terms of debate. The dialectic of the public sphere was such that groups of people who lacked control over property, and thus lacked private autonomy, came to be seen and heard in public. Since they had no interest in maintaining society as a private sphere, they came to embrace a countermodel, where autonomy was to have its foundation in the public sphere itself through the public control of socially necessary labor.[65]

62 Ibid., 125.
63 Ibid.
64 Ibid., 127.
65 Ibid., 128–29.

Having exposed its "moral self-interpretation" as an ideology, this dialectic of the bourgeois public sphere also implicitly called forth what Habermas, in his preface, had referred to as a "suppressed plebian public sphere,"[66] one that had already begun to function briefly during the French Revolution, and that surfaced again from time to time in Chartist and anarchist traditions. Since *The Structural Transformation of the Public Sphere* was concerned with the trajectory of the liberal model of the public sphere from emergence to crisis, it then became the project of Oskar Negt and Alexander Kluge, in *Public Sphere and Experience,* to describe the liberal public sphere's continued spectral existence after the fact, to explore what purposes its illusory existence had been put to, and to propose and theorize the emancipatory potential of counter-publics.

Negt and Kluge on Possible Counter-Publics

Throughout Habermas's investigation into the structure of the public sphere, from his account of its emergence, to its functioning, and then its continued trajectory of dialectic, dissolution, and crisis, the problem of false consciousness consistently lurks just below the surface. We see it when he admits that the bourgeois public sphere, in its classical liberal phase, functions as ideology, even if it is also "more than ideology." We see it when he says that its functioning relied on a "fictive unity" of the bourgeois as both *citoyen* and *homme*. We certainly see it in his account of the "dialectic of societalization," which disrupts the conditions necessary for the public sphere to credibly maintain its central political functioning. We see it again in his 2016 introduction, where he acknowledges the existence of a suppressed plebian public sphere. It is also evident in his discussion of what he calls "manipulative publicity." Finally, we also see it clearly in his account of our contemporary, occupational, pseudo-public sphere, which is also now also entering a state of collapse.

---

66 Ibid., xviii.

To understand what is really going on when we start to talk about a collapsing "pseudo-public sphere," however, we still need an account of how the bourgeois public sphere can remain a source of domination and control, even long after its structural dissolution. The final twist in this story, therefore, is to specifically address the issues of *the public sphere's ideological functioning under condition of its dialectic and crisis.* By addressing the meaning of crisis today, where the functioning of the public sphere appears to be almost entirely spectral, where the idea of the public sphere — its central notion of publicity — now functions almost exclusively as an ideological mask for domination by the capitalist class, it becomes theoretically possible to imagine how the public sphere might yet be reconstituted.

In *Public Sphere and Experience: Analysis of the Bourgeois and Proletarian Public Sphere* (1972), Oskar Negt and Alexander Kluge make all of this their explicit jumping off point. If we start with Habermas's recognition that "the task of providing a rational justification for political domination can no longer be expected from the principle of publicity,"[67] and we further recognize that publicity has gone from "a critical principle wielded by the public" into "a principle of managed integration wielded [...] by special interest groups,"[68] then, per Negt and Kluge, we can also go on to show the purposes to which this illusory existence has been put, and then propose and theorize the potential for establishing counter-publics.

In their formative years, Negt and Kluge had been assistants to Habermas and Adorno, respectively. Negt's previous focus was on the problem of working-class consciousness, and Kluge's was the emancipatory potential of alternative film and media culture, so their common concern with overcoming false consciousness led them to the problem of the public sphere.[69] With the contemporary history of the public sphere under condition of dialectic and crisis clearly in view, Negt and Kluge are

67 Ibid., 180.

68 Ibid., 206–207.

69 Negt and Kluge, *Public Sphere and Experience,* x.

unequivocal about its significance: "The decaying forms of the bourgeois public sphere can neither be salvaged nor interpreted through reference to the emphatic concept of a public sphere of the early bourgeoisie[....] what needs to be done [...] is to investigate the ideal history of the public sphere together with the history of its decay in order to highlight their identical mechanisms."[70]

To see how the spectral public sphere functions as an ideology today, therefore, we need a clearer-eyed view of how it has always functioned as such, despite its liberal, "moral self-interpretation." We need to recognize, Negt and Kluge say, that "the concept of the public sphere is originally one of the revolutionary rallying cries of the bourgeoisie," and as such, it is the "only medium within which the politics of the revolutionary bourgeoisie can articulate itself."[71] As the ideology of a revolutionary bourgeoisie, the claim of the public sphere to represent a general will actually functions as a powerful mechanism of exclusion. Contrary to liberal ideology, "the construction of the public sphere derives its entire substance from the existence of owners of private property," and "the bourgeois property owners," they point out, "were not interested in the formulation of public experience"—their prime interest lies in mitigating any "possible countereffects of this public sphere upon their private interests [...] they want to become involved in public works [...] so as to strengthen and protect property interests."[72]

At the heart of our investigation, Negt and Kluge write, "lies the use-value of the public sphere [...] which interests do ruling classes pursue by means of it?"[73] If and when we acknowledge that the public sphere, in its functioning, "fluctuates between denoting a façade of legitimation, and denoting a mechanism for controlling perceptions of what is relevant for society," then we must also come to the unequivocal conclusion that the bour-

70 Ibid., 3.
71 Ibid., 9.
72 Ibid., 10–12.
73 Ibid., 1.

geois public sphere is the "organizational form of the dictatorship of the bourgeoisie."[74] Put another way, the idea of the public sphere has as its actual goal the prevention of "Kant's dream of the political public sphere" from ever existing, by manufacturing "only the appearance of a collective will."[75]

When Negt and Kluge say that the public sphere "has use-value," they are also making the sociological observation that "social experience gets organized within it."[76] As a result, they add that "dominant interests can link *the experience of the majority of the population to the illusion of a public sphere*" (my emphasis), and in this way organize the suspension of this experience. Once we see the functioning of the public sphere in this way, then the organization of social experience can be undertaken for purposes of emancipation as well as for the creation of manipulative publicity on behalf of dominant interests.[77]

Per the film critic Miriam Hansen, as things stand under the early post-Fordist conditions in which they were writing, Negt and Kluge thought that it might be possible to "re-conceptualize the very notion of the public separate from the perspective of the present dominated by industrially produced, electronically mediated forms of publicity."[78] Where today market forces have learned "to plunder the interior décor of intimate thought," and "spiritual forces that had only been formally appropriated by capital" and are now being subsumed on a grand scale, they see a kind of a double movement.[79] As it pertains to matters of production, the experience of subordinate classes of people are under a kind of repression.[80] Where it pertains to leisure, desire for meaning, and ideology creation, on the other hand, they seek to erect a façade. With the public sphere, Negt and Kluge see "an "oscillation between exclusion, and intensified

74 Ibid., 55.
75 Ibid., 56.
76 Ibid., 3.
77 Ibid., 3n5.
78 Hansen, "Foreword," xxix.
79 Negt and Kluge, *Public Sphere and Experience*, xliv.
80 Ibid., 31.

incorporation:"[81] on the one hand, the rejection of the proletarian context of living;[82] on the other hand, the pre-organization of those parts of existence that had not hitherto been directly valorized by capital.[83]

Under contemporary conditions, Negt and Kluge identify two other fundamental modes of publicity for organizing social experience beyond the traditional public sphere. First, there is what they refer to as "the public sphere of production."[84] The public sphere of production recalls what Habermas referred to as "manipulative publicity," which Negt and Kluge say involves a set of unholy alliances between industry and mass media along with the disintegrating public sphere, rather than issuing from a concrete bourgeois form of life. This Hansen describes as being for the purposes of reproducing the dominant ideology and above all, to simulate the fictive coherence and transparency of a public sphere that is not one.[85] The second mode is what Negt and Kluge refer to as "the proletarian public sphere," which seeks to leverage Adorno's negative dialectics as a means to perform a kind of jujitsu move on the alienation, fragmentation, and confusion that the public sphere of production generates to suppress, delegitimize, or assimilate autonomous organizations of experience.[86] Where the public sphere of production continually organizes a suspension of proletarian experience, the systematic negation of large realms of social experience by the dominant pseudo-public sphere can be seen in some sense to "call forth" an alternative proletarian public sphere.[87]

When we consider the effects of industrial production and cultural reproduction under capitalism (alienation), and the systemic blockage of this experience, the dialectic of the bourgeois public sphere, that is, its continued dissolution, has the potential

---

81 Ibid., 14.
82 Ibid., 17.
83 Ibid., 18.
84 Ibid., 12–13.
85 Hansen, "Foreword," xxvii.
86 Ibid., xxxi–xxxii.
87 Negt and Kluge, *Public Sphere and Experience*, 31–32.

to become a broader play of negative dialectics, resulting in new forms of resistance and counterhegemonic practice. Here we see Negt and Kluge trading on Marx's claim that the proletariat is not an empirical category, but rather a category of the negation of the totality of existing conditions through a more all-encompassing historical and collective process experience. In doing so, they are foreshadowing the admixture of aspects of Adorno and Gramsci and the theorists of *Operaismo/Autonomia* that we find in later theorists of a politics of refusal, such as John Holloway. Negt and Kluge write in their 2016 introduction, "Where spiritual forces that have hitherto only been formally appropriated by capital have now undergone real subsumption on a grand scale [...] this is, in our opinion, precisely the point at which a countermovement can begin to take shape."[88]

Since Negt and Kluge were writing in what were still the early days of the globalized information age, the direction of their questioning, as sketched here, is perhaps more compelling than their further analyses, which likely needs supplementation by up-to-date media studies. After considering what interests the ruling classes pursue through the spectral existence of the public sphere, they go on to ask, "To what extent can the working class utilize this sphere?" Negt and Kluge's claim that the dissolution and crisis of the public sphere presents an opportunity for an "autonomously produced public sphere," or, as they later admit, in their introduction to the 2016 edition, a plurality of counter-publics,[89] has turned out to be prescient rather than just merely possible. We need only look at the (dismaying) achievement of the MAGA crowd in this regard, who now exist empirically as a genuine counter-public of the extreme Right, forcefully unraveling every aspect of the dominant pseudo-public sphere.

88 Ibid., xliv

89 Ibid., xlii–xliv.

Whether to Mourn Our Collapsing, Pseudo-Public Sphere

If Habermas and Negt and Kluge are correct, the bourgeois public sphere ceased to be primarily an organ for the self-articulation of civil society quite some time ago. Ever since the bourgeoisie lost its claim to being a revolutionary class, it has functioned for the most part hegemonically, as a powerful tool for reproducing ideologies supportive of entrenched and dominant interests. Accordingly, it makes sense to argue that our experience of a crisis of the public sphere today has mostly to do with the unraveling of various aspects of a "pseudo-public sphere."

For example, as the de facto social contract of liberalism's wage-based society has been increasingly dissolved and/or revoked, and the occupational, pseudo-public sphere has become degraded, it becomes possible to also recognize how our social experience has become increasingly constrained. Our public sphere is defined by market competition and the quest for enhanced, work-related human capital, and our private sphere is characterized by intimate experiences, happiness management, and personal projects of self-optimization. When we look for the conditions for genuine self-renewal rather than highly commodified projects of wellness and recovery, we perceive everywhere the loosening of weak-tie social bonds and are hard pressed to find any alternative mode of publicity. The phenomenology of this experience is something like that of being on the inside of a collapsing bubble, entombed in privacy, but with a strong visceral sense that conditions for individual self-renewal can't be separated from our collective experience of the crisis of the public sphere.

And yet the challenge of sorting out the diversity of definitions of the public sphere, and ideas about its process of dissolution and impending collapse, has turned out to be a long and winding road. The precise meaning of the phrase "crisis of the public sphere" is surprisingly elusive. If we look to the sociological literature on changing modern social character, we find an array of studies addressing generalized anxiety about the fading of our weak-tie sociability—everything from the loss of expressions of collective joy to the withering of widespread civic engagement, and the increasingly vexing problem of how to communicate with or get along with strangers. Common to all of these perspectives, there is a tacit acceptance of the assumption that categories of private and public are transhistorical constants, and that society should be exhorted to find and establish the right balance between them once again.

Where the moralist critics of hyper-individualism fail to produce a specific understanding of what constitutes the public sphere, historically oriented critics such as Arendt and Sennett describe the crisis of the public sphere through starkly differing accounts of a *querelle des Anciens et des Modernes.* According to Arendt, it is only meaningful to speak of a properly public realm when describing the ancient Greek pattern of political publicity. The *polis* offered a life of excellence for the few, for those "free to be seen and heard in public," and to contest for renown over matters of collective importance among an elite class of equals. By contrast, she contends, the modern public realm is inherently a pseudo-public sphere, characterized by "the private in public," thereby hopelessly blurring the distinctions necessary for a properly common world. Arendt uses the ancient *res publica* as a yardstick by which to compare the modern experience of public and private, with the result that the modern is found wanting, but Sennett's version of the *querelle* is framed as a warning about civilizational rise and fall in the manner of Gibbon. The increasing modern preoccupation with private selves is made to stand out in relief via an allusion to the collapse of ancient Rome. In both of Sennett's accounts of public culture tragically "gone positive," as Hegel would say, the public realm is seen generically as standing for "bonds of mutual commitment which exist between people who are not joined together by ties of family or intimate association."

Habermas really stands alone in asserting the existence of a distinctly modern public sphere, one that begins with an epochal idea—that of political legitimation grounded only in the bourgeois civil society's prospect for a common will. He describes the modern public sphere as a social space that is created between civil society and the state, which grows out of the collective awareness of the private autonomy of participants in the marketplace, with its densely complex social division of labor. The story of the crisis of the public sphere in Habermas concerns the fate of this idea, how it falls into dialectic, becoming itself primarily an ideology of manipulation and control. Despite his declaration that "the task of providing a rational justification for political domination can no longer be expected from the principle of publicity,"[90] Habermas nonetheless writes that "the outcome of the struggle between a critical publicity and one that is merely staged for manipulative purposes, remains open."[91] It was left to Negt and Kluge to propose an emancipatory potential arising specifically in and through the public sphere's spectral, ideological functioning under condition of its dialectic and crisis. Once we recognize the entirely hegemonic functioning of the semicollapsed public sphere, "we arrive at the point at which a countermovement can begin to take shape."[92]

In the years since *Public Sphere and Experience,* a literature has grown up around the notion of counter-publics as a site of resistance. Nancy Fraser and others have attempted to rectify the total absence of women's experience in changing notions of public and private, a glaring and unacceptable oversight in need of correction.[93] There is also a proliferation of work on the possibility of an environmental counter-public. Finally, the explosion of right-wing populism in recent years, paid for and directed by economic elites, has now raised the specter of how even nascent counter-publics can be colonized and appropriated by capital. The vector of a possible counterhegemonic practice, instantiated through the establishment of various counter-public spheres, provides a direction for answering a question that has haunted this chapter throughout: *What can it mean to mourn the loss*

90 Habermas, *The Structural Transformation of the Public Sphere,* 180.
91 Ibid., 235.
92 Negt and Kluge, *Public Sphere and Experience,* xliv.
93 Nancy Fraser, "Rethinking the Public Sphere: A Contribution to the Critique of Actually Existing Democracy," *Social Text* 25–26 (1990): 56–80.

of something almost entirely spectral? Despite the fact that the public sphere's idea has long since ceased to function, betraying its promise, it is nonetheless the case that the sense of crisis has entered a new and dangerous phase. As a kind of canary in the coal mine, heightened "stranger danger" provides us with tangible evidence that along with the public sphere's political functioning, the norms and rules underlying the civil society are now also entering a state of dissolution.

Negt and Kluge pointed out that bourgeois society does not need the public sphere in order to formulate its synthesis of society. "Competition and the law determining value create a centripetal tendency that holds society together."[94] The relative durability of civil society itself, therefore, as the foundation of civic nationhood, accounts for the paradoxical notion of "spectral functioning." Is it simply misguided, therefore, to mourn the increasing loss of the norms and rules of the bourgeois world's civil society? Unless one still believes in some sort of an iron-clad dialectic of history leading inexorably toward a classless society, the answer should probably be no. One should mourn the end of liberalism as a functioning ideology today, because the demise of its already-spectral public sphere heralds a likely descent into authoritarianism and neofeudalism, what Michael Hudson and others call "the big crunch."

If Negt and Kluge and also Habermas are right, rather than abandoning the idea of the public sphere in the realm of the political because of its present spectral function, we should instead recommit to the political reconstruction of a common world on a different, presumably postbourgeois, set of terms, one that meets the need for working-class recomposition. Whatever its specific features and characteristics, it would have to be a domain where it would be ridiculous not to decry the punching of nurses and stewardesses, the threatening of teachers and school board members, and the general loss of the assumption that one can simply go wherever one wants to carry on one's business in public, dispassionately, and impersonally. To enjoy a

94 Negt and Kluge, *Public Sphere and Experience*, 73.

common world, one replete with individual and collective possibilities, we should refuse to accept a modern world where we can no longer rely on the kindness of strangers.

17

Operaismo and the Postwork Political Imaginary

> Class doesn't exist naturally [...] Class is not a question of stratification, but of counter-position [...] class means class antagonism. As Tronti says, there is no class without class struggle. [Class struggle] [...] is never based on ideology or on the satisfaction of [...] identity, but is always a political wager rooted within a historically determined class composition [...] there is no class struggle without class recomposition.
>
> —Gigi Roggero, "An Interview on the Actuality of *Operaismo*," *Viewpoint Magazine*, 2020

The postwork political imaginary begins to unfold with a generational change in attitude that opens up a cultural space of refusal. This change is brought on (among other things) by a singularization of historical experience for younger generations, now facing the near-term prospect of ecological collapse. It also includes the development of strategies of resistance to conditions of precarity, arbitrary/purposeless jobs, authoritarian workplaces, and the harvesting of personal biopower. It further includes the social decolonization of key capitalist-realist notions that are important to the functioning of wage-based society, that is, necessary for capital's reproduction on the terrain of the so-called social factory. For example, there must be challenges to capitalist dogmas concerning usefulness, idleness and leisure, productivity and cycles of rest, and debt forgiveness, among other things (e.g., the degree to which wage-based society continues to be structured by gendered notions of productivity and the division of labor).[1] The postwork political imaginary also must include an understanding and appreciation of the transition from Fordism to post-Fordist patterns of work in the digital age, replete with new opportunities for both subjection and subjectification, and thus for the decommodification of labor. Finally, the postwork political imaginary and the politics of refusal also include the elaboration of approaches to an exodus — to the establishment of an autonomous, counter-public that could serve as an alternative to our currently collapsing, occupational pseudo-public sphere.

With all of this having been explored here as a conceptual terrain, the task that remains is to try to see what happens when these elements are cast into actual political practice. As a start, we should ask how well it conforms to our present, prepolitical situation. Looking out across the wide panorama of the world of work today, what does one see? A landscape of labor dramatically transformed as a result of post-Fordist, neoliberal capital's wholesale restructuring in the digital age. This includes technologies to enable automation and control of production, new management approaches, globalized, real-time, and 24/7 network communications, the financialization and globalization of markets, the unprecedented rise of the services sector, and other changes. Born out of the effects of this changing "technical composition of capital," one also encounters a new and different "class composition." As one might expect, along with the new experience of work, there is also becoming visible a yawning generation gap between the new subjects of wage labor and

1 Encouragement of a postwork political imaginary is oriented toward the establishment of a viable, broad-based politics of refusal of work-as-we-know-it. At the level of strategy, it also has to be responsive to the experiences and needs of specific communities of identity, and to things such as historical, regional, and cultural differences, for example.

their putative political leaders, organizations, and institutions. The generation gap reflects different needs, feelings, and forms of expression, and new attitudes and imperatives, including a new attitude of refusal. In connection with all of this, there is a recognition of an urgent need to challenge previously unquestioned work-related dogmas, to study and understand the new class composition, and to reframe previous narratives about the nature of political struggle, in order to imagine a path to some measure of worker autonomy from the commands of advanced technological capitalism.

I hope this summary, obviously just a sketch, serves as a reasonable description of the prepolitical situation in which we find ourselves today in postindustrial Western societies. Even the most cursory review of the posts of the 2.2 million people on the "anti-work subreddit" provides us with powerful supporting testimony to this effect. But it's also worth pointing out that this prepolitical landscape (with some obvious caveats) can also serve just as well as a description of the situation in northern Italy in the late 1960s, at the birth of the movement of *Operaismo* (Workerism). The scene of *Operaismo* is important here, because it is perhaps the only time when a genuine mass movement of the refusal of work and wage-based society has played out in the industrial West in the postwar period. Getting a clear sense of the real-world trajectory of *Operaismo* and post-*Operaismo* (*Autonomia*) in both theory and practice, here in this final chapter, can help to pull together the threads of the various explorations included in this book. An understanding of the real-world career of *Operaismo* can focalize what is at stake in challenging capitalist realist notions about work, grasping the meaning and significance of work in the digital age, and establishing a postwork counter-public as a means to an exodus.

Operaismo and the Politics of Refusal of Work

What, then, was *Operaismo/Autonomia?* For those seeking to answer this question, there has been a commonly seen tendency to want to tell the story backward, starting with the effective dissolution of the movement after the terrible events of 1977–79. By this I mean the kidnapping and murder of the industrialist/Christian Democrat Party leader Aldo Moro by the Red Brigades (*Brigate Rosse*), and the subsequent imprisonment of *Autonomia* leaders by the Italian government, without trial, and under a state of exception. This retrospective approach, however, leads to an understanding of the political movement by way of the various splits. For example, there are the differences between post-*Operaismo* (the *Autonomia* group) and the Red Brigades (BR). There are the differences between the post-Operaismo of Antonio Negri and the previous *Operaismo* movement of the 1960s, championed by Mario Tronti. Tronti, for example, says that *Operaismo* refers only to the activity that took place in and around the two journals *Quaderni Rossi* (*Red Notebooks*) and *Classe Operaia* (*Working Class*) between 1961 and 1966: "*Operaismo* starts with the *Quaderni Rossi* and stops with the death of *Classe Operaia*. End of story."[2]

These various distinctions certainly matter, especially for political historians. Once it's clear how *Operaismo* and *Autonomia* diverge from the Marxist-Leninist position of the BR, however, it's actually the throughline that connects the movement of the 1960s to the post-*Operaismo* of Negri and others in the late 1970s that is more relevant to the question of the politics of refusal today than the various causes of schism (the different attitudes and positions, and priorities and practices that make *Autonomia* distinct from *Operaismo*). One can applaud Roman Alquati's empirically grounded studies of class composition that belong to the early movement of *Operaismo*, for example, while still recognizing that their nearly exclusive focus on industrial labor in the factories becomes less relevant under post-Fordist conditions, where the reproduction of capital increasingly involves the entire "social factory." Likewise, one can agree with *Autonomia* that the subject of labor is now the "socialized worker" (i.e., all wage laborers under post-Fordist conditions

2 Mario Tronti, "Our *Operaismo*," in *Workers and Capital*, trans. David Broder (London: Verso, 2019), 327.

in the knowledge economy) and still find that the poststructuralist-inspired general social theory found in Hardt and Negri's *Empire* (2000) suffers, as Paul Thompson argues, from a lack of empirical grounding in real political economy.[3] For purposes of establishing the elements of the postwork political imaginary and a politics of refusal, there are thus critical lessons, both pro and con, to be learned from both the early *Operaismo* and the subsequent post-*Operaismo/Autonomia.*

In his introduction to Negri's *Marx Beyond Marx* (1978), Harry Cleaver summarizes the basic thrust of post-*Operaismo* in a way that expresses its essential continuity with the original *Operaismo*. When rendered as an ordered list, the summary looks something like this:

1. Capitalism is a social system with two subjectivities.
2. Capital controls the working class through the imposition of work.
3. The logic of this control is the dialectic which constrains human development within the limits of capitalist valorization.
4. Therefore, the central struggle of the working class as an independent subject is to break capitalist control through the refusal of work.
5. The logic of this refusal is the logic of antagonistic separation to undermine the dialectic.
6. In the space gained by this destruction, the class builds its own independent projects, its own self-valorization.
7. The refusal of work becomes the planned abolition of work as the basis of the constitution of a new mode of producing and a new multi-dimensional society.[4]

---

3 Paul Thompson, "Foundation and Empire: A Critique of Hardt and Negri," *Capital and Class* 29, no. 2 (2015): 74.

4 Harry Cleaver, introduction to Antonio Negri, *Marx Beyond Marx: Lessons on the Grundrisse,* ed. Jim Fleming, trans. Harry Cleaver, Michael Ryan, and Maurizio Virano (New York: Autonomedia/Pluto Press, 1991), xxvii.

For the purpose of extracting what can be learned that is relevant to a possible politics of refusal of work and wage-based society today, therefore, it is not unreasonable to refrain from worrying too much about labels, and thus, for the most part, to refer to the movement and its various articulations, splits, and factions, basically everything that happened in the movement from 1961 to 1977 and beyond, simply as *"Operaismo."* Where I have indicated that there is an essential throughline that binds the various articulations and moments of *Operaismo*, I have in mind the continuity of certain key concepts across its trajectory. Here I mean the "Copernican reversal" of capital and labor, class composition, the mass worker, the social factory, the socialized worker, the problem of recomposition, general intellect and immaterial labor, working-class self-valorization or autonomy, and refusal of work. Before delving into these formal constituents, however, it is useful to have some initial sense of the history and trajectory of *Operaismo* as a real political movement.

The Semiotext(e) anthology of historically important collected writings titled *Autonomia* (2007) begins with a series of journal entries from the culture critic Sylvère Lotringer, who met with members of the movement in the summer of 1979. Lotringer's journal and introductory essay are somewhat kaleidoscopic but include a number of statements that, in loose paraphrase, can also provide a starting point. They are intended as a description of post-*Operaismo/Autonomia*, but they can be seen to hold for the previous *Operaismo*. *Operaismo*, per Lotringer's impression, therefore, is Marxism reformulated to elude the imperative of production, the verticality of institutions, and the traps of political representation. It is an extraparliamentary movement of the Left, seeking to define a new way of doing politics, addressing specific and concrete needs without delegation. It is the search for a new class composition, capable of acting outside the party system, and as such the search for a new political terrain, where diverse strata could join and recompose a front against capital and wage labor. Finally, it is thus an intention to assume a revolutionary position inside and against capitalism through a struggle against work, that is, through a refusal of work.[5]

Operaismo as a Political Movement: The Historical Context

To understand what all this really means on the ground, it becomes necessary to grasp some important things about the movement's historical context and material preconditions, and then also how *Operaismo* as an intellectual formation arose in response to these. To begin with, the intelligibility of *Operaismo* is inseparable from the condition of the classes (both labor and capital) in Italy following World War II. Reflecting on the origins of the movement out of the new, postwar class composition, Sergio Bologna says that after the war, the party system in Italy inherited powerful tools for interference in the process of the reproduction of classes from the fascist government. As a result, it came to control key sectors of the economy. The Christian Democrats (CD) were able to negotiate with the United States and multinationals regarding the international division of labor and "to organize class relations in a way that corresponded to the plans for political stability."[6]

Especially in the north, this meant "top-down planning for the massification of labor power in large-scale industry," something that ran headlong into serious conflict with traditional village life as it existed up to that point.[7] "It was only in the late 50s and early 60s," Tronti writes, "that modern capitalism really took off in Italy, and the ancient little world of civil society embedded in the memory of the 19th century, finally came to an end."[8] For its part, the Italian Communist Party (PCI), already at that time (1945–46), made the fateful choice, along with the

5 Sylvère Lotringer, "In the Shadow of the Red Brigades," in *Autonomia: Post-Political Politics,* eds. Sylvère Lotringer and Christian Marazzi (Los Angeles: Semiotext(e), 2007), v–xvi.

6 Sergio Bologna, "The Tribe of Moles," in Lotringer and Marazzi, eds., *Autonomia,* 37.

7 Ibid.

8 Tronti, *Our Operaismo,* 338.

other parties, Tronti says, "to replace their relations with [...] the masses by mutual relation among themselves."[9] As Steven Wright has also emphasized, *Operaismo* must be seen to have evolved in response to the distance of the PCI from working-class composition and politics.[10] The cultural and political space for the assertion of working-class autonomy and a politics of refusal in the factories began with this opening up of new political space to the left of the PCI, a rolling crisis of the Left that reached its apotheosis with the so-called historic compromise of 1976 when the PCI entered into explicit partnership with the CD.

With respect to the overall *Operaismo* timeline of events, there is a generally recognized first period. Here, resistance and new thinking is focused on changing technological and management conditions in the northern factories, the changing class composition of the new Italian mass worker (which included the importation of large numbers of younger workers from the south), and the role of a broader social reproduction of capital in the changing patterns of life in the surrounding areas. Per Tronti, the theoretical work during this period involved close rereadings of Marx, with an intentionally foregrounded emphasis on labor struggles and class antagonism. In particular, *Operaismo* was reading *Capital,* the *Economic and Philosophical Manuscripts,* and the newly available translations of the *Grundrisse*. The work also involved performing sociological micro-analyses of worker experience, class composition, and changing attitudes on the shop floor, especially those published by Romano Alquati in the *Quaderno Rossi.* In "Our *Operaismo,*" Tronti himself summed up the new attitude and ethos during this period: "Our workers were not like those of Engels's Manchester [...]

---

9 Bologna, "The Tribe of Moles," 37.

10 Steven Wright, "Foreword," in Tronti, *Workers and Capital,* viii. *Operaismo's* central precepts were developed over the course of the early 1960s, during which its advocates differentiated themselves from the mainstream Left in Italy. They were united, he says, by a common belief that the leadership of the local Communist (PCI) and Socialist (PSI) parties did not understand the recent massive changes in working-class composition and politics.

we didn't bring *The Condition of the Working Class in England in 1844* with us to the factories, we brought the struggle against work in the *Grundrisse*."[11] Along with the Marx, Wright also emphasizes that Tronti's *Operai e Capitale* (1966) served as a kind of a bible for the group *Potere Operaio* (Worker's Power) during this time.[12]

Following this first phase, there is what might be called a middle, post-*Operaismo* period, fueled by the youth revolt of 1968, which was more focused on the world of broader social resistance beyond the factory, which, as Lotringer wrote in his journal, comprised "young intellectuals, young workers, and the unemployed, and was opposed to the work ethic, hierarchy, and ideological rigidity, and engaged in pranks, squats, reappropriations, and pirate radio."[13] It's important to note that the group *Potere Operaio* had included figures such as Antonio Negri, Franco Piperno, and Oreste Scalzone, all of whom later went on to be leading "Autonomists" after *Potere Operaio's* dissolution in 1973 over conflicting approaches to organizational forms and movement militarization (i.e., over Marxist-Leninist tendencies of some parts of the rank and file).[14]

The final *Autonomia* period begins with the economic stagnation of the mid-1970s, and begins to play out in the wake of the so-called historic compromise, where the PCI joined with the CD, and when some of the Left, under increasing pressure from irregular groups of the Right and from the state, actively embraced violent struggle (Red Brigades).[15] Subsequent to the mass arrests of militants and leaders in the late 1970s, *Autonomia* in the 1980s and beyond becomes mostly post-Fordist theory, concerned with establishing the emancipatory potential that may be found within the changing conditions of advanced technological capitalist society as a whole.

11 Tronti, "Our *Operaismo*," 335.
12 Wright, "Foreword," vii.
13 Lotringer, "In the Shadow of the Red Brigades," v.
14 Ibid., xii.
15 Ibid., vi.

Operaismo as a Distinctive Intellectual Formation

According to Tronti, again in "Our *Operaismo*," the key date for marking the beginning of the "workerist tendency" was 1956, the year in which there was a kind of a confrontation on the left. On one side, as Tronti said, there were those who recognized that the factory worker as he existed in Italy at that time "was a 20th-century figure,"[16] and so sought to filter Marxism through the reality of the Italian workforce experience. On the other, there was the leftist (PCI) establishment of the Instituto Gramsci, which promoted a distinctly Hegelian-idealist reading of Marx (one consistent with a line of influence in Italy that stretched back to the early influence of Benedetto Croce). "At the *Instituto Gramsci*," Tronti wrote scathingly, "they didn't write books [...] they read books, and between each initiative, they discussed what they thought of them."[17] The problem was not so much with Gramsci's analysis of the differences between the prerevolutionary situation of the West versus Russia, and with his recognition of the many trenches and fortresses of decentralized hegemonic power upon which the capitalist society and state rests. The problem had to do with what was made of this analysis in the hands of the PCI, who accepted the implication of a slow process of establishing working-class hegemony after a protracted "war of position." The eventual historic compromise with the CD thus reflected a recognition of the need for a system of alliances within the representative bourgeois democracy to help bring about an incremental transition to socialism through gradual reforms.

Tronti and the *Operaismo* groups in Turin, Bologna, and Padua, who were living a contemporary experience of class antagonism, were thus seeking what Wright has called a "theoretical rebirth of the working-class viewpoint" in support of autonomous committees in the factories.[18] For these groups, a

16 Tronti, "Our *Operaismo*," 335.

17 Ibid., 329.

18 Wright, "Foreword," x.

dialectical understanding of class positions, relative to an overall concept of totality, was at odds with the understanding of capitalist development as a repeating cycle of struggles between labor and capital. It was thus considered to be incapable of yielding an adequate notion of proletarian self-valorization, which instead depended upon on a stance of refusal and separation. In an early piece, Negri said that the compatibility of self-valorization with productive structuration is a myth. "Class self-valorisation has nothing to do with the structuration of capital [...] proletarian self-valorisation is the power to withdraw from exchange value and the ability to reappropriate the world of use values."[19]

Fleming also wrote in the preface to Negri's *Marx Beyond Marx* that where the term "hegemony" had come to imply "a static and passive working class, determined by its relation to capital," class composition and its political recomposition was focused instead on the tenuousness of capitalist control. It thus referred to "the process of the socialization of the working class, and the extension, unification, and generalization of its antagonistic tendency against capital, in struggle, and from below."[20] For *Operaismo*, as Tronti had already said in *Operai e Capitale*, "the society of capital and the workers party [...] [exist] as two opposite forms with one and the same content," that is, they represent an irreducible antagonism.[21] In substantive agreement with Tronti on this point, Negri, also in "Domination and Sabotage," said that there is "no homology [...] between the reality of the movement [of resistance] and the overall framework of capitalist development, with its contents and objectives."[22]

The "Copernican reversal of capital and labor," which figures so prominently in *Operai e Capitale*, and which emerged out of a close reading of the *Grundrisse*, finds its essential urgency in this need to intensify class antagonism in the interest of the project

19 Antonio Negri, "Domination and Sabotage," in Lotringer and Marazzi, eds., *Autonomia*, 66.
20 Jim Fleming, "Editor's Preface," in Antonio Negri, *Marx Beyond Marx*, xi.
21 Tronti, *Workers and Capital*, 242.
22 Negri, "Domination and Sabotage," 64.

of proletarian self-valorization and autonomy. In the chapter "The Strategy of Refusal," Tronti begins by noting that although working-class power is indeed closely tied to the productive power of wage labor, "capital is rather a social power," that is, a power of domination and exploitation. As such, the existence of the capitalist class ultimately derives from the productive power of labor, and because the activity of organizing labor through industry is the very thing that "provokes capitalists to constitute their own class interests, via the state," capitalist class consciousness is also therefore derived in similar fashion.[23]

The meaning of bourgeois revolution, Tronti says, is nothing more than the process whereby the capitalist class seeks to emancipate itself by using the state to enforce working-class subordination. Likewise, where technological innovation appears as the primary means whereby capital seeks emancipation from dependence upon labor power, the man–machine relationship, as "the history of the interaction between working class struggles and capitalist initiatives," Tronti says, shows us that industry is really the working-class history of capital.[24] Despite unrelenting efforts on the part of the capitalist class to make it appear otherwise, Tronti says that it is class antagonism, in the end, that is the driver of technological innovation, and he sums up his position by saying flatly that the antagonism of capital and its continuous attempts to free itself shows that "the capitalist class is in fact subordinate to the working class."[25]

As a politics of refusal of work, therefore, *Operaismo* finds its major theoretical significance in and through recognition of the significance of this intensified, oppositional but nondialectical class antagonism — the essential class relationship that is everywhere obscured by its stealthy inversion through capitalist social hegemony.[26] Where workers struggle against their employers,

23 Tronti, *Workers and Capital,* 243.

24 Ibid., 244.

25 Ibid., 246.

26 In the first part of this book, my focus was on breaking the spell of capitalist realism as a condition for bringing forth the postwork political imaginary; the second part described how capitalism reproduces itself

Tronti says, they are actually saying "no" to the transformation of labor power into labor.

Refusing to receive work from the capitalist, he says, as occurs in the strike, does not signify a refusal to give capital the use of one's labor power, since it has already been so given, per contract, nor does it represent a refusal to allow capital the product of labor, since this is already capital's property. Rather, stopping work implies a refusal of the command of capital as the organizer of production. Refusal, so understood, is thus intimately tied to the notion of autonomy, to the recognition that it is labor that produces capital. As autonomous (i.e., as nonsubordinate) the working class can refuse, because without labor power, so the story goes, capital—as dead labor—remains dead.[27] With this last part, we also see why *Operaismo* is concerned primarily, Negri says, with the search for the laws that govern proletarian self-valorization as a parallel and opposed process to the valorization of capital.[28] Once autonomy is understood in and through the nonparallelism of these two opposing processes of valorization, one can also come to the conclusion, as does Tronti, that the proletariat does not need institutions, only organization and tactics.[29]

Automation, General Intellect, and the Subsumption of Living Labor

Even before the political events of the late 1970s had shattered the momentum of the original *Operaismo's* project of "working-class recomposition" (which was grounded in the ebb and flow

through an abstract and impersonal form of domination. Here everyday class antagonism is also largely de-emphasized. In the third part, which concerns how to frame a possible exit from our collapsing, occupational pseudopublic sphere (a politics of refusal) the essential connection between value and class is foregrounded, along with the need to reassert and intensify class antagonism.

27 Tronti, *Workers and Capital,* 244.

28 Negri, "Domination and Sabotage," 65.

29 Tronti, *Workers and Capital,* 248–49.

of shop floor struggles, and which was ultimately decimated by mass arrests, the firing of shop stewards, and the purging of worker assemblies), it had already been largely overtaken by another form of extraparliamentary politics. It was eclipsed, as Henri Weber pointed out, by the potency of various unilateral administrative actions taken in the service of financial globalization — the withdrawal of investments, the flight of capital, and speculation against the lira, leading to massive unemployment, galloping inflation, and so on.[30] The arrival of post-Fordism, therefore, replete with increasingly immaterial labor and the effects of globalized flows of capital, defines a transition within *Operaismo,* a change in emphasis from Tronti's *Grundrisse*-inspired investigations into industrial working-class antagonism to the search for a new form of worker agency lurking in the "not-so-hidden abode" of post-Fordist production in the digital age.

The lodestone for this post-*Operaismo* analysis, it turns out, was a short section of Marx's *Grundrisse,* spanning the end of Notebook VI and the beginning of Notebook VII, which has come to be known as "The Fragment on Machines."[31] "The Fragment" begins with a juxtaposition between the role of living labor in the production process as it was before machine automation, and then after the adoption of automatic machine technologies as a form of fixed capital in the labor process. For perhaps all of human history, up to and including the early phases of the industrial revolution, fixed capital serves as a means of transforming raw material into products in such a way that it functions, first and foremost, as a use value for aiding the virtuoso craftsperson or worker. In the industrial age, before automated, machinic labor processes, one finds capital, the means of labor, the production process, and living labor. Materially, they function together in what Marx calls a "moving unity."[32]

30 Henri Weber, "In the Beginning Was Gramsci," in Lotringer and Marazzi, eds., *Autonomia,* 89.

31 Karl Marx, *Grundrisse* (London: Pelican Books, 1993), Notebook VII, 690–710.

32 Ibid., 691.

But when the production process becomes "machinic," living labor becomes literally a part of the production process rather than just the indispensable but foreign element around which it revolves. Through this metamorphosis, Marx writes, "workers are recast as conscious linkages in relation to automatic mechanisms."[33] What has occurred, Marx wants us to understand, is that the direct means of labor is superseded by a form of capital (fixed capital). In no way, he says, does the machine appear here as the individual's means of labor. Instead, the previous use value of the machine is thereby "transformed into an existence adequate to fixed capital."[34] This is the essential meaning of the first salvo in "The Fragment": with automation, machines can no longer be construed as a use value for living labor — they are now fixed capital in a value-producing process that is streamlined for the valorization of capital.

Whereas an instrument is made into an extension of living labor under the previous regime of machinic use value, and the worker handles it with virtuosity, Marx says, under this new regime, the machine's action is transmitted to the new material, and labor merely supervises and guards against interruptions. The worker's activity is determined and regulated by the movement of machinery, and so is reduced to an abstraction, or a "mere accessory" because the "science behind automation" does not actually exist in the consciousness of the worker, but rather acts upon him through the machine "as an alien power."[35] As for the nature of the automated machinery itself, Marx says that as fixed capital, it represents a capture of the accumulated knowledge and skill of the "general productive forces of the social brain," absorbed into capital itself, as opposed to a use value for labor, appearing henceforth as an attribute of capital. As such, it fulfills the antagonistic "tendency of capital" to increase labor's

33 Ibid., 692.
34 Ibid.
35 Ibid., 693.

productive force while "achieving the greatest possible negation of necessary labor."[36]

Per Marx in "The Fragment," therefore, fixed capital as machinery produces value in two ways: first, inasmuch as it *has value* (is a product of labor in an objectified form), and second, insofar as it enables labor to create more product in a shorter time, enabling the worker to produce more product per hour. As a result, she or he can effectively work a larger part of their time producing surplus value for capital. Here we see another variation of Marx's articulation of the contradictions of capitalism, with only the most ambiguous sense that the inherent antagonism must lead to the working-class becoming its revolutionary gravediggers. On the one hand, labor time is posited as the sole determinant of value; on the other, direct labor is reduced to a smaller and smaller proportion and subordinate element in relation to scientific and technical fixed capital. All of this, Marx wants to insist, can only result in increasing alienation and the unsustainability of the rate of profit (compound annual growth rate/CAGR).

If this early dystopian portrait of the worker as an accessory to machines in order to increase surplus value were all that "The Fragment" contained, it would probably have still have ended up being a touchpoint for understanding the nature of work in the post-Fordist age of cybernetization and networked digital communications. But it would not have gone on to play a major role in the post-*Operaismo* effort to identify and contest a new opening for a project of working-class recomposition. The decisive additional content starts with the analysis of machinic fixed capital as representing a kind of a capture of the accumulated knowledge and skill of the "general productive forces of the social brain." In this transformation, where the human being becomes the watchman and regulator of science- and technology-driven production, Marx says, it is neither the direct labor performed nor the time spent working that is appropriated, but rather "his own general productive power, his understanding of

36 Ibid.

nature and his mastery over it" as embedded in science- and technology-based processes and their management.[37] Where the power of knowledge becomes a direct force of production, Marx says, social life itself, as embedded in this fixed capital and folded into the production process, is seen to be transformed into what Marx calls *general intellect.*[38]

It can be easy to want to glide over this strange term, to dismiss it as just some sort of a German idealist monstrosity, something thus lacking a real-world referent. But it is precisely the opposite of this. Here Marx is actually naming something quite new under the sun, however awkwardly. What makes it especially difficult for us to grasp, in our knowledge-saturated technological society, is not its novelty, but rather the extent to which today we so thoroughly take for granted what this term actually means.

In his 2001 entry on general intellect for the *Lexicon of Post-Fordism,* Paolo Virno writes that the term "general intellect" should be taken in a sense that is parallel to what Rousseau had in mind with his use of the term *volonté générale* (the general will), which is to be understood "as the collective, public expression of something otherwise individual and private." For the first time, Virno says, knowledge itself has become abstracted, much in the same way that labor is abstracted in industrial production. Virno recognizes Marx to be describing a new social form of knowledge, knowledge that actually exists in the world objectively, knowledge that can create worldly effects all on its own, and is therefore something "not just in people's heads" or in books.[39] Negri explains in *Marx Beyond Marx* that the subsumption of labor by automatic machinery, which transforms living labor into capital (as an accessory to the machine as fixed capital) is nothing less than the subsumption of all of society, since it harnesses the forces of science which are the product of

37 Ibid., 705

38 Ibid., 706.

39 Paolo Virno, "General Intellect," trans. Arianna Bove, in *Lessico Postfordista* (Milan: Feltrinelli, 2001), https://www.generation-online.org/p/fpvirno10.htm.

society as a whole. It represents the subsumption of the social productive forces in their totality.[40]

Lest for a moment we forget all the just completed talk about "becoming accessories to machines," and find ourselves instead held in the thrall of scientific and technical progress, which is a perfectly natural thing to do, it must be reiterated here that Marx's view of this new "abstract knowledge" is an unremittingly gloomy one. When living labor (having previously been only partially subsumed into production by its transformation into abstract labor) becomes through this fully subsumed within the process of the valorization of capital, something indeed monstrous has occurred, something much worse than the linguistic awkwardness of the term "general intellect." *Operaismo* theorists, simply leveraging Marx here, do not want us to forget that this process, which Negri refers to as a "dialectic of living labor," which "finds itself inserted into the labor process," must be seen as one of thoroughgoing class antagonism.[41] Negri says that "The Fragment" is "without a doubt the highest example of the use of an antagonistic and constitutive dialectic the we find [...] in the whole of Marx's work."[42]

Immaterial Labor and the Struggle for Class Recomposition

If this is indeed the content of "The Fragment on Machines," as it pertains to the general intellect, it is reasonable to go on to ask next how these reflections could somehow serve as a catalyst for post-*Operaismo's* search for a new basis for class recomposition and effective resistance. The solution to this problem turns out to be a simple one. The theorists of *Operaismo,* even in appreciating Marx for his "prophetic powers," as James Steinhoff has remarked, nonetheless insist that they can see something today, revealed in the fullness of time, that Marx could not.[43]

40 Negri, *Marx Beyond Marx,* 142.

41 Ibid., 140.

42 Ibid., 139.

43 James Steinhoff, *Autonomy and Automation: Labour, Capital, and Machines in the Artificial Intelligence Industry* (Cham: Palgrave Macmillan,

Post-*Operaismo* inaugurates and catalyzes its project of class recomposition by picking a fight with Marx. "We need to level a fundamental criticism at *The Fragment*," Virno writes. "According to Marx, the general intellect — knowledge as the main productive force — fully coincides with fixed capital, the scientific power objectified in the system of machinery." But Marx thus neglects "the way in which *the general intellect manifests itself as living labor*" (italics mine). Under post-Fordist conditions, Virno says, "it becomes clear that the relation between knowledge and production is articulated in the linguistic cooperation between men and women acting-in-concert, *rather than being exhausted in the system of machinery*" (my emphasis).[44]

The general intellect, therefore, includes "formal and informal knowledge, imagination, ethical tendencies, mentalities, and language games," along with, one must presume, socially enabling technologies such as software and firmware, and hardware networks and their knowledge-based conditions of development. Writing from the horizon of the techno-optimism of the early 2000s, Virno says that conceptual and logical schemas cannot be reduced to fixed capital, because they are inseparable from "the interaction of a plurality of living subjects." Post-Fordist living labor, which cannot be objectified in machinery, is the prominent form in which the general intellect is manifest today. With this in the background, "conditions for conflict must be found in the progressive rupture between general intellect and fixed capital in this process, because it is clearly a new form of domination and exploitation."[45]

This set of assertions brings us back to Bifo Berardi's post-*Operaismo* reflections in *The Soul at Work* from my chapter 10, on the equivocal condition of the "cognitariat" in the struggle against work in the post-Fordist digital age. At least from a certain angle, Berardi says, it appears as if the mentalization of labor

2021), 79.

44 Paolo Virno, "General Intellect," in *Lessico Postfordist*, https://www.generation-online.org/p/fpvirno10.htm.

45 Ibid.

is actually less alienated than the Fordist, disciplined body. For a certain subset, the work is more personalized, so tech workers, for example, are more identified with it.[46] Also, there is a kind of an enrichment that comes with cognitive labor that is heavy on communication, and the work can be less hierarchical, and deterritorialized, at least at the nodal, team level.[47] All of this perhaps goes some distance to explain why there have been voluntary increases in the length of the working day, lower levels of absenteeism and disaffection reported over recent decades. But Berardi can see the downsides too, and thus the assignment of an equivocal role. Where communication becomes an economic necessity, it loses its spontaneous character, and becomes a form of impoverishment. So too with the apparent workplace independence, which masks a neo-Taylorist form of dependency. Computerized society, he says, increasingly "becomes the realization of a kind of a panlogism, in which we may see the total subjection of human beings by semiocapitalism" (i.e., infocentric, networked mental labor).[48]

Given the rise of the knowledge economy in the 1990s and 2000s, one can see here, in this generalized attempt to explicate the meaning and significance of the new immaterial labor, a restless effort to find a possible opening, at least in theory, with respect to class recomposition. It is one that plays out by following the — seemingly ineluctable — contour of the development of advanced technological capitalism, and one that seeks to somehow exploit its new contradictions to perform a kind of a jujitsu maneuver. The central premise of immaterial labor theory, James Steinhoff writes in *Automation and Autonomy*, is that value no longer refers to the average socially necessary labor time for the production of commodities, but rather can be made to track the autonomy of labor from capital, because the problem of the measurability of immaterial labor reflects a

46 Franco "Bifo" Berardi, *The Soul at Work: From Alienation to Autonomy*, trans. Francesca Cadel and Giuseppina Mecchia (Los Angeles: Semiotext(e), 2009), 25, 75–76.

47 Ibid., 88–89.

48 Ibid., 73.

fundamental change in the phenomenology of labor as such. Post-*Operaismo* theory, Steinhoff says, identifies a redefinition of value and advocates for a countertheory of valorization."[49] Negri had already articulated this basic position: "In the capitalist project, labor is commanded by surplus value, whereas in the revolutionary proletarian project, reappropriated surplus labor is commanded by necessary labor."[50]

But what is it about "immaterial labor," as irreducibly "living labor," contra Marx, that is supposed to create this reversal, and therefore provide some sort of a passage to effective, mass resistance to capitalist domination over labor in the digital age? Without a fuller account, this can sound a bit like the conviction, on the part of some contemporary technological futurists, that we must be approaching some sort of a "singularity." Worse yet, it could be taken as strangely reminiscent of the later Heidegger's still shocking assertion that "only a god can save us" [51]from technicity's closure of human historicity—only here, with the formula given in reverse, with technicity somehow doing the saving. At some points, for want of a clear explanation, it appears as if post-*Operaismo* just seeks to "make it so" through the magic of hypostatization, as if what could be shown to be possible in concept, could also thereby be shown, without further ado, to be true in reality. At other times, there seems to be some sense that post-*Operaismo* at this stage is quietly reading Habermas on the emancipatory potential of the sphere of interaction as separate and distinct from instrumental rationality derived from labor. By positing the existence of two independent spheres (labor and interaction), it almost seems as if they are here laying the groundwork for a variation on the Habermasian account of "system versus lifeworld."

---

49 Steinhoff, *Automation and Autonomy,* 83.

50 Negri, *Marx Beyond Marx,* 147.

51 Martin Heidegger, "Only a God Can Save Us," interview conducted by Rudolph Augstein and Georg Wolff, *Der Spiegel,* September 23, 1966.

Critiques of the Post-*Operaismo* Account of Immaterial Labor

In the opening paragraphs of the third chapter of Steinhoff's *Autonomy and Automation,* "Post-*Operaismo* and the New Autonomy of Immaterial Labor," there is a nice summary of the post-*Operaismo* terrain that has been covered thus far. It begins with *Operaismo's* understanding of automation as capital's antagonistic reaction to the collective power of the industrial mass worker. In relation to this antagonistic, changing technical composition of capital, the class composition of labor also continually changes, producing unanticipated new social capacities. In relation to this enlarged concept of class (following from the mass worker and the social factory), *Operaismo* theorizes the socialized worker, whose new level of social cooperation, in the social factory and in the production process, is drawn into the circuit of the valorization of capital. Following from technological changes resulting in a new class composition, the new capacities are referred to by means of the term "immaterial labor." In response to this transformation of labor, post-*Operaismo* identifies an underlying change to the nature of value now operating in capitalist society, and on the basis of a new subjectivity or class composition, advocates for a countertheory of valorization by means of a politics of collective refusal.[52]

In the remainder of the chapter, Steinhoff goes on to criticize two main aspects of what he refers to as "immaterial labor theory," as found, for example, in the first and third sections of Hardt and Negri's *Empire* (2000). First, Steinhoff denies the claim that immaterial labor reflects a change in capitalist society's theory of value that could serve as the foundation for a project of worker self-valorization and autonomy. Second, he denies the claim that immaterial labor, as living labor, is as irreducible to processes of machine automation as *Operaismo* supposes, with the implication that it has no special potential for being able to resist the command of capital. Although the structure of Steinhoff's argument can be a bit difficult to make out at

52 Steinhoff, *Automation and Autonomy,* 76–80.

times, it's worth following along because it contains a good deal of important nuance.

He begins his analysis by questioning the "immateriality" of immaterial labor. All forms of capitalist work, as we recall, actually have a double aspect—both concrete specificity and abstract significance. So-called immaterial labor isn't really that different in this regard. What gives labor weight and significance, Steinhoff says, is not the content of the labor per se (what kind it is) but rather its commodity form, the manner in which products, as bearers of value, support processes of capital valorization.[53] Where post-*Operaismo* wants to special plead for immaterial labor in this respect, because it produces in a way that is outside and beyond traditional and measurable workplace conditions, Steinhoff is markedly unimpressed. The value of so-called immaterial labor can in fact be calculated in practice by its realization in exchange, even if the number of hours put into the production of the commodity can't be precisely qualified.[54]

In response to the claim for irreducibility and emerging autonomy, Steinhoff next responds with a reality check to see if there is any sense in which the balance of technological power is shifting in favor of workers. How does labor obtain the ability to take control of the process of machinic metamorphosis? Hardt and Negri answer, Steinhoff says, by pointing to the advent of a "machinic humanity," that is, by saying that with the arrival of immaterial labor, becoming visible first at the social level, we are seeing what amounts to a hybridization of living labor with machine technology.[55] Technology is becoming a collective human prosthesis embedded in the general intellect-cum-social knowledge/social individual. When we say that fixed capital is reappropriated by labor, Steinhoff says, we do not mean that it "becomes their possession." We mean that as a "machinic assem-

53 Ibid., 84.
54 Ibid., 85.
55 Ibid., 87.

blage" it is integrated into subjectivity as one of its constituents.[56] Only on the assumption that the human element in immaterial labor is irreducible, it should be noted, can post-*Operaismo* affirm this supposed hybridization as an expression of labor's capacity rather than just another moment in capital's evolving technical composition.[57]

Borrowing from a certain discourse within the AI community, Steinhoff refers to this set of assertions as a version of "centaur theory."[58] In relation to it, he says there are really two meaningful positions: either there are machine/human hybrids (centaurs), and this will lead to greater autonomy; or else there are no centaurs, and capital still has, and will have, the last word. With respect to the pro-centaur option, Steinhoff completes the basic argumentative circuit: machine automation, so the story goes, is only one component of the general intellect; it also includes things such as networked immaterial labor and the communicative competence of acting-in-concert (abstract cooperation), which is something that can't be completely subsumed by capital.[59] The upshot of human/machine hybridization as a social force is that there is now a capacity for autonomous production that capital cannot command.[60] As a result of this opening, exploitation should be redefined as the expropriation of this cooperation by capital, after the fact.[61] Finally, as a result of this new found power and dignity, labor can now potentially *refuse* the form of valorization that has been imposed upon it. The essential self-valorization of immaterial labor sets the stage, therefore, for a politics of refusal.[62]

After making the case for centaurs, Steinhoff directs our attention to the deep ambiguity contained in this projection of a social future beyond capital. Does *Operaismo* mean to say

56 Ibid., 87–88.
57 Ibid., 88.
58 Ibid., 89.
59 Ibid., 90–91.
60 Ibid., 91–92.
61 Ibid., 91.
62 Ibid., 92.

that these revolutionary changes have already occurred, or are underway, or that they might occur in the future? With regard to the first, Steinhoff says flatly what we all must also admit: labor, as a global totality, has definitely *not* achieved autonomy from capital.[63] As an aside, for those of us who have worked in Silicon Valley over the last twenty years, the notion is, quite frankly, simply laughable. If laughter was something on the scrum manager's agenda for this week's sprint, my friends working in Silicon Valley tech companies would definitely need to find the time to stop and laugh. It is rather more plausible, he continues, that some limited degree of autonomy has been obtained, perhaps temporarily, by a subset of immaterial laborers.[64]

As for the final option, namely, that labor will *eventually* achieve full autonomy, Steinhoff opts to exhaust the remaining possibilities for centaur theory (either it might plausibly occur in the future, or else there are no centaurs) by reviewing the current tendency of the AI industry today under three rubrics: machine/human hybridization, abstract cooperation, and emergent autonomy. Under the first heading, Steinhoff acknowledges that the new productivity of immaterial labor has led to certain kinds of technical workers having special prerogatives—for example, choices about how to accomplish assigned goals and the ability to direct the course of their own work day under agile development methodologies. And yet, it nonetheless remains true that management is able to keep firm control by means of things such as scrums, tracking engines, and scrum team peer-to-peer accountability for maintaining adherence to standards and time norms.[65] The productivity of AI work, Steinhoff says, "remains strictly dominated by capital, even if the form of control is de-territorialized."[66] Since the research and production of AI continues to be dominated by an oligopoly of large capitalist firms, it's hard to imagine this so-called hybridization leading

63 Ibid., 94.
64 Ibid.
65 Ibid., 213–14.
66 Ibid., 210.

to autonomy. If anything, the tendency in AI work is toward the continuing annexation of novel production capacities of labor by capital.[67]

Under the second rubric, Steinhoff sees something similar. The update of "general intellect theory" to include the creative and communicative capacities of immaterial laborers leads to the assertion that because immaterial labor exists in the form of networks and communication flows, and the collective knowledge is everywhere and nowhere, it can't ultimately be controlled by traditional Fordist/Taylorist management techniques. To this Steinhoff replies, once again, that though the abstract communication of immaterial labor may be decentralized, it is still structured by the value form.[68]

Scanning the real world of AI work today, Steinhoff addresses the third rubric by searching for some real evidence of emergent autonomy for immaterial labor. Instead of a new cyborg subjectivity, however, he says that AI work evinces a new wave of "deskilling, fragmentation, and automation" similar to what Marx noted with respect to industrial labor. From "the high skill work of data scientists and machine learning engineers, to the digital manual labor of ghost workers who label training data," he says, the organic composition of capital is increasing, without augmenting the power of labor to resist.[69] If anything, the development of machine learning (ML) and AutoML indicate that capital may be on the way to overcoming its dependence on living labor. Where a user may click buttons in an end-to-end AutoML program, and witness the automatic generation of a functional ML model, "this is far from merging with the machine."[70] The AI industry, Steinhoff concludes, "does not

67 Ibid., 208.
68 Ibid., 214.
69 Ibid., 209.
70 Ibid., 210. It should be noted here that with the recent emergence of generative AI applications, such as ChatGPT, we are now seeing similar effects unfolding for various kinds of soft-skilled labor along with things such as AI development.

appear to possess the qualities that post-*Operaismo* attributes to immaterial labor."[71]

As should be clear, Steinhoff's analysis relies almost exclusively on "the argument from technology" to validate or deny post-*Operaismo*'s claims for immaterial labor's potential for autonomy. He uses the apparent lack of real-world evidence for emergent autonomy as a basis to reject "the strong case," that is, the assertion that immaterial labor "will eventually achieve full autonomy." From there, he moves immediately to entertaining the most dystopian alternative, namely, that of the achievement of "the real autonomy of capital" via the trajectory of its technical composition. Under the dystopian option, where "labor and valorization processes can be planned, executed, and completed, and their results integrated back into capital, all without living labor," he says, we would see "a world where nothing exists outside the market," a "teleological identity of capitalism and artificial intelligence," and thus a world of total subjugation.[72] Steinhoff even goes so far as to speculate about how many generations of machines produced by machines it might take before the residual contributions of labor become negligible, so that, "as Marshal McLuhan put it, humans become just the sex organs of the machine world [...] and we see the proletarianization of machines that can have their surplus value extracted." In making this dystopian speculation, however, he skips over the weaker case, that of the "could achieve" or "has the potential to achieve autonomy" through effective changes in subjectivity wrought by immaterial labor.[73]

But if it were the case that post-*Operaismo* really had nothing at all to offer between "centaurs and proletarian machines," that is, no third option, then there would have been little reason to provide a detailed account of it here in this chapter. Luckily, post-*Operaismo* does provide another option, which I like to call "the weak case," a path explored by both Virno and by Hardt

71 Ibid., 208.
72 Ibid., 220.
73 Ibid., 221.

and Negri (each in their own fashion). The weak case for immaterial labor moves the discourse on prospects for resistance and refusal beyond this apparent dead end, and does so in a way that advances the discussion we left off from chapter 16 concerning the politics of refusal and possible counter-publics.

General Intellect and the Project of an Autonomous Public Sphere

Early on in Hardt and Negri's *Empire,* in the section "Biopolitical Production," and almost as an aside, the authors make their first mention of post-*Operaismo's* immaterial labor theory: "In the work of a group of contemporary Marxist authors who recognize the new nature of productive labor," and use terms such as "immaterial labor and the Marxian concept of general intellect, we recognize two coordinated research projects."[74] The first consists "in the analysis of recent transformations of productive labor and its tendency to become increasingly immaterial."[75] The second research project consists in the analysis of the "immediately social and communicative dimension of living labor in contemporary society," and thus poses "the problem of the new figures of subjectivity, in both their exploitation and their revolutionary potential."[76] There are those who legitimately worry about whether the articulation of these two projects represent a kind of a problematic break in the analysis (e.g., Paul Thompson[77]), but it is clear that for Hardt and Negri at least, they are simply complementary, or perhaps even in a relationship that can be described as dialectical: "The immediately social dimension of the exploitation of living immaterial labor [...] activate[s] the critical elements that develop the potential for

74 Michael Hardt and Antonio Negri, *Empire* (Cambridge: Harvard University Press, 2000), 29.

75 Ibid.

76 Ibid.

77 Thompson, "Foundation and Empire," 74, 87–88.

insubordination and revolt [...] after a new theory of value, then a new theory of subjectivity must be formulated."[78]

It is this "second project," therefore, that I have in mind when I refer to "the weak case." The weak case is simply the version of post-*Operaismo,* beginning from the new class composition arising out of the knowledge economy, which considers the effects of changes in both subjection and subjectification, and then posits the possibility of a politics of refusal and the demand for an exodus, that is, for a counter-public alternative to what I have been calling the occupational, pseudo-public sphere. The hallmark of the weak case, therefore, is the assertion that we need not entertain a wholesale or total revolution in the theory of value in capitalist society to argue for a politics of refusal born from the new subjectivity wrought by immaterial labor.

A clear slant in support of this weaker case for immaterial labor's potential is already on display in Virno's entry on "general intellect" that we saw earlier this chapter. Per Virno, the issue facing us today is whether and to what extent "the progressive rupture between general intellect and fixed capital" via immaterial labor, in terms of both new social capacities and their exploitation (i.e., in terms of both subjection and subjectification) has "set up a search for conditions of conflict" in relation to the new forms of domination. Virno says that where social relations are increasingly ordered by abstract knowledge, we find an overall social condition of extreme cynicism, a condition of "atrophied solidarity and belligerent solipsism" that he says is an adaptation to the hypertrophic growth of (technocratic) administrative apparatus as an authoritarian concretion of general intellect. The question, therefore, is whether cynical indifference to "the search for an intersubjective foundation for *praxis*" can be overcome by tapping these new potentials, over and against the manner in which they have been made to serve post-Fordist capitalism and its occupational, pseudo-public sphere. In Virno's terms, the question is "whether the peculiar character of the intellect, as the technical requirement of the

78 Hardt and Negri, *Empire,* 29.

production process, can be the basis for a radical new form of democracy and public sphere that is the antithesis of the one pivoting on the state." The general intellect "can affirm itself as an autonomous public sphere only if its bond to the production of commodities and wage labor is dissolved."[79]

Virno Reading Arendt: Work, Intellect, and Action (Revisited)

Since the mid-2000s, both Virno and Hardt and Negri have each gone on to develop their ideas on how the post-Fordist general intellect and immaterial labor set the stage for a revitalized project of radical republicanism at the twilight of liberalism's world order. The most extensive development of these ideas can be found in Virno's *A Grammar of the Multitude* (2003), and Hardt and Negri's *Multitude: War and Democracy in the Age of Empire* (2004) and *Assembly* (2018). To unpack the central concept of the multitude and then situate it in relation to other projects seeking to recover a radical republican form of sovereignty would be quite a substantive undertaking, beyond the my scope in this book. It makes sense, instead, to conclude with some final thoughts on Virno's short piece "Virtuosity and Revolution: The Political Theory of Exodus" from the mid-1990s.[80] Here Virno again takes up the central question of post-*Operaismo,* that of how the rise of the general intellect (as a harnessing of public knowledge and the communicative competence of immaterial labor) also transforms production/work in ways that lead to new possibilities for collective political action, and an exodus from the capitalist form of society.

Virno's basic approach is to use Arendt's account of "action, work, and intellect," in both antiquity and in the modern age, as

79 Paolo Virno, "General Intellect," in *Lessico Postfordista,* https://www.generation-online.org/p/fpvirno10.htm.

80 Paolo Virno, "Virtuosity and Revolution: The Political Theory of Exodus," in *Radical Thought in Italy: A Potential Politics,* eds. Paolo Virno and Michael Hardt (Minneapolis: University of Minnesota Press, 1996), 189–212.

his foil for getting at the new configuration of these key aspects of social life under post-Fordist conditions. Since I have already presented Arendt as just such a foil here in this book, it is fitting to close this study with Virno's post-*Operaismo* confrontation with Arendt over the problem of political action, especially since Arendt's chapter on action is really the only significant part of *The Human Condition* that I have not previously touched upon.

Virno's starting point, once again, is the status of immaterial labor. But this time, the meditation takes off in an unexpected direction. In *Capital,* Virno reminds us, Marx identified two kinds of immaterial/intellectual labor. There is immaterial activity that results in commodities that are separate from the producer, and there is immaterial activity where the product is not separable from the producing activity.[81] In this second kind, fulfillment is found in the virtuoso performance of the activity, without it being objectivized in a finished work of art outside and beyond the performance itself. Here Marx has in mind the virtuoso performance-as-work that characterizes the activity of orators, teachers, doctors, and priests. Along with the rest of the modern age going back to Adam Smith, Marx rated the first kind, which he recognized as part of productive labor, as something standing higher than the sort of wage labor that is not strictly productive. By contrast, virtuoso immaterial/intellectual labor, pretty much as an afterthought, was awkwardly placed on a par with service work.[82]

Thinking about this standard modern account, Virno next lights upon a set of passages from Arendt's *Between Past and Future* concerning the nature of political action in general, and the strong connection that was recognized in premodernity between the performing arts, as virtuoso performance, and ethics and politics. Arendt writes that both performing artists (dancers, stage actors, musicians, and the like) and the man of political action "need an audience to show their virtuosity [...] both need a publicly organized space for their work [...] the

81 Virno, *Virtuosity and Revolution,* 191.

82 Ibid., 192.

Greek *polis* once was precisely that form of government which provided men with a space of appearances where they could act, with a kind of theater where freedom could appear."[83] Finding confirmation of this in the *Nicomachean Ethics,* book 6, Virno quotes Aristotle: "The aim of action, as virtuous conduct, is an end in itself, whereas with production, there is a difference between the aim of production, and production itself."[84] Virno wants to understand the ways in which the post-Fordist general intellect has transformed both labor/work and action.

One can see, therefore, how Arendt's highly unusual remarks on the relationship between premodern political action and virtuosity of performance draws Virno irresistibly into a deeper reflection on the differences among political action and labor and work, and on her account of the degradation of action in the modern age, the subject so provocatively explored as the central concern of Arendt's *The Human Condition.* Speech and action, Arendt tells us in chapter 5, are disclosive of human beings, qua human. With both word and deed, "we insert ourselves into the human world; it is not forced upon us by necessity, like labor, and it is not prompted by utility, like work."[85] Structurally, human action is radically different than other pure forms of activity. In the presence of others, "we begin something new, on our own initiative." To act, to begin, to found, to rule (the Greek *arché*). These are the things that show out political action in its distinctiveness.[86] Pure action, then, as concerns "starting something," is also marked by its connection to the unexpected. The new appears, in freedom, she writes, as if by a miracle.[87] But acting is also beset by frustrations and great uncertainty, which make it different from more reliable activities like fabrication and contemplation. One who acts begins a chain of events, and

83 Hannah Arendt, *Between Past and Future* (London: Penguin Books, 1977), 154.

84 Ibid., 192.

85 Hannah Arendt, *The Human Condition* (Chicago: University of Chicago Press, 1998), 176.

86 Ibid., 177, 189.

87 Ibid., 178.

one can't know precisely where they will lead, because of what can happen to the best laid plans of mice and men. Deeds create a particular kind of burden, that of irreversibility and unpredictability. As such, "to do and to suffer are sides of a coin." Since one who acts never quite knows what she or he is doing, one becomes guilty of unintended consequences that can never really be undone, and the meaning of the deed is never fully disclosed to the actor, but only to the retrospective glance of the historian.[88]

It's also important to recognize, Arendt continues, that to act, as a primary form of self-disclosure, also concerns the things (worldly realities) that exist between people. As an actor, announcing what one does, has done, and will do, with virtuosity, and making decisions about the conduct of human affairs, is something that shines most brightly and consistently only in the public realm. The *polis* should be recognized as the Greek solution to the problem of how to manage action's delicate tissue.[89] The frailty of human affairs was made stable by having a permanent space for demonstrating and witnessing excellence and renown, in both word and deed. With the end of the *polis,* Arendt identifies a set of subsequent solutions that have been offered as a way to deal with the general problem of political action's unpredictability, irreversibility, and fleetingness/anonymity. With the Romans, we see stabilization of action by means of the *pacta sunt servanda,* the institution of promise keeping and private contract.[90] There is also the discovery (which she attributes to Jesus of Nazareth at the level of widespread cultural influence) of the power of forgiveness.[91] Finally, in the Middle Ages, the solution is that of monarchy, which Arendt says banishes plurality as such, by limiting the public realm to the purview of the ruler alone, leaving everyone else to attend only to their own private affairs.[92]

---

88 Ibid., 190–92, 233.
89 Ibid., 179, 196.
90 Ibid., 243.
91 Ibid., 238.
92 Ibid., 220–222.

Because Virno's interest in Arendt's haunting narrative on the structure and history of action pivots upon her account of what she calls "the instrumentalization of action and the degradation of politics"[93] in the modern period," it's worth summarizing here a bit further. In the modern age, Arendt says, the comparatively low opinion of occupations that rest on virtuoso performance derive from the new preeminence of *homo faber,* and the conviction of the age that "a man's products" are what matter most. In the age of *homo faber,* there is a sense that action and speech are species of idleness, and that we should judge public actions, first and foremost, in terms of their orientation toward higher, utilitarian ends.[94] The people who meet in the public space of the exchange market, she says, meet not as persons, but as producers. What shows forth is their products to exchange, and not themselves, which becomes alienated through this primary public concern with commodities. The modern solution to the problem of how to eliminate the uncertainty of action in the domain of the social, Arendt says, is to replace acting with making, by channeling the capacity for action into things like exploring natural laws and fabricating objects.[95]

Arendt's narrative, as Virno observes, has modernity muddle up the traditional differences among the distinct human spheres of labor/work, intellect, and action. Work undergoes transformation under capitalism, and the fortunes of action in the modern age are thereby changed, but intellect, he points out, remains largely unchanged. Arendt, Virno says, "rejects out of hand the very idea of a public intellect."[96] In her judgment, "reflection and thought (the life of the mind) bear no relation to the care for common affairs," whereas Marx sketches "the insertion of intellect into the world of appearances" in the concept of general intellect. With this discussion, Virno says, Marx provides the first account of how it is that labor steps to the side of

93 Ibid., 230.
94 Ibid., 208.
95 Ibid., 231.
96 Virno, *Virtuosity and Revolution,* 194.

the production process, providing oversight and coordination of tasks, and a modulator of social cooperation through the harnessing of communicative competences and its various markers of virtuosity.[97]

Virno agrees with Arendt that the paralysis of political action today reflects a breakdown in the distinctions between action, work, and intellect, because "the customary frontiers" separating them "as *theory, poesis,* and *praxis* have given way."[98] His objection, however, has to do with precisely how and why the dividing line between work and action has disappeared. Arendt's position, Virno writes, "is that modern political praxis has internalized the model of work, so that it has come to resemble making, where the product is history, the state, the party, etc." This diagnosis, he declares, "must be inverted."[99]

The symbiosis of work with general intellect is what has led to the eclipse of action. What's important "is not that political action has become a form of producing, but that producing has embraced within itself many of the prerogatives of action."[100] Since the post-Fordist process of production requires virtuosity, the mass intellectuality of the post-Fordist job, Virno says, continually calls upon wage earners to exercise the art of the possible, to deal with the unforeseen, and to make the most of opportunities. As a result, under the auspices of the post-Fordist organization of production, action without a finished work moves from a special, problematic case to becoming a prototype for waged labor in general (what David Graeber has referred to as "bullshit jobs").[101] Understood in this way, the consequences for political action start to come into focus. Where work takes on action-like characteristics, Virno says, action proper comes to be seen as "falling short, or as a superfluous duplication."[102] Since its means/ends structure now appears poorer than the

97 Ibid., 193.
98 Ibid., 190.
99 Ibid., 190–91.
100 Ibid., 191.
101 Ibid., 193.
102 Ibid., 191.

one found in production, because action is either less complex than work or too similar, it comes to be seen as something less desirable. Where the labor that produces surplus value becomes politics, "politics in the narrow sense becomes discredited or paralyzed."[103]

Exodus: Forging the Alliance between General Intellect and Political Action

With these consequences brought into view, Virno goes on to propose the elaboration of a new model of political action, one that he says will "draw nourishment precisely from what today is creating its blockage."[104] He begins with two hypotheses. First, "the potential of the general intellect has to be our starting point for a re-definition of political praxis [...] we must counter-pose a coalition between intellect and action to that of intellect and work."[105] Second, whereas the symbiosis of knowledge and production today produces "an extreme legitimation pact of obedience to the capitalist state," it also enables us to glimpse the possibility of a nonstate public sphere.[106] The subversion of capitalist relations of production, Virno says, henceforth develops only with the institution of "a non-state public sphere, a political community that has as its hinge, the general intellect." The key to extracting political action from its present state of paralysis, therefore, consists in developing the publicness of the intellect "outside of work, and in opposition to it."[107]

Similar to André Gorz, Virno chooses the term "exodus" as a name for this model of political action. "Exodus" refers to the alliance between general intellect, political action, a mass defection from the capitalist state, and a movement toward what he calls "the public sphere of intellect."[108] This movement is a tak-

103 Ibid., 193.
104 Ibid., 189.
105 Ibid., 190.
106 Ibid.
107 Ibid., 196.
108 Ibid., 197.

ing command of the novel post-Fordist interweaving of work, action, and intellect, "which up to now, we have only suffered." Writing in a way that calls to mind Jenny Odell's inauguration of a modern revival of ancient cynicism, Virno says that "exodus" stands for "the founding of a republic by means of an engaged withdrawal."[109]

As for the "who" of exodus, Virno says it is "the multitude," conceived as a post-Fordist public intellect that is radically heterogeneous to the state. In sharing in a general intellect, the multitude is by definition something that can never converge into the general will of bourgeois popular sovereignty. The public sphere of intellect, which he also calls the "republic of the many," represents the potential to make good on a "democracy of the multitude" by means of things such as leagues, councils, and soviets, which give political expression to activity-in-concert that already enjoy a publicness different from that of traditional sovereignty.[110] Further stating that "only those who open a way of exit for themselves can do the founding,"[111] Virno spends the remaining part of the piece elaborating his own version of the "post-work political imaginary" by means of a table of virtues suitable for engaged withdrawal as founding leave-taking. Among the cardinal virtues for this politics of refusal, Virno references things such as radical disobedience (i.e., to develop the aspects of the general intellect that are at odds with the continued existence of wage labor, as was done in *Operaismo*); intemperance (to develop the full potential of nonservile virtuosity); and an invocation of a related "right to resistance." The founding of the republic, he says, eschews the prospect of civil war, but postulates an unlimited *ius resistentiae.*[112]

---

109 Ibid.
110 Ibid., 202–3.
111 Ibid., 197.
112 Ibid., 198–200, 206.

The Postwork Political Imaginary and the Politics of Refusal

In this final chapter, I have tried to present *Operaismo* (including post-*Operaismo/Autonomia*) as a kind of a living laboratory for understanding the dynamics of the politics of refusal in relation to its underlying postwork political imaginary. By dynamics, I have in mind an interplay: on the one hand, *Operaismo* can help to validate the basic conceptual elements of the postwork political imaginary; on the other hand, the real-world political struggle of *Operaismo* can be seen as a prism through which these concepts are then leavened by real-world considerations.

To start with the most proximate case: Virno's account of the paralysis of political action by the post-Fordist symbiosis of work with the general intellect is consistent with the assertions made here about the need to overcome the "occupational, pseudo-public sphere" as a part of the postwork political imaginary. Additionally, in Virno's calls for an exodus, as an engaged withdrawal from the terms of capitalist society that leverages new digital-age subjectivities, I likewise find validation for the idea that in the progressive collapse of this pseudo-public sphere, we find conditions for a politics of refusal and the establishment of new, postwork counter-publics. Cast into less relentlessly conceptual terms, if it is the case that capital is abandoning the terms of its own capitalist society, then it should be possible, out of the new subjectivity and class composition, to refuse its harsh conditions and develop alternative, postcapitalist socioeconomic structures. What comes immediately to mind are the many postwork imaginaries elaborated by others—everything from guaranteed basic income as part of the redistribution of work and the liberation of free time, to employee stock option plans (ESOPS), to alternative food networks (AFNS), to the myriad ways in which we might encourage new modes of socialization beyond the wage relation.

Validation for the other elements in the postwork political imaginary is also on display in the overall real-world trajectory of *Operaismo,* from Mario Tronti to post-Fordist *Autonomia.* For example, the "reversal of capital and labor," designed to intensify class antagonism and empower autonomy, maps nicely to the confrontation with the panoply of capitalist realist dogmas that was the subject of the first part of this book. The notion that capital is actually a parasite on the body of labor is a confrontation with capitalist realism, par excellence. With the post-*Operaismo* analysis of immaterial labor, we see the second major conceptual element, that is, what Berardi calls "the equivocal condition of the new cognitariat," or what I have referred to here generally as the need for a nuanced appreciation for the meaning and significance of the transformations of wage labor in the digital age.

Beyond validation for the overarching conceptual structures that make up the postwork political imaginary, the yield in the opposite direction is equally important. The *experience* of *Operaismo,* as an actual politics of refusal, has things to tell us about the application of these various conceptual elements to political practice. For example, when we think about the experience of work-as-we-know-it today, in its precarity, arbitrariness, workplace authoritarianism, and as something that harvests our personal biopower, we should also be mindful of the experience of *Operaismo* in the 1960s. When placed in the context of real political struggle, recognizing and understanding these conditions also means developing strategies and tactics for collective resistance to them. This can mean using the tools and capacities of the digital age "general intellect" for sharing and interpreting common experiences (understanding the new class composition). It can mean performing micro-analyses of real-world, workplace dynamics to frame strategies and tactics, and it also means confirming and reflecting significant generational shifts in order to mount effective resistance. In addition, it can be seen to mean the social-scientific evaluation of the limits of solidarities generated in a digital domain, since wage laborers in postindustrial societies can't rely on the residue of premodern community ties to form the basis of worker solidarity. For example, what actually happens when some workers start posting on Reddit that they have informed prospective employers of their refusal to do more than twenty hours of interviews without some sort of compensation? The trajectory of these things urgently requires analysis and critical understanding.

With respect to the various cultural critiques that can be marshaled to challenge capitalist realist dogmas about work, *Operaismo* shows the importance of real social interventions, that is, creating tools, mechanisms, institutions, venues, and public art and street performance for the dissemination of these sorts of critical rejoinders. Along with the Situationist International in the 1960s, Radio Alice from the late 1970s, and other movements, there are also the examples of Culture Jamming from the 1980s, elaborations upon T.A.Z (temporary autonomous zones) in the 1990s, and the Occupy movement in the 2000s. With these practices in mind, *Operaismo* teaches the importance of having a clear-eyed understanding of what happens when "the empire strikes back," that is, when the regular and irregular forces of the capitalist state become threatened and start to activate vast resources to pressurize the politics of refusal. Under pressure, decentralized movements from below quickly have to confront what *Operaismo* called "the problem of organization." In relation to various kinds of reactionary provocations, the Marxist-Leninist tendency appears, and in response to calls for militarization, movements are seen to fracture. The problem of nonvanguardist organizational forms is therefore something to be elaborated along with the other aspects of the political imaginary, because it's something that can't just be left until "the witching hour."

Today, with the recognition of cultural events such as the Great Resignation, quiet quitting, and the like, we are seeing some signs that the current round of innovations in the technical composition of capital (which are really only weigh stations on the road to capital's dream of autonomy from labor) are, in their turn, giving rise to a new class composition. It remains to be seen whether this widespread but informal wildcat behavior can become a form of the Great Refusal. Becoming self-aware, the new class composition, recognized as a generational event, becomes, almost ineluctably, a will to class recomposition by means of struggle. The elements of the postwork political imaginary, taken as a totality, are the bridge connecting this mere collection of signs to a real politics of refusal.

Bibliography

Adorno, Theodor. *Negative Dialectics.* Translated by E.B. Ashton. New York: Continuum, 2007.

Anderson, Elizabeth. *Private Government: How Employers Rule Our Lives (and Why We Don't Talk about It).* Princeton: Princeton University Press, 2017.

Áras an Uachtaráin. "Young Philosophers Awards Speech." *YouTube,* November 17, 2017. https://www.youtube.com/watch?v=Os20UivqNBI.

Arendt, Hannah. *Between Past and Future.* London: Penguin Books, 1977.

———. *On Revolution.* London: Penguin, 1977.

———. *The Human Condition.* Chicago: University of Chicago Press, 1998.

———. *The Life of the Mind.* San Diego: Harcourt Brace Jovanovich, 1978.

Aschoff, Nicole. *The New Prophets of Capital.* London: Verso, 2015.

Bellah, Robert. *Habits of the Heart: Individualism and Commitment in American Life.* Berkeley: University of California Press, 2008.

Berardi, Franco "Bifo." "Anatomy of Autonomy." In *Autonomia: Post-Political Politics,* edited by Sylvère Lotringer and Christian Marazzi, 148–70. Los Angeles: Semiotext(e), 2007.

———. *Breathing: Chaos and Poetry.* Los Angeles: Semiotext(e), 2018.

———. *Futurability: The Age of Impotence and the Horizon of Possibility*. London: Verso, 2017.

———. *The Soul at Work: From Alienation to Autonomy.* Translated by Francesca Cadel and Giuseppina Mecchia. Los Angeles: Semiotext(e), 2009.

Bologna, Sergio. "The Tribe of Moles." In *Autonomia: Post-Political Politics,* edited by Sylvère Lotringer and Christian Marazzi, 36–61. Los Angeles: Semiotext(e), 2007.

Boltanski, Luc, and Ève Chiapello. *The New Spirit of Capitalism.* Translated by Gregory Elliot. London: Verso, 2018.

Braverman, Harry. *Labor and Monopoly Capital: The Degradation of Work in the Twentieth Century.* New York: Monthly Review Press, 1998.

Breines, Wini. *Community and Organization in the New Left.* New Brunswick: Rutgers University Press, 1982.

Buhayar, Noah. "Buffett's $11 Million Beach House Is Still on the Market." *Bloomberg,* February 27, 2018. https://www.bloomberg.com/news/articles/2018-02-27/buffett-s-11-million-beach-house-is-still-on-the-market.

Čapek, Karel. "In Praise of Idleness." Translated by Norma Comrada. In *Toward the Radical Center: A Karel Capek Reader,* edited by Peter Kussi, 241–43. North Haven: Catbird Press, 1990.

Carey, Benedict. "Science Plays the Long Game: But People Have Mental Health Issues Now." *The New York Times,* April 1, 2021. https://www.nytimes.com/2021/04/01/health/mental-health-treatments.html.

Carrette, Jeremy, and Richard King. *Selling Spirituality: The Silent Takeover of Religion.* London: Routledge, 2005.

Castoriadis, Cornelius. *The Imaginary Institution of Society.* Translated by Kathleen Blamey. Cambridge: Polity Press, 1975.

———. *World in Fragments: Writings on Politics, Society, Psychoanalysis, and the Imagination.* Edited and translated by David Ames Curtis. Stanford: Stanford University Press, 1997.

Chaplin, Charlie. "The Final Speech from the Great Dictator." *charliechaplin.com*. 2018. https://www.charliechaplin.com/en/films/7-The-Great-Dictator/articles/29-The-Final-Speech-from-The-Great-Dictator.

Christopher, Rebecca. "I Cannot Recommend My Former Co-Worker Bartleby for Your Scrivening Position." *McSweeney's*, March 22, 2018. https://www.mcsweeneys.net/articles/i-cannot-recommend-my-former-coworker-bartleby-for-your-scrivening-position.

Cleaver, Harry. "Introduction." In Antonio Negri, *Marx Beyond Marx: Lessons on the Grundrisse*, edited by Jim Fleming, translated by Harry Cleaver, Michael Ryan, and Maurizio Virano, xix–xxvii. New York: Autonomedia/Pluto Press, 1991.

Colagrossi, Mike. "You Weren't Born Just to Be 'Useful,' Irish President Tells Students." *Big Think*, May 17, 2019. https://bigthink.com/the-present/young-philosophers/.

Cook, Ian. "Who Is Driving the Great Resignation?" *Harvard Business Review*, September 2021. https://hbr.org/2021/09/who-is-driving-the-great-resignation.

Cox, Hannah. "What Is the Great Resignation of 2021? (If You Don't Know, You'll Want to Read This)." *FEE Stories*, July 8, 2021. https://fee.org/articles/what-is-the-great-resignation-of-2021-if-you-dont-know-you-ll-want-to-read-this/.

Crippen, Alex. "Warren Buffett Buys This with His Billions… And It Makes Him Happy." *CNBC*, November 12, 2012. https://www.cnbc.com/id/49787452.

Davies, William. *The Happiness Industry: How the Government and Big Business Sold Us Well-Being*. London: Verso, 2015.

Davis, Angela Y. "Foreword." In *The Great Refusal: Herbert Marcuse and Contemporary Social Movements*, edited by Andrew T. Lamas, Todd Wolfson, and Peter N. Funke, vii–xi. Philadelphia: Temple University Press, 2017.

Debord, Guy. "A User's Guide to Détournement." In *Situationist International Anthology,* edited and translated by Ken Knabb, 14–21. Berkeley: Bureau of Public Secrets, 2006.

———. "*Détournement* as Negation and Prelude." In *Situationist International Anthology,* edited and translated by Ken Knabb, 67–68. Berkeley: Bureau of Public Secrets, 2006.

———. "Theory of the *Dérive*." In *Situationist International Anthology,* translated by Ken Knabb, 62–66. Berkeley: Bureau of Public Secrets, 1989.

Deleuze, Gilles. "Bartleby; or, The Formula." In *Essays Critical and Clinical,* translated by Daniel W. Smith and Michael A. Greco, 68–90. Minneapolis: University of Minnesota Press, 1997.

———. "Postscript on the Societies of Control." *October* 59 (Winter, 1992): 3–7. https://www.jstor.org/stable/778828.

Derrida, Jacques. *The Gift of Death, Second Edition / Literature in Secret.* Translated by David Wills. Chicago: University of Chicago Press, 2008.

Devon, Cheyenne. "Billionaire Warren Buffett Still Lives in the Same Home He Bought for $31,500 More Than 60 Years Ago." *CNBC,* March 3, 3032. https://www.cnbc.com/2023/03/03/warren-buffett-lives-in-the-same-home-he-bought-in-1958.html.

Dobb, Maurice. *Theories of Value and Distribution Since Adam Smith.* Cambridge: Cambridge University Press, 1973.

Eaton, George. "Noam Chomsky: We're Approaching the Most Dangerous Point in Human History." *The New Statesman,* April 6, 2022. https://www.newstatesman.com/encounter/2022/04/noam-chomsky-were-approaching-the-most-dangerous-point-in-human-history.

Ehrenreich, Barbara. *Dancing in the Streets: A History of Collective Joy.* New York: Holt Paperbacks, 2006.

———. *Natural Causes.* New York: Hatchette Book Group, 2018.

Epstein, Brian. "Social Ontology." *Stanford Encyclopedia of Philosophy,* edited by Edward N. Zalta and Uri Nodelman.

March 21, 2018. https://plato.stanford.edu/entries/social-ontology/.

Felner, Robert D., Tweety Yates Felner, and Morton M. Silverman. "Prevention in Mental Health and Social Intervention." In *Handbook of Community Psychology,* Vol. 1, edited by Julian Rappaport and Edward Seidman, 9–42. New York: Springer Science and Business Media, 2000.

Feola, Giuseppe. "Degrowth and the Unmaking of Capitalism: Beyond 'Decolonization of the Imaginary'?" *Acme: International Journal for Critical Geographies* 18, no. 4 (2019): 977–97. https://acme-journal.org/index.php/acme/article/view/1790.

Fisher, Mark. *Capitalist Realism: Is There No Alternative?* Winchester: Zero Books, 2008.

Fisher, Mark, and Jeremy Gilbert. "Capitalist Realism and Neoliberal Hegemony: A Dialogue." *New Formations* 80–81 (2013): 89–101. https://muse.jhu.edu/article/529454.

Fleming, Jim. "Editor's Preface." In Antonio Negri, *Marx Beyond Marx: Lessons on the Grundrisse,* edited by jim Fleming, translated by Harry Cleaver, Michael Ryan, and Maurizio Viano. New York: Autonomedia/Pluto Press, 1991.

Fleming, Peter. *Resisting Work: The Corporatization of Life and Its Discontents.* Philadelphia: Temple University Press, 2014.

Foucault, Michel. *Discipline and Punish: The Birth of the Prison.* Translated by Alan Sheridan. New York: Vintage Books, 1979.

———. "Technologies of the Self." In *Technologies of the Self: A Seminar with Michel Foucault,* edited by Luther H. Martin, Huck Gutman, and Patrick H. Hutton, 16–49. Amherst: University of Massachusetts Press, 1988.

Franzen, Jonathan. *Freedom.* New York: Picador Paperbacks, 2011.

———. *Purity.* New York: Picador Paperbacks, 2016.

———. *The Corrections.* New York: Picador Paperbacks, 2001.

Fraser, Nancy. "Rethinking the Public Sphere: A Contribution to the Critique of Actually Existing Democracy." *Social Text* 25–26 (1990): 56–80. DOI: 10.2307/466240.

Funke, Peter N., Andrew T. Lamas, and Todd Wolfson. "Bouazizi's Refusal and Ours: Critical Reflections on the Great Refusal and Contemporary Social Movements." In *The Great Refusal: Herbert Marcuse and Contemporary Social Movements,* edited by Andrew T. Lamas, Todd Wolfson, and Peter N. Funke, 1–25. Philadelphia: Temple University Press, 2017.

Gardner, John W. *Self-Renewal: The Individual and the Innovative Society.* London: W.W. Norton, 1995.

Garland, Merrick. "Attorney General Merrick B. Garland Delivers Remarks on the First Anniversary of the Attack on the Capitol." *U.S. Department of Justice,* January 5, 2022. https://www.justice.gov/opa/speech/attorney-general-merrick-b-garland-delivers-remarks-first-anniversary-attack-capitol.

Giddens, Anthony. "Introduction." In Max Weber, T*he Protestant Ethic and the Spirit of Capitalism,* translated by Talcott Parsons, 1–12(b). New York: Charles Scribner's Sons, 1976.

Gladwell, Malcolm. *Talking to Strangers: What We Should Know About the People We Don't Know.* New York: Back Bay Books, 2019.

Graeber, David. *Bullshit Jobs: A Theory.* New York: Simon and Schuster, 2018.

———. "Bullshit Jobs and the Yoke of Managerial Feudalism." *The Economist,* June 29, 2018. https://www.economist.com/open-future/2018/06/29/bullshit-jobs-and-the-yoke-of-managerial-feudalism.

———. "Culture as Creative Refusal." *Cambridge Anthropology* 31, no. 2 (2013): 1–19. https://www.jstor.org/stable/43612879.

Gramsci, Antonio. "The Art and Science of Politics." In *An Antonio Gramsci Reader: Selected Writings, 1916–1935,* edited by David Forgacs, translated by Quintin Hoare and Geoffrey Nowell-Smith, 222–30. New York: Schocken Books, 1988.

Gray, Thomas. "Elegy Written in a Country Churchyard." In *The Norton Anthology of English Literature,* 3 vols., 5th edn.,

edited by M.H. Abrams, 1:2480–83. New York: W.W. Norton, 1986.
Greenhouse, Steven. "Striketober Is Showing Workers' Rising Power — but Will It Lead to Lasting Change?" *The Guardian*, October 21, 2021. https://www.theguardian.com/us-news/2021/oct/23/striketober-unions-strikes-workers-lasting-change.
Greif, David. *Against Everything*. New York: Vintage Books, 2016.
Gorz, André. *Reclaiming Work: Beyond the Wage-Based Society.* Translated by Chris Turner. London: Polity Press, 2005.
Habermas, Jürgen. *Knowledge and Human Interests*. Translated by Jeremy J. Shapiro. Boston: Beacon Press, 1973.
———. *The Structural Transformation of the Public Sphere: An Inquiry into a Category of Bourgeois Society.* Translated by Thomas Burger. Cambridge: MIT Press, 1994.
———. *The Theory of Communicative Action*, Vol. 1: *Reason and the Rationalization of Society.* Translated by Thomas McCarthy. Boston: Beacon Press, 1984.
———. *Theory and Practice*. Translated by John Viertel. Boston: Beacon Press, 1973.
Hadot, Pierre. *Philosophy as a Way of Life*. Edited by Arnold I. Davidson. Translated by Michael Chase. Malden: Blackwell, 1995.
Han, Byung-Chul. *The Burnout Society.* Translated by Erik Butler. Stanford: Stanford University Press, 2015.
Hansen, Miriam. "Foreword." In Oskar Negt and Alexander Kluge, *Public Sphere and Experience: Analysis of the Bourgeois and Proletarian Public Sphere*. London: Verso, 2016.
Harris, Malcolm. *Kids These Days: Human Capital and the Making of Millennials*. New York: Little, Brown and Co., 2017.
Hardt, Michael, and Antonio Negri. *Assembly.* Oxford: Oxford University Press, 2017.
———. *Empire*. Cambridge: Harvard University Press, 2000.

———. *Multitude: War and Democracy in the Age of Empire.* New York: Penguin, 2005.

Hart, Andrew. "Against Generational Politics." *Jacobin,* February 28, 2018. https://jacobin.com/2018/02/generational-theory-millennials-boomers-age-history.

Hegel, G.W.F. *Phenomenology of Spirit.* Translated by A.V. Miller. London: Oxford University Press, 1977.

———. *Philosophy of Right.* Translated by T.M. Knox. London: Oxford University Press, 1962.

Heidegger, Martin. "Building, Dwelling, Thinking." In *Poetry, Language, Thought,* translated by Albert Hofstadter, 145–61. New York: Harper Colophon, 1971.

———. "Only a God Can Save Us." Interview conducted by Rudolph Augstein and Georg Wolff. *Der Spiegel,* September 23, 1966.

Heller, Ágnes. *Beyond Justice.* Cambridge: Basil Blackwell, 1987.

Heller, Kenneth, Richard A. Jenkins, Ann M. Steffen, and Ralph W. Swindle, Jr. "Prospects for a Viable Community Mental Health System." In *Handbook of Community Psychology,* Vol. 1, edited by Julian Rappaport and Edward Seidman: 445–70. New York: Springer Science and Business Media, 2000.

Hodgkinson, Thom. *How to Be Idle: A Loafer's Manifesto.* New York: Harper Perennial, 2007.

Holloway, John. *Crack Capitalism.* London: Pluto Press, 2010.

Houriet, Robert. *Getting Back Together.* London: Abacus, 1973.

Hudson, Michael. "A Debt Jubilee Is the Only Way to Avoid a Depression." *The Washington Post,* March 21, 2020. https://www.washingtonpost.com/opinions/2020/03/21/debt-jubilee-is-only-way-avoid-depression/.

———. *And Forgive Them Their Debts: Lending, Foreclosure, and Redemption from Bronze Age Finance to the Jubilee Year.* Dresden: ISLET-Verlag, 2018.

———. *Killing the Host: How Financial Parasites and Debt Bondage Destroy the Global Economy.* Petrolia: Counterpunch Books, 2015.

Huizinga, Johan. *Homo Ludens: A Study of the Play-Element in Culture.* Mansfield Centre: Martino Publishing, 2014.

Illich, Ivan. *The Right to Useful Unemployment.* London: Marion Boyars Ltd., 2000.

Imbert, Fred. "Warren Buffett's Favorite Steakhouse Fits His Modest Style." *CNBC,* May 19, 2018. https://www.cnbc.com/2018/05/19/gorats-warren-buffetts-favorite-steakhouse-fits-his-modest-style.html.

Jameson, Fredric. *Postmodernism, or, the Cultural Logic of Late Capitalism.* Durham: Duke University Press, 1991.

Kallis, George, and Hugh March. "Imaginaries of Hope: The Utopianism of Degrowth." *Annals of the Association of American Geographers* 105 (2015): 360–68. DOI: 10.1080/00045608.2014.973803.

Kant, Immanuel. *Critique of Judgment.* Translated by Werner S. Pluhar. Indianapolis: Hackett, 1987.

———. *Groundwork of the Metaphysics of Morals.* Translated by H.J. Paton. New York: Harper Torchbooks, 1956.

———. "Idea for a Universal History with a Cosmopolitan Purpose." In *Kant: Political Writings,* edited by H.S. Reiss, translated by H.B. Nisbet, 41–53. Cambridge: Cambridge University Press, 2016.

———. "On the Common Saying, 'This May be True in Theory, but It Does Not Apply in Practice.'" In *Kant: Political Writings,* edited by H.S. Reiss, translated by H.B. Nisbet,61–92. Cambridge: Cambridge University Press, 2016.

———. "Perpetual Peace: A Philosophical Sketch." In *Kant: Political Writings,* edited by H.S. Reiss, translated by H.B. Nisbet, 93–130. Cambridge: Cambridge University Press, 2016.

———. "The Contest of Faculties." In *Kant: Political Writings* edited by H.S. Reiss, translated by H.B. Nisbet, 176–90. Cambridge: Cambridge University Press, 2016.

———. *The Metaphysics of Morals.* Translated and edited by Mary Gregor. Cambridge: Cambridge University Press, 2000.

———. "What Is Enlightenment?" In *Kant: Political Writings,* edited by H.S. Reiss, translated by H.B. Nisbet, 54–60. Cambridge: Cambridge University Press, 2016.

Katznelson, Ira. *City Trenches: Urban Politics and the Patterning of Class in the United States.* New York: Pantheon, 1981.

Kierkegaard, Søren. *Either/Or.* 2 Vols. Translated by Howard V. Hong and Edna H. Hong. Princeton: Princeton University Press, 1978.

Kinderman, Peter. *A Prescription for Psychiatry: Why We Need a Whole New Approach to Mental Health and Wellbeing.* New York: Palgrave Macmillan, 2014.

King, Rachel. "What's Fueling 'The Great Resignation' among Younger Generations?" *Fortune Daily,* August 26, 2021. https://fortune.com/2021/08/26/pandemic-burnout-career-changes-great-resignation-adobe/.

Klein, Ezra. "That Anxiety You're Feeling? It's a Habit You Can Unlearn." *The New York Times,* April 20,2021. https://www.nytimes.com/2021/04/20/podcasts/ezra-klein-podcast-judson-brewer-transcript.html.

Klotz, Anthony. "The Great Resignation with Molly M. Anderson, Anthony C. Klotz, PhD & Elaine Welteroth." *The Washington Post,* September 24, 2021. https://www.washingtonpost.com/washington-post-live/2021/09/24/transcript-great-resignation-with-molly-m-anderson-anthony-c-klotz-phd-elaine-welteroth/.

Kocka, Jürgen. *Capitalism: A Short History.* Translated by Jeremiah Riemer. Princeton: Princeton University Press, 2016.

Kolakowski, Leszek. *Main Currents of Marxism,* Vol. 1: *The Founders.* Translated by P.S. Falla. Oxford: Oxford University Press, 1978.

Komlosy, Andrea. *Work: The Last 1,000 Years.* Translated by Jacob K. Watson and Loren Balhorn. London: Verso, 2018.

Krugman, Paul. "Is the Great Resignation a Great Rethink?" *Seattle Times,* November 7, 2021. https://www.seattletimes.com/opinion/is-the-great-resignation-a-great-rethink/.

Lacan, Jacques. *Ecrits.* Translated by Bruce Fink. New York: W.W. Norton, 2006.

———. *The Seminar of Jacques Lacan, Book XI: The Four Fundamental Concepts of Psychoanalysis.* Edited by Jacques-Alain Miller. Translated by Alan Sheridan. New York: W.W. Norton, 1998.

Lafargue, Paul. *The Right to Be Lazy.* Translated by Charles Hope Kerr. Edited by Bernard Marszalek. Chicago: Charles H. Kerr Company and AK Press, 2011.

Larmore, John. "The Idea of a Life Plan." *Social Philosophy and Policy Foundation Journal* 16, no. 1 (1999): 96–112. DOI: 10.1017/S0265052500002260.

Latouche, Serge. "Imaginary, Decolonization of." In *Degrowth: A Vocabulary for a New Era,* edited by Giacomo D'Alisa, Federico Demaria, and Giorgios Kallis, 117–24. New York: Routledge, 2014.

Lichtenstein, Nelson. "Are We Witnessing a 'General Strike' in Our Own Time?" *The Washington Post,* November 18, 2021. https://www.washingtonpost.com/outlook/2021/11/18/are-we-witnessing-general-strike-our-own-time/.

Lis, Catharina. "Perceptions of Work in Classical Antiquity: A Polyphonic Heritage." In *The Idea of Work in Europe from Antiquity to Modern Times,* edited by Joseph Ehmer and Catharina Lis, 33–68. New York: Routledge, 2009.

Lorenz, Taylor. "Stop Trying to Be Productive." *The New York Times,* April 1, 2020. https://www.nytimes.com/2020/04/01/style/productivity-coronavirus.html.

Lotringer, Sylvère. "In the Shadow of the Red Brigades." In *Autonomia: Post-Political Politics,* edited by Sylvère Lotringer and Christian Marazzi, v–xvi. Los Angeles: Semiotext(e), 2007.

Malik, Nesrine. "There Is Revolution in the Air Now, But History Shows the Old Order Will Fight Back." *The Guardian,* May 18, 2020. https://www.theguardian.com/commentisfree/2020/may/18/revolution-history-fight-back-coronavirus-policies-vulnerable.

Malone, Noreen. "The Age of Anti-Ambition." *New York Times Magazine,* February 15, 2022. https://www.nytimes.com/2022/02/15/magazine/anti-ambition-age.html.

Mancini, Jeannine. "Warren Buffett's Salary Is $100,000 Per Year — He Hasn't Had a Raise in 40 Years, and He Gives Half of It Back to Berkshire Hathaway." *Yahoo Finance,* July 13, 2013. https://finance.yahoo.com/news/warren-buffetts-salary-100-000-150916458.html.

Marcuse, Herbert. *An Essay on Liberation.* Boston: Beacon Press, 1969.

———. *Five Lectures.* Translated by Jeremy J. Shapiro and Shierry M. Weber. Boston: Beacon Press, 1970.

———. *One-Dimensional Man: Studies in the Ideology of Advanced Industrial Society.* Boston: Beacon Press, 1991.

Martin, Nick. "Against Productivity in a Pandemic." *New Republic,* March 2020. https://newrepublic.com/article/156929/work-home-productivity-coronavirus-pandemic.

Marx, Karl. *Capital.* Vol. 1. Translated by Ben Fowkes. London: Penguin, 1976.

———. *Grundrisse.* Translated by Martin Nicolaus. London: Penguin, 1973.

Marx, Karl, and Frederick Engels. *The Economic and Philosophic Manuscripts of 1844.* Translated by Martin Milligan. New York: Prometheus, 1988.

Mau, Søren. *Mute Compulsion: A Marxist Theory of the Economic Power of Capital.* London: Verso, 2023.

Mazzucato, Mariana. *The Value of Everything: Making and Taking in the Global Economy.* New York: Public Affairs, 2018.

McAlevey, Jane. *No Shortcuts: Organizing for Power in the New Gilded Age.* Oxford: Oxford University Press, 2019.

McGranahan, Carole. "Theorizing Refusal: An Introduction." *Cultural Anthropology* 31, no. 3 (2016): 319–25. DOI: 10.14506/ca31.01.

Melville, Herman. "Bartleby, the Scrivener: A Story of Wall Street." In *Billy Budd, Sailor, and Other Stories,* 103–44. New York: Bantam Classics, 2006.

Menon, Tara. "What Jane Eyre and Oliver Twist Tell Us about Talking to Strangers." *Psyche,* September 29, 2021. https://psyche.co/ideas/what-jane-eyre-and-oliver-twist-tell-us-about-talking-to-strangers.

National Institutes of Health (NIH) News Release. "NIH Awards $20 Million over Five Years to Bring Together Music Therapy and Neuroscience." *NIH,* September 19, 2019. https://www.nih.gov/news-events/news-releases/nih-awards-20-million-over-five-years-bring-together-music-therapy-neuroscience.

Negri, Antonio. "Domination and Sabotage," translated by Red Notes. In *Autonomia: Post-Political Politics,* edited by Sylvère Lotringer and Christian Marazzi, 62–71. Los Angeles: Semiotext(e), 2007.

———. *Marx Beyond Marx: Lessons on the Grundrisse.* Edited by Jim Fleming. Translated by Harry Cleaver, Michael Ryan, and Maurizio Viano. New York: Autonomedia/Pluto Press, 1991.

Negt, Oskar, and Alexander Kluge. *Public Sphere and Experience: Analysis of the Bourgeois and Proletarian Public Sphere.* Translated by Peter Labanyi, Jamie Owen Daniel, and Assenka Oksiloff. London: Verso, 2016.

Nietzsche, Friedrich. *The Birth of Tragedy.* Translated by Walter Kaufmann. New York: Vintage Books, 1967.

Nussbaum, Martha. *The Fragility of Goodness: Luck and Ethics in Greek Tragedy and Philosophy.* Cambridge: Cambridge University Press, 1986.

O'Connor, Brian. *Idleness: A Philosophical Essay.* Princeton: Princeton University Press, 2018.

Odell, Jenny. *How to Do Nothing: Resisting the Attention Economy.* Brooklyn: Melville House, 2019.

Paquot, Thierry. *The Art of the Siesta.* Translated by Ken Hollings. London: Marion Boyars, 2003.

Petersen, Anne Helen. "How Millennials Became the Burnout Generation." *Buzzfeed News,* January 5, 2019. https://www.buzzfeednews.com/article/annehelenpetersen/millennials-burnout-generation-debt-work.
Pieper, Joseph. *Leisure: The Basis of Culture.* Translated by Alexander Dru. San Francisco: Ignatius, 2009.
Postone, Moishe. *Time, Labor, and Social Domination: A Reinterpretation of Marx's Critical Theory.* Cambridge: Cambridge University Press, 2003.
Prádanos, Luis. *Post-Growth Imaginaries: New Ecology and Counter-Hegemonic Culture in Post-2008 Spain.* Liverpool: Liverpool University Press, 2019.
Price, Devon. *Laziness Does Not Exist: A Defense of the Exhausted, Exploited, and Over-Worked.* New York: Atria Books, 2022.
Purser, Robert. *McMindfulness: How Mindfulness Became the New Capitalist Spirituality.* London: Repeater Books, 2019.
Putnam, Robert. *Bowling Alone: The Collapse and Revival of American Community.* New York: Simon & Schuster Paperbacks, 2000.
Rauschning, Hermann. *The Voice of Destruction.* New York: G.P. Putnam and Sons, 1940.
Rawls, John. *A Theory of Justice.* Cambridge: Harvard University Press, 1999.
Reisman, David, with Nathan Glaser and Deuel Denny. *The Lonely Crowd.* New Haven: Yale University Press, 2001.
Roggero, Gigi. "A Science of Destruction: An Interview with Gigi Roggero on the Actuality of *Operaismo*," with David Gallo Lassere. *Viewpoint Magazine,* April 30, 2020. https://viewpointmag.com/2020/04/30/a-science-of-destruction-an-interview-with-gigi-roggero-on-the-actuality-of-operaismo/.
Rose, Nikolas. *Governing the Soul: The Shaping of the Private Self.* London: Free Association Books, 1999.
Rosenberg, Jacob. "Workers Got Fed Up. Bosses Got Scared. This Is How the Big Quit Happened. And What It Means." *Mother Jones,* January–February 2022. https://www.

motherjones.com/politics/2022/01/record-quits-great-resignation-labor-workers-pandemic/.
Russell, Bertrand. *In Praise of Idleness.* London: Routledge, 2004.
Schneebaum, Tobias. *Wild Man.* New York: Viking Press, 1979.
Schulz, Kathryn. "The Moral Judgments of Henry David Thoreau." *The New Yorker,* October 12, 2015. https://www.newyorker.com/magazine/2015/10/19/pond-scum.
Schürmann, Reiner. "Ultimate Double Binds." *Graduate Faculty Philosophy Journal* 14, no. 2/1 (1991): 213–36.
Sennett, Richard. *The Fall of Public Man.* New York: W.W. Norton, 2017.
Skinner, B.F. *Walden Two.* New York: Macmillan, 1948.
Slater, Nick, and Oren Nimni. "Bullshit Jobs." *Current Affairs,* August 20, 2019. https://www.currentaffairs.org/2019/08/bullshit-jobs.
Smart, Tim. "Study: Gen Z, Millennials Driving 'The Great Resignation.'" *US News & World Report,* August 26, 2021. https://www.usnews.com/news/economy/articles/2021-08-26/study-gen-z-millennials-driving-the-great-resignation.
Smith, Adam. *The Wealth of Nations.* New York: Bantam Classics, 2003.
Smith, Jason. "Preface: Soul-Strike." In Franco "Bifo" Berardi, *The Soul At Work: From Alienation to Autonomy,* 9–19. Los Angeles: Semiotext(e), 2009.
Smucker, Jonathan Matthew. *Hegemony How-To: A Roadmap for Radicals.* Chico: AK Press, 2017.
Srnicek, Nick, and Alex Williams. *Inventing the Future: Post-Capitalism and a World without Work.* London: Verso, 2016.
Standing, Guy. "The Left Should Stop Equating Labor with Work." *SocialEurope,* March 23, 2018. https://www.socialeurope.eu/why-work-not-labour-is-ecological-imperative.
Steinhoff, James. *Automation and Autonomy: Labour, Capital, and Machines in the Artificial Intelligence Industry.* Cham: Palgrave Macmillan, 2021.

Strauss, William, and Neil Howe. *Millennials Rising: The Next Generation*. New York: Vintage Books, 2000.
Stross, Charles. *Singularity Sky*. New York: Ace Books, 2003.
Styles, Harry. "As It Was." Track 4 from *Harry's House*. Columbia Records, 2022.
Taussig, Michael. *Shamanism, Colonialism, and the Wild Man*. Chicago: University of Chicago Press, 1991.
Thompson, E.P. *The Making of the English Working Class*. New York: Vintage Books, 1966.
Thompson, Paul. "Foundation and Empire: A Critique of Hardt and Negri." *Conference of Socialist Economists* 29, no. 2 (2005): 73–98. DOI: 10.1177/030981680508600105.
Thoreau, Henry David. *Walden*. San Bernadino: Black and White Classics, 2004.
Tronti, Mario. "Our *Operaismo*." In *Workers and Capital*, 327–48. London: Verso, 2019.
———. "The Strategy of Refusal." In *Autonomia: Post-Political Politics*, edited by Sylvère Lotringer and Christian Marazzi, 28–35. Los Angeles: Semiotext(e), 2007.
———. *Workers and Capital*. Translated by David Broder. London: Verso, 2019.
Van den Hoven, Birgit. *Work in Ancient and Medieval Thought*, Amsterdam: J.C. Gieben, 1996.
Veblen, Thorstein. *The Theory of the Leisure Class*. Edited by Martha Banta. Oxford: Oxford University Press, 2009.
Vinge, Vernor. "Technological Singularity." *Whole Earth Review*. Winter 1993. https://ntrs.nasa.gov/citations/19940022856.
Virno, Paolo. *A Grammar of the Multitude: For Contemporary Forms of Life*. Translated by Isabella Bertoletti, James Cascaito, and Andrea Casson. Los Angeles: Semiotext(e), 2004.
———. "General Intellect," translated by Arianna Bove. In *Lessico Postfordista*. Milan: Feltrinelli, 2001. https://www.generation-online.org/p/fpvirno10.htm.
———. "Virtuosity and Revolution: The Political Theory of Exodus." In *Radical Thought in Italy: A Potential Politics*,

edited by Paolo Virno and Michael Hardt, 189–222. Minneapolis: University of Minnesota Press, 1996.

Wamsely, Laurel. "After a Six Year Battle, Florida Couple Wins the Right to Plant Veggies in Front Yard." *KCUR Radio,* July 3, 2019. https://www.kcur.org/2019-07-03/after-6-year-battle-florida-couple-wins-the-right-to-plant-veggies-in-front-yard.

Wang, Serenitie, and Daniel Shane, "Jack Ma Endorses China's Controversial 12 Hours a Day, 6 Days a Week Work Culture." *CNN Business,* April 15, 2019. https://www.cnn.com/2019/04/15/business/jack-ma-996-china/index.html.

Waskow, Arthur. *Godwrestling — Round 2: Ancient Wisdom, Future Paths.* Woodstock: Jewish Lights Publishing, 1995.

———. "Toward a Jubilee Economy & Ecology in the Modern World." *Shalom Center Legacy,* May 12, 2008. https://legacy4now.theshalomcenter.org/node/1396.

Weber, Henri. "In the Beginning Was Gramsci." In *Autonomia: Post-Political Politics,* edited by Sylvère Lotringer and Christian Marazzi, 84–91. Los Angeles: Semiotext(e), 2007.

Weber, Max. *The Protestant Ethic and the Spirit of Capitalism.* Translated by Talcott Parsons. New York: Charles Scribner's Sons, 1976.

Weeks, Kathi. "Karl Marx and the Problem with Work." *De Gruyter Conversations,* May 15, 2018. https://blog.degruyter.com/marx-and-the-problem-with-work/.

———. *The Problem with Work: Feminism, Marxism, Antiwork Politics, and Postwork Imaginaries.* Durham: Duke University Press, 2011.

Weir, Bill. "To My Son, Born during the Climate Crisis: Get Mad and Get Ready." *CNN Project Planet,* April 22, 2022. https://www.cnn.com/travel/article/climate-change-bill-weir-letter-to-son-wt-scn/index.html.

Welch, Gilbert, Lisa M. Schwartz, and Steven Woloshin. *Over-Diagnosed: Making People Sick in Pursuit of Health.* Boston: Beacon Press, 2012.

Williams, Brian. "Until We Meet Again." *American Rhetoric Online Speech Bank,* December 9, 2021.

https://www.americanrhetoric.com/speeches/brianwilliamsmsnbcnewssignoff.htm.
Wright, Steve. *Storming Heaven: Class Composition and Struggle in Italian Autonomist Marxism.* London: Pluto Press, 2017.
———. "Foreword." In Mario Tronti, *Workers and Capital,* translated by David Broder. London: Verso, 2019.
Zinn, John Kabat. *Full Catastrophe Living: Using the Wisdom of Your Body and Mind to Face Stress, Pain, and Illness.* Revised Edition. London: Bantam Books, 2013.
Žižek, Slavoj. *The Parallax View.* Cambridge: MIT Press, 2009.

Made in the USA
Coppell, TX
05 November 2026

11292668R00251